Student's Companion

to
Microeconomics for Managers

Student's Companion

to
Microeconomics for Managers

David M. Kreps

Graduate School of Business, Stanford University, and
Berglas School of Economics, Tel Aviv University

W. W. Norton & Company • New York • London

W. W. Norton & Company has been independent since its founding in 1923, when William Warder and Mary D. Herter Norton first published lectures delivered at the People's Institute, the adult education division of New York City's Cooper Union. The Nortons soon expanded their program beyond the Institute, publishing books by celebrated academics from America and abroad. By mid-century, the two major pillars of Norton's publishing program—trade books and college texts—were firmly established. In the 1950s, the Norton family transferred control of the company to its employees, and today—with a staff of four hundred and a comparable number of trade, college, and professional titles published each year—W. W. Norton & Company stands as the largest and oldest publishing house owned wholly by its employees.

ISBN 0-393-97679-3

W. W. Norton & Company, Inc., 500 Fifth Avenue, New York, NY 10110
www.wwnorton.com

W. W. Norton & Company Ltd., Castle House, 75/76 Wells Street,
London W1T 3QT

1 2 3 4 5 6 7 8 9 0

Contents in Brief

Contents

Introduction

This *Student's Companion* supplements the textbook *Microeconomics for Managers* in a number of ways.

- It contains, for most chapters, solutions to some of the problems in the textbook.

- It provides some long and complex exercises that complement material in the text.

- It provides some supplementary material that is too far from the main plot line in the text to be included there but that may be of interest to readers.

- It contains five sets of review problems and their solutions, following major blocks of material in the text, which will give students a chance to review their understanding of the material and to integrate across some of the chapters.

- It provides an appendix that reviews the calculus required in the text.

Following this introduction, material keyed to individual chapters in the text is provided in sequence. That is, immediately following this introduction is material related to Chapter 1, then Chapter 2, and so forth. Within each chapter, solutions to problems and "bonus" material are introduced as is expositionally appropriate. The first set of review problems, both the problems and their solutions, follows the material related to Chapter 7. Other sets of review problems follow the material related to Chapters 10, 14, 19, and 23. The Appendix concludes the *Companion*.

You can look for the solutions of specific problems, if you want. But readers of the text who want to go beyond what is in the text and, at the same time, strengthen their understanding of textual material will find that reading straight through the companion material is a good idea. In an ideal world of infinite time to devote to the study of microeconomics, you would (1) read a chapter in the text, (2) go to the material in the *Companion* related to that chapter and start to read, while (3) trying your hand at solving the problems before reading the solutions I offer here. As you try problems, if you find yourself getting stuck, you can start to read the solution if one is offered, to get a hint on how to proceed. Then, (4) as sets of review problems are reached, you would take each problem in turn and work through it, reading the solutions that are offered either after you formulate you own solution or, as needed, to provide hints.

Because I provide solutions to more than half the problems in the book and to all the review problems, you must resist the temptation to read through the answers or to give up too quickly on doing the work yourself. You will learn more and more effectively if you give the problems an honest effort. Some of the review problems are difficult, but if you find that, when you get to a set of review problems, you are able to do fewer than two-thirds on your own, you are *not* working hard enough at learning this material.

The numbering system for problems, figures, and spreadsheets continues from the text. For instance, the last figure in Chapter 3 of the text is Figure 3.11, so the first figure in *Companion Material for Chapter 3* is Figure 3.12. For the review problems, roman numerals are used, so that Problem II.3 is the third problem in the second set of review problems, and Figure II.1 is the first figure in these problems.

Let me reiterate from the text that some of the problems are difficult. If you find that, after reading the text, you can do all the suggested problems, you might consider giving up wealth and a career in management for a career as an academic. More realistically, you should expect to get stuck in places. But getting stuck and then unstuck is how to learn microeconomics.

Material for Chapter 1

Microeconomics? For Managers?

Using Solver for Multiple Parameterizations of a Given Problem

In both problems in this chapter, you are asked to use Solver to solve multiple parameterizations of a given spreadsheet model. This can be done without reinvoking Solver for each parameterization separately. I illustrate the technique with Problem 1.1.

In this problem we use the GM1 spreadsheet, in which we enter values for P, the posted price; X and x, the redemption values of the coupon; Q, the amount received by the seller for a coupon in the transferred-coupon market; and k, the amount in addition to Q that a buyer must pay for a transferred coupon. Problem 1.1 asks you to fix Q at $10 and k at $50 and maximize GM's profit by varying the posted price P, for three sets of coupon values X and x.

Values that vary within a scenario, which in this problem is P, are usually called *variables*. Values that go unchanged, Q and k, or that vary between scenarios, X and x in this problem, are called *parameters*. Each set of parameter values constitutes one scenario; in this problem, we have the initial scenario of $X = \$1000$ and $x = \$500$, and three additional scenarios:

$$X = x = \$1000; \qquad X = \$2000 \text{ and } x = \$1500; \qquad X = \$1000 \text{ and } x = \$200.$$

Begin with the basic spreadsheet for the problem, which is sheet 1 of GM1. It helps in using this technique that the calculations are all done in a single column (or row), although this is not crucial.

Copy the guts of the spreadsheet in different places on the spreadsheet for as many scenarios as you want to consider. When everything in the basic spreadsheet is in a single column, this means copying the column, once for each scenario. For each scenario, put in the appropriate values for the parameters. Setting the posted price

	A	B	C	D	E
7					
8	P: Posted price	$20,000	$20,000	$20,000	$20,000
9	X: value of coupon to original bearer	$1,000	$1,000	$2,000	$1,000
10	x: value of coupon to third-party buyer	$500	$1,000	$1,500	$200
11	Q: coupon price for seller in transferred-coupon market	$10	$10	$10	$10
12	k: price spread in transferred-coupon market	$50	$50	$50	$50
13					
14	OLD-TRUCK BUYERS				
15	Effective price they face	$19,010	$19,010	$18,010	$19,010
16	% change in this price from $20,000	-4.95%	-4.95%	-9.95%	-4.95%
17	% change in quantity from 600,000	19.80%	19.80%	39.80%	19.80%
18	total quantity bought (millions)	0.7188	0.7188	0.8388	0.7188
19	net profit to GM for one sale to this group	$4,000	$4,000	$3,000	$4,000
20	net profit to GM for sales to this group ($ billions)	$2.88	$2.88	$2.52	$2.88
21					
22	THIRD-PARTY BUYERS				
23	Effective price they face	$19,560	$19,060	$18,560	$19,860
24	% change in this price from $20,000	-2.20%	-4.70%	-7.20%	-0.70%
25	% change in quantity from 1,400,000	8.80%	18.80%	28.80%	2.80%
26	total quantity bought (millions)	1.5232	1.6632	1.8032	1.4392
27	net profit to GM for one sale to this group	$4,500	$4,000	$3,500	$4,800
28	net profit to GM for sales to this group ($ billions)	$6.85	$6.65	$6.31	$6.91
29					
30	GM SUMMARY FIGURES				
31	GM net profit for sales to both groups ($ billions)	$9.73	$9.53	$8.83	$9.78
32	cost to GM of this program relative to benchmark	$0.27	$0.47	$1.17	$0.22
33	($ billions)				

Sheet 1 / Sheet 2 \ Sheet 3 /

Figure 1.4. Four scenarios, in which the redemption values of the coupons vary. In these four scenarios, one each in columns B, C, D, and E, the posted price is set at an initial value of $20,000. The next step is to maximize GM's profit by varying the posted price in each scenario.

P at an initial value of $20,000, this gives us the spreadsheet shown in Figure 1.4.[1] (This is sheet 3 of GM1.)

The exercise now is to use Solver to maximize the entry in cell B31 by varying B8, to maximize C31 by varying C8, and similarly for columns D and E. I could simply run Solver four times.

Alternatively, in cell F31, I can put the entry = B31 + C31 + D31 + E31, which is the sum of GM's profits in the four scenarios. (You could also write = SUM(B31:E31).) Then I call Solver and ask it to maximize the contents of cell F31 by varying B8, C8, D8, and E8. To be sure you know what I have in mind, in Figure 1.5 I show you

---

[1] Let me remind you that figures for each chapter of the text are numbered consecutively. The last figure in Chapter 1 of the text was Figure 1.3. So the first number for a figure in this part of the *Companion* is Figure 1.4.

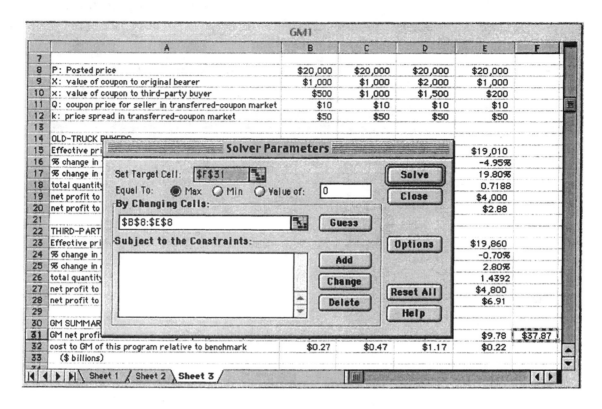

Figure 1.5. The Solver dialog box. After putting the sum of cells B31, C31, D31, and E31 into cell F31, we ask solver to maximize this sum, or cell F31, by varying the four posted prices.

what the Solver dialog box looks like, before I click Solve.

That's it. When Solver solves this one optimization problem, it will have solved all four of my scenarios at once. Why? Because the contents and calculations of the four columns are independent of one another. There are no trade-offs for the computer to make among the columns; it does not make (say) C31 bigger at the expense of B31. So, if I maximize the sum of the four profit figures, I maximize each profit figure individually. To put it more accurately, after Solver has maximized the sum, it will have maximized each of the four individually. This gives the answer.

Solution to Problem 1.1

If you do what is just described, you get back from Solver the spreadsheet shown in Figure 1.6. Note two things here. First, the cost to GM of the coupon program is the same in columns B and D. All that changes is that GM raises the posted price of its light truck by $1000. The explanation is simple: If GM offers every buyer of its light truck $1000 more in rebate, which is what changes from column B to column D, it can completely undo the impact of that additional rebate by raising the price of its light truck by the same $1000. And if it offers $1000 less in rebate to every customer, it can completely undo this by lowering the posted price by $1000.

	A	B	C	D	E
7					
8	P: Posted price	$20,627	$20,977	$21,628	$20,417
9	X: value of coupon to original bearer	$1,000	$1,000	$2,000	$1,000
10	x: value of coupon to third-party buyer	$500	$1,000	$1,500	$200
11	Q: coupon price for seller in transferred-coupon market	$10	$10	$10	$10
12	k: price spread in transferred-coupon market	$50	$50	$50	$50
13					
14	OLD-TRUCK BUYERS				
15	Effective price they face	$19,637	$19,987	$19,638	$19,427
16	% change in this price from $20,000	-1.81%	-0.06%	-1.81%	-2.86%
17	% change in quantity from 600,000	7.25%	0.25%	7.25%	11.45%
18	total quantity bought (millions)	0.64350054	0.60150018	0.64349949	0.66870076
19	net profit to GM for one sale to this group	$4,627	$4,977	$4,628	$4,417
20	net profit to GM for sales to this group ($ billions)	$2.98	$2.99	$2.98	$2.95
21					
22	THIRD-PARTY BUYERS				
23	Effective price they face	$20,187	$20,037	$20,188	$20,277
24	% change in this price from $20,000	0.94%	0.19%	0.94%	1.39%
25	% change in quantity from 1,400,000	-3.75%	-0.75%	-3.75%	-5.55%
26	total quantity bought (millions)	1.34750126	1.38950041	1.34749881	1.32230177
27	net profit to GM for one sale to this group	$5,127	$4,977	$5,128	$5,217
28	net profit to GM for sales to this group ($ billions)	$6.91	$6.92	$6.91	$6.90
29					
30	GM SUMMARY FIGURES				
31	GM net profit for sales to both groups ($ billions)	$9.89	$9.91	$9.89	$9.85
32	cost to GM of this program relative to benchmark	$0.11	$0.09	$0.11	$0.15
33	($ billions)				

Sheet 1 / Sheet 2 \ **Sheet 3** /

Figure 1.6. The four scenarios, optimized. Solver does its stuff and comes back with these answers. Now the task is to look at these optimized values and come to conclusions. See the text for the analysis of these numbers.

We conclude that as long as GM sets the posted price of its light truck, and fixing Q and k, what matters to GM in terms of the cost of the program is the difference in coupon face values for the two groups, or $X - x$. As long as that difference is constant, GM does not care about the magnitude of X and x, since it can undo any change in magnitude with a corresponding change in its posted price.

Three caveats to this conclusion should be noted.

1. This works as long as GM is sure that every customer will get his or her hands on a coupon. If some of the customers do not get a coupon, then changing the posted price does not neutralize an equivalent change in the face values of the

coupons; a rise in price of $1000, say, is a real rise in price for customers who for whatever reason have no coupon. If the number of customers who have no coupon is a small percentage of the total, they have little impact on GM's profit. But it will no longer be precisely true that all that matters, as long as GM controls P, is $X - x$.

2. In the paragraph on page 6 beginning "We conclude . . . ," do not miss the phrase "fixing Q and k." It is natural to expect that Q will depend on x if it is nonzero; Q, the market price of a coupon, is likely to be some percentage of x, the coupon's value to a third-party buyer. So changing x is likely to change Q, invalidating the conclusion that all that matters is $X - x$, unless $Q = 0$ for *all* values of x. More specifically, if Q rises with x, then an increase in X and x that leaves $X - x$ fixed will be (very) expensive for GM. (The reason for this is that Q acts like a tax for third-party buyers; see Chapter 13 for the impact of taxes on the profits of sellers.)

3. This takes place in a world—really, in a model—in which the automobile manufacturer sets the retail price of its vehicles and consumers are reasonably sophisticated about the effect of rebates. In the real world—and in different models that we could build of the real world—manufacturers sell cars via independent dealerships (see Chapter 6), getting consumers into the showroom can help make sales that otherwise would not be made, and consumers can sometimes be "fooled" by clever marketing ploys. Such factors as these, ignored entirely by our current model, provide other explanations for rebates and coupons and may complicate the glib conclusion we just reached. The simple model here is the start of a serious analysis, not the end.

Now, comparing the costs to GM of columns B, C, and E (D is the same as B), we see as well that *the cost of the program to GM increases in $X - x$.* The smaller is the difference in face values of the coupon, the lower the cost to GM. The bigger is the difference, the higher the cost. So if GM "sweetens" the settlement offer by, say, telling the judge it is willing to raise X to $1500 and push x way up to $1200, and GM optimizes in P, GM actually cuts its costs and lowers the value received by the plaintiffs. If you are not convinced of this, verify it with the spreadsheet.

Why do we see this pattern? To reiterate, $X - x$ is all that matters because GM can undo an equal increase in both X and x by increasing P the same amount. The reason GM is better off the smaller is the difference $X - x$ (if Q is independent of this difference), is that the larger is $X - x$, the greater is the amount of undesirable price discrimination that GM engages in. (This statement is unlikely to make sense to you until you read Chapter 7.)

Solution to Problem 1.2

Problem 1.2 asks you to do a similar analysis, where we hold X and x fixed at their "real" values of $1000 and $500, respectively, where Q is held fixed at $10, and where k varies, looking at the values k = $5, $50, and $100. The techniques are exactly as in Problem 1.1, so I proceed immediately to the "answer," or what you should see after you run Solver. (The pre-Solver spreadsheet, with P = $20,000 in all three scenarios, is sheet 4 of GM1.) This is depicted in Figure 1.7.

	A	B	C	D
7				
8	P: Posted price	$20,643	$20,628	$20,610
9	X: value of coupon to original bearer	$1,000	$1,000	$1,000
10	x: value of coupon to third-party buyer	$500	$500	$500
11	Q: coupon price for seller in transferred-coupon market	$10	$10	$10
12	k: price spread in transferred-coupon market	$5	$50	$100
13				
14	OLD-TRUCK BUYERS			
15	Effective price they face	$19,653	$19,638	$19,620
16	% change in this price from $20,000	-1.73%	-1.81%	-1.90%
17	% change in quantity from 600,000	6.93%	7.25%	7.60%
18	total quantity bought (millions)	0.64160997	0.6435	0.64560003
19	net profit to GM for one sale to this group	$4,643	$4,628	$4,610
20	net profit to GM for sales to this group ($ billions)	$2.98	$2.98	$2.98
21				
22	THIRD-PARTY BUYERS			
23	Effective price they face	$20,158	$20,188	$20,220
24	% change in this price from $20,000	0.79%	0.94%	1.10%
25	% change in quantity from 1,400,000	-3.17%	-3.75%	-4.40%
26	total quantity bought (millions)	1.35568993	1.34749999	1.33840008
27	net profit to GM for one sale to this group	$5,143	$5,128	$5,110
28	net profit to GM for sales to this group ($ billions)	$6.97	$6.91	$6.84
29				
30	GM SUMMARY FIGURES			
31	GM net profit for sales to both groups ($ billions)	$9.95	$9.89	$9.82
32	cost to GM of this program relative to benchmark	$0.05	$0.11	$0.18
33	($ billions)			

Sheet 1 / Sheet 2 / Sheet 3 \ **Sheet 4**

Figure 1.7. Problem 1.2: The numbers. For each of the three scenarios in this problem, which vary in terms of the value of k, the amount beyond Q that the buyer of a coupon must pay in the transferred-coupon market, this gives the optimal posted price and the optimized cost of the program to GM. It is clear that GM's costs rise with increases in k and that GM optimally posts a lower price the larger is k.

The pattern is clear: The cost of the program to GM rises the larger is k, and the optimal price for GM to post falls in k. To understand fully what is happening here, you must wait for Chapter 13 and the discussion of taxes; but to anticipate this, the quantity k is equivalent to a tax imposed on third-party buyers of a GM light truck. The buyer pays this amount, but it does not go to GM but to brokers, market markers, or whoever pockets the difference between what a buyer of a transferred coupon pays for the coupon and what the seller receives. And just as increased taxes—even imposed on a segment of a firm's customers—decrease the firm's profit, so this "tax" lowers GM's profit. Moreover, usually the seller of a good optimally "shares" in paying the tax by lowering the price it charges the higher is the tax, which is exactly what we see here.

Material for Chapter 2

The Most Famous Picture in Economics

Solution to Problem 2.1

In this problem, $X = \$1000$, $x = \$500$, and $k = \$50$. We want to find supply and demand figures for the transferred coupon market, for $P = \$20{,}630$ and for two prices for transferred coupons, $Q = \$10$ and $Q = \$300$.

The first things to realize are that every third-party buyer of a GM light truck wants a coupon on these terms, since buying a coupon costs $60 or $350, both of which are less than the rebate of $500 the coupon produces. And every original holder of a coupon *who does not plan to buy a GM light truck* wants to sell the coupon at either of these prices, indeed at any price above $0. It is perhaps worth noting here that demand falls to 0 when Q goes above $450, since then the coupon costs more than it provides in rebate, and supply jumps up to the full 4.7 million coupons when Q goes above $1000, since now holders of coupons can get more for selling them than by using them.

So, for the numbers requested, demand is simply the number of third-party buyers of GM light trucks, and supply is 4.7 million less the number of original-bearer buyers of GM light trucks. The spreadsheet GM1 gives us numbers for buyers of GM light trucks in each group.

- Figure 2.5(a) shows GM1 for the values $P = \$20{,}630$, $X = \$1000$, $x = \$500$, $k = \$50$, and $Q = \$10$. The number of sales of GM light trucks to original holders of coupons, read from cell B15, is 0.6432 million. Therefore supply of coupons is 4.7 million less this, or 4.0568 million. The demand is the entry in cell B23, which is the sales figure for third-party buyers, 1.3468 million. Note, of course, that supply of coupons far exceeds demand for them.

- Figure 2.5(b) shows GM1 for the same values of P, X, x, and k, and $Q = 300$. Supply of coupons to the transferred coupon market is 4.7 million less 0.6084 million, or 4.0916 million, while demand is 1.2656 million. Supply has gone up and demand down; moving from $Q = \$10$ to $Q = \$300$ is a move in the wrong direction, at least as far as reaching a point where supply equals demand in the transferred-coupon market.

	A	B	C
5	P: Posted price	$20,630	
6	X: value of coupon to original bearer	$1,000	
7	x: value of coupon to third-party buyer	$500	
8	Q: coupon price for seller in transferred-coupon market	$10	
9	k: price spread in transferred-coupon market	$50	
10			
11	OLD-TRUCK BUYERS		
12	Effective price they face	$19,640	
13	% change in this price from $20,000	-1.80%	
14	% change in quantity from 600,000	7.20%	
15	total quantity bought (millions)	0.6432	
16	net profit to GM for one sale to this group	$4,630	
17	net profit to GM for sales to this group ($ billions)	$2.98	
18			
19	THIRD-PARTY BUYERS		
20	Effective price they face	$20,190	
21	% change in this price from $20,000	0.95%	
22	% change in quantity from 1,400,000	-3.80%	
23	total quantity bought (millions)	1.3468	
24	net profit to GM for one sale to this group	$5,130	
25	net profit to GM for sales to this group ($ billions)	$6.91	
26			
27	GM SUMMARY FIGURES		
28	GM net profit for sales to both groups ($ billions)	$9.89	
29	cost to GM of this program relative to benchmark	$0.11	
30	($ billions)		

(a)

	A	B	C
5	P: Posted price	$20,630	
6	X: value of coupon to original bearer	$1,000	
7	x: value of coupon to third-party buyer	$500	
8	Q: coupon price for seller in transferred-coupon market	$300	
9	k: price spread in transferred-coupon market	$50	
10			
11	OLD-TRUCK BUYERS		
12	Effective price they face	$19,930	
13	% change in this price from $20,000	-0.35%	
14	% change in quantity from 600,000	1.40%	
15	total quantity bought (millions)	0.6084	
16	net profit to GM for one sale to this group	$4,630	
17	net profit to GM for sales to this group ($ billions)	$2.82	
18			
19	THIRD-PARTY BUYERS		
20	Effective price they face	$20,480	
21	% change in this price from $20,000	2.40%	
22	% change in quantity from 1,400,000	-9.60%	
23	total quantity bought (millions)	1.2656	
24	net profit to GM for one sale to this group	$5,130	
25	net profit to GM for sales to this group ($ billions)	$6.49	
26			
27	GM SUMMARY FIGURES		
28	GM net profit for sales to both groups ($ billions)	$9.31	
29	cost to GM of this program relative to benchmark	$0.69	
30	($ billions)		

(b)

Figure 2.5. Finding supply and demand figures in the transferred-coupon market, from the spreadsheet GM1. We can virtually read supply and demand figures from the spreadsheet by setting the values to the desired parameter levels and level of the variable Q: Then, as long as $Q + k \leq x$, demand for coupons in the transferred-coupon market equals demand for GM light trucks by third-party buyers, and as long as $Q \leq X$, supply of coupons is 4.7 million less the demand for GM light trucks by original bearers.

Solution to Problem 2.2

(a) If consumers pay precisely what producers receive, then $p = q$, and equilibrium is found where supply equals demand. Algebraically, this is where

$$S(p) = 1000(p - 4) = 2000(10 - p) = D(p),$$

where I substitute p for q in the demand side of this equation, since $p = q$. Dividing both sides of the equation by 1000, this gives

$$p - 4 = 2(10 - p) \quad \text{or} \quad p - 4 = 20 - 2p \quad \text{or} \quad 3p = 24 \quad \text{or} \quad p = 8,$$

at which point the quantity supplied and demanded is 4000 units. Figure 2.6 shows this in a picture.

(b) Let P denote the price on the price tag of the good. With a sales tax paid by the buyer, the "supplier price," or what the producer gets from the sale of a unit, is P.

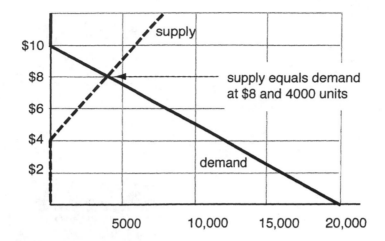

Figure 2.6. Supply equals demand in Problem 2.2.

And the "buyer price," or the net amount paid by a buyer, is P plus the tax. So, in this part of the problem,

$$p = P \quad \text{and} \quad q = 1.1P.$$

Hence, in terms of the price-tag price P, supply equals demand where

$$S(P) = 1000(P - 4) = 2000(10 - 1.1P) = D(1.1P),$$

which is P = \$7.50. The quantity supplied and demanded is 3500 units, and government revenue from the sales tax is 3500 × \$0.75 = \$2625.

(c) Keeping P as the price-tag price of the good, in this case, the consumer pays P, so $q = P$, but sellers of the good take in only $0.9P$ (with 10% going to the government). Therefore, supply equals demand in this case at

$$S(0.9P) = 1000(0.9P - 4) = 2000(10 - P) = D(P),$$

which is P = \$8.276, giving a quantity bought and sold of 3448 units and government tax revenues of 3448 × \$0.8276 = \$2853.79.

Challenge: Answer the following question. For the type of percentage sales tax used in part b of this problem, what percentage sales tax maximizes government revenues from the tax? (You can do this either algebraically or using Solver, although if you use Solver, you must be somewhat resourceful.)

Material for Chapter 3

Marginal This and Marginal That

Solution to Problem 3.1

This is a simple variation on the poiuyt problem from Section 3.2 so it merits little attention. The spreadsheet PROBLEM 3.1, sheet 1, gives the basic model, and sheet 2 computes discrete margins. Either by using the discrete margins or Solver, you should have no problem getting to the answer, which is shown in Figure 3.12. (Solver apparently gave up a tiny bit too soon.)

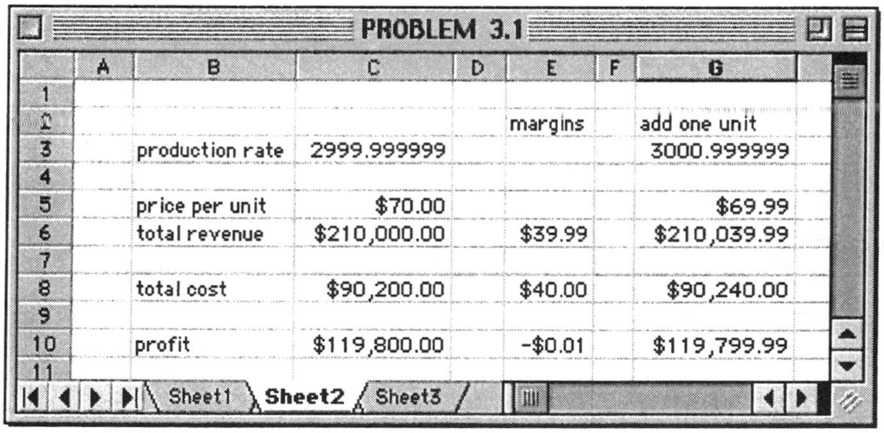

	A	B	C	D	E	F	G	
1								
2						margins	add one unit	
3		production rate	2999.999999				3000.999999	
4								
5		price per unit	$70.00				$69.99	
6		total revenue	$210,000.00		$39.99		$210,039.99	
7								
8		total cost	$90,200.00		$40.00		$90,240.00	
9								
10		profit	$119,800.00		-$0.01		$119,799.99	
11								

Sheet1 \ **Sheet2** / Sheet3

Figure 3.12. Solving Problem 3.1 with a spreadsheet.

Or, you can use calculus. Total revenue is $TR(x) = 100x - x^2/100$, so marginal revenue is $MR(x) = 100 - 2x/100$. Since $TC(x) = 200 + 20x + x^2/300$, marginal cost is $MC(x) = 20 + 2x/300$. Marginal revenue is a decreasing linear function, while marginal cost is an increasing linear function. They cross once (therefore), where

$$100 - \frac{2x}{100} = 20 + \frac{2x}{300},$$

which is $80 = 8x/300$, or $x = 3000$. Therefore, the production rate $x = 3000$ is profit-maximizing.

Solution to Problem 3.3

(a) We can do this using Excel or calculus. First, with Excel, sheet 1 of the spreadsheet FREEDONIAN STEEL, shown as Figure 3.13(a), gives various levels of production for CHI, its total costs, and its average cost. Clearly, the shape of average cost is this: For very low levels of production, average cost is very large. This is the result of amortizing the fixed costs of production over a very small base. Average cost declines and seems to bottom out at a production rate of 100,000, where average cost is $400 per ton. Then average cost begins to climb. In fact, if you graph average cost against production level for the numbers given, you get the shape shown in Figure 3.13(b), something of a bowl shape, with a pretty steep left-hand side. (I omit the first two production levels, since including them makes the range of values too large to see anything.)

Is 100,000 the rate that minimizes average cost? To be sure, you could ask Solver to minimize, say, cell C3 by varying A3. If you do, you find that, sure enough, $x = $ 100,000 does minimize average cost.

To use calculus, take the derivative of average cost:

$$AC'(x) = -\frac{10,000,000}{x^2} + \frac{1}{1000}.$$

This is an increasing function of x (the x^2 in the denominator gets larger, so the fraction gets smaller, but it has a negative sign, so the entire expression increases in x). It is 0 where

$$-\frac{10,000,000}{x^2} + \frac{1}{1000} = 0,$$

which is the solution to

$$x^2 = 10,000,000,000, \quad \text{or} \quad x = 100,000.$$

This means that average cost decreases up to production level 100,000 (its derivative is negative) and increases thereafter (its derivative becomes positive). Moreover, since its derivative increases, it has a bowl shape: Where it decreases, it decreases at a slower and slower rate; and once it starts increasing, the rate at which it increases itself increases. Finally, we can plug $x = $ 100,000 into the formula for average cost to learn that, at $x = $ 100,000, average cost (at its minimum) is $400.

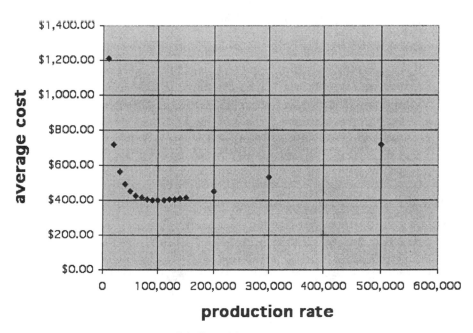

(a) Sheet 1 of FREEDONIAN STEEL

(b) Graphing average cost

Figure 3.13. Finding the shape of average cost for CHI. For a variety of production levels, total and average costs are computed. Then average cost is graphed.

Although it is more than you need to know right now, let me say a word more about this cost function. The marginal cost function is $MC(x) = 200 + x/500$, an increasing function. The combination of increasing marginal cost and a positive fixed cost (that is, $TC(0) > 0$) gives this sort of bowl-shaped average cost function, as you learn in Chapter 8.

(b) Begin with a simple spreadsheet, sheet 2 of FREEDONIAN STEEL, which takes a level of domestic production and computes domestic price, domestic revenue, total cost, and profit. (If you download sheet 2 from the website, you will find that it comes with $x = 100,000$.) Ask Solver to maximize profit by changing the domestic production rate, and it comes back with the answer shown in Figure 3.14, $x = 80,000$, for a domestic steel price of $680 and profit of $22 million.

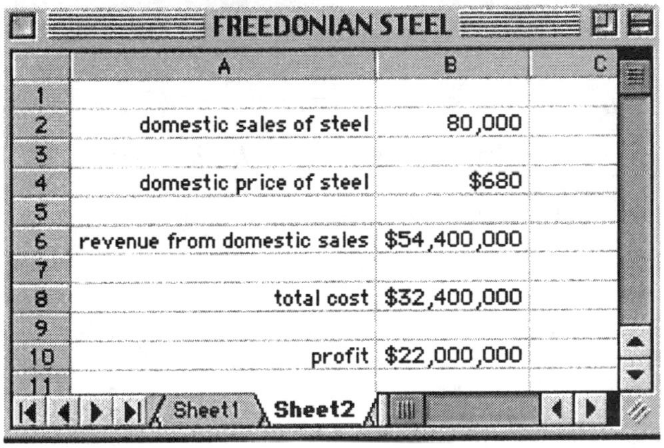

Figure 3.14. Finding the optimal production rate, if exports are ruled out.

Or, use calculus. Total revenue is $1000x - x^2/250$, so marginal revenue is $1000 - x/125$. Marginal cost is $200 + x/500$. Marginal revenue starts above marginal cost and falls, so the two intersect at one point, which must be the profit-maximizing point. This is where

$$1000 - \frac{x}{125} = 200 + \frac{x}{500} \quad \text{or} \quad 1000 - \frac{4x}{500} = 200 + \frac{x}{500},$$

which is

$$800 = \frac{5x}{500} \quad \text{or} \quad x = 80,000.$$

From here, simply plug the production level into the formula for price to find that this means a price of $680, multiply price times quantity to get revenue $54.4

million, plug 80,000 into the total cost function to find that total cost is $32.4 million, therefore the profit is $22 million.

(c) The spreadsheet called for in this case is sheet 3 of FREEDONIAN STEEL (which when downloaded has the starting values of 80,000 for domestic production and 0 for production for sale on the world market). When creating this spreadsheet, take care to sum domestic and export production rates and use the combined production rate in the computation of total cost. Once you create (or download) the spreadsheet, you can ask Solver to maximize profit by varying the two production rates. The answer is shown in Figure 3.15: domestic sales of 78,125, international sales of 9375, a domestic price of $688, and profit of $22,070,312. I do not claim that an increase in profit of $70,312 is a huge deal, but it is $70,312.

	FREEDONIAN STEEL	
	A	B
1		
2	domestic sales of steel	78,125
3	international sales of steel	9,375
4		
5	total production of steel	87,500
6		
7	total cost of production	$35,156,251
8		
9	domestic price of steel	$688
10		
11	revenue from domestic sales	$53,710,920
12	revenue from international sales	$3,515,644
13	total revenue	$57,226,564
14		
15	profit	$22,070,312
16		

Figure 3.15. Finding the optimal production plan, including exports.

(d) What is going on here? In Figure 3.16(a), I show you sheet 4 of FREEDONIAN STEEL for the initial values of sheet 3; that is, domestic sales equal to 80,000 and no exports. Note that, as called for in the problem, I added the discrete margins in the two variables. The margins tell the story: Regardless of what average cost is, marginal cost is $360. Note that this is marginal cost in both domestic and export production, which is entirely sensible: Total cost is a function of the sum of domestic and export production, so the impact on total cost of one more unit of domestic production must be identical to the impact of one more unit for export. Moreover, domestic marginal revenue, in terms of domestic production, is $360.

	A	B	C	D	E	F	G	H
				margs in domestic	margs in internat		one more domestic	one more internat.
2	domestic sales of steel	80,000					80,001	80,000
3	international sales of steel	0					0	1
4								
5	total production of steel	80,000					80,001	80,001
6								
7	total cost of production	$32,400,000		$360	$360		$32,400,360	$32,400,360
8								
9	domestic price of steel	$680					$680	$680
10								
11	revenue from domestic sales	$54,400,000		$360	$0		$54,400,360	$54,400,000
12	revenue from international sales	$0		$0	$375		$0	$375
13	total revenue	$54,400,000		$360	$375		$54,400,360	$54,400,375
14								
15	profit	$22,000,000		$0	$15		$22,000,000	$22,000,015

(a) Margins for the optimal domestic-only plan

	A	B	C	D	E	F	G	H
				margs in domestic	margs in internat		one more domestic	one more internat.
2	domestic sales of steel	80,000					80,001	80,000
3	international sales of steel	5,000					5,000	5,001
4								
5	total production of steel	85,000					85,001	85,001
6								
7	total cost of production	$34,225,000		$370	$370		$34,225,370	$34,225,370
8								
9	domestic price of steel	$680					$680	$680
10								
11	revenue from domestic sales	$54,400,000		$360	$0		$54,400,360	$54,400,000
12	revenue from international sales	$1,875,000		$0	$375		$1,875,000	$1,875,375
13	total revenue	$56,275,000		$360	$375		$56,275,360	$56,275,375
14								
15	profit	$22,050,000		-$10	$5		$22,049,990	$22,050,005

(b) Increasing exports to 5000 tons: New margins

	A	B	C	D	E	F	G	H
				margs in domestic	margs in internat		one more domestic	one more internat.
2	domestic sales of steel	78,100					78,101	78,100
3	international sales of steel	9,500					9,500	9,501
4								
5	total production of steel	87,600					87,601	87,601
6								
7	total cost of production	$35,193,760		$375	$375		$35,194,135	$35,194,135
8								
9	domestic price of steel	$688					$688	$688
10								
11	revenue from domestic sales	$53,701,560		$375	$0		$53,701,935	$53,701,560
12	revenue from international sales	$3,562,500		$0	$375		$3,562,500	$3,562,875
13	total revenue	$57,264,060		$375	$375		$57,264,435	$57,264,435
14								
15	profit	$22,070,300		$0	$0		$22,070,300	$22,070,300

(c) Margins at the "optimal" solution, found by trying to equate relevant margins

Figure 3.16. Using marginal analysis to understand the solution. Margins in domestic and export (international) sales are added to the spreadsheet, and we understand why we get the answers we do: Starting at the answer to part b of the problem, *marginal* profit for export sales is positive, so we increase exports. This raises marginal cost in both types of production, so we lower domestic production. We optimize when marginal profits for both domestic and export sale are 0.

But export marginal revenue, in terms of export production, is $375. No mystery about this figure: CHI can sell as much as it wants internationally at $375 per ton. So export marginal revenue in terms of export production is *always* going to be $375. Clearly, higher profit can be made on the margin. A marginal ton of steel, produced for export, costs $360 and nets $375 in revenue. (Look at the marginal profit figures: Marginal profit in export production is $15.)

So, on the margin, CHI wants to start to export. As it does this, the marginal cost of production rises, because CHI's marginal cost function increases. In Figure 3.16(b), I show you the results if we increase export sales to 5000, leaving domestic sales at 80,000. The rising marginal cost, now $370, is getting closer to export marginal revenue, but it still has a way to go; we can still increase profit by increasing export sales. But now domestic production is, on the margin, suboptimal: The marginal cost of a ton of steel for the domestic market is $370, while domestic marginal revenue is only $360. So CHI not only wants to increase exports; because increased production increases marginal cost, CHI wants to decrease production for domestic sales.

Please note carefully that this is true even though the domestic price of steel is $680, well above the price per ton CHI realizes overseas. Domestic price is domestic *average* revenue; domestic *marginal* revenue is what is important.

Where does this end? You need to find levels of domestic and export production such that the marginal cost of production—which, as we observed, is the same for production for the domestic market and for export—equals the marginal revenue from domestic sales and equals the marginal revenue from export sales. We know that the last (marginal revenue from export sales) is always going to be $375, so we are looking for production levels such that marginal cost equals domestic marginal revenue equals $375.

At this point, now that we know what we are looking for, we can solve this problem analytically fairly simply. Domestic marginal revenue depends on domestic sales only, and it is not hard to find that domestic marginal revenue is $375 when domestic sales total 78,125. The equation is $1000 - x_D/125 = 375$, where x_D is production for sale domestically. Marginal cost depends on total production, and it is not hard to solve the equation $MC(x) = 200 + x/500 = 375$ to find that marginal cost equals $375 when total production is 87,500. So, to maximize profit, total production must be 87,500 and domestic sales must be 78,125. Export sales must be what is left, or $87,500 - 78,125 = 9375$ tons.

In the spirit of substituting action for thought, you could also take sheet 4 of the spreadsheet and hunt for values that do what we want: make marginal cost equal domestic marginal revenue equal export marginal revenue, which is $375. The rule is simple: When domestic marginal profit is positive, increase domestic production. When it is negative, decrease domestic production. When export marginal profit is positive, increase production for export. When it is negative, decrease production for export.

Doing this, using just the spreadsheet and not looking at the "answer" that Solver produces, I get everything lined up with the numbers shown in Figure 3.16(c). As you can see, I am $12 in profit off the optimum. Which for this sort of model, is good enough.

Finally, for those of you who would like to see how to do this with calculus directly: There are two variables, x_D, for production for domestic sales, and x_E, for production for export sales. Total profit is

$$\pi(x_D, x_E) = 1000x_D - \frac{x_D^2}{250} + 375x_E - \left[10{,}000{,}000 + 200(x_D + x_E) + \frac{(x_D + x_E)^2}{1000} \right].$$

Take partial derivatives in this profit function in the two variables, set the two partial derivatives equal to 0 simultaneously, and you'll get the answer that Solver produced for us.

Solution to Problem 3.5

The "shape" of the profit function that goes with the marginal profit function in Figure 3.10 is shown here as Figure 3.17. Specifically, in the top part of Figure 3.17, I reproduce the marginal profit function, and directly below it I draw the (total) profit function.

Note the word *shape* in quote marks. In this figure, I assume that total profit at zero production level is 0. If we were told that total profit at zero production were, say, −$1000, then the total profit function in the bottom half of Figure 3.17 would look the same except for being shifted down by $1000 at all points. In general, if I tell you the marginal anything function, you can give me the shape but not the position of the original function; in fancy language, the derivative of a function determines the function *up to a constant of integration*.

Concerning the shape of total profit, the important point concerns the production level x^*. For production levels below x^*, marginal profit is positive, so profit is

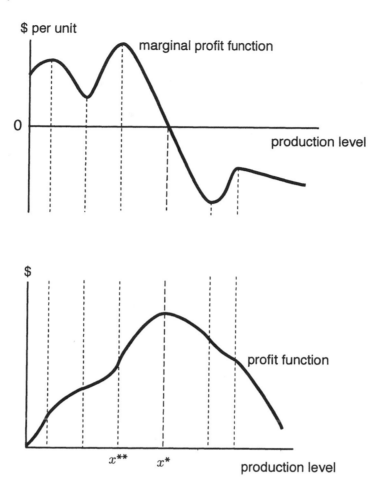

Figure 3.17. A marginal and corresponding total profit function.

rising. For production levels above x^*, marginal profit is negative, so profit is falling. Hence, profit is maximized at x^*.

Less important is the shape drawn at other marked production levels, such as x^{**}. These points mark local maxima and minima of the marginal profit function, and as such, they mark *points of inflection* of total profit. (A point of inflection is where the function changes from being convex to being concave or vice versa.) Note also the point x^{**}, which is the global maximum of the marginal profit function. At this point, the total profit function has its steepest (upward) slope.

Solution to Problem 3.6

The top panel of Figure 3.18 reproduces Figure 3.11; below it is my guess as to the shape of the total profit function.

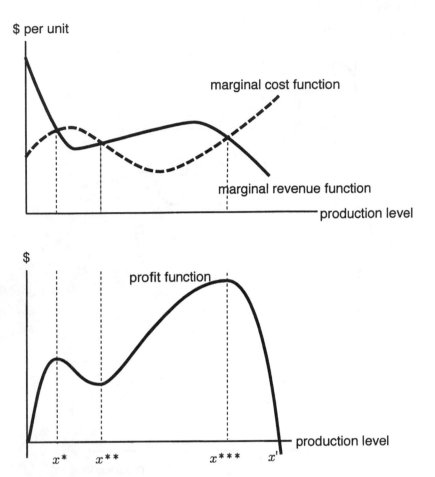

Figure 3.18. Marginal cost and revenue and the corresponding profit function.

You should be able to figure out the following:

1. Profit increases as production level increases from 0 to x^*, because marginal revenue exceeds marginal cost from 0 to x^*.

2. Profit falls from x^* to x^{**}, because marginal cost exceeds marginal revenue over this range.

3. Profit rises again from x^{**} to x^{***}, since over this range, marginal revenue exceeds marginal cost.

4. Profit falls past x^{***}, since beyond this level of production, marginal cost exceeds marginal revenue.

These facts imply that profit attains a local maximum at x^*, a local minimum at x^{**}, and a second local maximum at x^{***}. The remaining question is whether profit is greater at x^* or at x^{***}. Which of these is the global maximum? I drew the global maximum at x^{***}, and my justification for this involves the two shaded regions in the top part of Figure 3.18. The area of the shaded region between the marginal cost and marginal revenue function from x^* to x^{**} represents the amount by which profit falls over this interval. The area of the shaded region between marginal revenue and marginal cost from x^{**} to x^{***} represents the amount by which total profit rises over this interval. If you compare the size of these two regions, it is fairly clear that the second area is substantially larger than the first, so that profit rises more from x^{**} to x^{***} than it falls from x^* to x^{**}. This says that profit at x^{***} is higher than at x^*.

In this picture, I drew profit so that it becomes negative at x'. I do not really know this from the picture. If marginal cost stays above marginal revenue as the picture indicates, then eventually profit will become negative. To know where this will happen, I have to add up areas between curves and compare; not something easy to do. My drawing in of x' is meant to be suggestive but nothing more than that.

Once again, I assume that revenue and cost are 0 at $x = 0$; hence, profit is 0 there. If, say, total cost were negative at $x = 0$, the entire total profit function would be shifted down; this has no impact on the local maxima and minima, nor would it change the conclusion that profit at x^{***} is higher than at x^*. But if cost at $x = 0$ is large enough, profit is negative at all production levels. This then raises the question, Can the firm avoid this *fixed cost*, the total cost at $x = 0$, by ceasing operation altogether? If the firm could do this, it would then maximize profit by going out of business. We return to this issue in later chapters.

Solution to Problem 3.8

This problem is not much more difficult than the problem solved in Section 3.5. The only complication is that the total cost function is a bit more complex. But the spreadsheet CHAP3-2 is easily modified to work in this problem; and whether you find the optimal rates of production of poiuyts and qwerts by hand, using marginal profit figures, or using Solver, when it is all over, you should end up with the spreadsheet shown in Figure 3.19, which is the spreadsheet PROBLEM 3.8. The margins computed in the spreadsheet are not really necessary if you use Solver, but they are very useful if you find the optimal production rates by hand.

With calculus, total profit in this case can be written as

$$\left(100 - \frac{x_p}{100} - \frac{x_q}{400}\right)x_p + \left(80 - \frac{x_q}{50} - \frac{x_p}{200}\right)x_q - \left(300 + 20x_p + 10x_q + \frac{9x_p^2 + 6x_px_q + x_q^2}{1200}\right),$$

where I already began some algebraic manipulation by computing the squared term in the cost function. Skipping some algebraic steps, this simplifies to

$$80x_p + 70x_q - \frac{21x_p^2}{1200} - \frac{25x_q^2}{1200} - \frac{15x_p x_q}{1200} - 300.$$

We must compute the partial derivatives in x_p and x_q and set each to 0: This gives

$$\frac{\partial \pi(x_p, x_q)}{\partial x_p} = 80 - \frac{42x_p}{1200} - \frac{15x_q}{1200} = 0, \quad \text{and}$$

$$\frac{\partial \pi(x_p, x_q)}{\partial x_q} = 70 - \frac{50x_q}{1200} - \frac{15x_p}{1200} = 0.$$

We now have two simultaneous linear equations in two unknowns. With a bit of work, we get the solution

$$x_p = 1888 \quad \text{and} \quad x_q = 1113.6.$$

	A	B	C	D	E	F	G	H
1								
2				discrete margins	discrete margins		values for	values for
3		Basic values		in poiuyts	in qwerts		one more poiuyt	one more qwert
4								
5	number of poiuyts	1888.000087					1889.000087	1888.000087
6	number of qwerts	1113.599682					1113.599682	1114.599682
7								
8	price of a poiuyt	$78.34					$78.33	$78.33
9	price of a qwert	$48.29					$48.28	$48.27
10								
11	revenue from poiuyts	$147,898.37		$59.45	-$4.72		$147,957.82	$147,893.65
12	revenue from qwerts	$53,773.51		-$5.57	$26.00		$53,767.94	$53,799.50
13	total revenue	$201,671.88		$53.88	$21.28		$201,725.76	$201,693.16
14								
15	total cost	$87,475.88		$53.90	$21.30		$87,529.78	$87,497.18
16								
17	profits	$114,196.00		-$0.02	-$0.02		$114,195.98	$114,195.98

Sheet2 / Sheet3

Figure 3.19. The solution to Problem 3.8 in a spreadsheet.

Solution to Problem 3.10

This is a simple variation on the seat-allocation problem from Section 3.6, with a small twist added in part b. I do it with calculus; you can do it with your own spreadsheet if you wish.

(a) Total revenue from Wolverton supporters is $20W - W^2/2000$, so marginal revenue is $20 - 2W/2000$. Total revenue from Manteca supporters is $24M - M^2/3000$, so marginal revenue is $24 - 2M/3000$. Since seats trade one for one between the two groups, we cannot have optimized if the marginal revenues are not equal: At the optimal (gate-receipts-maximizing) allocation of seats,

$$20 - \frac{2W}{2000} = 24 - \frac{2M}{3000} \quad \text{or} \quad \frac{2M}{3000} = 4 + \frac{2W}{2000},$$

which is

$$4M = 24{,}000 + 6W, \quad \text{or} \quad 2M = 12{,}000 + 3W.$$

Assuming we want to allocate all 30,000 seats, we must also satisfy

$$M + W = 30{,}000, \quad \text{or} \quad M = 30{,}000 - W.$$

Substituting for $30{,}000 - W$ for M in the previous equation, this gives us

$$2(30{,}000 - W) = 12{,}000 + 3W \quad \text{or} \quad 48{,}000 = 5W \quad \text{or} \quad W = 9600,$$

and therefore $M = 20{,}400$. Just to check, the marginal revenue from a Maneteca seat when $M = 20{,}400$ is $24 - (2 \times 20{,}400/3000) = £10.40$, while the marginal revenue from a Wolverton seat when $W = 9600$ is $20 - (2 \times 9600/2000) = £10.40$.

(b) Here comes the twist. This looks just like part a, and we proceed to solve it the way we solved part a. The equal marginal revenue condition does not change at all:

$$2M = 12{,}000 + 3W.$$

But this time we have 60,000 seats instead of 30,000, so

$$M = 60{,}000 - W.$$

Therefore,

$$2(60{,}000 - W) = 12{,}000 + 3W \quad \text{or} \quad 108{,}000 = 5W \quad \text{or} \quad W = 21{,}600,$$

and so M = 38,400. To run the check, marginal revenue from a Manteca seat when M = 38,400 is $24 - (2 \times 38{,}400/3000) = -£1.60$; marginal revenue from a Wolverton seat when W = 21,600 is $20 - (2 \times 21{,}600/2000) = -£1.60$. The two marginal revenue figures are equal, *but they are negative.* This means that if we only sold, say, 21,599 seats to Wolverton supporters, we would make an additional £1.60 in gate receipts from Wolverton supporters. If we must allocate that seat to a Manteca supporter, we lose this gain, but why not instead leave the seat empty?

This is a case where marginal revenues hit 0 before all the seats are allocated. Assuming we need not sell all the seats (that is, assuming the constraint is $W + M$ is *less than or equal to* 60,000), in this case we want to leave some seats empty. We sell seats to Manteca supporters until the marginal revenue from that group hits 0:

$$0 = 24 - \frac{2M}{3000} \quad \text{or} \quad M = 36{,}000,$$

and we sell seats to Wolverton supporters until marginal revenue from them hits 0:

$$0 = 20 - \frac{2W}{2000} \quad \text{or} \quad W = 20{,}000,$$

which means that we sell only 56,000 of the 60,000 seats.

The moral is this: The check I ran at the end of part a, which looked like a check on my algebra—did I really equalize the marginal revenues?—has another purpose. I do not know, a priori, if I want to allocate all the seats between supporters of the two teams. So I assume that I do, then, after I get the gate-receipts-maximizing allocation of all the seats, I check to see if the marginal revenue from the seats is still positive. If so, I did want to allocate all the seats; on the margin, seats are still valuable and I'd like a venue with larger seating capacity. But, if the (equal) marginal revenues are negative, then I know that to maximize gate receipts, some seats should go empty, and I allocate to the point where the marginal revenue from a seat, to either group, is 0.

Solution to Problem 3.11

Adding the constraint that $x_p + x_q \leq 2000$ does *bind* on us, since we know from the solution to Problem 3.8 that without that constraint, the optimal production plan has $x_p + x_q = 3001.6$. This additional constraint means that there is a one-to-one trade-off between x_p and x_q, and so we can find the answer one of three ways:

1. Ask Solver to resolve the problem, adding in the constraint. Very easy to do, as long as Solver is handy.

2. Recognize that, since there is a one-to-one trade-off, we want to find x_p and x_q that sum to 2000 and such that the marginal profit figures for the two variables are identical. You can use the spreadsheet and hunt for the answer by hand or you might be able to come up with a more sophisticated way of doing this.

3. Do the problem analytically, using calculus. Because of the one-to-one trade-off, the two marginal profit figures, which are just partial derivatives, must be equalized. That is, at the optimum,

$$\frac{\partial \pi(x_p, x_q)}{\partial x_p} = 80 - \frac{42x_p}{1200} - \frac{15x_q}{1200} = 70 - \frac{50x_q}{1200} - \frac{15x_p}{1200} = \frac{\partial \pi(x_p, x_q)}{\partial x_q}.$$

This is

$$10 + \frac{35x_q}{1200} = \frac{27x_p}{1200}, \quad \text{or} \quad 12{,}000 + 35x_q = 27x_p.$$

We are guessing that, at the optimum, $x_q + x_p = 2000$, so we can replace x_p in the last equation by $2000 - x_q$. We get

$$12{,}000 + 35x_q = 27(2000 - x_q) \quad \text{or} \quad 62x_q = 42{,}000,$$

which gives $x_q = 677.419$ and therefore $x_p = 1322.581$. To check that this is right, we evaluate the two marginal profit figures at these values: The two marginal profit figures should equal one another and be positive. I suggest you try this using the spreadsheet PROBLEM 3.8. It works.

Solution to Problem 3.12

The reason this problem has no pat answer is that the decision by the head of the Poiuyt Division depends on what she thinks the head of the Qwert Division will decide and vice versa. And we have no way to know what each side thinks about the other.

To establish that each side's actions depend on what the division heads think the other would do, suppose the head of the Poiuyt Division believes that the head of the Qwert Division will choose $x_q = 3000$. Then Poiuyts sell for $90 - x_p/100 - 3000/300 = 80 - x_p/100$, and Poiuyt Division Revenue is

$$80x_p - \frac{x_p^2}{100}.$$

Division variable cost is $10x_p$. Therefore, the Poiuyt Division marginal revenue is $80 - x_p/50$, which equals the division marginal cost of 10 if $70 - x_p/50 = 0$, or $x_p = 3500$.

But, if the head of the Poiuyt Division believes that the Qwert Division will choose $x_q = 4500$, Poiuyt Division total revenue is $75x_p - x_p^2/100$. Equating divisional marginal revenue to marginal cost gives $x_p = 65 \times 50 = 3250$.

Similarly, the decision of the Qwert Division head depends on what he believes the Poiuyt Division will do.

In Chapters 21 and 22, we deal with problems of this sort, and we learn that even when you know how to attack this sort of problem, the answers are not clear. But, for the time being, we use the technique of looking for a *Nash equilibrium* of a one-shot game between the two divisional heads, where each chooses quantity, simultaneously and independently of the other. In a Nash equilibrium, each side correctly anticipates the optimal choice of the other party and optimizes given those anticipations. That is, we look for decisions x_p^* and x_q^* such that x_p^* maximizes Poiuyt Division variable profit, if the Poiuyt Division head anticipates that the Qwert Division will produce x_q^* qwerts, and vice versa.

The math goes as follows. (I tell you how to do this with a spreadsheet in a moment.) Given x_q^*, the Poiuyt Division's marginal revenue is

$$90 - \frac{x_q^*}{300} - \frac{x_p}{50}.$$

Set this equal to divisional marginal cost of 10, and you get the equation

$$80 = \frac{x_q^*}{300} + \frac{x_p^*}{50}. \tag{3.1}$$

The Qwert Division's marginal revenue given x_p^* is

$$120 - \frac{x_p^*}{150} - \frac{x_q}{50},$$

which, when set equal to the qwert marginal cost of $20, gives the equation

$$100 = \frac{x_p^*}{150} + \frac{x_q^*}{50}. \tag{3.2}$$

We have to solve equations (3.1) and (3.2) simultaneously; the answer is $x_q^* = 3882.3$ and $x_p^* = 3352.3$, approximately.

If you want to do this with a spreadsheet, the problem is to find quantities for the two divisions such that, for each division, *its* divisional marginal revenue (for its product) equals its product's marginal cost. If you conduct this search successfully, or if you plug in the numbers just derived, you will be looking at the spreadsheet shown in Figure 3.20.

	A	B	C	D	E	F	G	H
1								
2				discrete margins	discrete margins		values for	values for
3		Basic values		in poiuyts	in qwerts		one more poiuyt	one more qwert
4								
5	number of poiuyts	3352.3					3353.3	3352.3
6	number of qwerts	3882.3					3882.3	3883.3
7								
8	price of a poiuyt	$43.54					$43.53	$43.53
9	price of a qwert	$58.83					$58.82	$58.82
10								
11	revenue from poiuyts	$145,945.73		$10.00	-$11.17		$145,955.74	$145,934.56
12	revenue from qwerts	$228,389.24		-$25.88	$20.00		$228,363.36	$228,409.23
13	total revenue	$374,334.97		-$15.88	$8.82		$374,319.09	$374,343.79
14								
15	total cost	$112,169.00		$10.00	$20.00		$112,179.00	$112,189.00
16								
17	profits	$262,165.97		-$25.88	-$11.18		$262,140.09	$262,154.79

Figure 3.20. Spreadsheet CHAP3-2, used to solve Problem 3.12. We search for quantities of poiuyts and qwerts such that, for each product or division, the marginal revenue of the division in its product equals the marginal cost of its product; that is, we want D11 to equal D15 and E12 to equal E15. Note that this gives significantly less total profit, $262.155K, than obtained at the overall profit-maximizing solution of $x_p = 2000$ and $x_q = 4000$, which gives a profit of $279K.

The key comparison is between the overall profit figure with these production levels, $262K or so, and the overall profit figure from Figure 3.7 in the text, with the optimal production levels, which is $279K. The firm loses $17K, about 6% of what is possible, by decentralizing in this fashion.

Why does this happen? Neither division's management is taking into account the adverse effect its output has on the price, and hence the revenue, of the other division. The Poiuyt Division, by cutting back its production of poiuyts by one, would have a very small negative impact on its divisional profit, but it would improve the Qwert Division's profit by $25.88. And the Qwert Division, by pulling back its production by one, would improve the Poiuyt Division's profit by $11.18. The cost accounting done here does not pick up the *externality* that each division imposes on its sister division and so leads to production levels that are suboptimal from the point of view of the firm overall.

This is not simply a theoretical possibility; think, for instance, of different divisions of General Motors—Chevrolet, Pontiac, Oldsmobile, etc.—setting their prices without regard to the competition among them. To account properly in cases like this—in the sense that divisional managements have the interests of the greater firm in mind—something must be done so that each division internalizes the effect it has on the other division's prices and hence profits.

We return to this issue in Chapter 14. But, since the issue is raised here, I ought to say that cost accounts to deal with this problem can be very difficult to implement, since in real life (much more complex than this toy problem), this is very difficult to get right. In theory, a charge should be levied against each division equal to the impact it has on the profit of the other division. But how do you compute that charge? For instance, most people would think that increased sales by the Chevrolet Division of GM hurts the Pontiac Division because of interdivisional competition for customers. But, when General Motors was originally constructed by Alfred P. Sloan, he believed there would be *positive* effects on marketing between at least some divisions: Customers would progress from, say, Chevrolets to Pontiacs or Buicks to Oldsmobiles and finally to Cadillacs as they became richer, always staying within the GM family. If Sloan was right, Buick should *pay* a transfer price to Chevrolet for every additional Chevy sold.

Let me close by adding that this sort of problem in real life is even more complex than it may now seem to you. Why would the firm leave decisions in the hands of divisional managers? Why decentralize? The reason is that divisional managers presumably know more about their division's business than headquarters does. If headquarters could see these spreadsheets, it could dictate production quantities to the division in accordance with the optimal numbers, from Figure 3.7. Headquarters, almost by definition, does not know these numbers. Moreover, headquarters rewards division managers based on how well their division does, to motivate divisional manager behavior that is in the interest of the firm. This leads us almost immediately into questions about incentives, which we reach only in Chapter 19. Put it this way: Suppose the next CEO of this firm will be whichever of the two division managers does the best in terms of divisional profit. Then, from the position in Figure 3.20, both division managers might want to increase their production still further: Doing so diminishes their own division profit, but at least on the margin, it diminishes the division profit of the other division more quickly. And, if both divisions increase their output, the firm overall will do worse still.

Can you "solve" this problem right now? No, you lack some crucial tools. But, even after you acquire those tools, real-life examples of this sort of problem are dreadfully hard to solve. Solutions are often beyond the wits of experienced managers, who have a complete grasp of the economics of the situation. The key, once you understand how hard this problem is, is to take steps to avoid it: Design the organization (what goes in which division) to minimize the numbers of these externalities among the divisions created. But that takes us very far afield of current topics, so I leave this here with the clear message that managerial accounting is a lot harder and a lot more important than you might have thought.

Material for Chapter 4

Demand Functions

Solution to Problem 4.1

(a) Figure 4.3 depicts the optimized spreadsheet, PROBLEM 4.1, used to solve this problem with Excel and Solver. Note that price is the driving variable; that is, quantity is computed from the price entry. Then (a nice feature of Excel), total cost is computed from quantity. (You need to get the spreadsheet and look at the cell definitions to see this.) The answer is a price of \$30 and a corresponding quantity of 40,000 units.

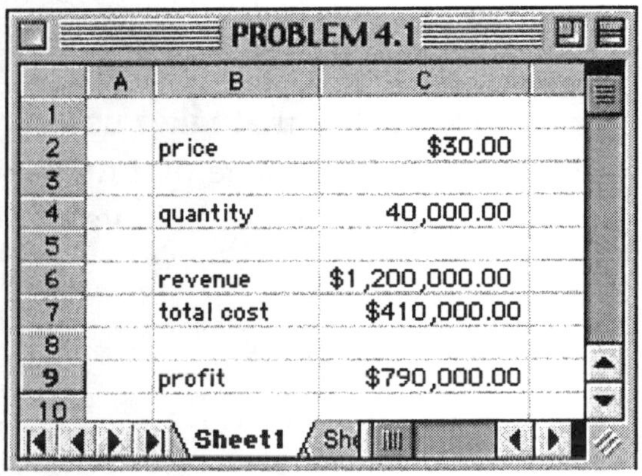

PROBLEM 4.1

	A	B	C
1			
2		price	\$30.00
3			
4		quantity	40,000.00
5			
6		revenue	\$1,200,000.00
7		total cost	\$410,000.00
8			
9		profit	\$790,000.00
10			

Figure 4.3. The spreadsheet solution to Problem 4.1.

(b) To solve this problem analytically in quantities, we have to express revenue as a function of quantity. This means taking the demand function $D(p) = 2000(50 - p)$ and inverting it, to get the corresponding inverse demand function, $P(x) = 50 - x/2000$. With this done, $\mathrm{TR}(x) = 50x - x^2/2000$, and marginal revenue is $\mathrm{MR}(x) = 50 - 2x/2000$. Since total cost is already expressed as a function of quantity, we simply take its derivative to get marginal cost, $\mathrm{MC}(x) = 10$. Then we note that marginal revenue is a decreasing linear function and marginal cost is constant. They cross once, with marginal revenue going from above to below marginal cost. They cross at the profit-maximizing quantity, which is the solution to

$$50 - \frac{2x}{2000} = 10 \quad \text{or} \quad 40 = \frac{2x}{2000} \quad \text{or} \quad x = 40{,}000.$$

It is easy to plug this quantity into the inverse demand function, to get the corresponding optimal price, $p = \$30$.

(c) To solve this problem analytically in price, it is easy to write total revenue as a function of price. This is just $p \times D(p)$, or $100{,}000p - 2000p^2$. The key is to write cost as a function of price. Given a price p, the quantity produced is $2000(50 - p)$, and total cost as a function of quantity is $10{,}000 + 10x$, so in terms of price, total cost is just

$$10{,}000 + 10[2000(50 - p)] = 1{,}010{,}000 - 20{,}000p.$$

Profit as a function of price is therefore

$$100{,}000p - 2000p^2 - [1{,}010{,}000 - 20{,}000p] = 120{,}000p - 2000p^2 - 1{,}010{,}000,$$

which is a parabola with a negative coefficient in the quadratic term. Thus, simple algebra plus calculus tells us that this expression for profit is maximized where its derivative is 0, which is the solution to

$$120{,}000 - 4000p = 0 \quad \text{or} \quad p = \frac{120{,}000}{4000} = 30.$$

Plugging a price of 30 back into the demand function gives the corresponding optimal quantity of 40,000 units.

Which did you find easier: method b or c? Most people think they are of roughly equal difficulty. But, for sundry reasons, we invariably use method b, working in quantities, in this book. One reason why can be gleaned from trying Problem 4.17; if total cost is a bit more complex, method c becomes very difficult. A second reason is that, for perfectly competitive firms, method c does not make sense. (Firms choose quantity; price is given to them.) Still, it is worth knowing that you can do this either way, if you want, because very occasionally, method c is analytically more convenient.

Solution to Problem 4.3

(a) Figure 4.4 shows a simple spreadsheet PROBLEM 4.3 that obtains the desired numbers. Column B lists the 11 prices, and column C computes the corresponding levels of demand. Column D adds one cent to the price in column B (a nice, small

	A	B	C	D	E	F
			PROBLEM 4.3			
1						
2		price	demand	price + .01	new demand	elasticity
3		$1.00	11000	$1.01	10990	-0.0909
4		$2.00	10000	$2.01	9990	-0.2000
5		$3.00	9000	$3.01	8990	-0.3333
6		$4.00	8000	$4.01	7990	-0.5000
7		$5.00	7000	$5.01	6990	-0.7143
8		$6.00	6000	$6.01	5990	-1.0000
9		$7.00	5000	$7.01	4990	-1.4000
10		$8.00	4000	$8.01	3990	-2.0000
11		$9.00	3000	$9.01	2990	-3.0000
12		$10.00	2000	$10.01	1990	-5.0000
13		$11.00	1000	$11.01	990	-11.0000

Sheet1 / Sheet2 / Sheet3 /

Figure 4.4. Computing elasticities along the demand function $D(p) = 1000(12 - p)$.

discrete change in price), and column E computes the corresponding (changed) quantity. Then, in column F, formula (4.1) is employed to calculate elasticity.

It is worth noting that, for low prices and large demands, elasticities are close to 0. At the midpoint of the linear demand function, elasticity is -1. For high prices and small levels of demand, elasticity becomes very large (negative).

Doing this with calculus and with price as the variable,

$$\nu(p) = D'(p)\frac{p}{D(p)} = -1000\frac{p}{1000(12 - p)} = -\frac{p}{12 - p}.$$

Note that this function is close to 0 for prices close to 0, and it explodes to $-\infty$ for prices close to 12. Also, it is -1 when $p = 12 - p$, which is the midpoint $p = 6$; it is less than -1 (demand is elastic) when $p > 6$ and it is greater than -1 (demand is inelastic) when $p < 6$.

With calculus and quantity as the variable, inverse demand is $P(x) = 12 - x/1000$, so

$$\hat{\nu}(x) = \frac{1}{P'(x)} \times \frac{P(x)}{x} = \frac{1}{-1/1000} \times \frac{12 - x/1000}{x}$$

$$= -1000\frac{12 - x/1000}{x} = -\frac{12{,}000 - x}{x},$$

where x runs between 0 and 12,000. For quantities of x close to 0, this is a very large negative number (very elastic demand); for quantities x close to 12,000, this is very close to 0 (very inelastic demand); it is -1 when $12,000 - x = x$ or $x = 6000$, which is the midpoint of the demand function; it is less than -1 (elastic demand; positive marginal revenue) for $x < 6000$; and it is greater than -1 (inelastic demand; negative marginal revenue), for $x > 6000$.

(b) The pattern observed in part a works precisely for all linear demand functions. First, let me write out the formulas for the relevant functions:

$$\nu(p) = -\frac{Bp}{A - Bp}, \quad \hat{\nu}(x) = -\frac{A - x}{x}, \quad \text{and} \quad \text{MR}(x) = \frac{A - 2x}{B}.$$

For high prices and low quantities ($p > A/(2B)$, $x < A/2$), demand is elastic (less than -1) and marginal revenue is positive. Marginal revenue hits 0 and elasticity hits -1 at the midpoint of the demand function, where $p = A/(2B)$ and $x = A/2$. And for large quantities (greater than $A/2$) and small prices (less than $A/(2B)$), demand is inelastic and marginal revenue is negative.

Examples with linear demand functions abound, so it may be helpful to summarize the last paragraph in a picture. See Figure 4.5.

Solution to Problem 4.4

(a) A \$0.10 drop in price on a base price of \$8.00 is a $0.1/8 = 0.0125 = 1.25\%$ drop in price. The problem states that a 1% change in price gives a 3% change in quantity— in other words, elasticity is -3—so this 1.25% drop in price means an increase in quantity sold of 3.75%. On the base of 10,000 units, 3.75% is 375 units, so quantity sold will increase to 10,375.

Therefore total revenue or receipts, which were previously \$80,000 (or \$8 times 10,000 units) change to $\$7.90 \times 10,375 = \$81,962.50$, or an increase of \$1,962.50.

(b) A 150-unit decrease in sales, on a base of 10,000 units, is a 1.5% decrease. Therefore, with elasticity equal to -3, this means a 0.5% increase in price. On a base of \$8.00 per unit, this means a \$0.04 rise in price. Therefore, total revenue, which was \$80,000, changes to $\$8.04 \times 9850 = \$79,194$, or a fall of \$806.

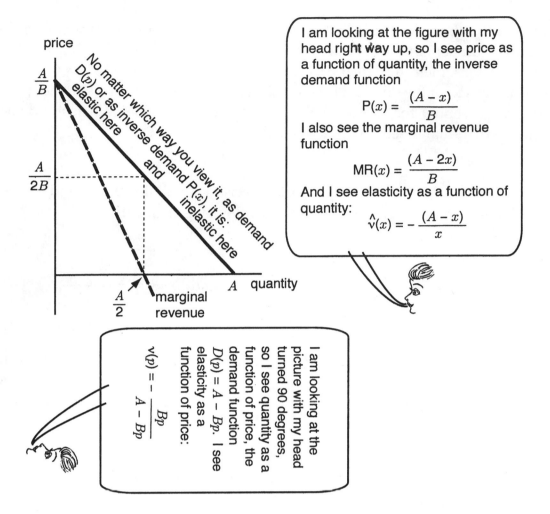

Figure 4.5. The case of linear (inverse) demand. All linear (inverse) demand functions—and you will see a lot of them—behave the same way when it comes to elasticity: Unit elasticity (= −1) at the midpoint; elastic for high prices–low quantities; inelastic for low prices–high quantities.

Alternatively, we can use the formula

$$\frac{\mathrm{dTR}(x)}{\mathrm{d}x} = P(x)\left[1 + \frac{1}{\hat{\nu}(x)}\right]$$

which in this case gives

$$\frac{\mathrm{dTR}(x)}{\mathrm{d}x} = 8\left[1 + \frac{1}{-3}\right] = \frac{16}{3}.$$

Thus, a decrease of 150 units means a change in total revenue of

$$\frac{16}{3}(-150) = -\$800,$$

or a fall of $800.

We do not get quite the same answer (the two methods approximate discrete changes from derivatives slightly differently) but either gets us a good guess, as long as the change contemplated is small.

Solution to Problem 4.7

The key is to find how many more units the firm would sell per month, if it dropped its price to $12.50. A very slick technique is to fit the constant elasticity of demand function with elasticity -2.5 to the data we are given, namely that demand at a price of $14 is 30,000. That is, solve for C in the equation

$$30{,}000 = C \times 14^{-2.5}.$$

This gives $C = 22{,}000{,}945$ (approximately) and hence $D(\$12.50) = 22{,}000{,}945 \times 12.50^{-2.5} = 39{,}826$. So production and sales increase by 9,826 per month. From here it is easy to compute total revenue, total cost, and therefore profit at the two prices $14 and $12.50. Do the math and you will find that profit goes up by $4,130.

I suspect that this is a bit too slick for many readers, so let me show you some other ways to get approximate answers. First, we have to compute how much production and sales increase when prices drop from $14 to $12.50. This is a $1.50 decline in price, which on a base of $14 is a $1.5/14 = 0.107 = 10.7\%$ decline in prices. An elasticity of -2.5 means that each percent drop in price is a 2.5% rise in quantity, so a 10.7% decline in price means a 26.8% rise in quantity. On a base of 30,000 units, this is an 8040 unit increase in sales.

The slick answer gave us almost 10,000 increase in sales; here we got only 8040. Why the difference? Because we based our calculation on a $1.50 fall in price on a base of $14.00. Suppose instead we had used $12.50 as the base price. Then, a $1.50 rise in price from $12.50 is a 12% change in price, which (with an elasticity of -2.5) means a 30% change in quantity. We are looking for the quantity x such that a 30% decrease in that quantity leaves us at 30,000 units, or $0.7x = 30{,}000$, or $x = 42{,}857$. That is, computing with $12.50 and the unknown quantity as the base for percentage calculations gives us an overestimate: the quantity changes by 12,857.

To the extent that elasticity truly stays at -2.5 for prices inside this range, the slick calculations give the precisely correct answer. But the two approximate answers are not bad approximations. And from either one, it is relatively easy to calculate the change in profit.

Solution to Problem 4.9

To get total demand, we need demand functions for each group, so the first step is to invert each inverse demand function:

- For the youth group, $P_y(x_y) = 10 - x_y/1000$. I assume (which is entirely standard in all examples of this sort) that this means that for prices above 10, there is no demand by this group. There is demand for prices from 10 to 0, given by solving $p = 10 - x_y/1000$ for x_y, which is $D_y(p) = 1000(10 - p)$.

- Similarly, demand for the middle-aged group is 0 for prices above 15, and for prices between 15 and 0, it is given by $D_m(p) = 2000(15 - p)$.

- Demand for seniors is 0 for prices above 12.5, and it is given by $D_s(p) = 800(12.5 - p)$ for prices from 12.5 down to 0.

Total demand is the sum of these three group demand functions. No group buys at prices above 15, only the middle-aged group buys from 15 to 12.5, the middle-aged and seniors buy from 12.5 to 10, and all three groups buy from 10 to 0. Therefore, total demand is

$$D(p) = \begin{cases} 0, & \text{if } p > 15, \\ 2000(15 - p), & \text{if } 15 \geq p > 12.5, \\ 2000(15 - p) + 800(12.5 - p), & \text{if } 12.5 \geq p > 10, \text{ and} \\ 2000(15 - p) + 800(12.5 - p) + 1000(10 - p), & \text{if } 10 \geq p \geq 0. \end{cases}$$

Collecting terms in each line yields

$$D(p) = \begin{cases} 0, & \text{if } p > 15, \\ 30{,}000 - 2000p, & \text{if } 15 \geq p > 12.5, \\ 40{,}000 - 2800p & \text{if } 12.5 \geq p > 10, \text{ and} \\ 50{,}000 - 3800p, & \text{if } 10 \geq p \geq 0. \end{cases}$$

Students sometimes worry, in defining the price ranges, whether weak or strict inequalities should be used. Since the demand function is continuous across each of those prices, it does not matter.

The problem also asked for inverse demand. To find this, we invert the demand function just computed. We do this in sections. First, note that, at $p = 0$, demand is 50,000 units, so this is an upper bound on the quantity that can be sold. (We say, in writing down the inverse demand function, that price at quantities above 50,000 is 0.) Now we have to break the quantity range, from 0 to 50,000, into quantity intervals that correspond to prices from 15 to 12.5, from 12.5 to 10, and from 10 to 0. To do this, we plug the prices 12.5 and 10 into the demand function, finding that $D(12.5) = 5000$ and $D(10) = 12{,}000$. Hence, from quantity level 0 to 5000, demand is $30{,}000 - 2000p$, so inverse demand is $P(x) = 15 - x/2000$. From quantity level 5000 to 12,000, demand is $40{,}000 - 2800p$, hence inverse demand is $P(x) = 40{,}000/2800 - x/2800 = 14.2857 - x/2800$. From quantity level 12,000 to 50,000, demand is $50{,}000 - 3800p$, hence inverse demand is $13.1579 - x/3800$. Putting together the pieces,

$$P(x) = \begin{cases} 15 - x/2000, & \text{for } 5000 \geq x \geq 0, \\ 14.2857 - x/2800, & \text{for } 12{,}000 > x > 5000, \\ 13.1579 - x/3800, & \text{for } 50{,}000 \geq x > 12{,}000, \text{ and} \\ 0, & \text{for } x > 50{,}000. \end{cases}$$

Solution to Problem 4.10

We are given demand for each of the two groups, so we can quickly write down aggregate demand:

$$D(p) = \begin{cases} 0, & \text{if } p > 20, \\ 5000(20 - p), & \text{if } 20 \geq p > 14, \text{and} \\ 5000(20 - p) + 10{,}000(14 - p) = 240{,}000 - 15{,}000p, & \text{if } 14 \geq p \geq 0 \end{cases}$$

In Figure 4.6, you see this demand function drawn in as a solid line. Ignore the dashed lines for the moment. (You will see in a moment that drawing this demand function is really useful.) Take careful note of the kink in the demand function at the price 14; note also that the quantity at this price is 30,000 units.

To solve the profit-maximization problem, we can use calculus or Excel and Solver. And there are two ways to use Excel and Solver, using a logical function or using constraints. I begin with the two ways to use Excel and Solver.

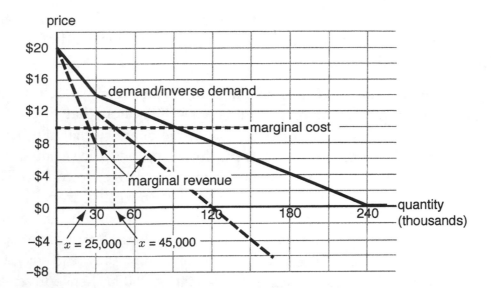

Figure 4.6. Problem 4.10 in a graph. The solid, kinked line is the demand/inverse demand function, from which we get the marginal revenue function (shown as a dashed line with large dashes). Note that marginal revenue jumps at the quantity 30,000, which corresponds to the price $14, where demand is kinked. Marginal cost is a constant $10, drawn in as a dashed line with small dashes: Because marginal revenue cuts marginal cost twice (three times if you count the jump), we have two candidates for the profit-maximizing quantity. The text describes how this is resolved.

The spreadsheet in question is PROBLEM 4.10. Begin with sheet 1, shown here as Figure 4.7(a). Cell B1 contains the price, entered as $12. Cell B2 gives demand, and this is the key entry. In Excel, the formula is

$$= IF(B1 > 14, 5000*(20 - B1), 240000 - 15000*B1)$$

That is, the computer takes the price and applies one of two formulas to calculate the quantity demanded, depending on whether the price is above or below $14. Cell B3 computes profit using the formula $= (B1 - 10)*B2$, making use of the fact that marginal cost is a constant $10. (While marginal cost is a constant $10, the problem statement leaves open the possibility that the firm has nonzero fixed cost. If there is a nonzero fixed cost, the entry in B3 is gross of that fixed cost, meaning with the fixed cost not included in the calculation.)

Ask Solver to maximize B3, changing cell B1, and you should get what is shown in Figure 4.7(b): The profit-maximizing price is $13, for a quantity sold of 45,000 and a profit of $135,000. (If you tried this on you own and Solver told you the answer was $15, do not despair. It may be Solver's fault and not yours. I explain in a bit.)

To solve the problem in Excel using constraints, move to sheet 2 of PROBLEM 4.10,

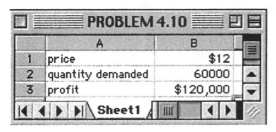

(a) Prior to optimization

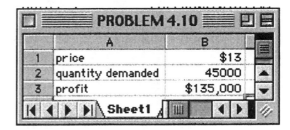

(b) After optimization

Figure 4.7. Solving Problem 4.10 with Excel, using a logical function. This figure shows sheet 1 of the spreadsheet PROBLEM 4.10, which solves Problem 4.10 using a logical function in Excel. The key is the formula for cell B2, which is based on a test of whether the price (the value in cell B1) is greater or less than $14. Panel a shows the spreadsheet with the initial value for price of $12, while panel b shows the spreadsheet after Solver was told to maximize profit, varying price.

depicted as Figure 4.8(a). Lines 3, 4, and 5 contain price, quantity demanded, and profit, where the quantity demanded is computed from the price using the demand function formula for prices above $14. Lines 10, 11, and 12 contain price, quantity demanded, and profit, once again, except that in line 11, the formula for quantity demanded as a function of the price is the formula appropriate for prices $14 and below, namely = 5000(20 − B10) + 10,000(14 − B10). I use trial values for the prices of $17 in the top half of the spreadsheet and $12 in the bottom half.

Now, call up Solver and optimize. The key is that, in the top part of the spreadsheet, I instruct Solver to maximize B5 by varying B3, *subject to the constraint that B3 must be greater than or equal to $14.* And I instruct Solver to maximize B12, by varying B10, subject to the constraint that B10 must be less or equal to $14. (As described at the start of *Companion Material for Chapter 1,* I could do this in one go with Solver. But, in this instance, I decided not to do so, so the exposition would be clearer.) The answers are in panel b of Figure 4.8. We see that, if constrained to a price above $14, the price $15 is best. For prices below $14, $13 is best. The grand optimizing price is $13, since it gives greater profit than $14. The two methods agree.

(I still reserve the explanation of how it might happen that, with sheet 1, Solver might give you $15 as the answer. I'll get there, but it will help to solve this problem analytically first.)

To do it analytically, with calculus, we use MC = MR. Marginal cost is a constant $10. What is the marginal revenue function? To find it, we first need inverse demand, so we go back to the demand function and invert it piece by piece, in

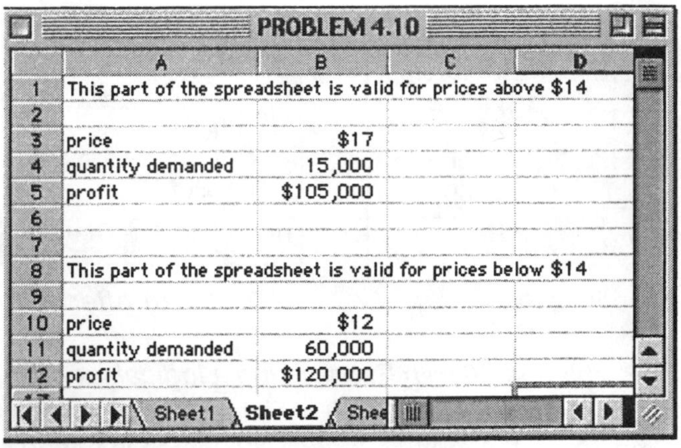

PROBLEM 4.10

	A	B	C	D
1	This part of the spreadsheet is valid for prices above $14			
2				
3	price	$17		
4	quantity demanded	15,000		
5	profit	$105,000		
6				
7				
8	This part of the spreadsheet is valid for prices below $14			
9				
10	price	$12		
11	quantity demanded	60,000		
12	profit	$120,000		

Sheet1 Sheet2 Shee

(a) Initial values

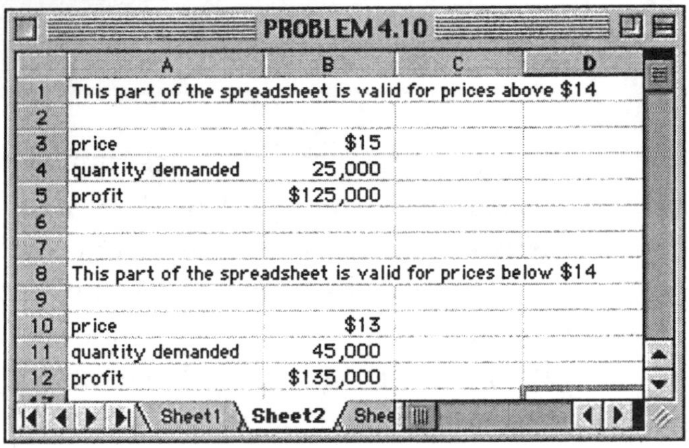

PROBLEM 4.10

	A	B	C	D
1	This part of the spreadsheet is valid for prices above $14			
2				
3	price	$15		
4	quantity demanded	25,000		
5	profit	$125,000		
6				
7				
8	This part of the spreadsheet is valid for prices below $14			
9				
10	price	$13		
11	quantity demanded	45,000		
12	profit	$135,000		

Sheet1 Sheet2 Shee

(b) Optimized Values

Figure 4.8. Solving Problem 4.10 with Excel using constraints. This figure shows sheet 2 of the spreadsheet PROBLEM 4-10, which solves Problem 4.10 using constraints. Rather than use a logical variable to get the formula for demand in one go, we set up two pieces of spreadsheet, one for prices above $14, and the second for prices below $14. When we optimize, using Solver, we optimize the top piece constraining price to be above $14 and the bottom piece constraining price to be below $14. Panel a shows the spreadsheet with the initial values for prices of $17 and $12, while panel b shows the spreadsheet after Solver maximized profit in each part, varying price, subject to the appropriate constraint.

exactly the manner described in the solution to Problem 4.9. The critical price of $14 corresponds to a quantity of 30,000. So we get the inverse demand function

$$P(x) = \begin{cases} 20 - x/5000, & \text{if } 0 \leq x < 30{,}000, \\ 240{,}000/15{,}000 - x/15{,}000 = 16 - x/15{,}000, & \text{if } 30{,}000 \leq x \leq 240{,}000, \text{ and} \\ 0, & \text{if } x > 240{,}000. \end{cases}$$

We get total revenue by multiplying inverse demand by x:

$$\text{TR}(x) = \begin{cases} 20x - x^2/5000, & \text{if } 0 \leq x < 30{,}000, \\ 16x - x^2/15{,}000, & \text{if } 30{,}000 \leq x \leq 240{,}000, \text{ and} \\ 0, & \text{if } x > 240{,}000. \end{cases}$$

Then we take derivatives to find marginal revenue:

$$\text{MR}(x) = \begin{cases} 20 - 2x/5000, & \text{if } 0 < x < 30{,}000, \\ 16 - 2x/15{,}000, & \text{if } 30{,}000 < x < 240{,}000, \text{ and} \\ 0, & \text{if } x > 240{,}000. \end{cases}$$

Read this very carefully and you will note that in writing down marginal revenue, I shifted from a mix of weak and strict inequalities for my ranges of x, to all strict inequalities. For inverse demand and total revenue, it does not matter which inequalities you use, since inverse demand and total revenue are continuous functions across these critical quantities. But, if inverse demand and total revenue are continuous, they also have kinks at the critical quantities and so, strictly speaking, marginal revenue, being the derivative of total revenue, is not defined.

If I just lost you in math speak, the thing to do is to graph the marginal revenue function just computed on the same graph as inverse demand. This is done in Figure 4.6; marginal revenue is the dashed line with large dashes. Note that marginal revenue "jumps up" at the critical quantity of 30,000. (It also jumps up to 0 at $x = 240{,}000$, but I am less concerned with this.) This jump is precise evidence of the kink in total revenue; as we approach the quantity level 30,000 from below, marginal revenue approaches \$8 per unit, but when the quantity goes from 30,000 to 30,001, total revenue suddenly increases by \$12.

Now, superimpose the marginal cost function, a constant \$10. This is drawn as a line of short dashes in Figure 4.6. Note that marginal cost cuts marginal revenue more than once. The first intersection is where $20 - 2x/5000 = 10$, which is $x = 25{,}000$. At this intersection, marginal revenue goes from above marginal cost to below it. Then, at $x = 30{,}000$, the "jump" passes from below marginal cost to above. And, at the solution to $16 - 2x/15{,}000 = 10$, or $x = 45{,}000$, marginal revenue again cuts marginal cost from above to below.

What does all this mean for profit? Since marginal revenue begins above marginal cost, profit rises initially. It rises until the first intersection point, $x = 25{,}000$, at which point profit begins to fall. Therefore, $x = 25{,}000$ is a local maximum of profit. Profit falls until $x = 30{,}000$, where marginal revenue suddenly jumps; profit suddenly shifts direction and starts rising again. It continues to rise until $x = 45,000$, where it begins to fall and, since marginal revenue is now forever below marginal cost, continues to fall for all subsequent production levels. Therefore, $x = 45,000$ is a second local maximum.

What is the profit-maximizing production level? It is clearly either $x = 25,000$ or $x = 45,000$, and the only way to choose between the two is to evaluate the two levels of profit that go with these quantities. First, compute the prices that correspond to these production levels: $x = 25,000$ goes with a price of $15, while $x = 45,000$ corresponds to a price of $13. Then, the corresponding profit levels are $25,000(15 - 10) = $125,000$, and $45,000(13 - 10) = $135,000$. The second intersection gives more profit.

Let me close with two remarks.

1. If you go back to the point made by Problem 3.6 and examine the graph in Figure 4.6 closely, you'll see unmistakeable graphical evidence that the second intersection point is profit maximizing, without doing the calculations.

2. I mentioned that the first method of using Excel, with a logical function, might come to grief or, at least, to the price $15, when running Solver. In fact, with my computer and Excel, if I begin Solver on sheet 1 of PROBLEM 4.10 at the value of $15.10 instead of $12, Solver happily reports back that $15 is the answer. Solver climbs hills by looking for directions to move that increase its objective function (if it is maximizing), and if it is started near a local maximum that is not a global maximum, it can easily get stuck at the local maximum.

Do Real-Life Marginal Revenue Functions Ever Increase?

An interesting feature of the previous problem is that, because of the kink in the demand and inverse demand functions, marginal revenue jumps up. This, ultimately, is the source of the multiple solutions of MC = MR. But this is only a toy example. You might wonder whether, in real-life applications, you can ever get multiple solutions of MC = MR, because of a marginal revenue function that, over some range at least, is increasing.

This can happen. Which means that a firm, even if it knows the demand function it faces near the price it charges (that is, even if it knows the elasticity of demand it faces where it is) might be at a local profit-maximizing price and quantity, rather than a global max. Here is how.

Equation (4.2) says that marginal revenue depends on price and elasticity. Of course, price is (generally) a decreasing function of quantity. But elasticity can change dramatically and in different directions, as quantity increases. In particular, demand can be fairly inelastic for a range of quantities, become fairly elastic for larger quantities, then become inelastic again, at least for some goods. Where demand is inelastic, equation (4.2) tells us that marginal revenue is negative, so this pattern means that marginal revenue is negative, positive, and then negative. This certainly is inconsistent with downward sloping marginal revenue.

An example concerns textbooks such as this one. As I discussed with publishers pricing strategies for this book, I was told (by many publishers, so I assume this is correct) that, if we charge a very high price relative to similar textbooks, most sales would be to libraries; at this price, the book would be too expensive for adoption by instructors in courses. This sort of textbook "sells" in a range of prices perhaps $20 wide, because this is where the competition has settled. If priced in this range, the book should, the publisher and I hope, rack up significant sales as an adopted textbook. For prices below the lowest price in this range, the publishers are all convinced that sales would not increase significantly as price declines; instructors would be no more likely to adopt the book for a lower price, once the price was in the "reasonable" range. Of course, a lower price means some increase in sales— students might be more likely to buy an unusued copy than a used copy, and greater nontextbook sales might be realized—but since most sales are as a textbook, the key to pricing the book was to hit a price in the "reasonable" range.

This is phrased in terms of prices, but as price and quantity are decreasing functions of one another, it implies the pattern of elasticities mentioned; inelastic demand for quantities that correspond to prices above or below the range, with a substantial piece of elastic demand within the range.

Having introduced this example, I can use it to make two other points.

1. I am not as convinced as the textbook publishers that demand remains inelastic for prices well below the standard range. In 2000 (when I first wrote these lines), the relevant range within the United States was $80 to $100. I concede that lowering the price a bit below $80 is unlikely to increase sales much; demand is probably fairly inelastic over the range from, say, $70 to $80. But I wonder whether demand becomes very elastic again over the range $30 to $50, because in that range, perhaps, students are a lot more apt to keep their copies of the book, so that new sales replace the sale of used books. Unfortunately, no textbook publisher that I know is willing to run such a drastic experiment. The point is that if I am right, this may be a case where publishers, just like Excel, are stuck

at a local maximum that is not a global maximum.

2. The profit-maximizing exercises we have been doing assume that firms know the relationship between the price they charge and the number of units they sell. This, in fact, is the basis for the observation made in the chapter and reinforced with Problem 4.1, that it does not matter for our models whether you think of the firm choosing the profit-maximizing price or the profit-maximizing quantity. In some cases, this is untrue, even as an approximation. For a brand new textbook, publishers are uncertain how many copies will be sold, largely because the number of adoptions is highly uncertain. Does this mean that publishers cannot use the ideas of this chapter? Not at all. While quantities are very unclear, publishers believe they have a very good fix on how elasticity varies with price. For publishers of new textbooks, price and quantity are not equally good in the role of the driving variable. Given what they know—or at least what they think they know—they are quite willing and, they believe, able to think in terms of the profit-maximizing price to set, as they hold their breath about quantity.

Solution to Problem 4.12

(a) We have to consider three ranges of prices. For prices above \$15, the firm sells no units. For prices from \$10 to \$15, it sells only to the older group, selling $250(15 - P)$ per 1000 women in this group. There are 25,000 women in this group in this market, so total sales to them are $25 \times 250(15 - P) = 6250(15 - P)$. Finally, for prices below \$10, the firm sells $25 \times 250(15 - P) = 6250(15 - P)$ to women in the older group and $40 \times 500(10 - P) = 20{,}000(10 - P)$ to women in the younger group, for total sales of

$$6250(15 - P) + 20{,}000(10 - P) = 293{,}750 - 26{,}250P.$$

Thus the demand function facing this firm is

$$D(P) = \begin{cases} 0 & \text{for } P > 15, \\ 93{,}750 - 6250P & \text{for } 10 < P \le 15, \text{ and} \\ 29{,}3750 - 26{,}250P & \text{for } P \le 10. \end{cases}$$

(b) To do part b, we first have to work out the levels of sales to each of the four groups at the price \$8.

- For the group of women aged 15–20, the firm sells $25 \times 600 = 15,000$ units.

- For the group of women aged 21–25, it sells $15 \times 500 = 7500$ units.

- For the group of women aged 26–30, it sells $10 \times 600 = 6000$ units.

- For the group of women aged 31–35, it sells $5 \times 300 = 1500$ units.

So its total sales at \$8 are $15,000 + 7500 + 6000 + 2400 = 30,000$ units.

To find the (approximate) level of sales at \$8.16, we need to compute the elasticity of total demand at \$8. To do this, we recall from the chapter that the elasticity of total demand is the weighted average of elasticities of pieces of demand, weighted by the demand by each piece. Since total demand is 30,000 units, this is

$$\nu(P) = (-1)\frac{15,000}{30,000} + (-1.2)\frac{7500}{30,000} + (-1.5)\frac{6000}{30,000} + (-2)\frac{1500}{30,000} =$$

$$(-1)(0.5) + (-1.2)(0.25) + (-1.5)(0.2) + (-2)(0.05) = -0.5 - 0.3 - 0.3 - 0.1 = -1.2.$$

The elasticity of demand at $P = 8$ for the entire population is -1.2. Therefore, if price increases from \$8 to \$8.16, which is an increase of 2%, the quantity would decrease by approximately $(2\%)(1.2) = 2.4\%$. Since the quantity is 30,000 at $P = 8$, this means that a rise in price to \$8.16 would give a fall in the quantity demanded of approximately $(30,000)(0.024) = 720$ units, to approximately 29,280 units.

(c) A price of \$8 is too low. We use the formula

$$\text{MR}(x) = P(x)\left(1 + \frac{1}{\hat{\nu}(x)}\right).$$

At a price of $P(x) = \$8$, the firm expects to sell 30,000 units, and the elasticity of demand at that price–quantity pair is -1.2. Marginal revenue is

$$\text{MR}(30,000) = 8\left(1 + \frac{1}{-1.2}\right) = 8 \times \frac{1}{6} = \$1.333.$$

This is less than marginal cost of \$2. Since the marginal cost function is constant at \$2 and marginal revenue falls as quantity increases, the firm, to maximize profit, must scale back production to a level at which marginal revenue equals \$2. (If, and it is a very big if, the firm had constant elasticity of demand, this would be the solution to $2 = p(1 + (5/-6)) = p/6$ or $p = \$12$. But we have no guarantee that the elasticity of demand stays the same for this big a change in price.) Scaling back the quantity means raising prices; $8 is too low a price for profit maximization.

Solution to Problem 4.14

Sheet 1 of the spreadsheet PROBLEM 4-14, with numbers supplied for the first part of the question, is found in Figure 4.9. Column B records what the items are, and Column C gives the various supplied and computed values. To see the formulas for Column C, get the spreadsheet. From Figure 4.9, you see that, with a posted price of $10 and a coupon of $0.50, profit improves by $1,050, or by 3.15%.

	A	B	C
1			
2		quantity sold	10000
3		market elasticity	-3
4		current price	$10.00
5			
6		implied MC	$6.67
7			
8		percentage getting coupon	30%
9		average elasticity this group	-6
10			
11		implied elasticity others	-1.714
12			
13		new posted price	$10.00
14		coupon value	$0.50
15			
16		sales w/o coupons	7,000.00
17		sales w/ coupons	3,900.00
18			
19		total sales	10,900.00
20			
21		implied changed in profits	$1,050.00
22		% change in profits	3.15%

Figure 4.9. The spreadsheet PROBLEM 4-14.

Figure 4.10 shows sheet 2 of the spreadsheet, with Column C from sheet 1 "copied" three times in successive columns. The first of the four columns with numbers repeats the results given in Figure 4.9, while in the next three columns, I used Solver to (1) optimize over the coupon value, (2) optimize over the posted price and coupon value, and (3) optimize over posted price and coupon value for the alternative assumptions on the couponing program. The numbers speak for themselves, but here are a couple of things to note:

	A	B	C	D	E	F
1						
2		quantity sold	10000	10000	10000	10000
3		market elasticity	-3	-3	-3	-3
4		current price	$10.00	$10.00	$10.00	$10.00
5						
6		implied MC	$6.67	$6.67	$6.67	$6.67
7						
8		percentage getting coupon	30%	30%	30%	40%
9		average elasticity this group	-6	-6	-6	-5.2
10						
11		implied elasticity others	-1.714	-1.714	-1.714	-1.533
12						
13		new posted price	$10.00	$10.00	$11.25	$11.59
14		coupon value	$0.50	$0.83	$2.08	$2.30
15						
16		sales w/o coupons	7,000.00	7,000.00	5,500.00	4,533.33
17		sales w/ coupons	3,900.00	4,500.00	4,500.00	5,466.67
18						
19		total sales	10,900.00	11,500.00	10,000.00	10,000.00
20						
21		implied changed in profits	$1,050.00	$1,250.00	$3,125.00	$3,372.35
22		% change in profits	3.15%	3.75%	9.37%	10.12%

Figure 4.10. Sheet 2 of PROBLEM 4-14. Answers to the questions asked.

- When we optimize over both the posted price and the coupon value, the total sales level does not change. This is a mathematical curiosity, having to do with how we figured out what discrete changes in quantity would result from discrete changes in price. Do not worry about why it happens or think that it would happen if we had fully specified (inverse) demand functions for the couponed and non-couponed groups.

- It was not clear a priori that we would be better off with the second couponing program, because although we hit a fraction closer to 50% of the market with the coupons, which is a good thing, we lose because their elasticity is closer to the overall figure of −3. In fact, if the numbers for the second program were that 40% of the population gets coupons, with an elasticity for that group of −5.1 (instead of −5.2), the optimized program would give us only a 9% increase in profit, slightly worse than the optimized values for the first program where 30% with an elasticity of −6 obtain coupons.

I close with three comments.

1. It would be relatively easy to adapt this spreadsheet to accommodate multiple couponing programs; that is, where one segment of the population gets a high-discount coupon and a second gets a low-discount coupon.

2. The answers obtained do not depend on the original number of units sold or the price charged for them, at least insofar as the percentage change in profit would not be sensitive to those parameters. All the important calculations in this problem can be conducted in percentage terms (What percentage of price should the coupon be for? What percentage rise should be used for the posted price? What percentage change is there in profit?), which is why I included that final row.

3. The key numbers in determining the "power" of an optimized couponing scheme are the overall elasticity of demand, the percentage size of the market that will get the coupons, and the elasticity of that group. These, of course, are all "guesstimates" by product marketing folks, and you might worry how sensitive profit changes are to misestimating these quantities. This is easy enough to figure out. For instance, suppose Marketing estimates that 30% of the population will get coupons, overall elasticity is -3, and the couponed group has an elasticity of -6. You compute the optimized values for the price and coupon value we derived. Then you can see how profit (and sales) would be affected if we use those optimized values, but any of the three parameters change. For instance, in Figure 4.11, I show you the results of the "optimized" program if, say, the couponed group is 40% of the population and has an elasticity of -5 (profit rises by nearly 8%), if only 20% get the coupons with an elasticity of -6 (profit up only 1.56%), and if only 20% get the coupons with an elasticity of -5 (profit falls by a bit over 3%). Note carefully; all these profit calculations are based on the posted price/coupon value computed under the initial assumptions; this tells us how "sensitive" is profit to misestimates by the Marketing Department, if we take seriously the estimates by the marketers. If, say, marketing gives ranges for the percentage of the market that will get the coupons and the elasticity of that group, we can look for a posted price/coupon value combination that gives relatively good results across the spectrum of possibilities for the parameters.

Solution to Problem 4.15

I did a linear regression of price on units sold, and my regression package (in Excel) gave me the estimated demand equation $D(p) = 1155.4 - 15.05p$, with an adjusted R^2 of 0.63. A 95% confidence interval on the slope coefficient is from -19.3 to -10.7. Although you were not asked for this, note that we can compute an estimate of the elasticity of demand at a price, for instance, at the price $50, by (1) finding an estimate for demand at that price: $D_e(50) = 1155.4 - 15.05 \times 50 = 402.9$, and (2) plugging it into the formula for elasticity estimates for demand and for the

PROBLEM 4-14

	A	B	C	D	E
1					
2		quantity sold	10000	10000	10000
3		market elasticity	-3	-3	-3
4		current price	$10.00	$10.00	$10.00
5					
6		implied MC	$6.67	$6.67	$6.67
7					
8		percentage getting coupon	40%	20%	20%
9		average elasticity this group	-5	-6	-5
10					
11		implied elasticity others	-1.667	-2.250	-2.500
12					
13		new posted price	$11.25	$11.25	$11.25
14		coupon value	$2.08	$2.08	$2.08
15					
16		sales w/o coupons	4,750.00	5,750.00	5,500.00
17		sales w/ coupons	5,660.00	2,996.00	2,830.00
18					
19		total sales	10,410.00	8,746.00	8,330.00
20					
21		implied changed in profits	$2,606.37	$520.82	-$1,040.57
22		% change in profits	7.82%	1.56%	-3.12%

Sheet1 / Sheet2 / Sheet3

Figure 4.11. Sheet 3 of PROBLEM 4-14: Some sensitivity analysis.

slope of demand:

$$\nu_e(50) = \text{estimate of } D'(50) \times \frac{50}{D_e(50)} = -15.05 \times \frac{50}{402.9} = -1.8677.$$

Note that, since the estimate of the slope and the estimate of $D(50)$ are correlated and we are taking a ratio, the estimate just computed for elasticity is probably biased. Also, finding standard errors or confidence intervals for our estimate of elasticity is not going to be a trivial matter. Your statistics professor can take it from here.

Solution to Problem 4.16

I do this using calculus, on the assumption that only calculus-friendly readers would have ventured into this problem, given my warnings. I write $\mathcal{TR}(p)$ for total revenue or receipts as a function of p. Of course,

$$\mathcal{TR}(p) = p \times D(p).$$

Apply the product rule, and

$$\frac{d\mathcal{TR}(p)}{dp} = D(p) + pD'(p) = D(p)\left(1 + \frac{pD'(p)}{D(p)}\right) = D(p)(1 + \nu(p)).$$

That was easy enough.

The confusing part (for some students) is this says that total receipts are a decreasing function when $\nu(p) < -1$; that is, when demand is elastic. But, in the text, it says that total revenue increases in precisely these circumstances. Why?

The resolution is simple, once you think hard about it. This formula says that total receipts are a decreasing function of *price* when demand is elastic, whereas in the text, it says that total revenue is an increasing function of *quantity* in precisely those cases. All this is for movement along the demand curve. Increasing quantity means decreasing price. So the two really say precisely the same thing.

Material for Chapter 5

Modeling Consumer Behavior

About the Natural Logarithm Function

The natural logarithm function, $\ln(\cdot)$, is very important in mathematics. For one thing, it is the inverse of the exponential function, which is to say that $\ln(e^x) = x$, where e is the transcendental number $2.718\ldots$ that mathematicians call *eee*. $\ln(x)$ is defined only for strictly positive x. It is strictly increasing, and its two limits are

$$\lim_{x \to 0} \ln(x) = -\infty \quad \text{and} \quad \lim_{x \to \infty} \ln(x) = \infty.$$

Being a bit sloppy, we sometimes write $\ln(0) = -\infty$. The value of this function at 1 is 0, or $\ln(1) = 0$. It has the following other properties:

$$\ln(x \times y) = \ln(x) + \ln(y),$$

$$\ln(x^a) = a \ln(x), \text{ and}$$

$$\frac{d \ln(x)}{dx} = \frac{1}{x}.$$

Since it comes up in some examples, note that

$$\frac{d \ln(ax + b)}{dx} = \frac{a}{ax + b}.$$

Using Solver with Logarithmic Utility

Because Solver is a trifle stupid in how it does stuff, you have to be careful when using the natural log function in conjunction with it. Think of Solver as, essentially, trying to maximize a function as follows: It sits at some point and looks in various directions, seeing in which direction the function is increasing. When it finds such a direction, it takes a step in that direction and evaluates the function at the new position. The step size gets progressively smaller, and when Solver evaluates all the directions in which it might go and finds that nothing seems worthwhile, in terms of how much the function increases, Solver reports back that it has the answer.

The stupidity in Solver arises when you constrain variables. Solver does what is just described and evaluates the function at the new point. Only then does it ask the question, Does this new point that has been reached satisfy all the constraints? When the answer is No, Solver pulls back on the step, going only as far as it can while respecting the constraint.

Suppose we asked Solver to maximize the function $= 3*LN(B2) + LN(B3) + .5*LB(B4)$, where the entries in the cells B2, B3, and B4 are the amounts of bread, cheese, and salami. When Excel tries to evaluate the natural log function and the argument it is given is 0 or negative, it shuts down, telling you that you asked it to do something it cannot do. So if we used the function above, it would be important to make sure that the entries in cells B2, B3, and B4 are never 0 or negative.

Seemingly, we could put in constraints that B2 must be greater than or equal to, say, 0.00001, and similarly for B3 and B4. (If we put in the constraint $B2 \geq 0$, in theory it is possible that B2 could be 0, which Solver would not like. So I use a slightly larger right-hand side in the constraint.)

Here Solver's stupidity can cause problems. Suppose that, from where it is currently sitting, the view looks to Solver as if decreasing the amount of salami (the entry in B4) is a good idea. Solver steps off in this direction, increasing either B2 or B3, presumably. But, before it checks whether its new value of B4 obeys the constraint that $B4 \geq 0.00001$, Solver evaluates $\ldots + .5*LN(B4)$. If the step it took, prior to checking the constraint, gave us a temporarily negative number in cell B4, Excel sees LN of a negative number and shuts itself down, scolding you for being so stupid. Clearly, it would be better if SOLVER checked its constraints before it evaluated the function.

How can we fix this problem? I put in the preceding constraints on B2, B3, and B4, but when I wrote out the utility function, I used the formula

$$= 3*LN(MAX(B2, 0.00001)) + \text{etc.}$$

That is, I made sure that whenever Excel computed LN of something, the something would be at least 0.00001, so that Excel would not shut down on me. Since Solver eventually makes sure that constraints are satisfied, this does not affect the value of the function at the points at which, eventually, it settles. In any case, this particular fix worked like a charm in all the examples I tried.

Solution to Problem 5.2

Equating bangs for the buck in just the manner of the example from pages 112–3 gives

$$\frac{6}{b}\frac{1}{1.2} = \frac{3}{c}\frac{1}{3} = \frac{1}{s}\frac{1}{4} \quad \text{or} \quad \frac{1.2b}{6} = \frac{3c}{3} = 4s \quad \text{or} \quad \frac{b}{5} = c = 4s.$$

Since utility is strictly increasing in all three goods, we know that the consumer will spend all her wealth, and so we also have

$$1.2b + 3c + 4s = 20.$$

Doing a bit of algebra, this gives us

$$6c + 3c + c = 20 \quad \text{or} \quad 10c = 20 \quad \text{or} \quad c = 2,$$

hence,

$$b = 5c = 10 \quad \text{and} \quad s = \frac{c}{4} = 0.5.$$

That is, the consumer will purchase 10 loaves of bread (cost $12.00), two kilos of cheese (cost $6.00), and half a kilo of salami (cost $2.00).

Solution to Problem 5.4

(a) Begin by hypothesizing that, at the solution, all three goods will be consumed in strictly positive amounts. Then, their bangs for the buck must be equal, or

$$\frac{8}{b+2} \times \frac{1}{1} = \frac{6}{c+1} \times \frac{1}{2} = \frac{2 \times 2}{2s+1} \times \frac{1}{4}.$$

Flipping these fractions over and simplifying gives

$$\frac{b+2}{8} = \frac{c+1}{3} = 2s+1.$$

Since utility is strictly increasing in all three goods, we know that the budget equation holds at the solution, or

$$b + 2c + 4s = \$18.$$

Using the equal-bangs-for-the-buck equations, we find that

$$2c = \frac{3b}{4} + 1.5 - 2 = \frac{3b}{4} - 0.5 \quad \text{and} \quad 4s = \frac{b}{4} + .5 - 2 = \frac{b}{4} - 1.5,$$

therefore the budget equation can be rewritten as

$$b + 0.75b - 0.5 + 0.25b - 1.5 = 2b - 2 = 18,$$

which gives $b = 10$. From this, we calculate

$$c = \frac{3}{8} \times 12 - 1 = \frac{28}{8} = 3.5 \quad \text{and} \quad s = \frac{1}{2} \times \left(\frac{12}{8} - 1 \right) = 0.25,$$

which is the answer.

(b) If the consumer has the same utility function but only \$6.50 to spend, and we begin with the hypothesis that she consumes all three goods in strictly positive amounts, we have the same equal-bangs-for-the-buck equations, but the budget equation becomes

$$b + 2c + 4s = 2b - 2 = \$6.50,$$

or $b = 4.25$. This gives

$$c = \frac{3 \times 4.25}{8} - \frac{1}{4} = \frac{10.75}{8} \quad \text{and} \quad s = \frac{3.75}{16} - \frac{1.5}{4} = -\frac{2.25}{16}.$$

This gives us a negative value for s, which violates the nonnegativity constraint. So the hypothesis that all three variables are strictly positive is false. We hypothesize next that s equals 0 at the solution but b and c are strictly positive. So the bangs for the buck of b and c must be equal, and $b + 2c = 6.50$ is the budget equation. Substituting $0.75b - 0.5$ for $2c$ (from the equal bangs-for-the-buck condition), this is

$$b + 0.75b - 0.5 = 6.50 \quad \text{or} \quad b = \frac{7}{1.75} = 4.$$

Corresponding to this is

$$c = 3 \times \left(\frac{4+2}{8}\right) - 1 = \frac{10}{8}.$$

To check that this is the answer, I evaluate the bangs for the buck of bread and cheese at the levels 4 and $\frac{10}{8}$, respectively, and compare with the bang for the buck of salami at $s = 0$. According to my calculator, these are $\frac{8}{6} = 1.333$, $3/(\frac{10}{8} + 1) = 3/(\frac{18}{8}) = \frac{24}{18} = \frac{4}{3} = 1.333$, and 1, respectively, so these are okay: The bangs for the buck of the commodities being consumed are equal, and they exceed the bang for the buck of the good not being consumed. Finally, just to check my math, I check the budget equation: 4 loaves of bread costs \$4, and $\frac{10}{8}$ of a kilo of cheese costs $\frac{20}{8} = \$2.50$, so the total expenditure is indeed \$6.50. We have the answer.

(c) Now the consumer has money left over in her utility function, entering as $\ldots + m$. So begin by assuming the consumer ends with money left over. The bang for the buck for money left over is 1. This is equal to the bang for the buck of bread if $8/(b + 2) = 1$, or $b = 6$. It is equal to the bang for the buck of cheese if $3/(c + 1) = 1$, or $c = 2$. And it is equal to that of salami if $1/(2s + 1) = 1$, which is true where $s = 0$. This bundle costs $6 \times \$1 + 2 \times \$2 + 0 \times \$4 = \$10$, so as long as the consumer has at least \$10 in her pocket, this is what she consumes: six loaves of bread, 2 kilos of cheese, and no salami, leaving the store with \$10 less than she entered with. This covers the case of initial wealths of \$50, \$500, and \$18. But, if the consumer begins with \$6.50 only, then she leaves the store having spent everything for lunch. And the answer is precisely the answer obtained for the second part of b: four loaves of bread and $\frac{10}{8}$ kilos of cheese.

Solution to Problem 5.6

(a) The utility that the consumer obtains from the bundle ($5.00, 1 stick) is $u(1, 5) = 4 - 1 + 5 = 8$. Hence, m^* must solve

$$u(1.5, m^*) = 4 \times 1.5 - 1.5^2 + m^* = 8 \text{ or}$$

$$6 - 2.25 + m^* = 8 \text{ or } m^* = 8 - 6 + 2.25 = \$4.25.$$

(b) The utility of ($5.00, 1 stick) = 8, hence, the indifference curve through this point is the set of points (m, c) such that $4c - c^2 + m = 8$, or $m = c^2 - 4c + 8$. And the utility of ($6.00, 1 stick) = 9, so the indifference curve through this point is the set of points (m, c) such that $m = c^2 - 4c + 9$. To graph the two indifference curve, we have to graph these two parabolas. Figure 5.11 depicts the two indifference curves. Notice that the direction of increasing preference is north only (more money left over is always better than less); past 2 sticks of cotton candy, more cotton candy (holding money fixed) takes the consumer on to lower and lower indifference curves.

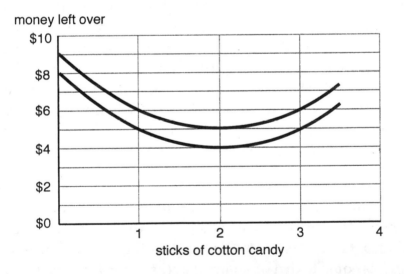

Figure 5.11. Indifference curves for Problem 5.6. More money left over is always good, but since cotton candy has subutility $4c - c^2$ which decreases for increasing c past $c = 2$, the indifference curves bend back up: Give the consumer more than two sticks of cotton candy, and to keep her on the same indifference curve, you have to give her more money.

Solution to Problem 5.8

The budget set is depicted in Figure 5.12. Note that we have a standard triangle-shaped budget set, where we find the budget line (the outer boundary of the budget set) by finding two points along the line. The easiest two to find are the all-bread bundle (with $24 to spend and bread costing $1.20 per loaf, the consumer can buy 20 loaves of bread if she buys no cheese) and the all-cheese bundle ($24 will buy 8 kilos of cheese at $3 per kilo). These two bundles correspond to the two heavy dots, draw a straight line joining them (the budget line), fill in the triangle (the shading), and you have Figure 5.12.

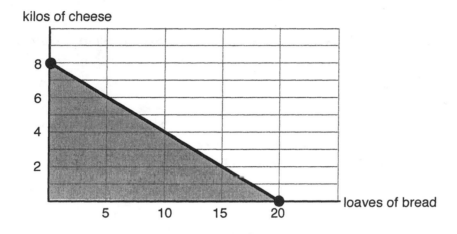

Figure 5.12. Problem 5.8: A budget set.

Solution to Problem 5.10

See Figure 5.13 for one sort of picture. This is a topographical contour map with a peak in the middle of the consumption plane.

The slanting of the ovals means something, but it is something that is not at all implied by what was in the problem. Can you figure out what that something is, and what it would mean if the ovals were slanted in the other direction? (Hint: As we increase the amount of cotton candy, what happens to the level of consumption of fudge that is best in combination with that amount of cotton candy?)

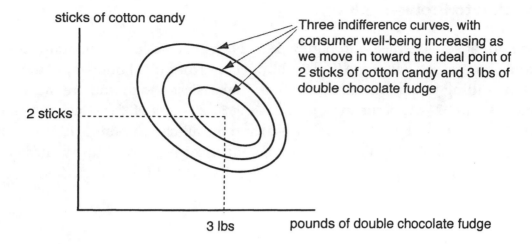

Figure 5.13. Problem 5.10: Some very strange indifference curves.

Solution to Problem 5.11

Because the consumer would have utility $-\infty$ if she consumed 0 of either bread or salami, we know she would consume strictly positive amounts of both of these. Their bangs for the buck at the prices $2 per loaf of bread and $2.50 per kilo of salami are

$$\frac{4}{2b} \quad \text{and} \quad \frac{0.5}{2.5s},$$

respectively. The bang for the buck of cheese is

$$\frac{1}{p_c(c+1)}.$$

Hypothesize momentarily that the consumer chooses a strictly positive amount of cheese, and the equal bangs-for-the-buck rule says that these three bangs must be equal. Flipping the fractions over, this is

$$\frac{b}{2} = 5s = p_c(c+1).$$

We also have the budget equation $2b + p_c c + 2.5s = 10$. From the equal bangs-for-the-buck equations,

$$2b = 4p_c(c+1), \quad \text{and} \quad 2.5s = 0.5p_c(c+1),$$

so the budget equation can be rewritten

$$4p_c(c+1) + p_c(c+1) + 0.5p_c(c+1) = 5.5p_c(c+1) = 10,$$

or

$$c(p_c) = \frac{10 - 5.5p_c}{5.5p_c}.$$

This is the demand curve for price p_c such that this quantity is nonnegative; when p_c exceeds $10/5.5$, the demand for cheese is 0.

Solution to Problem 5.12

(a) To find the inverse demand functions, we simply take the derivatives of the "subutility" functions. So,

- The inverse demand function for bread is $P(b) = 1/b$.

- The inverse demand function for cheese is $P(c) = 1/(c+3)$.

- The inverse demand function for fudge is $P(f) = 2 - 2f$. Note that this becomes negative when f goes above 1, which is correct; to get this consumer to choose to consume more than 1 kilo of fudge, we have to pay him.

If you want demand functions, you have to invert these:

- The demand function for bread is $D(p_b) = 1/p_b$.

- The demand function for cheese is $D(p_c) = (1/p_c) - 3$. Note that this becomes negative when $p_c > 1/3$, which means that the consumer buys no cheese at prices above $0.33 per kilo. (Either not a cheese lover or not very good cheese.)

- The demand function for fudge is $D(p_f) = (2 - p_f)/2$. Note that this becomes negative at $p_f = 2$, which means that the consumer buys no fudge at more than $2 per kilo.

(b) The expenditure on bread is a constant $1. The expenditure on cheese is $p_c[(1/p_c) - 3] = 1 - 3p_c$, which is maximized when $p_c = 0$. This is a bit meaningless, as at this price, the consumer demands an infinite amount of cheese. But as the price of cheese falls, the expenditure on cheese rises toward $1. So we take $1 as the maximal level of expenditure on cheese. And expenditure on fudge is

$(2p_f - p_f^2)/2$, which is maximized at $p_f = \$1$, for an expenditure of $0.50. There-fore, the most this consumer spends on these three items is $2.50; as long as the consumer has more than $2.50 to start with, his expenditures on these three items leave him with some money left over, whatever their prices.

Solution to Problem 5.13

For each of these cases, the consumer's demand function is "given" by the derivative of the subutility function. More precisely, the consumer's inverse demand function is $v'(x)$, where v' denotes the derivative of v.

(a) So when $v(x) = x^{1/2}$, $v'(x) = (1/2)x^{-1/2}$. Therefore, the consumer's inverse demand function is $P(x) = (1/2)x^{-1/2}$, and her demand function is the inverse of this, or $D(p) = 2/p^2$. Note that the quantity demanded approaches infinity as price approaches 0, and it is strictly positive for all prices.

(b) When $v(x) = 10\ln(x+1)$, $v'(x) = 10/(x+1)$. Therefore, the consumer's inverse demand function is $P(x) = 10/(x+1)$. Note that, at $x = 0$, this is 10, which means that, at prices above $10 (or whatever currency is in use for measuring money here), the consumer buys none of this good. As x goes to infinity, this stays positive. So demand is the "inverse" of this, or

$$D(p) = \begin{cases} 0, & \text{if } p > \$10, \text{ and} \\ (10/p) - 1, & \text{if } \$0 < p \le \$10. \end{cases}$$

(To get the expression $(10/p) - 1$, solve the equation $p = 10/(x+1)$ for x in terms of p.)

(c) When $v(x) = 6x - x^2$, $v'(x) = 6 - 2x$. Note that at $x = 0$, this is 6 and it hits 0 at $x = 3$. Hence, this consumer buys no x if its price is above $6, and even if x is given away for free, she takes only 3 units of it. This is the linear demand function

$$D(p) = \begin{cases} 0, & \text{if } p > 6, \text{ and} \\ 3 - (p/2), & \text{if } 0 \le p \le 6. \end{cases}$$

(d) For this subutility function v, $v'(x) = 1/x$ for $x \le 1$ and $3 - 2x$ for $x \ge 1$. It is perhaps worth checking that at the critical value of $x = 1$, this utility function approaches 0 from both sides; it is continuous. And its derivative approaches 1 from both sides; it is smooth. The point of including this example is that no matter how high is the price, demand is positive; for $p \ge 1$, $D(p) = 1/p$. But, at price

$p = 0$, the consumer wants only $x = 3/2$. So we have a demand function that never hits 0, no matter how high the price but goes to a finite level as price goes to 0.

To fill in the blanks, for this sort of problem, in which utility for x and money left over has the form $v(x) + m$:

- Demand is strictly positive no matter how high prices get if $v'(0) = \infty$, but if $v'(0)$ is a finite number, demand hits 0 when price rises to $v'(0)$.

- Demand approaches ∞ as the price declines to 0 if $v' > 0$ no matter how large x becomes. But if v' hits 0 at some finite level of x, then demand stops at that level when the price goes to 0.

Material for Chapter 6

Channels of Distribution and
The Problem of Double Marginalization

Solution to Problem 6.1

To begin, take the case of direct distribution from the manufacturer to consumers. The manufacturer's marginal cost in this instance is \$11+\$30 = \$41, or the marginal cost of manufacturing plus the marginal cost of retailing. (Retail) marginal revenue is $131 - 2x/100$, so marginal cost equals marginal revenue where

$$131 - \frac{2x}{100} = 41 \quad \text{or} \quad 90 = \frac{2x}{100} \quad \text{or} \quad x = 4500.$$

This makes retail price $P = 131 - 4500/100 = 131 - 45 = \$86$. And the manufacturer's profit is

$$(\$86 - \$41)(4500) - \$10,000 - \$5000 = \$187,500.$$

For the case of simple (wholesale-price only) two-step distribution, if the manufacturer sets the wholesale price at p, the retailer's marginal costs are $p+10$. Equating this to retail marginal revenue, the retailer purchases x units where x is the solution of

$$131 - \frac{2x}{100} = p + 10 \quad \text{or} \quad x = 50(121 - p).$$

Hence, the wholesale inverse demand function is

$$p(x) = 121 - \frac{x}{50},$$

and the wholesale marginal revenue function is

$$\mathrm{MR}_W(x) = 121 - \frac{2x}{50}.$$

Equating wholesale marginal revenue to the manufacturer's marginal cost of \$11 (for manufacturing only) gives

$$121 - \frac{2x}{50} = 11 \quad \text{or} \quad x = 2750.$$

This corresponds to a wholesale price $p = 121 - (2750/50) = \$66$ and a retail price of $131 - (2750/100) = \$103.50$. The manufacturer's profit is $(\$66 - \$11)(2750) - 10{,}000 = \$141{,}250$. And the retailer's profit is $(\$103.50 - 66 - 10)(2750) - 1000 = \$74{,}625$.

Note that, between these two options, the manufacturer prefers direct distribution. But there is one final option to try.

For the case of two-step distribution with a fixed-fee-per-unit charge, we know that the answer is $p = \$11$, the marginal cost of manufacture. But, to derive this: If the per-unit charge is p and the retailer pays the up-front fee, he purchases $50(121 - p)$ units. This leads to a retail price of

$$P = 131 - \frac{50(121 - p)}{100} = \frac{141 + p}{2}.$$

Therefore, the retailer's gross profit is

$$\left(\frac{141 + p}{2} - 10 - p\right)\left(50(121 - p)\right) - 1000 = 25(121 - p)^2 - 1000.$$

The retailer can set the fixed cost (for a given p) at $F = 25(121 - p)^2 - 1000 - 100$. This means that, as a function of p, the manufacturer's net profit is

$$25(121 - p)^2 - 1100 + (p - 11)(50(121 - p)) - 10{,}000.$$

This can be simplified to read

$$25(121 - p)[(121 - p) + 2(p - 11)] - 11{,}100 = 25(121 - p)[99 + p] - 11{,}100$$

$$= 25(121 \times 99 + 22p - p^2) - 11{,}100.$$

Take the derivative in p, set it equal to 0, and out pops $22 = 2p$ or $p = 11$.

To finish, if $p = 11$, the retailer purchases $50(121 - 11) = 5500$ units, retailing them for $P = 131 - 5500/100 = \$76$. The retailer's gross profit is $(76 - 11 - 10)5500 - 1000 = \$301{,}500$. The fixed fee is set at \$100 less than this, or \$301,400, and since the per-unit charge equals the marginal cost, the retailer's profit is this fee less the \$10,000 fixed cost of manufacturing, or \$291,400. The net profit of the retailer is, of course, \$100.

Solution to Problem 6.2

We did the necessary math in the solution of Problem 6.1. This is just to hammer the point home. Where the retailer has no marginal cost of retailing, if the wholesale price is p, the retailer buys (and resells) x units, where x equates the retailer's marginal cost p with his marginal revenue, $131 - 2x/100$, or $x = 50(131 - p)$. This gives the quantity the manufacturer can sell as a function of wholesale price, the wholesale demand function. To work in quantity units, we need the wholesale inverse demand function, which is (inverting this function) $p(x) = 131 - x/50$. So wholesale total revenue is $131x - x^2/50$, and wholesale marginal revenue is $131 - 2x/50$. Set this equal to manufacturing marginal cost, and you get

$$11 = 131 - \frac{2x}{50} \quad \text{or} \quad x = 25 \times 120 = 3000.$$

Put this quantity into wholesale inverse demand to find that $p = 131 - 3000/50 = \$71$, and put it into retail inverse demand, to find that $P = 131 - 3000/100 = \$101$.

Material for Chapter 7

Price Discrimination (and Surplus Extraction)

Solution to Problem 7.1

(a) First rewrite the two demand relationships as regular (rather than inverse) demand functions. For the seniors, it is

$$D_S(p) = 500(15 - p),$$

while for the rest of the population it is

$$D_R(p) = 2000(20 - p).$$

The first of these works for prices below 15, and the second for prices below 20. Therefore, total demand at price p is given by

$$D(p) = \begin{cases} 0, & \text{for } p > 20, \\ 2000(20 - p), & \text{for } 20 \geq p > 15, \text{ and} \\ 500(15 - p) + 2000(20 - p), & \text{for } p \leq 15. \end{cases}$$

Note that $500(15 - p) + 2000(20 - p) = 47,500 - 2500p = 2500(19 - p)$. At $p = 15$, total demand is 10,000, and thus we have, for inverse demand

$$P(y) = \begin{cases} 20 - y/2000, & \text{for } y < 10,000, \\ 19 - y/2500, & \text{for } 10,000 \leq y \leq 47,500, \text{ and} \\ 0, & \text{for } y > 47,500. \end{cases}$$

Hence, marginal revenue is

$$\text{MR}(y) = \begin{cases} 20 - y/1000, & \text{for } y < 10,000, \\ 19 - y/1250, & \text{for } 10,000 \leq y \leq 47,500, \text{ and} \\ 0, & \text{for } y > 47,500. \end{cases}$$

Note that marginal revenue is discontinuous at $y = 10{,}000$ and jumps *up* there, from 10 to 11.

Since the marginal cost of production is $5, marginal cost equals marginal revenue only on the second branch of the marginal revenue function, where

$$5 = 19 - \frac{y}{1250} \quad \text{or} \quad y = 17{,}500.$$

At this quantity, the price is

$$p = 19 - \frac{17{,}500}{2500} = \$12.$$

The firm's profit is

$$17{,}500 \times (12 - 5) = \$122{,}500.$$

A graphical analysis is shown in Figure 7.4

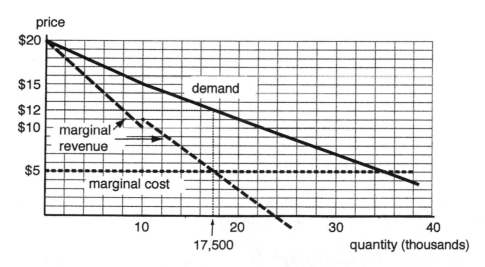

Figure 7.4. Problem 7.1(a): Demand, marginal revenue, and marginal cost.

(b) If this monopolist could discriminate by group, it would proceed as follows. From the seniors, its marginal revenue function is

$$MR_S(y) = 15 - \frac{y}{250}$$

which it equates to marginal cost of $5 to get $y_s = 2500$ and a price of $10.

From the regular customers, the monopolist's marginal revenue function is

$$\text{MR}_R(y) = 20 - \frac{y}{1000}.$$

Equating this to the marginal cost of $5 gives a quantity of 15,000 and a price of $12.50.

As for profit, the monopolist makes $5 \times 2500 = \$12{,}500$ off of the seniors and $7.50 \times 15{,}000 = \$112{,}500$ off of the regulars, for a total profit of $125,000. This is slightly better than before.

Solution to Problem 7.3

If $Q = k = 0$, under the terms of the initial deal, all customer would have a coupon when they go to purchase a GM light truck. Therefore, if GM posts a price P, it is really setting a price of $P - 1000$ for the original truck owners and $P - 500$ for the third-party buyers. In other words, GM is engaging in price discrimination by groups.

But, in the model of demand that we used, there is no difference in the demand characteristics of the two groups. In particular, they have precisely the same elasticities of demand. So, if GM charges them different prices, it is engaging in adverse price discrimination. Put it this way, from the formula $\text{MR} = P(1 + 1/\nu)$, if the two groups have the same elasticities and face different prices, they are generating different marginal revenues. But the marginal costs of supplying cars to them is the same. So GM is not equating marginal cost and marginal revenue for both groups; it would do better to push prices back together, so it can do so.

As for the observation that the cost to GM rises in the difference between $X - x$, this is just saying that a little bit of price discrimination is a bad thing for GM in this case and more price discrimination is worse.

Things would change, perhaps dramatically, if the two groups had different elasticities of demand. More specifically, since GM is charging the old truck owners a lower price than third-party buyers, if old truck owners had more elastic demand than third-party buyers, the sort of price discrimination that GM is engaged in could even wind up making extra profit for GM. You have to make a judgment here: Is it reasonable to think that old truck owners have more elastic demand? Usually,

I think the answer is No: Old customers are more likely to be "loyal" customers, which means less elastic. Still, in this instance, perhaps the old truck owners who are unhappy with GM have more elastic demand.

Solution to Problem 7.6

For each utility function $u(0) = 0$, so the gain in utility from the consumption of x units (gross of any changes in money left over) is always just $u(x)$. More generally, this gross gain in utility would be $u(x) - u(0)$.

(a) The procedure for each consumer is to (1) find where his or her marginal utility equals the marginal cost, (2) compute the total gross utility the consumer obtains from this, and (3) set the take-it-or-leave-it terms as this: You (the consumer) can take the number of units computed in step (1) if you pay the dollar amount computed in step (2).

- For Larry, we set $10 - 2x = 2$ or $x = 4$ for a gross utility gain of $10 \times 4 - 4^2 = 40 - 16 = 24$, and Larry is told, "You may purchase 4 units for $24, take it or leave it." This nets a profit of $16.

- For Mae, we set $8/(x + 1) = 2$ or $x = 3$ for a gross utility gain of $8 \ln(4) = 11.09$. Mae is told, "You may purchase 3 units for $11.09, take it or leave it," for a profit to the firm of $5.09.

- For Curly, set $4x^{-1/2} = 2$ or $x = 4$ for a gross utility gain of $8\sqrt{4} = 16$. Curly's terms are these: "You may purchase 4 units for $16, take it or leave it," for a net profit of $8.

- For Shepp, set $8 - 2x = 2$ or $x = 3$ for a gross utility gain of $8 \times 3 - 3^2 = 15$. So Shepp is told, "You may purchase 3 units for $15, take it or leave it." This gives the firm a net profit of $9.

Therefore total profit from the four is $16 + $5.09 + $8 + $9 = $38.09.

(b) As discussed in the text, when you can tailor the entry fee and the per-unit price to the individual consumer, you set the per-unit price to each consumer equal to marginal cost, and you set the entry fee so that the consumer has no net gain in utility. Thus

- For Larry, the entry fee is $16 and the per-unit price is $2.

- For Mae, the entry fee is $5.09 and the per-unit price is $2.

- For Curly, the entry fee is $8 and the per-unit price is $2.

- For Shepp, the entry fee is $9 and the per-unit price is $2.

This gives precisely the same outcome as in part a; the firm sells 4 units to Larry, 3 to Mae, 4 to Curly, and 3 to Shepp, for a net profit of $38.09.

(c) To solve this, I set up a simple Excel spreadsheet, sheet 1 of PROBLEM 7.6, with the following entries: First, a numerical entry for the price p. Then, the demand by each of the four, gotten by solving $u'(x) = p$ for each, or *Demand by Larry* = $(10-p)/2$, *Demand by Mae* = $(8/p) - 1$, and so on for Curly and Shepp. Next, find the total demand, equal to the sum of the four individual demand entries. Profit equals to $(p - 2)$ times the sum of the four individual demand entries. (If you download this spreadsheet, you will find that it comes with the initial value of p = $4.00.)

Having constructed this spreadsheet, I call up Solver and ask it to maximize profit (cell C14), by varying price (cell C5). The solution is p = $5.22, for total sales of 4.89 units and a profit of $15.78. Figure 7.5 shows the spreadsheet after Solver has optimized.

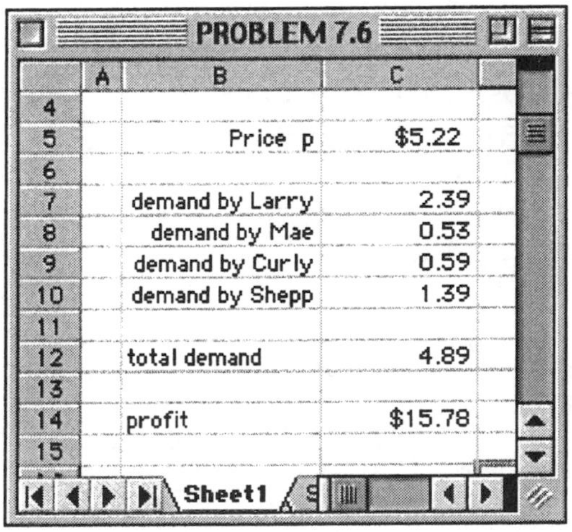

Figure 7.5. Problem 7.6(c): Finding the optimal single price to charge. If a single price must be charged Larry, Mae, Curly, and Shepp and they are allowed to select the quantity they wish to buy at that price, the profit-maximizing price is $5.22, giving a profit of $15.78.

(d) For this part, the more complex spreadsheet depicted in Figure 7.6 is used. It begins with two numerical entries: the entry fee and the per-unit price. Then for each of the four consumers, I compute in turn:

1. The number of units the consumer buys, if he or she enters, gotten by solving $u'(x)$ = per-unit price.

2. The gross gain in utility from that number of units, taking into account the per-unit cost of the goods (so, for example, in the case depicted in the figure, the $0.76 for Mae is $8 \ln(0.6) - 5.00 \times 0.6$).

3. A 0/1 variable, set equal to 0 if the gross gain in utility in row 2 is less than the entry fee, and set equal to 1 otherwise (if this variable is 0, the consumer will not purchase the goods, but will if it is 1).

4. The net gain in consumer utility (gross from line 2 less entry fee, if the entry fee is paid, and 0 if the entry fee is not paid).

5. The net demand by the consumer, taking into account that he or she purchases 0 if line 3 is 0.

6. The revenue from the consumer from per-unit sales, if the consumer purchases anything at all.

7. The entry fee paid, if it is paid, and 0 if not.

Then there are entries for the total sold (the sum across row 13), total revenue (the sum of rows 14 and 15), and total profit for the firm (total revenue less total sold times the $2 marginal cost). The spreadsheet is shown with initial values of $0.50 for the entry fee and $5 for the per-unit price.

	B	C	D	E	F
4					
5	entry fee	$0.50			
6	per-unit price	$5.00			
7					
8		Larry	Mae	Curly	Shepp
9	gross demand	2.50	0.60	0.64	1.50
10	gross utility	$6.25	$0.76	$3.20	$2.25
11	pays entry fee?	1	1	1	1
12	net utility	5.7500	0.2600	2.7000	1.7500
13	net demand	2.5000	0.6000	0.6400	1.5000
14	revenue from unit sales	$12.50	$3.00	$3.20	$7.50
15	revenue from entry fee	$0.50	$0.50	$0.50	$0.50
16					
17	total units sold	5.24			
18	total revenue	$28.20			
19	TOTAL PROFIT	$17.72			

PROBLEM 7.6

Sheet1 Sheet2 Sheet3

Figure 7.6. Problem 7.6(d): A complex spreadsheet.

From this starting point, Solver is asked to maximize profit, varying the entry fee and per-unit price. Solver returned the answer shown in Figure 7.7.

	B	C	D	E	F
4					
5	entry fee	$0.74			
6	per-unit price	$5.03			
7					
8		Larry	Mae	Curly	Shepp
9	gross demand	2.48	0.59	0.63	1.48
10	gross utility	$6.17	$0.74	$3.18	$2.20
11	pays entry fee?	1	1	1	1
12	net utility	5.4324	0.0000	2.4387	1.4628
13	net demand	2.4848	0.5904	0.6323	1.4848
14	revenue from unit sales	$12.50	$2.97	$3.18	$7.47
15	revenue from entry fee	$0.74	$0.74	$0.74	$0.74
16					
17	total units sold	5.19233893			
18	total revenue	$29.09			
19	TOTAL PROFIT	$18.70			

Figure 7.7. Problem 7.6(d): The spreadsheet after running Solver.

Note that at this "solution," row 11 in the table is always 1, and row 12 for Mae equals 0. At these values, the entry fee has been raised to the point where Mae is just indifferent between buying or not. Note, though, that this leaves Larry, Curly, and Shepp with net utilities of 5.4324, 2.4387, and 1.4628, respectively. Suppose we raise the entry fee by $1.46, keeping the per-unit price at $5.03. We make an extra 1.46×3 from Larry, Curly, and Shepp (now Shepp is barely willing to pay the entry fee). We lose $3.71 in revenue from Mae (who will drop out), but save an additional $1.18, because we are not producing units for Mae. Clearly, this is a worthwhile change, so I changed the entry fee to $2.20, getting the spreadsheet in Figure 7.8. Profit is up to $20.55.

I have no reason to think that this is optimal, so I can try Solver again, starting from this point. When I did this, Solver extracted the last bit of surplus from Shepp (raising the entry fee) and told me it was at the optimum. So maybe this is the answer.

It is not. Go back to the starting per-unit price of $5.00 and try an entry fee of $2.25, which is the largest entry fee Shepp would pay with this per-unit price. Profit goes up to $20.67. Oops. Start Solver from that point, and it tells you it does not need to

	B	C	D	E	F
4					
5	entry fee	$2.20			
6	per-unit price	$5.03			
7					
8		Larry	Mae	Curly	Shepp
9	gross demand	2.48	0.59	0.63	1.48
10	gross utility	$6.17	$0.74	$3.18	$2.20
11	pays entry fee?	1	0	1	1
12	net utility	3.9744	0.0000	0.9807	0.0047
13	net demand	2.4848	0.0000	0.6323	1.4848
14	revenue from unit sales	$12.50	$0.00	$3.18	$7.47
15	revenue from entry fee	$2.20	$0.00	$2.20	$2.20
16					
17	total units sold	4.60198391			
18	total revenue	$29.75			
19	TOTAL PROFIT	$20.55			

Sheet1 **Sheet2** Sheet3

Figure 7.8. Problem 7.6(d): Adding $1.46 to the entry fee.

move; it is at the optimum. But it is wrong: If you try a per-unit price of $4.99 and the largest entry fee that keeps Shepp in the game, $2.265, profit rises to $2.71.

Solver is not a good tool for this problem because the objective function is so discontinuous. So to solve this problem, it is necessary to resort to some logic combined with brute-force programming. The logic is simple. Whatever per-unit price is charged, the entry fee will be set to extract the last bit of surplus from one of the four consumers. It could be set to leave Larry with no net gain in utility, which, since Larry generally gets the most (dollar-measured) value from this good, means the other three will not pay the entry fee. It could be set to extract the last bit of surplus from Mae, which, since Mae tends to get the least (dollar-measured) value, means all four will be buying. But the point is this: Fix the per-unit price, and there are only four entry fees that need to be tested.

A spreadsheet can be constructed that takes the per-unit price, computes the four candidate entry fees, evaluates the firm's profit with each one, and finds the best entry fee. Sheet 3 of PROBLEM 7.6 does just this. (I am not going to show this to you here. It is a pretty complex spreadsheet, not the least because I constructed it so all these computations are done in a single line.) If you get the spreadsheet, you can see how it is done by examining sheet 3. Once this is done, and especially if it is done so that all the computations are done in a single row, then by copying that row many times and varying the per-unit price, you can see how profit varies with the per-unit price, and therefore find the optimal per-unit price.

Sheet 3 of PROBLEM 7.6 does this as well. It computes profit as a function of per-unit price for prices between $0.80 and $4.60 in two cent increments, which shows that the optimum per-unit price seems to be in the range $1.50–$1.60. Then it computes profit as a function of per-unit price for prices in that range, in increments of $0.0025. (I found that the optimal price is somewhere between $0.80 and $4.60 by trying every price from $0.10 to $10.00, using $0.10 increments.) The answer appears to be a per-unit price of $1.530 or so, with a corresponding entry fee of $10.46, for a net profit of $24.65.

It is worth pointing out that profit as a function of per-unit price is not a very well-behaved function. It rises, then falls, then rises, and finally falls, as per-unit price increases. This is not the only reason that Solver was unable to handle this problem, but it certainly makes Solver's life even harder.

It is also worth pointing out that a per-unit price of $1.53 is less than the firm's marginal cost of production. This firm loses money on every unit it sells, but makes it up and more on the entry fees it is able to charge.

At this point, the obvious remark is that optimal second-degree price discrimination is hard to do. Even if you restrict yourself to a simple scheme of an entry fee plus a per-unit price, it can be hard to work out the optimal scheme. Also, let me admit the obvious, that when it comes to second-degree price discrimination in the real world, firms usually do not approach the problem as we did here, where it enumerates its customers and (knows) their utility functions.

Solution to Problem 7.8

The problem talks about percentages of the buying population with particular utility functions, rather than numbers of consumers. But it is fairly clear that the profit figures we get scale with the size of the market, so we can solve for optimal prices assuming, say, there are nine consumers of the first type and one of the second.

The first step is to find the optimal single linear price scheme. This price p is 30, or 29, or 20.

- If the price is $p = 30$, then 1 unit is sold, for a profit of $1(30 - 3) = 27$.

- If the price is $p = 29$, 2 units are be sold, for a profit of $2(29 - 3) = 52$.

- If the price is $p = 20$, 11 units are be sold, for a profit of $11(20 - 3) = 187$.

So a price of $p = 20$ is optimal.

Next is to compute the optimal first-degree discrimination scheme. For each of the nine consumers of the first type, we make a take-it-or-leave-it offer of 1 unit at price 20, netting $9(20-3) = 153$. For the 10th consumer, we offer 2 units for 59 on a take-it-or-leave-it basis, netting $59-6 = 53$. Therefore, total profit is $153+53 = 206$.

Finally, we show that the claimed nonlinear price scheme is the optimal way to second-degree price discriminate. We already know that we want to sell 1 unit to each of the first nine, since the most we can make out of the tenth consumer is $53; and we can do substantially better than that with a linear price. To get the nine to buy a unit, the cost of the first unit can be no higher than $20. There is no point to making it lower, so this sets the price of the first unit.

Having done that, we wish to price the second unit so that the 10th consumer buys it. This consumer gets the first unit for $20, and the best we can do is extract all the marginal utility he gets from the second unit, by setting its price at $29.

Finally, we want to sell no more units, since to get consumers to buy them their price would have to be 1 or less, below our marginal costs. So the optimal scheme is as described in the problem, and the net profit is $10(20 - 3) + (29 - 3) = \$196$.

Solution to Problem 7.10

It is very easy to compute the optimal prices to charge the two groups. We want to equate marginal cost to marginal revenue, group by group. Marginal revenue is given by the formula $MR = P(1 + 1/\nu)$. Marginal cost is a constant $40. Elasticity for the first group is -2, so we have to solve

$$40 = P_1\left(1 + \frac{1}{-2}\right), \quad \text{which is} \quad P_1 = \$80.$$

For the second group, elasticity is -5, so

$$40 = P_2\left(1 + \frac{1}{-5}\right), \quad \text{which is} \quad P_2 = \$50.$$

To find the percentage increase in profit is a good deal more work. First, we have to know what percentage of the entire market (at the price $60) is in the first group, and what percentage is in the second. We do this as follows: Since $60 is the profit-maximizing price and $40 is marginal cost, marginal revenue at $60 must be $40.

This means the overall elasticity of demand at $60 must be -3. (Use the formula again.) Now the overall elasticity -3 is a weighted average of the elasticities of the two groups, weighted by the sizes of the two groups at the price $60. But, for -3 to be a weighted average of -2 and -5, the weights must be two-thirds on -2 and one-third on -5. (If you cannot see this, solve for α in the equation $-2\alpha + -5(1 - \alpha) = -3$.)

The next step is to see how total sales to the two groups changes when the price is moved from $60 for both groups to $80 for the first group and $50 for the second. For this, we need the demand functions.

For group 1, we know that a constant-elasticity demand function with elasticity -2 takes the form

$$D_1(P_1) = K_1 P_1^{-2} = \frac{K_1}{P_1^2}.$$

To find the constant K_1, we need to know the level of demand at the price $P_1 = \$60$. I assume that total demand at $60 is 3000 units (see the final paragraph) so $D_1(60) = 2000$. Then I can solve for K_1 by solving

$$\frac{K_1}{60^2} = 2000 \quad \text{or} \quad K_1 = 2000 \times 60^2.$$

Similarly, demand for the second group is

$$D_2(P_2) = K_2 P_2^{-5} = \frac{K_2}{P_2^5},$$

where, since $D_2(60) = 1000$,

$$\frac{K_2}{60^5} = 1000 \quad \text{or} \quad K_2 = 2000 \times 60^5.$$

With this, we can work out (1) demand by the two groups at the new prices, (2) the profits from the two groups at the new prices, (3) the change in total profit, and (4) the percentage change in profit. This is a job for Excel; see Figure 7.9 and the spreadsheet PROB7-10. The last row (the sum of the three profits) is there to check the spreadsheet: I asked Solver to maximize this entry, varying the three prices (cells D16, D21, and D25) and am happy to get back the prices shown as optimal.

A final word on this; I ran the spreadsheet assuming sales of 3000 at the price $60. This is okay because everything scales by this number (double it, and all profit figures double; halve it and they all halve) so that the percentage increase in profit is unaffected by the number. If you do not believe me, try the spreadsheet.

	PROB7-10			
	A	B	C	D	E
2					
3		Total quantity sold		3000	
4					
5		GROUP 1 CALCULATIONS			
6			group 1 elasti	-2	
7			percentage of	67%	
8			k =	7,200,000.00	
9					
10		GROUP 2 CALCULATIONS			
11			group 2 elasti	-5	
12			percentage of	33%	
13			k =	7.776E+11	
14					
15		PROFIT SINGLE PRICE			
16			price =	$ 60.00	
17			profit =	$ 60,000.00	
18					
19					
20		PROFIT GROUP 1			
21			price =	$ 80.00	
22			profit =	$ 45,000.00	
23					
24		PROFIT GROUP 2			
25			price =	$ 50.00	
26			profit =	$ 24,883.20	
27					
28		TOTAL PROFIT		$ 69,883.20	
29					
30		PERCENTAGE INCREASE		14.14%	
31					
32		SUM OF THREE PROFITS		$ 129,883.20	
33					

Sheet1 / Sheet2 / Sheet3

Figure 7.9. The spreadsheet PROB7-10: Computations for Problem 7.10. This spreadsheet computes demand functions, demand levels, and profit levels for Problem 7.10

Review Problems I

This is the first of five sets of review problems. It reviews material through Chapter 7. If you have been learning the material, you should find this set of problems relatively straightforward, except perhaps for I.3(b), I.4, and I.12. Solutions to all these review problems follow their statement, beginning on page 82.

I.1 A firm has total cost function $TC(x) = 10{,}000 + 10x$, and faces demand function $D(p) = 1000(50 - P)$. What is its profit-maximizing price, quantity, and profit level?

I.2 (a) Consider a firm that sells its product in two markets. Inverse demand in the first market is given by $P_1(x_1) = 20 - x_1/1000$, while inverse demand in the second market is given by $P_2(x_2) = 30 - x_2/400$. The firm can charge different prices in the two different markets. Its total cost depends on its total production level, $X = x_1 + x_2$, and is given by $TC(X) = 1000 + 10X + X^2/1000$. What production plan and prices in the two markets maximize this firm's profit? What is its (maximized) profit level?

(b) When the firm has optimized, it will charge different prices in the two markets and, in fact, P_2 will exceed P_1. What can you tell me (without doing any calculations with numbers) about the elasticities of demands that it will face in the two markets?

I.3 (a) A firm manufacturers two products, moiuyts and noiuyts. If it produces and sells x_m moiuyts and x_n noiuyts, the prices that pertain for the two goods are $p_m = 100 - x_m/100 - x_n/200$ and $p_n = 150 - x_n/100$, respectively. That is, the price of noiuyts depends only on the number of noiuyts produced and sold, but more noiuyts depresses the price of moiuyts. The marginal cost of a moiuyt is 20, and the marginal cost of a noiuyt is 25. What is the profit-maximizing production plan (prices and profit level) for this firm?

(b) Suppose that each moiuyt or noiuyt produced requires an oiuyt frame. The marginal cost of an oiuyt frame is 10, and the firm from part a felt it could procure all the oiuyt frames it wanted at this marginal cost. But it turns out that the firm can procure only 6000 oiuyt frames. Note well, if an oiuyt frame is used to make a moiuyt, there is an additional marginal cost of 10 (in addition to the cost 10 of the oiuyt frame), while if it is used to make a noiuyt, the additional (marginal) cost is 15. With the additional constraint imposed by the unavailibility of oiuyt frames, what is the profit-maximizing plan for the firm?

I.4 Consider the demand function $D(p) = 1000p^{-2.5}$. What is the inverse demand function that goes with this demand function? What is the elasticity of demand at the price $p = 10$? What is the elasticity of demand that goes with the quantity $x = 32,000$? What is the marginal revenue function that goes with this demand function? (Can you answer the last question without computing total revenue and taking a derivative? How?)

I.5 (a) Demand for a particular product (sold by a single firm) has elasticity -2.5 at the price $5.00, at which price demand equals 50,000 units. If the firm wishes to sell 52,500 units, approximately what price must be charged?

(b) This firm faces falling marginal revenue and rising marginal cost. Its marginal cost at the production level of 50,000 units is $4.00 per unit. Is the profit-maximizing production quantity for this firm more than, less than, or precisely equal to 50,000 units?

(c) In particular, suppose that marginal costs and marginal revenues are close to constant over the range from 49,900 units to 50,100 units. What will be the impact on the profit of this firm if it produces 50,010 units instead of 50,000? (Note, I am not saying that this firm, if it maximizes its profit, would choose to produce at 50,000 units. You discovered whether it would or not in part b of this problem.)

I.6 A profit-maximizing firm produces 10,000 units per month and sells them for $10.50 each. This firm's marginal cost at 10,000 units is $4.20. What is the firm's elasticity of demand at the price $10.50?

I.7 A profit-maximizing firm charges $20 for its good, at which price it sells 50,000 units per year. It estimates that, if it raised its price by $0.10, it would decrease demand by 750 units. What is its marginal cost of production at 50,000 units?

I.8 A firm sells its product to both commercial and industrial clients. Demand by industrial clients is $D_I(p) = 3000(550 - p)$ for $p \leq 550$. (Industrial demand is 0 for prices above $550.) Demand by commercial clients is $D_C(p) = 1000(750 - p)$ for $p \leq 750$. (Commercial demand is 0 for prices above $750.) Marginal costs are $100 per unit.

(a) What single price maximizes profit, taking both groups into account? What is the firm's profit at that price?

(b) If the firm can set separate prices for the two types of customers, what pair of prices maximizes the firm's profit? How much profit (in total) does the firm make?

I.9 Suppose that a vendor of cotton candy faces the marginal revenue function shown in Figure I.1. The discontinuities are due to kinks in the inverse demand curve. This vendor has the following total cost function: For levels of production between zero and 200 sticks, $TC(C) = C + 50$. For levels of production above 200 sticks, $TC(C) = 1.5C - 50$. What is the profit-maximizing level of production for the vendor, given this total cost function (and the marginal revenue function shown in Figure I.1)? (As a challenge, if I tell you that the inverse demand curve is continuous, can you reconstruct it from Figure I.1?)

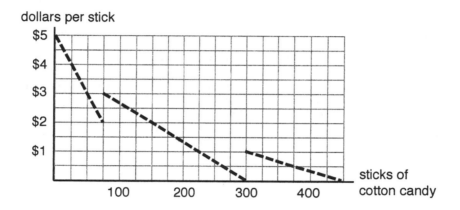

Figure I.1. Problem I.9: A marginal revenue function.

I.10 A consumer must choose a bundle consisting of bread, cheese, and salami, the prices of which are $p_b = \$2$, $p_c = \$10$, and $p_s = \$20$. This consumer has $20 to spend. His utility function is

$$u(b, c, s) = 6 \ln(b + 1) + 2 \ln(c + 2) + \ln(s + 3).$$

What does this consumer choose?

I.11 A consumer must choose a bundle consisting of bread, cheese, salami, and fudge, the prices of which are $p_b = \$2$, $p_c = \$10$, $p_s = \$20$, and $p_f = \$10$. This consumer has $500 in her pocket, but she values money left over, so she may not spend the whole $500 on this meal. Her utility function is

$$u(b, c, s) = 60 \ln(b + 1) + 30 \ln(c + 2) + 10 \ln(s + 3) + 0.2f - 0.2f^2 + m.$$

What does this consumer choose?

I.12 A firm sells its product to 5000 consumers. Remarkably, each of these consumers has a utility function of the form

$$u(x, m) = kx - x^2 + m$$

where x is the amount of the good consumed, m is money left over, and k is a constant that is different for different consumers. Specifically, 1000 consumers have $k = 4$, 1000 have $k = 5$, and the other 3000 have $k = 6$. Each consumer has at least $100 in his or her pocket. The marginal cost of producing this good is $1.

(a) If the firm sets a price per unit p and lets consumers decide how much to purchase, what price p maximizes the firm's profit?

(b) If the firm could engage in first-degree price discrimination, what would it do, and how much profit would it make?

Solution to Problem I.1

The marginal cost is 10. To find marginal revenue, first find inverse demand: $x = D(p) = 1000(50 - P)$, so $x/1000 = 50 - P$ so

$$P(x) = 50 - \frac{x}{1000},$$

then total revenue and marginal revenue:

$$TR(x) = 50x - \frac{x^2}{1000} \quad \text{so} \quad MR(x) = 50 - \frac{2x}{1000}.$$

Equate marginal cost and marginal revenue:

$$50 - \frac{2x}{1000} = 10 \quad \text{or} \quad 40 = \frac{2x}{1000} \quad \text{or} \quad x = 20,000.$$

Plug this back into the inverse demand function to find the price $P(20,000) = 50 - 20,000/1000 = \$30$, and use the formulas for total revenue and total cost to find that profit equals $390,000.

Solution to Problem I.2

(a) Marginal revenue in the first market is $MR_1(x_1) = 20 - 2x_1/1000$, and marginal revenue in the second market is $MR_2(x_2) = 30 - 2x_2/400$. Marginal cost is $MC(X) = 10 + 2X/1000 = 10 + 2(x_1 + x_2)/1000$. The solution is where marginal revenue in each market equals marginal cost (in each market):

$$20 - \frac{2x_1}{1000} = 30 - \frac{2x_2}{400} = 10 + \frac{2(x_1 + x_2)}{1000}.$$

If you solve these two equations in two unknowns, the answer is $x_1 = 1250$ and $x_2 = 2500$, which, using the inverse demand functions, gives prices $P_1 = \$18.75$ and $P_2 = \$23.75$, for a profit of \$30,250.

(b) Since the marginal cost of an extra unit of x_1 (output for market 1) equals the marginal cost of an extra unit of x_2 (because total cost is a function of $x_1 + x_2$), the marginal revenues in the two markets must be equal. But, since $MR = P(1 + 1/\nu)$, this implies that the term $(1 + 1/\nu_1) > (1 + 1/\nu_2)$, therefore $1/\nu_1 > 1/\nu_2$. Hence, $\nu_2 > \nu_1$. (Since elasticities are negative, this means that market 2, the market charged the higher price, has less elastic demand than market 2).

Solution to Problem I.3

(a) Total revenue is

$$TR(x_m, x_n) = 100x_m - \frac{x_m^2}{100} - \frac{x_m x_n}{200} + 150x_n - \frac{x_n^2}{100},$$

so marginal revenues in the two products are

$$MR_m(x_m, x_n) = 100 - \frac{2x_m}{100} - \frac{x_m}{200} \quad \text{and} \quad MR_n(x_m, x_n) = 150 - \frac{x_m}{200} - \frac{2x_n}{100}.$$

We have to solve for x_m and x_n, where we equate the marginal revenue in moiuyts to their marginal cost of 20 and the marginal revenue in noiuyts to their marginal cost of 25. This gives $x_m = 2600$ and $x_n = 5600$, for prices $p_m = \$46$ and $p_n = \$94$ and profit equal to \$454,000.

(b) The solution to this problem requires that you equate the marginal profits for the two products. Marginal profit for moiuyts is the marginal revenue for moiuyts less their \$10 variable marginal cost:

$$M\pi_m(x_m, x_n) = 90 - \frac{2x_m}{100} - \frac{x_n}{200},$$

while marginal profit for noiuyts is the marginal revenue for noiuyts less their \$15 variable marginal cost:

$$135 - \frac{x_m}{200} - \frac{2x_n}{100}.$$

You need not subtract off the marginal cost of the oiuyt frames, since that would be the same in the two, so would cancel out when you equate them. This gives one equation; the second equation is that the total production run has to be 6000, or $x_m + x_n = 6000$. Solve these and you'll find $x_m = 1500$ and $x_n = 4500$, hence $p_m = \$62.50$, $p_n = \$105$, and the profit equals \$423,750. Note that this gives marginal profit figures of \$37.50, more than the \$10 marginal cost of an oiuyt frame, so the firm certainly wishes to use all 6000.

Solution to Problem I.4

To find the inverse demand function, invert the relationship $x = 1000p^{-2.5}$ as follows:

$$\frac{x}{1000} = p^{-2.5} \quad \text{so} \quad \left(\frac{x}{1000}\right)^{-1/2.5} = p,$$

and the inverse demand function is therefore

$$P(x) = \left(\frac{x}{1000}\right)^{-0.4}.$$

Rather than find the elasticity at a price of \$10 or at a quantity of 32,000, let me compute the entire elasticity function:

$$\nu(p) = D'(p) \times \frac{p}{D(p)} = -2500p^{-3.5} \times \frac{p}{1000p^{-2.5}} = -2.5.$$

That is, the elasticity of demand is -2.5 at all prices and so at all quantities.

This makes it relatively easy to give the marginal revenue function:

$$\text{MR}(x) = P(x)\left(1 + \frac{1}{\hat{\nu}(x)}\right) = \left(\frac{x}{1000}\right)^{-0.4}\left(1 + \frac{1}{-2.5}\right) = 0.6\left(\frac{x}{1000}\right)^{-0.4}.$$

Solution to Problem I.5

(a) An increase of 2,500 units on a base of 50,000 is an increase of 5%. If elasticity is -2.5, this means a 2% decrease in price. On a base of $5.00, a 2% decrease is $0.10, so price must fall to $4.90.

(b) By the formula, $\text{MR}(50,000) = \$5(1 - \frac{1}{2.5}) = \$3$. Since marginal cost is $4, 50,000 is a point at which marginal costs exceed marginal revenues. Since marginal cost rises and marginal revenue falls, to maximize profit, this firm must decrease its level of production.

(c) In particular, an increase in production by 10 units means (approximately) a rise in revenues by $30 and a rise in costs of $40, for a net decrease in profit of $10.

Solution to Problem I.6

Because the firm maximizes its profit at 10,000 units per month, its marginal cost equals its marginal revenue at that level of production. Since its marginal cost is $4.20, this is also its marginal revenue. But marginal revenue is $P(1+1/\hat{\nu})$, therefore

$$4.2 = 10.5\left(1 + \frac{1}{\hat{\nu}(10,000)}\right).$$

The solution to this equation is $\hat{\nu}(10,000) = \nu(\$10.50) = -1.6667$.

Solution to Problem I.7

A $0.10 raise in price is a 0.5% raise on a base of $20. A decrease of 750 in demand on a base of 50,000 is a 1.5% fall. Hence, the elasticity of demand at this price–quantity pair is -3. Therefore, the firm's marginal revenue at 50,000 units is $20(1 + \frac{1}{-3}) =$

$\frac{40}{3} = \$13.33$. Since this firm maximizes its profit at this level of production, this is also its marginal cost.

Solution to Problem I.8

(a) Demand at prices below \$550 is the sum of the two pieces of demand, or $3000(550 - p) + 1000(750 - p) = 2{,}400{,}000 - 4000p$. Inverse demand for these prices (corresponding to a quantity of 200,000 or more) is $P(x) = 600 - x/4000$. Therefore, marginal revenue over this range is $MR(x) = 600 - x/2000$. Equate this to marginal cost, and you get

$$600 - x/2000 = 100 \quad \text{or} \quad x = 1{,}000{,}000.$$

This corresponds to a price of \$350, and thus a profit of $(350 - 100)(1{,}000{,}000) = \$250$ million.

To be sure this is the profit-maximizing production plan, we check to see whether marginal cost ever equals marginal revenue for prices above \$550 and quantities below 200,000. But, at $x = 200{,}000$, marginal revenue (in the first segment, for prices between \$750 and \$550) has fallen to \$350, still well above the \$100 marginal cost.

(b) For commercial customers, set a price of \$425, selling 325,000 units, for a profit of \$105,625,000. For industrial customers, set a price of \$325, selling 675,000 units, for a profit of \$151,875,000. With the ability to discriminate between the two groups, the firm makes \$257.5 million, a 3% gain over the nondiscrimination solution.

Solution to Problem I.9

In Figure I.2, we superimpose on the picture of marginal revenue the marginal cost function, which is $MC(c) = 1$ for $c < 200$ and $MC(c) = 1.5$ for $c > 200$. In this case, marginal revenue exceeds marginal cost for all levels of production below 200 and marginal cost exceeds marginal revenue for all levels above 200 units, so the profit-maximizing point will be 200 units. (As for the challenge, I graph the corresponding continuous inverse demand function in Figure I.3 as a dashed line. It is up to you to see how I got it.)

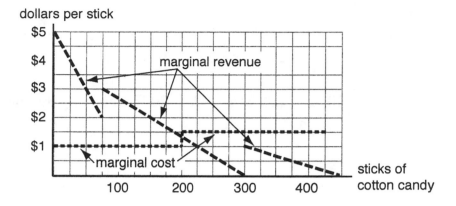

Figure I.2. Problem I.9: Marginal revenue and marginal cost.

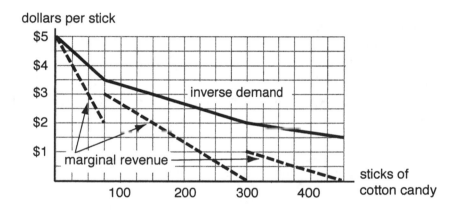

Figure I.3. Problem I.9 challenge: The inverse demand function.

Solution to Problem I.10

Assuming the consumer consumes a positive amount of each good, the equal-bangs-for-the-buck equation is

$$\frac{6}{2(b+1)} = \frac{2}{10(c+2)} = \frac{1}{20(s+3)},$$

which is

$$\frac{b+1}{3} = 5(c+2) = 20(s+3).$$

The budget equation is

$$2b + 10c + 20s = 20.$$

Now $10c = 2(b+1)/3 - 10$, and $20s = (b+1)/3 - 20$, so the budget equation can be rewritten

$$2b + \frac{2(b+2)}{3} - 10 + \frac{b+1}{3} - 20 = 20,$$

or

$$2b + b + 2 = 50,$$

or $3b = 48$, or $b = 16$. This gives a negative value for s, so the solution cannot have all three commodities strictly positive.

Perhaps, therefore, the solution has $s = 0$ and both b and c strictly positive. The equal-bangs-for-the-buck equation in bread and cheese is $(b+1)/3 = 5(c+2)$, and the budget equation is $2b + 10c = 20$, which becomes

$$2b + \frac{2(b+1)}{3} - 10 = 20, \quad \text{or} \quad \frac{8b}{3} = \frac{88}{3},$$

or $b = 11$. Therefore, $10c = 2(b+1)/3 - 10 = 2(12/3) - 10 = -2$, and c comes out negative. So this cannot be the solution.

We could try $c = 0$ and b and s strictly positive, but instead I try b strictly positive and both c and s equal to 0. Since all \$20 is spent on bread, $b = 10$. At this level of b, the bang for the buck in bread is $\frac{3}{22}$. And the bang for the buck in cheese at $c = 0$ is $\frac{2}{20} = 0.1$, while the bang for the buck in salami at $s = 0$ is $\frac{1}{60}$. So $b = 10$, $c = 0$, and $s = 0$ works: The bangs for the buck of the goods consumed in strictly positive amounts are equal—trivially so, because there is only one such good—and this bang for the buck exceeds that of the other goods, at 0 levels of consumption. That is the answer.

Solution to Problem I.11

This is a $\ldots + m$ money-left-over utility function, so we begin hypothesizing that the consumer has some money left over at the end of her purchases. The bang for the buck for money left over is 1, so equating this to the bang for the buck for bread, cheese, salami, and fudge gives

$$\frac{60}{2(b+1)} \text{ or } b = 29, \quad \frac{30}{10(c+2)} = 1 \text{ or } c = 1,$$

$$\frac{10}{20(s+3)} = 1 \text{ or } s = \frac{-5}{2}, \quad \text{and} \quad 0.2 - 0.4f = 1 \text{ or } f = -0.2.$$

The last two violate the nonnegativity constraints and lead us to notice that, at $s = f = 0$, the bangs for the buck of those two commodities are already less than 1. Hence, the answer, subject to checking on whether the consumer has money left over, is $b = 29$, $c = 1$, $s = f = 0$. And, sure enough, at these quantities, the consumer's expenditure is $68, a good deal less than the $500 she possesses. This is indeed the answer.

Solution to Problem I.12

This is a long problem, but it contains almost everything we have done so far.

(a) To answer part a, we need to work out the total demand function facing the firm. We first find demand, consumer by consumer.

Group 1 consumers have the utility function $u(x,m) = 4x - x^2 + m$. Inverse demand for a consumer from this group is then $P(x) = 4 - 2x$, and demand is $d_1(p) = 2 - p/2$ (for prices below 4, of course).

Group 2 consumers have the utility function $u(x,m) = 5x - x^2 + m$. Inverse demand for a consumer from this group is then $P(x) = 5 - 2x$, and demand is $d_2(p) = 2.5 - p/2$ (for prices below 5).

Group 3 consumers have the utility function $u(x,m) = 6x - x^2 + m$. Inverse demand for a consumer from this group is then $P(x) = 6 - 2x$, and demand is $d_3(p) = 3 - p/2$ (for prices below 6).

(We have to check that the consumers spend no more than $100 at any price. Let me remind you how this is done for group 3 consumers. Expenditure by a member of this group for prices from 0 to 3 is $3p - p^2/2$, so expenditure is maximized where the derivative of this function is 0, or $p = 3$. At that point, the quantity purchased is 1.5, for a total expenditure of $4.50, which is a good deal less than $100.)

Next we write out total demand:

$$D(p) = \begin{cases} 0, & \text{for } p > 6, \\ 3000(3 - p/2), & \text{for } 6 \geq p \geq 5, \\ 3000(3 - p/2) + 1000(2.5 - p/2), & \text{for } 5 \geq p \geq 4, \\ 3000(3 - p/2) + 1000(2.5 - p/2) + 1000(2 - p/2), & \text{for } p \leq 4. \end{cases}$$

From this we can find total inverse demand. First we find the quantities that correspond to the prices of $5 and $4: At $p = \$5$, total demand is 1500, while at $p = \$4$, total demand is $3000 + 500 = 3500$. Therefore,

- For quantities from 0 to 1500, inverse demand is the inverse of $x = 9000 - 1500p$, which is $P(x) = 6 - x/1500$. Note that marginal revenue over this range of quantities is $MR(x) = 6 - x/750$. Equate this to marginal costs of 1, and you get $6 - x/750 = 1$ or $x = 750 \times 5 = 3750$, which is much more than 1500. Marginal cost does not intersect marginal revenue for this range of quantities.

- For quantities from 1500 to 3500, inverse demand is the inverse of $x = 3000(3 - p/2) + 1000(2.5 - p/2) = 11{,}500 - 2000p$, which is $P(x) = 5.75 - x/2000$. Marginal revenue over this range of quantities is $MR(x) = 5.75 - x/1000$. Set this equal to marginal cost, and you get $5.75 - x/1000 = 1$ or $x = 4750$, which is outside the range, so that there is no intersection of marginal cost and marginal revenue for this range of quantities either.

- For quantities above 3500, inverse demand is the inverse of $x = 3000(3 - p/2) + 1000(2.5 - p/2) + 1000(2 - p/2) = 13{,}500 - 2500p$, which is $P(x) = 5.4 - x/2500$. Marginal revenue in this range is $MR(x) = 5.4 - x/1250$. Equate this to marginal cost, and you get $x = 1250 \times 4.4 = 5500$. Since this is the only place that marginal cost equals marginal revenue, this must be the profit-maximizing quantity. This corresponds to a price of $5.4 - 5500/2500 = \$3.20$ and a profit of $(3.20 - 1)(5500) = \$12{,}100$.

(b) You can do this part of the problem with take-it-or-leave-it offers, or with fixed-fee plus per-unit price offers. I use the latter.

First, we work out how much to sell to each consumer. For a consumer with $u(x, m) = kx - x^2 + m$, set marginal utility equal to marginal cost: $k - 2x = 1$, or $x = (k - 1)/2$. So, for group 1 ($k = 4$), $x = 1.5$. For group 2, $x = 2$. For group 3, $x = 2.5$.

Next we compute the gross gain in utility for each sort of consumer. If a consumer with utility function $u(x, m) = kx - x^2 + m$ consumes $(k - 1)/2$ units of the x good, the gross gain in utility is

$$\frac{k(k-1)}{2} - \frac{(k-1)^2}{4} = \frac{2k^2 - 2k - k^2 + 2k - 1}{4} = \frac{k^2 - 1}{4}.$$

We set the per-unit price at marginal cost, or $p = 1$, for every consumer. And we set the fixed fee at the gross gain in utility less what the consumer must pay for her goods:

$$\frac{k^2 - 1}{4} - \frac{k-1}{2} = \frac{k^2 - 2k + 1}{4}.$$

The firm's profit comes entirely from the fixed fees, so

- From group 1, where $k = 4$, the firm makes $\frac{9}{4}$ in profit for each of the 1000 members of this group, or $2250.

- From group 2, where $k = 5$, the firm makes 4 in profit for each of the 1000 members of this group, or $4000.

- From group 3, where $k = 6$, the firm makes $\frac{25}{4}$ in profit for each of the 3000 members of the group, or $18750.

The total profit is $25,000. (First-degree price discrimination is really powerful.)

Material for Chapter 8

Averages and Margins

Solution to Problem 8.1

(a) This is a case with strictly positive fixed cost and rising marginal cost, so the picture will be similar in shape to Figure 8.4.

(b) Since $TC(x) = 10\,\text{million} + 50x + x^2/16{,}000$, average cost is $AC(x) = 10\,\text{million}/x + 50 + x/16{,}000$. A variety of techniques can be used to find where marginal cost exceeds average cost and where it is less:

1. The difference is $MC(x) - AC(x)$

$$= \left(50 + \frac{2x}{16{,}000}\right) - \left(\frac{10\,\text{million}}{x} + 50 + \frac{x}{16{,}000}\right) = \frac{x}{16{,}000} - \frac{10\,\text{million}}{x}.$$

This is positive where

$$\frac{x}{16{,}000} > \frac{10\,\text{million}}{x} \quad \text{or} \quad x^2 > 160\,\text{billion} \quad \text{or} \quad x > 400{,}000$$

and it is negative where $x < 400{,}000$.

2. Marginal cost exceeds average cost where average cost is increasing. So we find the derivative of the average cost function,

$$AC'(x) = \frac{1}{16{,}000} - \frac{10\,\text{million}}{x^2},$$

which is positive where $1/16{,}000 > 10\,\text{million}/x^2$, which is where $x^2 > 160\,\text{billion}$, which is where $x > 400{,}000$.

3. Since the picture is as in Figure 8.4, we know that average cost starts above marginal cost and stays there until marginal cost cuts through it, after which

average cost increases, chasing after (rising) marginal cost. To find the value that separates these two regions, we equate marginal cost and marginal revenue:

$$50 + \frac{2x}{16{,}000} = \frac{10\text{ million}}{x} + 50 + \frac{x}{16{,}000}.$$

You can do the math from here; the answer is $x = 400{,}000$.

4. Or you can use a spreadsheet. See Figure 8.14. (The spreadsheet is PROB8-1. Note that I compute discrete margins for a discrete increase of 100 in quantity, which explains the "extra" cent in the marginal cost column.)

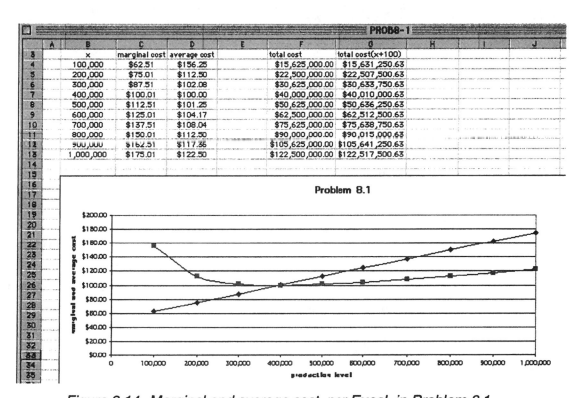

Figure 8.14. Marginal and average cost, per Excel, in Problem 8.1.

(c) We know that the efficient scale is $x = 400{,}000$ from part b. We can find this analytically in two ways. We can equate marginal cost and average cost, following method 3 in part b. Or, we can differentiate the average cost function and set its derivative equal to 0, following method 1 in part b. Without calculus, you can find the answer with a spreadsheet.

However we find that efficient scale is 400,000, we then plug this into either average cost or marginal cost to find minimum average cost. That is, we compute either

$$AC(100{,}000) = \frac{10\,\text{million}}{400{,}000} + 50 + \frac{400{,}000}{16{,}000} = 25 + 50 + 25 = \$100$$

$$\text{or} \quad MC(100{,}000) = 50 + \frac{2 \times 400{,}000}{16{,}000} = 50 + 50 = \$100.$$

(d) (I solve this with calculus. It can be done with a spreadsheet and Solver, but I leave that to those who wish to do it that way.) The firm's profit level is $250x - x^2/4000 - (10\,\text{million} + 50x + x^2/16{,}000) = 200x - 5x^2/16{,}000 - 10\,\text{million}$. This is a quadratic function with a negative squared term, so it is positive between its two roots, which by the quadratic formula are

$$x = \frac{-200 \pm \sqrt{40{,}000 - 4 \times 5 \times 10{,}000{,}000/16{,}000}}{(2)(-5/16{,}000)} = \frac{200 \pm \sqrt{27{,}500}}{10/16{,}000}.$$

These two roots are 54,670 and 585,330, so for x between those two numbers, profit is positive.

Profit increases where marginal revenue exceeds marginal cost. Marginal revenue is $250 - 2x/4000$, while marginal cost is $50 + 2x/16{,}000$, so marginal revenue exceeds marginal cost when $250 - 2x/4000 > 50 + 2x/16{,}000$ which is where $200 > 10x/16{,}000$ or $x < 320{,}000$. And profit is maximized where marginal cost equals marginal revenue, which is $x = 320{,}000$.

Solution to Problem 8.3

This is a case of strictly positive fixed cost and rising marginal cost, so the picture is as in Figure 8.4. More specifically, marginal cost is linear, so the picture is shaped very much like the graph in Figure 8.14. To find efficient scale, the hard part is the first step, finding the total cost function. To do this, you have to integrate marginal cost and add the fixed cost:

$$TC(x) = F + \int_0^x MC(y)\,dy = F + \int_0^x (a + by)\,dy = F + ax + \frac{bx^2}{2}.$$

Thus average cost is

$$AC(x) = \frac{F}{x} + a + \frac{by}{2}.$$

Now equate marginal cost to average cost, to get

$$\frac{F}{x} + a + \frac{bx}{2} = a + bx \quad \text{or} \quad \frac{2F}{b} = x^2 \quad \text{or} \quad x = \sqrt{\frac{2F}{b}},$$

for efficient scale. The problem does not ask you to compute minimum average cost, but this is easy: Evaluate marginal cost at efficient scale, to get

$$\text{minimum } AC = a + b\sqrt{\frac{2F}{b}}.$$

Solution to Problem 8.5

The profit function corresponding to Figure 8.11(a) is in panel a of Figure 8.15, with Figure 8.11(a) reproduced in panel b. Note the region of positive profit, the region of rising profit, and the point of maximum profit. (For those who know a bit of math, the shape of the cost function is a parabola. You can see this by integrating the difference between marginal revenue and marginal cost or, even more easily, by noting that profit is quantity times profit margin. Profit margin, the difference between AR and AC, is a function of the form $M - mx$ for positive constants M and m, so profits take the form $Mx - mx^2$.)

The profit function corresponding to Figure 8.11(b) is shown in Figure 8.16(a), with Figure 8.11(b) reproduced directly below it. Again note the point of profit maximization and the regions in which profit is positive and negative and rising and falling. (Once again the profit function is a parabola, which intersects the vertical axis at $-K$, where K is the level of fixed costs.)

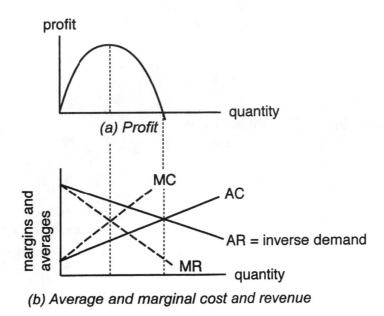

(b) *Average and marginal cost and revenue*

Figure 8.15. Problem 8.5: The profit function for the four functions in Figure 8.11(a).

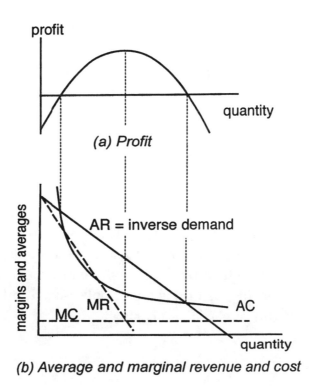

(b) *Average and marginal revenue and cost*

Figure 8.16. Problem 8.5: The profit function for the four functions in Figure 8.11(b).

Solution to Problem 8.6

(a) Since the marginal cost and revenue functions do not shift as K shifts, the profit function simply shifts up (lower K) and down (higher K). The point of maximum profit remains precisely the same, although any increase in K gives a corresponding decrease in the level of maximum profit. The region over which profit is positive shrinks (symmetrically, around the point of maximum profits).

(b) As we increase k, we increase costs at every level (except $x = 0$), and so profit decreases at every level (except $x = 0$). (At $x = 0$, profit stays at the level $-K$.) Accordingly, the region of positive profit must shrink. Moreover, the point at which MC hits MR shifts to the left (in the picture, think of shifting the MC line up), so that profit maximization occurs at lower and lower scales of production. (Because we know that profit has the shape of a parabola, we know that the region of positive profit is symmetric around the point of maximal profit, so we can be a bit more precise about how the region of positive profit shrinks away.)

(c) The quick answer is this: When this level of K is reached, AC is tangent to inverse demand at precisely the level of production where MC equals MR. This is an easy corollary of part a: As K shifts, the profit-maximizing level of production does not shift but stays at the same point (where MC equals MR). When fixed costs get so high that a single point achieves nonnegative profits, that point is the profit-maximizing level of production, which is where MC equals MR.

Solution to Problem 8.8

This uses the graphical procedure described on pages 194–5. First we find that AC(100) = $50 and AR(100) = $80. The procedure is to draw tangents (see Figure 8.17) to the AC and AR functions and extend those tangents back to the price axis: They hit at around $20 and $104, respectively. (If your numbers are slightly different, do not worry.) Then MC at 100 is found by moving in the direction opposite from AC, in an amount equal to the difference between AC(100) and the price-axis intercept of the tangent. Therefore MC(100) = $80. Similarly, MR(100) = AR(100) − [$104 − AR(100)] = $56.

Solution to Problem 8.10

The argument for Figure 8.10(a) is very quick. The region where profits are positive includes production levels only below efficient scale, so profit must be maximized at less than efficient scale.

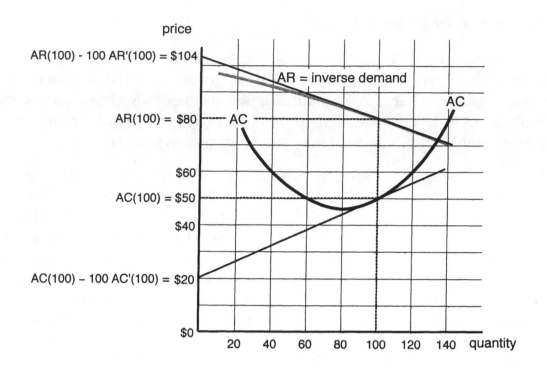

Figure 8.17. Problem 8.8: Finding marginal cost and revenue from average cost and revenue. To find MC(100), note first that AC(100) = $50, and AC(100) − 100AC′(100) = $20. Therefore, we know that 100AC′(100) = $30, and hence MC(100) = AC(100) + 100AC′(100) = $80. The value of MR(100) is computed similarly.

The argument for Figure 8.10(b) is one degree harder. Assuming (as you were told you may do) MC is rising, profit is maximized where MC = MR (since MR is falling). MC equals AC at efficient scale, and AC is less than MR at efficient scale, so the intersection of MC and MR must occur to the right of efficient scale; that is, at greater than efficient scale.[1]

The argument for Figure 8.10(c) is a simple adaptation of the argument for Figure 8.10(b). We start the same way, concluding that profit is maximized at the single point where MC equals MR. Since MR equals AC at efficient scale, and AC must equal MC at efficient scale, MR equals MC at efficient scale.

Can we prove this if we do not assume that MC is rising? It can be done, but it is a bit complex: Profit maximization must occur to the right of the point of maximum profit margin; see Problem 8.11. You can find the point of maximum profit margin by looking for where the slope of AC matches the slope of AR. This is a bit before the point of minimum average cost; now use the facts that (1) we are looking for where MC = MR and (2) MC < AC where average costs are falling and > AC where average costs are rising; obviously, the only possible intersection points for MC and MR beyond the point of maximum profit margin is where MC > AC, which means where AC is rising, which is beyond efficient scale.

Solution to Problem 8.12

Total revenue is

$$\mathrm{TR}(s, p) = 200s - s^2 + 200p - 2p^2.$$

Hence, marginal revenue equals marginal cost in skets is

$$200 - 2s = 50 + 2(s + p),$$

while marginal revenue equals marginal cost in plorts is

$$200 - 4p = 50 + 2(s + p).$$

Solve for s and p, and you get $s = 30$ and $p = 15$.

Material for Chapter 9

Technology and Cost Minimization

Solution to Problem 9.1

(a) The four- and six-chair isoquants are shown in Figure 9.10. Let me explain the six-chair isoquant: We must have at least 12 labor hours and 6 lathe hours, and the number of hours must be at least 36 in total. This gives the shapes shown.

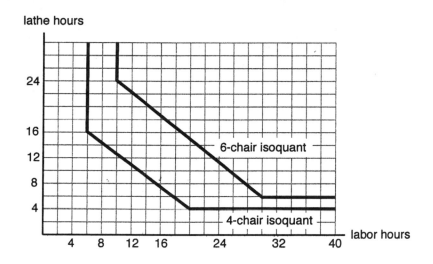

Figure 9.10. Problem 9.1: An isoquant diagram.

(b) In Figure 9.11, I determine the cheapest way to make six chairs. First I lay out an iso-cost line to get its slope. I pick the $240 iso-cost, which is 24 labor hours and no lathe or 16 lathe hours and no labor, or anything on the line between those points. Then I push out parallel to this line and find that I hit the isoquant at the corner shown. This makes sense. Labor is less costly per hour than the lathe, and as long as I can reduce my lathe time and increase labor in a one-to-one ratio, I want to do so. The only thing that stops me is that, for six chairs, I have an unavoidable minimum of 6 hours on the lathe. Note that this point (30 hours labor and 6 hours lathe) has a cost of $\$10 \times 30 + \$15 \times 6 = \$390$.

(c) We have constant returns to scale, so total costs are a straight line and average cost and marginal cost are the same, both flat. From the answer to b, I see that it

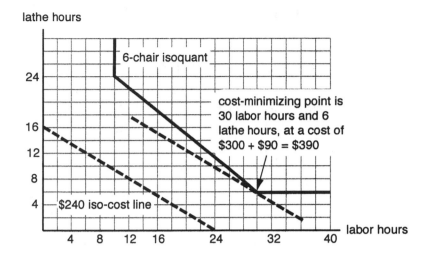

Figure 9.11. Problem 9.1: Determining the least-cost way to make six chairs.

costs $65 to make one chair (65 = 390/6), so I get the total cost and marginal and average cost curves shown in Figure 9.12.

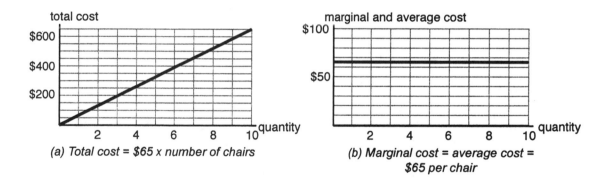

Figure 9.12. Problem 9.1: Total, average, and marginal cost functions.

Solution to Problem 9.3

(a) This is a no-substitutions production function. One way to see this is to fix x, a desired amount of output. To get $f(y_1, \ldots, y_n)$ to equal x, you need $g_i(y_i) \geq x$ for each i. To get x, y_i must be (at least) the solution to $g_i(y) = x$. Any more y_i would go to waste, as long as some other j satisfies $g_j(y_j) = x$, as then the minimum would be determined by j. (At least, the minimum would be no larger than x, which is less than $g_i(y_i)$.)

(b) This is a fixed-coefficients production function. Since G is strictly increasing,

$$G\left(\min\left\{\frac{y_1}{a_1}, \ldots, \frac{y_n}{a_n}\right\}\right) = \min\left\{G\left(\frac{y_1}{a_1}\right), \ldots, G\left(\frac{y_n}{a_n}\right)\right\}.$$

Therefore, we have a special case of a; this is a no-substitutions production function. Moreover, the ratio of the different inputs at the right-angle kinks never changes: If $x = G(y_i/a_i)$ and $x = G(y_j/a_j)$, then $y_i/a_i = y_j/a_j$, or $y_i = a_i y_j/a_j$.

(c) This is a constant marginal rate of substitution production function. If $x = G(y_1/a_1 + \ldots + y_n/a_n)$ and we, say, decrease y_i to y_i', then the necessary compensating increase in y_j is $a_j(y_i - y_i')/a_i$. That is, if we increase y_j by this amount, the sum stays the same, so G(the sum) stays the same. Since this compensating increase in input j is independent of the original values of y_i and y_j and depends only on the amount that input i is decreased, the rates of substitution of one input for another are constant.

Solution to Problem 9.5

(a) Part a asks you to solve the problem graphically, then with a spreadsheet, and then algebraically, using calculus.

To solve the problem graphically, take the 100-unit isoquant, which is reproduced as Figure 9.13, and draw on it some iso-cost line to get the slope. I choose to begin with the $800 iso-cost, given by the two points ($m = 0$, $l = 200$) and ($m = 400$, $l = 100$). (You can choose any level of cost and two points giving that cost that you wish.)

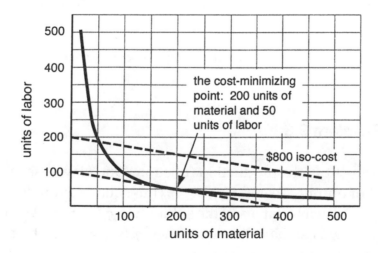

Figure 9.13. Problem 9.5(a): Graphical solution.

Next, we slide this iso-cost line, keeping the slope the same, in or out until it is just tangent to the isoquant. If you, too, picked the $800 iso-cost, you have to slide inward (in the direction of the heavy arrows).

When tangency is achieved, read off the coordinates of the point of tangency ($m = 200$ and $l = 50$) and cost out this set of inputs to get the (cost-minimizing) total cost of producing 100 units:

$$TC(100) = \$1 \times 200 \ + \ \$4 \times 50 = \$400.$$

To solve the problem with a spreadsheet, you have to build a spreadsheet that computes, for given levels of m and l, the total amount of output, given by the production function, and the cost of m and l, given by the formula total cost = $m + 4l$. Then ask Solver to minimize the cell containing the total cost, holding the cell containing the output level at 100 (or more). Figure 9.14 shows the results of this; if you obtain the spreadsheet PROB9-5, it will give (in sheet 1) the spreadsheet with initial values of $m = l = 100$. Note the small amount of "round-off" error.

	A	B	C
3			
4		amount of m	200.011332
5		amount of l	49.9971669
6			
7		output level	99.9999997
8			
9		price per unit of m	$1
10		price per unit of l	$4
11			
12		cost of inputs	$400

Figure 9.14. Problem 9.5(a): The solution obtained by Solver.

To solve the problem algebraically, note first that, to produce a strictly positive amount of output, you need strictly positive levels of each input. Thus the rule applies:

$$\frac{r_l}{\text{MPP}_l} = \frac{r_m}{\text{MPP}_m}.$$

The two marginal physical product functions are

$$\text{MPP}_l = \frac{\partial f}{\partial l} = \frac{1}{2}l^{-1/2}m^{1/2} \quad \text{and} \quad \text{MPP}_m = \frac{\partial f}{\partial m} = \frac{1}{2}l^{1/2}m^{-1/2}.$$

Therefore, the rule says that

$$\frac{4}{\frac{1}{2}l^{-1/2}m^{1/2}} = \frac{1}{\frac{1}{2}l^{1/2}m^{-1/2}}.$$

Invert each of the fractions in the last equality, to get

$$\frac{1}{8}l^{-1/2}m^{1/2} = \frac{1}{2}l^{1/2}m^{-1/2}.$$

Collect all the ls on the right and all the ms on the left, to get

$$\frac{1}{8}m = \frac{1}{2}l, \quad \text{or} \quad m = 4l.$$

So, at the cost-minimizing production plan, four units of material will be used for each unit of labor.

If we wish to produce x units of output and use l^* units of labor, we use $4l^*$ units of material, giving us output $f(l^*, 4l^*) = (l^*)^{1/2}(4l^*)^{1/2} = 2l^*$. That is, to produce x units of output in a cost-minimizing fashion, we use $x/2$ units of labor and $2x$ units of material. The cost of this is

$$\text{TC}(x) = \$4 \times \frac{x}{2} + \$1 \times 2x = \$4x.$$

To finish part a, TC(100) = $400.

(b) If you did part a graphically or with a spreadsheet, at this point you need to invoke my assertion that this technology has constant returns to scale, to conclude that, if 100 units cost $400, then the marginal cost of production is a *constant* $4 per unit. If you did part a algebraically, you know the entire total cost function $\text{TC}(x) = 4x$, so you know that $\text{MC}(x) = \$4$. In either case, we go on to equate marginal cost and marginal revenue.

Inverse demand is $P(x) = 12 - (x/2000)$, so total revenue is $TR(x) = 12x - (x^2/2000)$, and marginal revenue is $MR(x) = 12 - (2x/2000) = 12 - (x/1000)$. $MC = MR$ where

$$12 - \frac{x}{1000} = 4 \quad \text{or} \quad 8 = \frac{x}{1000} \quad \text{or} \quad x = 8000,$$

at which point the price charged is

$$P(8000) = 12 - \frac{8000}{2000} = \$8.$$

Note that $x = 8000$ implies $l = 4000$ and $m = 16{,}000$.

Solution to Problem 9.7

In general, we are looking at production functions of the form

$$f(y_1, y_2, \ldots, y_m) = (y_1)^{\alpha_1}(y_2)^{\alpha_2} \cdot \ldots \cdot (y_m)^{\alpha_m}.$$

(This is the general form of a Cobb-Douglas production function. If we increase all the inputs by a given multiple, say, $\lambda > 1$, we get

$$f(\lambda y_1, \ldots, \lambda y_n) = (\lambda y_1)^{\alpha_1} \cdot \ldots \cdot (\lambda y_m)^{\alpha_m}$$

$$= \lambda^{\alpha_1 + \ldots + \alpha_m} \cdot (y_1)^{\alpha_1} \cdot \ldots \cdot (y_m)^{\alpha_m} = \lambda^{\alpha_1 + \ldots + \alpha_m} f(y_1, \ldots, y_m).$$

Hence, whether we have increasing, decreasing, or constant returns to scale depends on whether

$$\lambda^{\alpha_1 + \ldots + \alpha_m} \geq, \leq, \text{ or } = \lambda.$$

This, in turn, depends on whether

$$\alpha_1 + \ldots + \alpha_m \geq, \leq, \text{ or } = 1.$$

Hence,

- In the case $f(k, l, m) = k^{1/2}l^{1/8}m^{1/4}$, the sum of the exponents is $\frac{1}{2} + \frac{1}{8} + \frac{1}{4} = \frac{7}{8}$ which is less than 1; we have decreasing returns to scale (and increasing average costs).

- In the production function of Problem 9.2, the sum of the exponents is 1, and we have constant returns to scale.

- In the production function $f(k, m) = k^{1/2}m^{2/3}$, the sum of the exponents is $\frac{7}{6}$; we have increasing returns to scale and decreasing average costs.

Solution to Problem 9.9

(a) Figure 9.15 shows one iso-cost line (the $200 iso-cost line), which is shifted while maintaining its slope until it is just tangent to the 10-unit isoquant. The point of tangency is at 60 units of material and 20 units of labor, which has a total cost of

$$\$10 \times 20 \ + \ \$2 \times 60 = \$320,$$

so we know that TC(10) = $320.

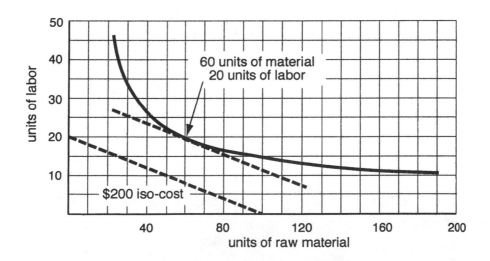

Figure 9.15. Problem 9.9: Finding the cheapest way to make 10 rewps.

(b) If we suppose that the firm has decreasing returns to scale, then we know that its average costs are rising (to be more accurate, not falling). The average cost at 10 units of output is $32, so the average cost at 15 units can be no less than $32, which means that the total cost of producing 15 rewps can be *no less than* $32 \times 15 = $480.

Solution to Problem 9.10

Marginal revenue is $MR(x) = 20 - (2x/3000)$. We have to set this equal to marginal cost, and I guess that MC will equal MR on the second segment of MC. So we have to solve

$$20 - \frac{2x}{3000} = \frac{8000 + x}{833.333} = 9.6 + \frac{x}{833.333}.$$

This gives us

$$10.4 = \frac{x}{833.333} + \frac{x}{1500} = \frac{2333.333x}{833.333 \times 1500},$$

which is

$$x = \frac{10.4 \times 833.333 \times 1500}{2333.333} = 5571.4284.$$

The corresponding c or marginal cost figure is $13571.4284/833.333 = 16.2857$; you can plug this value into the X_1^* and X_2^* functions to see how much should be produced at each facility.

Solution to Problem 9.12

You can make up to 400 kg of final output in the hydration–distillation process at a cost of $4.00 per kilogram. Why 400 and $4? Because you can process up to 1000 kg of input, and each kilogram of input provides 0.4 kg of output; moreover, each kilogram of input costs $1.00 for raw materials and $20 \times 0.03 = \$0.60$ in labor costs, or $1.60 total, so the cost per kilogram of output is $1.6/0.4 = \$4$. And you can make up to 250 kg of final output in the catalytic process at a cost of $5.60 per kilogram of output: You can process up to 500 kgs of input, getting .5 kgs of output for every kilogram of input; the cost per kilogram of input is $1.00 for raw materials and $20 \times 0.09 = \$1.80$ for labor, or $2.80 per kilogram of input total, or $5.60 per kilogram of output total.

What are your total costs? For up to 400 kg of output, you should use the hydration–distillation process only; your total cost rises linearly at a rate of $4 per kilogram. At 400 kg of output, you have to shift to the more expensive catalytic process, since you have no more capacity for hydration–distillation; your costs rise at a rate of $5.60

per kilogram. This works up to an additional 250 kg of output, at which point you can make no more. So we get a total cost function as shown in Figure 9.16(a): linear up to 400 kg, then kinked and linear with a bigger slope up to 650 kg, then vertical, meaning you can get no more output. Figure 9.16(b) graphs the corresponding marginal cost function. Note the staircase character of marginal cost.

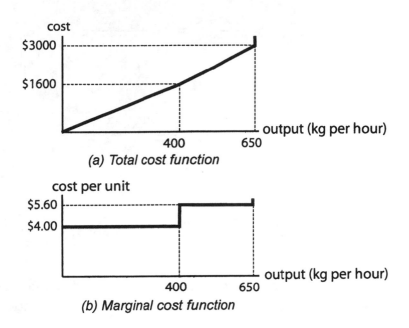

Figure 9.16. Problem 9.12: Total and marginal cost functions.

Solution to Problem 9.14

Let me begin by saying that this is an extremely hard problem. In particular, the two technologies are not cost independent, since each uses up shared, scarce inputs to production; namely, cheap and somewhat cheap labor time. If you got close to the answer, you are doing great.

As long as the marginal cost of using additional labor is 0, which is up to where the firm is using 18 labor hours per factory hour, the catalytic process is cheaper per unit output; it has cost of $2.00 per kilogram of output, while the hydration–distillation process has a cost of $2.50 per kilogram. The 18 labor hours stretch to processing 200 kg of raw material in the catalytic process, or 100 kg of output. So, at up to 100 kg of output per hour, we use the catalytic process only, with a marginal cost of $2.00 per kilogram of output.

Once we move beyond 100 kg of output, we have a choice. We can continue to process 200 kg of raw material using the catalytic process and produce additional output using the hydration–distillation process. This, as we computed in Problem 9.12, has a marginal cost of $4.00 per kilogram of output. Alternatively, we can decrease the amount of of catalysis we use, since this uses labor time faster than hydration–distillation, getting back more output with hydration–distillation. How does this work? If we drop 1 kg of output using catalysis, this frees up 0.18 labor hours. With those 0.18 labor hours, we can process 6 kg of input using hydration–distillation, getting 2.4 kg of output. Therefore, the net impact on output is an additional 1.4 kg. The effect on costs is this: We save $2 on the raw material inputs to catalysis, but we spend an extra $6 on raw materials for hydration–distillation, or a net spending of $4. So, we can get 1.4 kg of final output on the margin at a cost of $4 on the margin, for a cost of $2.86 (approximately) per kilogram of final output. This is better than the marginal cost of $4.00 per kilogram if we increase labor hours, so this is what we do.

This substitution works until we are use all our "free" labor hours on hydration–distillation. The 18 labor hours per factory hour can be used to process 600 kg of input to hydration–distillation, or 240 kg of output. So from 100 kg to 240 kg of output, the marginal cost is $2.86 per kilogram of output (approximately).

Once we get to 240 kg of output, there is nothing to do but to start employing labor at $20 per hour. Now, the least marginal cost involves using hydration–distillation, with a marginal cost of $4 per kilogram of final output. This is good until we process 1000 kg of input for 400 kg of output using hydration–distillation. Note that this employs 30 hours of labor per factory hour, so we have not reached the point at which the price of labor goes up.

Above 400 kg of output, we have to go back to using catalysis. Now, the marginal cost per kilogram of output is $5.60 (see Problem 9.12), up to the point where labor usage is 60 hours. Since 30 hours of labor go to hydration–distillation, we have 30 hours that can be used at catalysis, which gives 333.33 kg of input to catalysis, or 166.67 kg of output from catalysis. That is, the marginal cost stays at $5.60 up to total production of 566.67 kg of output.

Beyond this level, we have to employ premium labor, at $30 per hour. We continue to want to run as much hydration–distillation as we can; a higher marginal labor cost only reinforces this, so we continue to run a full 1000 kg of input, for 400 kg of output and 30 hours of labor, through hydration distillation. To move beyond 566.67 kgs of output, we have to increase catalysis. The marginal cost of a unit of input to catalysis is $1 for materials plus $30 × 0.09 = $2.70 labor costs, or $3.70

total, or $7.40 per unit output. So, up to the overall capacity of 650 kg of output, marginal costs rise to $7.40 per unit.

Putting all this together, we get the total and marginal cost functions shown in Figure 9.17. Note the fixed cost for those first 18 labor hours.

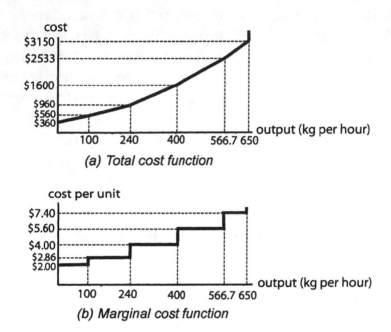

(a) Total cost function

(b) Marginal cost function

Figure 9.17. Problem 9.14: Total and marginal cost curves.

Once again, we have a total cost curve that is composed of a number of linear segments (with increasing slope) and a marginal cost curve that looks like a staircase.

Few readers will be able to reason their way through this problem, as we just did. However, if you know how to do linear programming, you can formulate the computation of total cost as a linear programming problem. Six variables are needed:

- x_0: the hourly amount of kilograms of input per hour, processed using catalysis and fixed-cost labor.

- x_1: the hourly amount of kilograms of input per hour, processed using catalysis and $20 per hour (marginal) labor.

- x_2: the hourly amount of kilograms of input per hour, processed using catalysis and $30 per hour (marginal) labor.

- y_0: the hourly amount of kilograms of input per hour, processed using hydration–distillation and fixed-cost labor.

- y_1: the hourly amount of kilograms of input per hour, processed using hydration–distillation and \$20 per hour (marginal) labor.

- y_2: the hourly amount of kilograms of input per hour, processed using hydration–distillation and \$30 per hour (marginal) labor.

The objective function is to minimize hourly costs:

$$\text{minimize } x_0 + x_1 + x_2 + y_0 + y_1 + y_2 + 20(0.09x_1 + 0.03y_1) + 30(0.09x_2 + 0.03y_2) + 18 \times 20,$$

which you should recognize as the costs of the raw material, plus labor costs (where the fixed 18×20 at the end is the fixed cost of the first 18 hours of labor), subject to the following constraints:

- The amount output should equal or exceed the total amount desired: $0.5x_0 + 0.5x_1 + 0.5x_2 + 0.4y_0 + 0.4y_1 + 0.4y_2 \geq C$, where C is a constant for the amount of output being sought.[1]

- the total amount of catalysis input is bounded by 500: $x_0 + x_1 + x_2 \leq 500$.

- The total amount of hydration–distillation input is bounded by 1000: $y_0 + y_1 + y_2 \leq 1000$.

- The amount of fixed-cost labor is bounded above by 18 hours: $0.09x_0 + 0.03y_0 \leq 18$.

- The amount of \$20 labor is bounded above by 42 hours (above the 18 hours of fixed cost labor): $0.09x_1 + 0.03y_1 \leq 42$.

- All the variables are nonnegative: $x_0, x_1, x_2, y_0, y_1, y_2 \geq 0$.

One final note: The "shape" of the total and marginal cost functions (the first composed of a number of linear segments with increasing slope and the other a staircase) is typical of cost functions computed from linear programming formulations. The

---

[1] Why use a $\geq$ instead of =? In fact, I know (how?) this constraint binds at the solution, so it does not matter. But, if this is not true (if the cheapest way to get C units of output is to overproduce), why not do that? (One reason might be that it is costly to dispose of unsold output, but the problem says nothing about that.)

jumps in marginal cost, corresponding to changes in the slope of total cost, represent basis changes in the optimal solution, as we increase the amount that has to be produced. If you do run this linear program, note that the shadow price on the output constraint, as a function of C, is precisely the marginal cost function.

Solution to Problem 9.15

(a) Except for the constraints that the amount of each input must be nonnegative, the problem

$$\text{maximize } \text{TR}\big(f(y_1, y_2, y_3)\big) - \big(r_1 y_1 + r_2 y_2 + r_3 y_3\big)$$

is an unconstrained maximization problem. Hence, if we are not concerned with this constraint (if we know that all three inputs are used in positive amounts), the condition for a maximum would be that the partial derivatives of the objective function (profit) in each variable (the amount of each input) must be 0, or

$$\text{MR}\big(f(y_1, y_2, y_3)\big) \times \text{MPP}_i(y_1, y_2, y_3) - r_i = 0,$$

for $i = 1, 2,$ and 3. I take the partial derivative of $\text{TR}\big(f(y_1, y_2, y_3)\big)$ in y_i pretty quickly there, using the chain rule. In any case, this is often rewritten by economists as

$$\text{MR}\big(f(y_1, y_2, y_3)\big) \times \text{MPP}_i(y_1, y_2, y_3) = r_i.$$

Economists sometimes call the product on the left-hand side the *marginal revenue product* of input i; when they do, the equation given is therefore read "the marginal revenue product of input i should equal its price."

If we take into account the nonnegativity constraint on the level of input i, the equation just given becomes an inequality:

$$\text{MR}\big(f(y_1, y_2, y_3)\big) \times \text{MPP}_i(y_1, y_2, y_3) \leq r_i,$$

with equality required if $y_i > 0$. This is sometimes written compactly as

$$y_i \times \big[\text{MR}\big(f(y_1, y_2, y_3)\big) \times \text{MPP}_i(y_1, y_2, y_3) - r_i\big] = 0.$$

(b) In Problem 9.5(b), marginal revenue is $MR(x) = 12 - x/1000$, so the optimality condition for input l (for instance) is

$$\left(12 - \frac{l^{1/2}m^{1/2}}{1000}\right)\frac{1}{2}m^{1/2}l^{-1/2} = r_m = 4.$$

This is

$$\left(\frac{6m^{1/2}}{l^{1/2}} - \frac{m}{2000}\right) = 4.$$

Similarly, the optimality condition for input m is

$$\left(\frac{6l^{1/2}}{m^{1/2}} - \frac{l}{2000}\right) = 1.$$

Multiply the first of these by l and the second by m. You get

$$4l = \left(6m^{1/2}l^{1/2} - \frac{ml}{2000}\right) = m.$$

Replace m in the first equation (say) by $4l$. You get

$$\left(\frac{12l^{1/2}}{l^{1/2}} - \frac{4l}{2000}\right) = 4, \text{ or}$$

$$8 = \frac{4l}{2000} \quad \text{or} \quad l = 4000.$$

Therefore $m = 16{,}000$. This agrees with the solution we obtained in two steps for Problem 9.5.

(c) If the price of input i depends on the amount of input i used and is given by the function $r_i(y_i)$, then the optimality condition we derived earlier becomes

$$y_i \times \left[MR\big(f(y_1, y_2, y_3)\big) \times MPP_i(y_1, y_2, y_3) - \big(r_i'(y_i)y_i + r_i(y_i)\big)\right] = 0.$$

In words, the price of input i is replaced by the marginal cost of purchasing input i.

Solution to Problem 9.16

Most parts of Problem 9.16 are "solved," although the context is slightly different, in Chapters 11 and 12. I leave it to you to put the pieces together—if you are trying this problem, you are almost surely capable of doing so. But part c of this problem is not found in Chapter 11 or 12. So I provide that part here. Suppose, contrary to what is claimed, we have $q' > q$, $x' \in X_i^*(q')$, and $x \in X_i^*(q)$, with $x > x'$. Since x is optimal for facility i at the transfer price q, $qx' - \text{TC}_i(x') \leq qx - \text{TC}_i(x)$. Rewrite this as

$$\text{TC}_i(x) - \text{TC}_i(x') \leq q(x - x').$$

Since $x > x'$ (by assumption) and $q' > q$, $q'(x - x') > q(x - x')$. Therefore,

$$q'(x - x') > \text{TC}_i(x) - \text{TC}_i(x'),$$

which we can rewrite as

$$q'x - \text{TC}_i(x) > q'x' - \text{TC}_i(x'),$$

which contradicts the assumption that x' is optimal at transfer price q'. (If you find this sort of thing intriguing, look for books that discuss *monotone comparative statics*.)

Material for Chapter 10

Multiperiod Production and Cost

Solution to Problem 10.1

(a) If the firm is stuck employing $l = 64$ in the short run, its short-run production function is $x = f(m, 64) = m^{1/3}64^{1/6} = 2m^{1/3}$. So to produce x units of output in the short run, the amount of m needed is the solution to $2m^{1/3} = x$, or $m = x^3/8$. Hence, the short-run total cost of producing x units is

$$\text{SRTC}(x) = \$300 + \$4 \times 64 + \$1\frac{x^3}{8} = 556 + \frac{x^3}{8},$$

the sum of the fixed cost, the cost of the short-run-fixed 64 units of l, and the cost of the variable amount of m required to obtain x units of output.

(b) The requested graphs are shown in Figure 10.8. (To improve picture quality, I "traced" a spreadsheet graph with a more sophisticated drawing tool.) This is the sort of picture expected.

(c) Recall from Problem 9.7 that at the status quo, $x = 16$, $P = 128$, $m = 512$, $l = 64$, and profit equals $16 \times 128 - 300 - 3 \times 16^2 = 980$.

When inverse demand shifts to $180 - 2x$, marginal revenue shifts to $\text{MR}(x) = 180 - 4x$. In the short run, $\text{SRMC}(x) = 3x^2/8$, so the firm maximizes profit by producing at the level x that solves

$$180 - 4x = \frac{3x^2}{8} \quad \text{or} \quad \frac{3}{8}x^2 + 4x - 180 = 0.$$

Using the quadratic formula, the two roots of this equation are

$$x = \frac{-4 \pm \sqrt{16 - (4)(3/8)(-180)}}{(2)(3/8)} = \frac{-4 \pm \sqrt{286}}{3/4} = \frac{-4 \pm 16.91153}{3/4}.$$

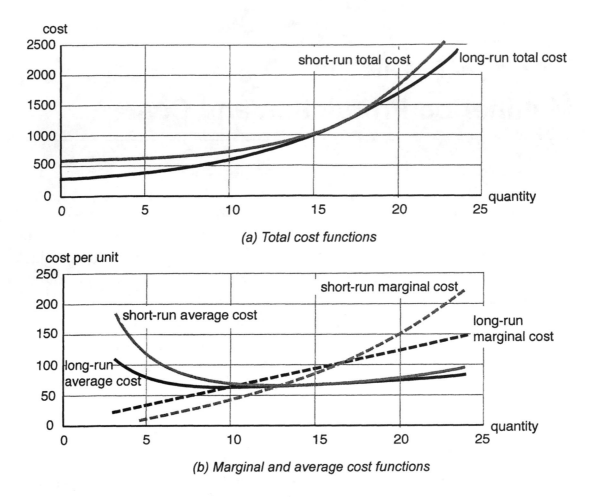

(a) Total cost functions

(b) Marginal and average cost functions

Figure 10.8. Problem 10.1: Long-run and short-run cost functions.

The root we want is (obviously, because the other root is negative) the one where you add the 16.91153, which is

$$x = \frac{16.91153 - 4}{3/4} = 17.2154.$$

So, in the short run, the firm produces $x = 17.2154$, which gives a price of $P = 180 - 2(17.2154) = \$145.57$. Profit is $17.2154 \times 145.57 - 556 - 17.2154^3/8 = 1312.28$, and material utilitization is 637.76.

In the longer run, marginal cost becomes $\mathrm{LRMC}(x) = 6x$, so profit is maximized where

$$\mathrm{MC}(x) = 6x = 180 - 4x = \mathrm{MR}(x) \quad \text{or} \quad 180 = 10x \quad \text{or} \quad x = 18,$$

for a price of $P = 180 - 2(18) = \$144$, profit of $144 \times 18 - 300 - 3 \times 18^2 = 1320$, material utilitization of 648, and labor utilization of 81.

Solution to Problem 10.2

I leave the work for you to do, but so you can check your work, here are the answers to the first question:

$$\text{SRTC}(x) = 684 + \frac{x^3}{8} \quad \text{and} \quad \text{LRTC}(x) = 300 + 3.4344x^2.$$

It is worth noting that, if we compute long-run and short-run total costs at $x = 16$, we get

$$\text{LRTC}(16) = \$1179.21 \quad \text{and} \quad \text{SRTC}(16) = \$1196.00.$$

Total costs are not equal at the status quo. Assumption 10.2 does not hold. The reason is that the status quo production plan (64 units of l and 256 units of m) is not the cost-minimizing long-run production plan at the new input prices. In the short run, we are stuck with $l = 64$, so to continue to produce 16 we do not change the level of m. But in the long run, because l has become more expensive, we increase m and decrease l. This saves $17 or so. (Is there any level of production at which the new SRTC equals the new LRTC? Yes; and if you have derived the LRTC function I've provided, you should be able to tell what it is under 10 seconds with a calculator only.)

Solution to Problem 10.3

(a) The long run is unchanged from Problem 10.1, so the long-run analysis is unchanged, and $\text{LRTC}(x) = 300 + 3x^2$. Short-run total cost is more complex, however. For levels of x below the status-quo level $x_0 = 16$, the analysis of Problem 10.1 applies because the short-run rules of Problem 10.1 apply for decreases in production level: $\text{SRTC}(x) = 556 + x^3/8$.

For $x > 16$, however, we reason as follows. The firm can add labor but at a marginal cost of $6 per unit. Starting from the status quo of 16 units of output, 64 units of labor, and 512 units of material, the firm increases only material usage until

$$\frac{\$1}{\text{MPP}_m} = \frac{\$6}{\text{MPP}_l},$$

where the latter is evaluated at $l = 64$. The displayed equation is

$$\frac{1}{\frac{1}{3}m^{-2/3}l^{1/6}} = \frac{6}{\frac{1}{6}m^{1/3}l^{-5/6}},$$

which when simplified gives $m = 12l$. Therefore, m is increased, holding l at 64, until $m = 12 \times 64 = 768$. At this point, production is $x = 768^{1/3}64^{1/6} = 18.315$, so over the range $16 \leq x \leq 18.315$, $\mathrm{SRTC}(x) = 556 + x^3/8$. At this level of x and m, it makes sense on the margin to hire more labor via overtime, keeping the ratio of m to l at 12 to 1. Substituting $m = 12l$ into the production function gives

$$x = (12l)^{1/3}l^{1/6}, \quad \text{thus} \quad l = 0.1908x^2 \text{ and } m = 12 \times 0.1908x^2.$$

This continues until we reach the upper limit of 16 units of overtime, or $l = 80$ and $m = 960$, at which point $x = 960^{1/3}80^{1/6} = 20.477$. Total cost over this range is computed as $\mathrm{SRTC}(x) = \$300 + \$4 \times 64 + \$6 \times [0.1908x^2 - 64] + \$1 \times 12 \times 0.1908x^2 = 172 + 3.4344x^2$. Beyond level 20.477, no more labor can be added in the short-run, so material use must solve $x = m^{1/3}80^{1/6}$ or $m = x^3/80^{1/2} = 0.1118x^3$, hence, total cost is $\mathrm{SRTC}(x) = 300 + 4 \times 64 + 6 \times 16 + 0.1118x^3$. Putting all the pieces together, we get

$$\mathrm{SRTC}(x) = \begin{cases} 556 + x^3/8, & \text{for } x \leq 18.315, \\ 172 + 3.4344x^2, & \text{for } 18.315 \leq x \leq 20.477, \text{ and} \\ 652 + 0.1118x^3, & \text{for } 20.477 \leq x. \end{cases}$$

(b) If inverse demand shifts to $180 - 2x$, marginal revenue shifts to $180 - 4x$. In the long run, we get the same answer as in Problem 10.1. But for the short run, we have to equate marginal revenue and short-run marginal cost, which is

$$\mathrm{SRMC}(x) = \begin{cases} 3x^2/8, & \text{for } x \leq 18.315, \\ 6.8688x, & \text{for } 18.315 \leq x \leq 20.477, \text{ and} \\ 0.3354x^2, & \text{for } 20.477 \leq x. \end{cases}$$

To figure out where marginal revenue cuts through marginal cost, I build a spreadsheet, PROB10-3, which computes marginal revenue and marginal costs for each

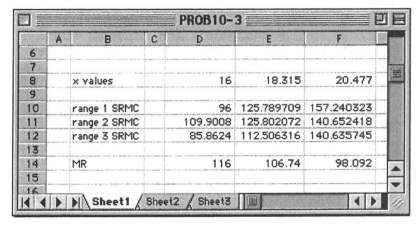

Figure 10.9. Problem 10.3: Spreadsheet PROB10-3.

of the three "segments" of the marginal cost function, for the values $x = 16, 18.315$, and 20.477. This is shown in Figure 10.9.

The spreadsheet tells us that at $x = 16$, SRMC, given by range 1 SRMC, is \$96, while marginal revenue is \$116. When we get to $x = 18.314$ (the level of x at which point it is cost-effective to add overtime labor), short-run marginal cost has risen to \$125.79 or so, while marginal revenue has fallen to \$106.74. It is worth noting that the marginal cost function over this "regime shift," from a constant $l = 64$ to where labor is added at overtime, is continuous; the slight differences in value you see are round-off error.

This means that marginal revenue cuts through marginal cost somewhere in the region of $16 \le x \le 18.315$. We need to identify precisely where this happens, but before doing so, let me continue with the spreadsheet a bit. Over the range $18.315 \le x \le 20.477$, marginal cost is given by the range 2 SRMC function, running from \$125.80 or so, to \$140.65. Marginal revenue falls from \$106.74 to \$98.09. We know that marginal revenue is falling throughout, and over this range, short-run marginal cost is the increasing function $\text{SRMC}(x) = 6.8688x$, so there are no intersections in this range.

Note next that, at the boundary between range 2 and range 3, where $x = 20.477$, SRMC is again continuous. At the start of range 3, marginal revenue is well below SRMC, and since marginal revenue is falling and marginal cost, given now by $0.3354x^2$, is rising, again there are no further intersections.

Therefore, the only intersection, and the short-run profit-maximizing position, is where

$$180 - 4x = \frac{3}{8}x^2,$$

which we know from Problem 10.1(c) is $x = 17.2154$, and so forth.

Solution to Problem 10.4

(a) To produce x units of output requires $3x$ units of m, at a total cost of $\$3m$, and $x/5$ units of l, at a total cost of $\$2x$, so that LRTC$(x) = \$5x$.

(b) With the given inverse demand function, marginal revenue is $23 - 2x/5$, so marginal cost equals marginal revenue where

$$5 = 23 - \frac{2x}{5} \quad \text{or} \quad 18 = \frac{2x}{5} \quad \text{or} \quad x = 45.$$

At this quantity, price is $\$14$ and profit is $\$405$.

(c) If the firm cannot vary l, there is no way (with a fixed-coefficients production function) for it to increase the level of x it produces above the status-quo level of $x = 45$. It can decrease production below $x = 45$ and save $\$3$ per unit, but it must pay a fixed $\$90$ for the full 9 units of l used. Hence, its short-run total cost function is

$$\text{SRTC}(x) = \begin{cases} 90 + 3x, & \text{for } x \leq 45, \text{ and} \\ \infty, & \text{for } x > 45, \end{cases}$$

where the ∞ is mathematical shorthand for, You cannot do it at any price. If a picture is desired, we would have something like Figure 10.10.

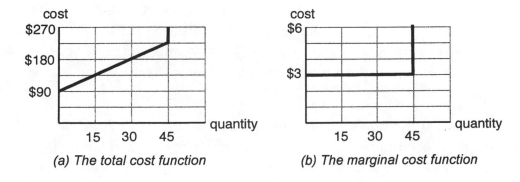

(a) The total cost function   *(b) The marginal cost function*

Figure 10.10. *Problem 10.4: Short-run total and marginal cost functions for a no-substitutions technology, with one input fixed in the short-run.*

If inverse demand rises to $23.5 - x/5$, this increases marginal revenue to $23.5 - 2x/5$. In the short run, the firm is unable to increase its output beyond $x = 45$, so it simply increases the price per unit by \$0.50 per unit to \$14.50, enjoying an extra \$22.50 in profit, or a profit of \$427.50. In the long run, the firm equates long-run marginal cost and long-run marginal revenue, or

$$5 = 23.5 - \frac{2x}{5} \quad \text{or} \quad 18.5 = \frac{2x}{5} \quad \text{or} \quad x = 46.25.$$

Therefore, the price is pulled down slightly, to \$14.25, and profit rises to \$427.8125.

(d) As in part c, we look at the problem in two parts: for increases in production beyond the status-quo level of $x = 45$ and for decreases from $x = 45$. For increases, we need \$3x worth of materials and $90 + 15(x - 45)/5 = 3x - 45$ worth of labor (the \$90 is for the first 9 units of l). For decreases from 45, we need \$3x worth of materials, and $10x/5 + 5(45 - x)/5 = 2x + 45 - x = x + 45$ worth of labor. The latter is the cost of the labor that is employed at \$10 per unit, plus the cost of furloughed labor, at \$5 per unit. Hence, we get the short-run total cost function

$$\text{SRTC}(x) = \begin{cases} 4x + 45, & \text{for } x \leq 45, \text{ and} \\ 6x - 45, & \text{for } x \geq 45. \end{cases}$$

Note that this total cost function is continuous but has a kink at $x = 45$. Therefore, the short-run marginal cost function is

$$\text{SRMC}(x) = \begin{cases} 4, & \text{for } x < 45, \text{ and} \\ 6, & \text{for } x > 45. \end{cases}$$

Short-run marginal cost is discontinuous at the status quo. The pictures of short-run and long-run cost functions (total and marginal) are given in Figure 10.11.

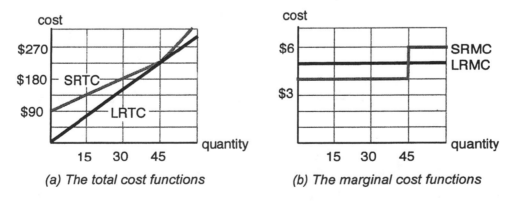

(a) The total cost functions   (b) The marginal cost functions

Figure 10.11. *Problem 10.4: Long-run and short-run total and average cost functions, for a no-substitutions technology, with one input semi-fixed in the short run.*

If inverse demand shifts up to $P(x) = 23.5 - x/5$, marginal revenue shifts up to $P(x) = 23.5 - 2x/5$. In the short run, this rise of $0.50 in marginal revenue is not enough to hit short-run marginal cost at the upper level of $6, so the firm does not react in terms of quantity. In other words, the short-run reaction is the same as in part c. (And, of course, so is the long-run reaction.)

If inverse demand shifts up to $P(x) = 25 - x/5$, on the other hand, marginal revenue shifts up to $P(x) = 25 - 2x/5$. This exceeds $6 at $x = 45$, so the firm increases production (in the short run) until $25 - 2x/5 = 6$, or $19 = 2x/5$, or $x = 47.5$. This gives a price of $15.50 and a short-run profit of $15.50 \times 47.5 - (6 \times 47.5 - 45) = \$496.25$. Then, in the long run, the firm adds l at the regular time rate of $10 per unit, which lowers its marginal costs to $5. So long-run profit maximization occurs where $25 - 2x/5 = 5$, or $x = 50$, at which point the price is $15 and profit is $500. The dynamics are depicted in Figure 10.12.

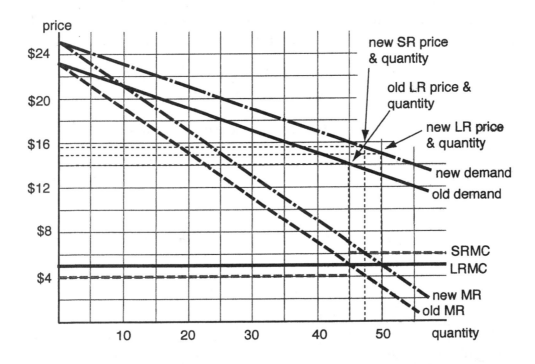

Figure 10.12. Problem 10.5(d): Dynamics for a shift in inverse demand.

(e) There is no kink in the short-run total cost function in Problem 10.3; we essentially verified this numerically using Excel. Alternatively, you could differentiate the total cost function, to find that the derivative is continuous across the "break points" in the function definition. To account for why we have a kink in this problem but not in Problem 10.3, note that, in this problem, there is no possible substitution of one input for another. Hence, to increase production (say), you must add l at the higher marginal rate. In the problem in the text, substitution is possible, and at the status quo, the ratio of input prices to marginal physical products are equalized. Hence with a "premium price" for one input, you need not use the premium-priced input but can substitute the second input, at a second-order loss in marginal productivity. In effect, this is an application of the so-called envelope theorem. For more on this point, see a Ph.D.-level book on price theory or constrained optimization, looking for a discussion on differentiability of the optimal value function.

Deriving the Formula for the Experience Curve

In the text, I asserted that a pure experience-curve total cost function takes the form

$$TC(x, X) = \frac{c_1[(X + x)^\beta - X^\beta]}{\beta}, \quad \text{for } \beta = \frac{\ln(\gamma)}{\ln(2)} + 1,$$

where x is output in the given period and X is cumulative prior output. The constant γ is the "slope" of the experience curve, in the sense that costs fall to γ of their previous level every time cumulative production doubles; that is, the sequence c_n of unit cost figures has the property $c_{2n} = \gamma c_n$ for all n.

To derive this formula, we note first that, with an experience-curve effect, the sequence of unit costs takes (roughly) the form $c_n = c_1 n^{\beta-1}$, for some constant β. (In fact, this is really the defining characteristic of an experience-curve effect. Simply knowing that costs fall by γ for every doubling of cumulative output does not quite pin things down.) Now, the property $c_{2n} = \gamma c_n$ tells us that $2^{\beta-1} = \gamma$, which you can solve for β in terms of γ, to get the formula $\beta = [\ln(\gamma)/\ln(2)] + 1$. To find $c_{X+1} + \ldots + c_{x+X}$, we approximate the sum with $\int_x^{X+x} c_1 y^{\beta-1} dy$, which when evaluated gives the formula we provided.

Pricing Down the Experience Curve?

The following is a fairly long, involved "problem," so long and involved that I left even its statement for the *Student's Companion*. Despite its length and complexity, I recommend it highly as a great way to wrap up the discussion of the experience curve and the first ten chapters of the book, as it contains a very nice final example of thinking intelligently about marginal this and marginal that.

As noted in the text, in the late 1970s and early 1980s, the big "strategy" fad in manufacturing was the experience curve. High-priced consulting firms pitched their clients the notion that a winning strategy was to become the market-share leader in the early days of a product, to become the "experience leader" and have the lowest unit costs. Eventually the market-share leader would have such a cost advantage over rivals that all the rivals would be driven out—or at least become docile—and the leader would reap large profits.

How do you become the market share leader? By selling your product at very low cost. *Buy market share!* was the short-form version of this strategy. Firms were exhorted to price down the experience curve, keeping margins no more than razor thin, lest someone take away some of your market share and, eventually, beat your brains out with their experience-based cost advantages. These ideas mutated from business strategy to trade policy, when NICs (newly industrialized countries) put in place tariff barriers to "protect" their infant industries from the ravages of more experienced global competitors.

We are not ready to address the merits of this bit of business strategy, because until we get to Chapter 22, we are in no position to discuss seriously competition among industrial rivals. Even after Chapter 22, questions of appropriate business strategy when firms have experience-curve technologies are not easy to answer. But we can, at least, take on a simpler question: Set aside all notions of rivals and competition and buying market share. If a single producer faces a stable market with an experience-curve-driven cost structure, should the producer price down the learning curve?

Imagine a firm that develops a new product, with a clear, well-defined market: If the firm produces x units of the good for sale in a given quarter, the price per unit that the firm receives is $P(x) = 1000 - 0.08x$. The market for this item lasts for precisely 5 years (20 quarters), and the firm must decide on production levels for each of the 20 quarters; let x_1 denote the level of production in quarter 1, x_2 the level of production in quarter 2, and so on.

The complicating feature in this problem is that the firm's production technology exhibits a substantial experience-curve effect. Specifically, the cost to produce the nth cumulative unit is approximately 80% of the cost of producing the $n/2$th cumulative unit. The firm has produced five prototype units, so the first unit it produces in the first quarter of sales is its sixth.

Cost engineers at this firm, who are very good at these sorts of problems, have been able to give Marketing the following formulas: Suppose that in quarter 1 the firm produces x_1 units. Then its total costs of production in that quarter are

$$\$22166\left[(x_1 + 5)^{0.6767} - 5^{0.6767}\right].$$

If it goes on to produce x_2 units in the second quarter, its total costs for the second quarter are

$$\$22166\left[(x_2 + x_1 + 5)^{0.6767} - (x_1 + 5)^{0.6767}\right],$$

and so on. Write X_{n-1} for the *total* or *cumulative* number of units produced through period $n-1$, including the five prototypes; that is,

$$X_{n-1} = 5 + x_1 + x_2 + \ldots + x_{n-1}.$$

Then, if the firm goes on to produce an additional x_n units in quarter n, its total costs for quarter n are

$$\$22166\left[(x_n + X_{n-1})^{0.6767} - (X_{n-1})^{0.6767}\right].$$

What values of x_1, x_2, ..., and x_{20} maximize the sum of the firm's cash flows over the 20 quarters? (Do not discount the cash flows, at least not at the start.) In particular, since costs fall as more units are made, this means costs in the last quarter are below costs in early quarters. Since demand and therefore marginal revenue do not shift, does this imply that the firm should produce less in early years, so that the prices it charges fall as costs come down the experience curve?

To investigate this question, build a spreadsheet. In column B, simply record the quarter number. (Leave a few blank rows on top of the spreadsheet.) In column C, for each quarter put in the quantity to be produced in that year. In column D, use the inverse demand function to find the price the firm gets in each quarter as a function of the number in column C. In column E, put total revenue for the quarter (column C times column D). In column F, put the cumulative output to the end of that quarter. Remember the five prototypes. In column G, compute the total cost incurred during the quarter, using the formula given previously. In column H, compute the profit for the quarter (column E minus column G). Then, in a cell below this table, add the 20 profit figures.

So there is no misunderstanding, Figure 10.13 shows the desired spreadsheet, for the values $x_1 = 250$, $x_2 = 500$, $x_3 = 750$, and so on. (Note that the particular production plan I filled in gives total profit of $3,554,388.) First try to replicate this spreadsheet. (If you wish simply to copy it, it is named EXPERIENCE-CURVE.)

Now for the fun; try different values for x_1 through x_{20} to see how high you can push the 5-year profit figure. So you have a goal to shoot for, I got them as high as $8,443,585. Use Solver if you wish, although I warn you that Solver does not always work, at least not from all starting values, and this is a case where you might learn more by playing around with the numbers a bit.

quarter #	quantity	price	revenue	cum prod	cost	profit
				5		
1	250	$ 980.00	$ 245,000	255	$ 876,440	$ (631,440)
2	500	$ 960.00	$ 480,000	755	$ 1,021,929	$ (541,929)
3	750	$ 940.00	$ 705,000	1505	$ 1,168,516	$ (463,516)
4	1000	$ 920.00	$ 920,000	2505	$ 1,289,672	$ (369,672)
5	1250	$ 900.00	$ 1,125,000	3755	$ 1,393,594	$ (268,594)
6	1500	$ 880.00	$ 1,320,000	5255	$ 1,485,258	$ (165,258)
7	1750	$ 860.00	$ 1,505,000	7005	$ 1,567,729	$ (62,729)
8	2000	$ 840.00	$ 1,680,000	9005	$ 1,643,019	$ 36,981
9	2250	$ 820.00	$ 1,845,000	11255	$ 1,712,522	$ 132,478
10	2500	$ 800.00	$ 2,000,000	13755	$ 1,777,243	$ 222,757
11	2750	$ 780.00	$ 2,145,000	16505	$ 1,837,938	$ 307,062
12	3000	$ 760.00	$ 2,280,000	19505	$ 1,895,185	$ 384,815
13	3250	$ 740.00	$ 2,405,000	22755	$ 1,949,442	$ 455,558
14	3500	$ 720.00	$ 2,520,000	26255	$ 2,001,077	$ 518,923
15	3750	$ 700.00	$ 2,625,000	30005	$ 2,050,388	$ 574,612
16	4000	$ 680.00	$ 2,720,000	34005	$ 2,097,624	$ 622,376
17	4250	$ 660.00	$ 2,805,000	38255	$ 2,142,994	$ 662,006
18	4500	$ 640.00	$ 2,880,000	42755	$ 2,186,674	$ 693,326
19	4750	$ 620.00	$ 2,945,000	47505	$ 2,228,817	$ 716,183
20	5000	$ 600.00	$ 3,000,000	52505	$ 2,269,551	$ 730,449
					sum of quarterly profits	$ 3,554,388

Figure 10.13. An experience-curve spreadsheet.

In the optimal production plan, $x_1 = x_2 = \ldots = x_{20}$. Can you figure out why this is? What about MC = MR in this problem?

Then, to bring a bit more reality into the problem, redo the analysis where you try to maximize the discounted sum of cash flows, discounting at (say) 2.5% per quarter. What does the optimal production plan look like?

As noted already, we are not ready to think formally about how competition in the product market might affect the results of this simple exercise. But you might wish to think about this informally; the analysis I am about to offer has a few things to say on this.

Analysis: Pricing Down the Experience Curve?

Figure 10.14 illustrates the production plan with a total profit of $8,443,585. Note that the level of production is the same in each period, 3765.3 units per quarter. This means that the price per unit, $698.78, does not change. The firm does not price down the experience curve. Instead it sets and sticks to a price, taking substantial losses in the first year ($4.3 million) to make substantial profits in later years.

EXPERIENCE-CURVE

quarter #	quantity	price	revenue	cum prod	cost	profit
				5		
1	3765.3	$ 698.78	$ 2,631,101	3770.3	$ 5,766,177	$ (3,135,075)
2	3765.3	$ 698.78	$ 2,631,101	7535.6	$ 3,486,175	$ (855,073)
3	3765.3	$ 698.78	$ 2,631,101	11300.9	$ 2,940,042	$ (308,941)
4	3765.3	$ 698.78	$ 2,631,101	15066.2	$ 2,633,375	$ (2,274)
5	3765.3	$ 698.78	$ 2,631,101	18831.5	$ 2,426,531	$ 204,571
6	3765.3	$ 698.78	$ 2,631,101	22596.8	$ 2,273,477	$ 357,625
7	3765.3	$ 698.78	$ 2,631,101	26362.1	$ 2,153,610	$ 477,491
8	3765.3	$ 698.78	$ 2,631,101	30127.4	$ 2,056,045	$ 575,056
9	3765.3	$ 698.78	$ 2,631,101	33892.7	$ 1,974,382	$ 656,719
10	3765.3	$ 698.78	$ 2,631,101	37658	$ 1,904,563	$ 726,539
11	3765.3	$ 698.78	$ 2,631,101	41423.3	$ 1,843,865	$ 787,236
12	3765.3	$ 698.78	$ 2,631,101	45188.6	$ 1,790,382	$ 840,719
13	3765.3	$ 698.78	$ 2,631,101	48953.9	$ 1,742,732	$ 888,369
14	3765.3	$ 698.78	$ 2,631,101	52719.2	$ 1,699,882	$ 931,219
15	3765.3	$ 698.78	$ 2,631,101	56484.5	$ 1,661,043	$ 970,059
16	3765.3	$ 698.78	$ 2,631,101	60249.8	$ 1,625,598	$ 1,005,504
17	3765.3	$ 698.78	$ 2,631,101	64015.1	$ 1,593,058	$ 1,038,043
18	3765.3	$ 698.78	$ 2,631,101	67780.4	$ 1,563,031	$ 1,068,071
19	3765.3	$ 698.78	$ 2,631,101	71545.7	$ 1,535,193	$ 1,095,908
20	3765.3	$ 698.78	$ 2,631,101	75311	$ 1,509,280	$ 1,121,822
					sum of quarterly profits	$ 8,443,585

Sheet1 Sheet2 Sheet3

Figure 10.14. The optimal production plan.

This is the optimal production plan. If you found an alternative that beats my plan by more than round-off error, you made a mistake in setting up your spreadsheet. Here is the logic that tells me this and allows us to derive the answer analytically.

Let x_1, x_2, through x_{20} be the levels of production in each of the 20 quarters. For total profit over the 20 quarters, we have the formula

$$\pi(x_1, \ldots, x_{20}) = x_1 P(x_1) + x_2 P(x_2) + \ldots + x_{20} P(x_{20})$$
$$- 22166[(5 + x_1 + x_2 + \ldots + x_{20})^{0.6767} - 5^{0.6767}],$$

where $P(x) = 1000 - 0.08x$. Let me explain this: First, we add the 20 revenue terms, one for each quarter. The last term is the total cost over the 20 quarters. We get this by writing down the total cost for quarter 1,

$$22166[(5 + x_1)^{0.6767} - 5^{0.6767}],$$

adding the cost for quarter 2,

$$22166[(5 + x_1 + x_2)^{0.6767} - (5 + x_1)^{0.6767}],$$

and so on. The point is that the term $22166(5 + x_1)^{0.6767}$ which is added for the first quarter is subtracted for quarter 2, and similarly for like terms in quarters 3 through 20, leaving the total cost expression shown.

Let me state that another way. In this "pure experience-curve" technology, each unit produced has a production cost c_z regardless of when it is produced, depending only on its cumulative number z in the sequence of production. The formula given to Marketing by Production may hide this, but it is true. If the firm makes X_{n-1} units in the first $n - 1$ quarters, so the first unit made in quarter n is number $5 + X_{n-1} + 1$, and if the firm goes on to make x_n units in this quarter, then its total costs in this quarter are

$$c_{5+X_{n-1}+1} + c_{5+X_{n-1}+2} + \ldots + c_{5+X_{n-1}+x_n}.$$

Since we do not discount revenues or costs, the total cost incurred by the firm in the 20 quarters is just the sum of the costs of the units made, or

$$c_6 + c_7 + \ldots + c_{x_1+x_2+\ldots+x_{20}},$$

which (those smart folks in Production tell us) is

$$2216[(5 + x_1 + \ldots + x_{20})^{.6767} - 5^{.6767}].$$

Knowing that the (undiscounted) sum of the costs of these units is given by this formula is a bit of magic, unless you understood the derivation of the formula given just before the start of this problem. While the formula might be magic, the idea that undiscounted total costs depend only on the total amount produced and not on how that production is divided among the quarters, well, that is a basic property of pure experience-curve technology costs.

To maximize profit, we take partial derivatives in x_1 through x_{20}, and simultaneously set each equal to 0. Rewriting $x_1 P(x_1)$ as $1000x_1 - 0.08(x_1)^2$, the partial derivative in x_1 is

$$1000 - 0.16x_1 - (22166)(0.6767)[5 + x_1 + x_2 + \ldots + x_{20}]^{0.6767-1} =$$

$$1000 - 0.16x_1 - 15000[5 + x_1 + x_2 + \ldots + x_{20}]^{-0.3233}.$$

Setting this equal to 0 gives us

$$x_1 = \frac{\left(1000 - 15000[5 + x_1 + x_2 + \ldots + x_{20}]^{-0.3233}\right)}{0.16}.$$

Similarly, we will get

$$x_2 = \frac{\left(1000 - 15000[5 + x_1 + x_2 + \ldots + x_{20}]^{-0.3233}\right)}{0.16}$$

when we set the partial derivative with respect to x_2 equal to 0, and so on.

Note that the right-hand sides of the two previous equalities are the same. Therefore the two left-hand sides must be equal, or $x_1 = x_2$. The same applies for all the other quarterly production levels, or $x_1 = x_2 = \ldots = x_{20}$. And this in turn means that, if x is the common value of these 20 terms, x must solve the single equation

$$x = \frac{1000 - 15000[5 + 20x]^{-0.3233}}{0.16}.$$

To find this value of x, I got out Excel and created two entries. The first was a value for the variable x; the second computed

$$\frac{1000 - 15000[5 + 20x]^{-0.3233}}{0.16} - x.$$

To find a value of x for which the second term is 0, use Solver or hunt for the solution by successive approximation: Whichever you try, you will come to the answer $x = 3765.3$ plus or minus some round-off error.

Actually, things are not quite that easy. If you do this by hand, you will find two different answers, $x = 245\pm$ and $= 3765.3\pm$. If you use Solver, starting from some values takes you to one solution while starting from others takes you to the other. By plugging these values back into the spreadsheet, you find that the second gives the higher profit. But, if I did not tell you that there are two solutions and you just used Solver, you might come up with just the first.

This is a lot of math, but the intuition is really quite simple. Suppose that, in any year, the firm decides to produce one additional unit. We know what this means in terms of marginal revenue: If the firm is already producing x units that year, its marginal revenue is $1000 - 0.16x$. The marginal cost of an additional unit of production, no matter what year it is produced, is just the marginal cost of the last unit produced in the last period. In this model of production, speed of production is irrelevant. The total costs to the firm of producing 10,000 units the first year and none thereafter are the same as the costs of producing 2,000 in each of the 5 years, and the marginal cost is just the derivative of total costs, or $15000(5 + X)^{-0.3223}$, where X is the total amount produced in the 5 years. So the firm wants to choose x_1 through x_{20} so that

$$1000 - 0.16x_n = 15000(5 + X)^{-0.3223} = 15000(5 + 20x_n)^{-0.3223},$$

or marginal revenue equals marginal cost, for $n = 1, 2, \ldots, 20$. The fancy part here is that marginal cost depends on the total amount produced over 5 years and not on the rate of production in any particular quarter.

That is the theory. What about the facts? In fact, we do not see firms whose production processes have an experience-curve structure pricing in this fashion: producing the same amount each year over the horizon of the product, charging the same price year after year, taking enormous losses early on. Instead, when products have an experience-curve production structure, we often see prices declining as time passes and experience builds up. And we see profit (and profit margin) rising as time passes. There are several reasons for this, some of which can be put into our model and some of which are more complex:

1. In the simple model of costs we created, the cost to produce any unit depends only on the number of units produced prior to this one. The rate of production

does not affect costs in the slightest. Compare this with the "standard model," in which the cost of production depends on the rate, where (with rising marginal costs) faster rates mean higher marginal costs. Both are models, and neither is completely accurate. In particular, while many production processes exhibit the basic experience-curve effect (costs declining with cumulative output), it is not true that costs are independent of rate. If Boeing tried to produce 10 times the number of 747s in January as it did in December, its average unit costs would probably rise, even though there is a tendency for its costs to fall with experience. Indeed, part (only part) of the reason that costs fall with experience is that production processes can be speeded up, lowering labor time and hence labor costs per unit. Insofar as this is what drives down unit costs, it can be expensive for a firm to maintain a flat rate of production; it is more efficient (in terms of costs) to increase the speed of production as experience is gained. Another (big) part of the cost savings from experience comes in improved product and process design. Insofar as these improvements must be built into capital equipment (say, with the redesign of jigs and fixtures), it can become (cost) efficient to produce at lower speed, on a single prototype production line, then spread the fruits of what is learned over several other lines. This again means that, on efficiency grounds, the production rate may increase over the production life cycle. If, for either reason, production rates increase, then prices decline, if demand does not shift and goods cannot be backordered at the current-delivery price.

2. We did not discount revenues and costs. Therefore, the firm is happy to lose $1 today if it means even $1.01 more in profit 5 years hence. In the real world, firms discount cash flows (at least, they do not trade off $1 today for $1 in 5 or 10 years). This discounting causes the firm to cut back on production (and losses) early on. Without too much trouble, we can incorporate this into our spreadsheet analysis: Take the spreadsheet with which we began, and instead of adding the quarterly profit figures, sum the discounted profit figures, discounted at whatever quarterly rate is appropriate. Sheet 2 of EXPERIENCE-CURVE computes discounted profits in the final column and then sums. Employing Solver to maximize the sum of discounted profits gives the answer shown in Figure 10.15, where profits are discounted at a rate of 2.5% per quarter. Note that production increases slowly over the 5 years.

3. An important reason for discounting and for refusing to invest too much in early production is that the product life of many experience-curve goods is very uncertain. In the example, the firm knows it has 19 quarters to recoup losses it takes in the first quarter. But, in many real-world examples, firms have to

quarter #	quantity	price	revenue	cum prod	cost	cash flow		cash flow discounted	
				5					
1	3293.141	$ 736.55	$2,425,559	3298.141	$5,261,344	$	(2,835,786)	$	(2,766,620)
2	3390.009	$ 728.80	$2,470,636	6688.149	$3,268,301	$	(797,665)	$	(759,229)
3	3454.392	$ 723.65	$2,499,766	10142.54	$2,797,715	$	(297,949)	$	(276,676)
4	3503.27	$ 719.74	$2,521,438	13645.81	$2,533,252	$	(11,813)	$	(10,702)
5	3542.511	$ 716.60	$2,538,560	17188.32	$2,354,097	$	184,463	$	163,038
6	3574.976	$ 714.00	$2,552,540	20763.3	$2,220,701	$	331,839	$	286,143
7	3602.319	$ 711.81	$2,564,183	24365.62	$2,115,442	$	448,741	$	377,510
8	3625.595	$ 709.95	$2,574,000	27991.21	$2,029,039	$	544,961	$	447,275
9	3645.527	$ 708.36	$2,582,338	31636.74	$1,956,049	$	626,288	$	501,487
10	3662.637	$ 706.99	$2,589,444	35299.38	$1,893,029	$	696,416	$	544,039
11	3677.313	$ 705.81	$2,595,502	38976.69	$1,837,670	$	757,832	$	577,578
12	3689.852	$ 704.81	$2,600,652	42666.54	$1,788,360	$	812,291	$	603,984
13	3700.492	$ 703.96	$2,605,001	46367.03	$1,743,929	$	861,072	$	624,639
14	3709.418	$ 703.25	$2,608,635	50076.45	$1,703,502	$	905,133	$	640,587
15	3716.783	$ 702.66	$2,611,625	53793.23	$1,666,413	$	945,212	$	652,637
16	3722.712	$ 702.18	$2,614,025	57515.95	$1,632,139	$	981,886	$	661,423
17	3727.307	$ 701.82	$2,615,882	61243.25	$1,600,266	$	1,015,615	$	667,457
18	3730.654	$ 701.55	$2,617,232	64973.91	$1,570,460	$	1,046,771	$	671,154
19	3732.823	$ 701.37	$2,618,105	68706.73	$1,542,446	$	1,075,659	$	672,855
20	3733.873	$ 701.29	$2,618,528	72440.6	$1,515,998	$	1,102,531	$	672,842
						NPV of cash flows	$	4,951,421	

Figure 10.15. The optimal production plan with 2.5% per quarter discounting.

worry that "tomorrow" may not come for a particular good. This effectively increases the rate at which they discount profits and losses; firms are less willing to sustain early losses.

4. The analysis assumes that demand does not shift over the 5-year period. In fact, in many cases, demand grows as the product matures, and the firm produces more in later periods simply because demand is greater at any given price. Note, however, that while this may mean that production levels should increase, it does not mean that prices should fall. In fact, insofar as the firm can affect the size of the market it faces later by building a customer base, it has increased incentives to price low early on. On the other hand, as we saw in Chapter 7, it may be possible to use slowly declining prices as a way to discriminate among customers.

5. The model assumes that a single firm faces consumers. In real-world applications, the firm must be concerned with the actions of competitors. The impact of competition is quite complex and can push the "solution" we obtained in either direction. For example, if a firm has an early lead in a particular product and there is little or no spillover from one firm to another in terms of experience, then the leading firm may price very aggressively (that means, low prices) early on to forestall the entry of competitors. The large airframe manufacturers are some-

times seen as acting in this fashion; Boeing priced 747s very aggressively and captured the market for large-jumbo planes for a long period of time, leaving McDonnell-Douglas, Lockheed, and later Airbus to compete in the medium-jumbo segment. On the other hand, when competition is hard to restrain or there is spillover from one firm to another of the fruits of experience, firms are less inclined to invest in knowledge, because knowledge is correspondingly less proprietary. This results in pricing strategies that look more like pricing down the experience curve.

We can fairly easily incorporate effects 1 and 2 into the model and, with some heroic assumptions, incorporate effect 3. But, to handle 4 and 5, we need more tools than we have at our disposal. So we leave production at this point and move on to equilibrium.

Review Problems II

These problems review material in Chapters 8 through 10.

II.1 The total cost function $TC(x) = x^3 + 4x^2 + 10x + 99$ gives rise to a U-shaped average cost function, where average costs first fall and then rise. Is the production level $x = 3$ above or below efficient scale? Justify your answer. (Hint: You *do not* need to find the level of efficient scale to answer this question.)

II.2 Consider the total cost function $TC(x) = 5000 + 2x^2$.

(a) What is the marginal cost function?

(b) What is the average cost function?

(c) Which value of x is the efficient scale of production, and what is the (minimum) average cost at the efficient scale?

II.3 Figure II.1 shows the 100-unit isoquant of a firm that produces fasdip out of material and labor. The production process of this firm has constant returns to scale.

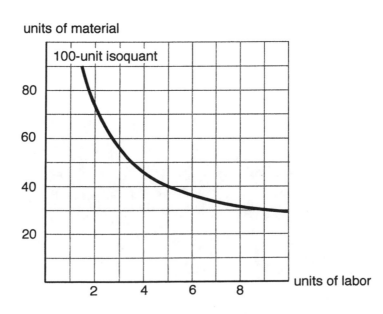

Figure II.1 Problem 11.3: The 100-unit isoquant for the manufacture of fasdip

(a) If the price of materials is $2.50 per unit and the price of labor is $10 per unit, approximately what is the (least-cost) total cost of producing 100 units of fasdip?

(b) Suppose this firm faces the inverse demand curve

$$P = 5 - \frac{x}{200}.$$

(Input prices are as in part a of the problem.) What price should it charge, and what quantity should it sell, to maximize its profit?

(c) Suppose that, in the short run, the firm in question cannot change the amount of labor it hires, although it can change the amount of material. Beginning from the profit-maximizing position you calculated in part b, find the short-run total cost of producing half the amount produced in part b. (This is difficult.)

II.4 The very strange looking isoquant in Figure II.2 goes with the following story. The firm in question has a choice of two different fixed-coefficient, constant-returns-to-scale production technologies. In the first, each unit of output requires 2 units of labor and 3.5 units of material, while in the second, each unit of output requires 3 units of labor and 2 units of material. This technology has constant returns to scale (so the one isoquant describes the technology completely). The firm must use only one of the two technologies at any time; it cannot produce some fraction of its output with one technology and the rest with the second technology. (Something worth thinking about, if you get the problem: If the firm can shift between the two technologies at negligible cost, say, using one technology one month and the other the next, does it matter that the firm is unable to use both technologies at the same time?)

(a) Suppose the price of labor is r_l = $1 and the price of material is r_m = $1. The firm wishes to produce 20 units of output. How many units of labor and how many units of material would the firm employ? What would be the total cost of the 20 units? (Throughout this problem, assume that this firm makes profit-maximizing choices.)

(b) Suppose that, under the same conditions as in part a, the firm wishes to produce 40 units of output. How many units of labor and material would the firm employ? What will be the total cost of the 40 units?

(c) Suppose the firm faces the inverse demand curve $P = 25 - x/100$. What would the firm do (in terms of quantity produced and price charged)?

units of material

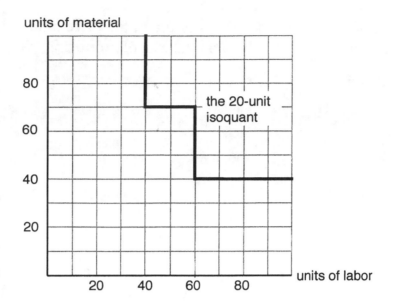

Figure II.2 Problem II.4: An isoquant.

(d) Suppose the firm reaches the position you found in part c. Suddenly the price of labor doubles to $2 per unit. In the short run, the firm can freely change the amount of labor and material it employs, but it cannot change the technology it uses; that is, if it previously used inputs in the fixed ratio of 2 labor to 3.5 capital (per unit of output), it must stay with this ratio, and if it used the fixed ratio of 3 labor to 2 material (per unit of output), it must stay with this. What does the firm do in the short run in response to the rise in the cost of labor?

(e) In the longer run, the firm is able to change technologies if it wishes to. What is its long-run response to the new price of labor?

II.5 The manufacture of trewqs requires both labor and raw material. Specifically, each trewq requires 5 hours of labor time, at a cost of $10 per labor hour. (Therefore, x trewqs require $5x$ labor hours and has a labor total cost of $50x$.) The material requirements of trewqs is more complex. To produce x trewqs per day requires $2x + x^2/10$ units of material, at a cost of $2 per unit. No substitution is possible between labor and materials. There are no fixed costs.

(a) What is the long-run total cost function for trewqs?

(b) Suppose that inverse demand function for trewqs is given $p = 198 - 0.4x$. How many trewqs does the manufacturer sell to maximize profit, and what price do they sell for?

(c) The government imposes a tax of $4 per trewq, collected directly from the manufacturer. (That is, for each trewq produced, the firm must pay the government $4.) What effect does this have on the total cost of trewq production? What effect does this have on the marginal cost?

(d) In the short run, although this firm can freely change the number of units of raw material that it uses (at the market price of $2 per unit), it cannot easily change the amount of labor time it employs: It cannot, in the short run, discharge anyone it has been employing; and it can add labor hours only by paying a premium overtime wage of $15 per hour. What is the impact of this tax of part c on the price and quantity of trewqs supplied by the manufacturer in the short run?

(e) What is the impact of the tax on the price and quantity of trewqs supplied by the manufacturer in the long-run?

For the remainder of this problem, forget about the tax: You are back to the situation described in part b. Suddenly it becomes feasible to produce trewqs by a second technology, which uses inputs in fixed proportions and has constant returns to scale. In this technology, each trewq requires 4 units of labor and 6 units of material. However to use this technology, a third input, a machine known as a *bliffilator*, is required. To make one trewq requires (in addition to the 4 units of labor and 6 units of material) 6 minutes of bliffilator time. Bliffilator time can be leased by the firm, at a cost of $140 per hour. (Bliffilator time can be rented in any units you desire, including fractions of an hour.)

(f) What is the total cost of making 120 trewqs entirely by this new method?

(g) Suppose the firm converted its production *entirely* to this new method. What quantity would it produce and what price would it charge? What would be its profit?

(h) Suppose the firm could use both technologies simultaneously. That is, it can make some of its trewqs by the first method and others by the second. (Let me be very precise here: Suppose the firm makes x_1 trewqs by the first method and x_2 by the new, second method. Then, it would require $5x_1 + 4x_2$ units of labor, $2x_1 + x_1^2/10 + 6x_2$ units of material, and $0.1x_2$ hours of bliffilator time.) To maximize its profit, what quantity would it produce and what price would it charge? What would be its profit? Explain your answer.

II.6 Recall Problem 9.6, in which a firm, whose production function was given by $f(m, l) = m^{1/3}l^{1/6}$, had fixed costs of $300 and faced prices for material and labor of $1 and $4, respectively. Although the answer is not supplied in this *Student's Companion*, let me give you the bottom lines: The firm's total cost function is $TC(x) =$

$300 + 3x^2$ and if it faces the inverse demand function $P = 160 - 2x$, it maximizes profit by producing 16 units of output, using 64 units of labor and 512 units of material. Suppose that, from this starting point, the price of materials suddenly rises to $1.20 per unit.

(a) What happens in the short run (when the firm can vary the amount of materials it employs but not the amount of labor)?

(b) What happens in the long run?

Warning: The numbers in this problem are not guaranteed to come out nicely (which is to say, they will not be nice). Do not conclude that you have screwed up if you get ugly looking numbers.

II.7 (a) Consider the total cost function graphed in Figure II.3. Starting at 0, it is linear up to some level of production x^* (at which point its value is c^*); thereafter it is linear with higher slope. Draw the marginal and average cost functions that go with this total cost function. You should supply as much detail as you can on your graphs.

(b) Suppose you are told that this total cost function comes from a technology that has either increasing, constant, or decreasing returns to scale. (Remember, increasing returns to scale includes constant returns as a special case, as does decreasing.) Which of these three would be most descriptive? Why?

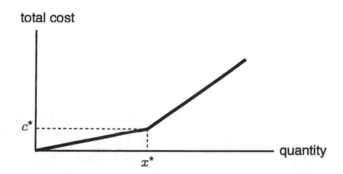

Figure II.3. Problem II.7: A total cost function.

II.8 A firm has two cost-independent facilities at which it can make a particular item. If it makes x_1 units at the first facility, its total cost there is $5x_1 + x_1^2/2000$, which means a marginal cost of $5 + x_1/1000$. If it makes x_2 units at the second facility, its total cost there is $8x_2 + x_2^2/4000$, which means a marginal cost of $8 + x_2/2000$. In addition, the firm can purchase this item from a foreign vendor, who is willing to sell the domestic firm as much as it (the domestic firm) wishes at a price of $15 per unit.

(a) Since marginal costs are rising for this firm at both facilities, there is a limit to how many it will make domestically, before it moves to purchasing units from the foreign vendor. What is that limit?

(b) Suppose the firm wished to produce or procure 15,000 units. What would be the cost-minimizing way to do this?

(c) Suppose this firm faces inverse demand function $P(x) = 24 - x/6000$. What should the firm do to maximize its profit?

Solution to Problem II.1

For the given total cost function, marginal cost is $MC(x) = 3x^2 + 8x + 10$, while average cost is $AC(x) = x^2 + 4x + 10 + 99/x$. Therefore, at $x = 3$, $MC(3) = 27 + 24 + 10 = 61$, while $AC(3) = 9 + 12 + 10 + 33 = 64$. Hence, at $x = 3$, average cost exceeds marginal cost and average cost is falling. Since we know average cost is U-shaped, this means that $x = 3$ is below the efficient scale.

Solution to Problem II.2

(a) $MC(x) = 4x$

(b) $AC(x) = 5000/x + 2x$

(c) To find the efficient scale, you can either (1) take the derivative of average cost and set it equal to 0, or (2) look for where marginal cost equals average cost. Following plan (1), we get

$$-1 \times \frac{5000}{x^2} + 2 = 0 \quad \text{or} \quad 2 = \frac{5000}{x^2} \quad \text{or} \quad 5000 = 2x^2.$$

Following plan (2), we get

$$\frac{5000}{x} + 2x = 4x \quad \text{or} \quad \frac{5000}{x} = 2x \quad \text{or} \quad 5000 = 2x^2.$$

(Of course, they lead to the same equation.) This gives $x^2 = 2500$ or $x = 50$, at which point, average cost = marginal cost = $4 \times 50 = 200$.

Solution to Problem II.3

(a) Figure II.4 shows the $100-isocost line, which is moved parallel until it hits the 100-unit isoquant. It does so at the point where labor usage is 5 and material usage is 40, a bill of materials that costs $10 × 5 + $2.50 × 40 = $150. So the total cost of making 100 units of fasdip is $150.

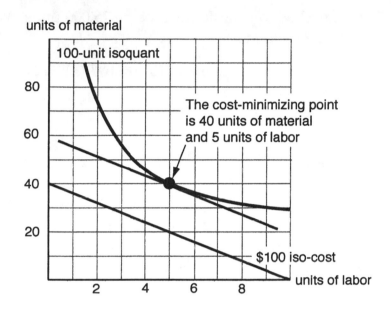

Figure II.4. Problem II.3: Finding the least-cost way to make 100 units of fasdip.

(b) Since this technology has constant returns to scale, average cost = marginal cost is constant, and from part a, we know this constant average cost = marginal cost is $1.50. Marginal revenue (from inverse demand) is $MR(x) = 5 - x/100$, so marginal cost equals marginal revenue where $5 - x/100 = 1.5$ or $x = 350$, at which point the price is $3.25.

(c) By constant returns to scale, $x = 350$ means $3.5 × 5 = 17.5$ units of labor input. Hence, we want to find the level of material usage m so that the point (17.5 labor, m material) lies on the 175-unit isoquant. By constant returns to scale, this is the same m that (17.5/1.75 labor, $m/1.75$ material) lies on the $175/1.75 = 100$-unit isoquant (we scale by 1.75 to get to the one isoquant we have). But, for 10 units of labor, we need approximately 29 units of material to be on the 100-unit isoquant, so $m/1.75 = 29$, or $m = 50.75$. Therefore, the short-run total cost for producing 175 units (at a status quo of 17.5 units of labor) is

$$\$10 × 17.5 + \$2.50 × 50.75 = \$301.875.$$

Solution to Problem II.4

(a) Figure II.5 shows an iso-cost at these prices for total cost of $50, slid parallel to find the minimum cost way to make 20 units: 60 units of labor and 40 units of material, for a total cost of $100.[1]

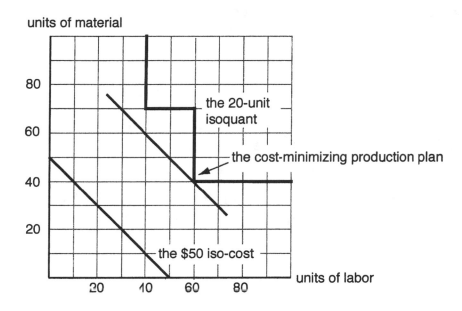

Figure II.5. Problem II.4: Finding the cost-minimizing way to produce 20 units.

(b) Since this production technology has constant returns to scale, the 40-unit isoquant is shaped exactly like the 20-unit isoquant, except that it is twice as far out from the origin. Hence, the cost-minimizing way to produce 40 units is with 120 units of labor and 80 units of material, for a total cost of $200.

(c) From part a (or b) and the fact of constant returns to scale, the firm has constant

---

[1] To answer the parenthetical question posed in this problem, if we allowed for convex combinations of the two technologies, the 20-unit isoquant would just be the convex hull of the 20-unit isoquant depicted; that is, the line joining the two corners would be added. Then, the least-cost iso-cost line hitting the isoquant would hit at one of the two "corners" first. If the iso-cost lines are parallel to the line segment joining the two corners, then the least-cost iso-cost hits the entire line segment all at once; in that case, either corner is as cheap as any convex combination of the two. So, as long as the firm can switch between the two technologies freely, allowing convex combinations does not reduce costs. Note: There are two complications of this simple story, either of which could make convex combinations useful—(1) if the separate technologies had rising marginal costs (decreasing returns to scale), or (2) if the firm had an effect on the cost of its inputs (that is, if the cost of an input rose the more the firm bought), so that iso-cost *lines* would become iso-cost *curves*.

average and marginal costs of $5 per unit. Marginal revenue is

$$MR(x) = 25 - \frac{2x}{100},$$

so marginal cost equals marginal revenue where

$$25 - \frac{2x}{100} = 5 \quad \text{or} \quad 20 = \frac{2x}{100} \quad \text{or} \quad x = 1000.$$

Note that this entails using the 3 units of labor to 2 of material technology, with 3000 units of labor and 2000 units of material. The price of the good is $25 - (1000/100) = \$15$, so the profit margin on each unit is $10 and the total profit is $10,000.

(d) In the short run, the firm must continue to produce with fixed coefficients of 3 units of labor to 2 units of material per unit output. At the new input prices, this means that the marginal cost of each unit of output is

$$\$2 \times 3 + \$1 \times 2 = \$8.$$

So marginal cost equals marginal revenue where

$$25 - \frac{2x}{100} = 8 \quad \text{or} \quad 17 = \frac{2x}{100} \quad \text{or} \quad x = 850.$$

This gives a price for the good of $25 - (850/100) = \$16.50$, for a profit margin of $8.50 per unit and a total profit of $7225.

(e) In the longer run, at these prices, it makes sense for the manufacturer to switch to the 2 labor to 3.5 materials technology (draw the iso-cost if you do not see this), which gives a constant marginal cost of $\$2 \times 2 + \$1 \times 3.5 = \$7.50$ per unit. The firm maximizes profit where

$$25 - \frac{2x}{100} = 7.50 \quad \text{or} \quad 17.5 = \frac{2x}{100} \quad \text{or} \quad x = 875.$$

This gives a price of $25 - (875/100) = \$16.25$ per unit, for a profit margin of $8.75 per unit and total profit of $7656.25.

Solution to Problem II.5

(a) Labor costs for producing x trewqs are $\$10 \times 5 \times x = \$50x$. Material costs are $\$2 \times (2x + x^2/10) = \$4x + (x^2/5)$. So total costs are

$$TC(x) = \$54x + \frac{x^2}{5}.$$

(b) This inverse demand function gives a marginal revenue function of $MR(x) = 198 - 0.8x$. Marginal cost is $MC(x) = 54 + 0.04x$. So marginal cost equals marginal revenue where

$$198 - 0.8x = 54 + 0.4y \quad \text{or} \quad 144 = 1.2x \quad \text{or} \quad x = 120.$$

This gives a price of

$$198 - 0.4 \times 120 = \$150.$$

This implies the use of 600 units of labor and $240 + 1440 = 1680$ units of material.

(c) This acts as an increase in the marginal cost of a trewq of $4, or an increase in total costs of $\$4x$ when you produce x trewqs. That is, the (long-run) total cost function becomes $TC(x) = 58y + x^2/5$ and the (long-run) marginal cost function becomes $58 + 2x/5$.

(d) If the firm wishes to produce precisely 120 trewqs, it would employ the same amount of labor as before, so that its (short-run) total costs would be $58x + x^2/5$ at $x = 120$. If it wishes to reduce the amount of trewqs it produces, it must continue to employ all 600 labor hours, but it can reduce its materials to the appropriate level of $2x + x^2/10$, so its total costs would be

$$\$10 \times 600 + \$2 \times [2x + x^2/10] + \$4 \times x = 6000 + 8x + x^2/5.$$

If it wishes to increase trewq production beyond 120 trewqs, it must increase the amount of labor it hires by $5(x - 120)$ at a cost of $15 per unit, for a total cost of

$$\$10 \times 600 + \$15 \times (5[x - 120]) + \$2 \times [2x + x^2/10] + \$4 \times x =$$

$$75x - 3000 + 8x + 2x^2/10 = 83x + 2x^2/10 - 3000.$$

In this last string of equalities, the leftmost expression is the key: This is the sum of the wages paid at regular time (for the "fixed" 600 hours), plus the wages paid for overtime work, plus material costs, plus the cost of the tax. (The rest is algebra.)

Therefore, the firm has a discontinuous short-run marginal cost function. For levels of production x less than 120 units, the short-run marginal costs are

$$\text{SRMC}(x) = 8 + 0.4x.$$

For levels of x greater than 120 units, the short-run marginal costs are

$$\text{SRMC}(x) = 83 + 0.4x.$$

This discontinuity in short-run marginal costs occurs because, on the margin, adding production beyond 120 units involves overtime labor, while subtracting production below 120 units gives no labor cost relief.

Figure II.6 graphs the short-run marginal cost and marginal revenue functions. Note that marginal revenue exceeds short-run marginal cost for all levels x below 120 and marginal cost exceeds marginal cost for all levels x above 120, so the profit-maximizing level of production remains at 120 units. All that changes is that the firm pays $480 in taxes to the government.

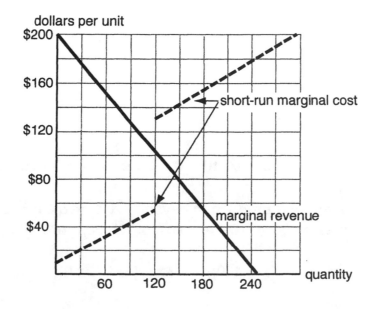

Figure II.6. Problem II.5: Short-run marginal cost and marginal revenue.

(e) In the long run, the firm's total cost function becomes $58x + x^2/5$ at all levels of x. So, in the long run, marginal cost equals marginal revenue where

$$58 + 0.4x = 198 - 0.8x \quad \text{or} \quad 140 = 1.2x \quad \text{or} \quad x = 116.667.$$

This leads to a price of $151.33.

(f) Because the new technology has constant returns to scale, it has constant marginal = average cost. This marginal = average cost is

$$\$10 \times 4 \;+\; \$2 \times 6 \;+\; \$140 \times 0.1 \;=\; \$66.$$

Making 120 trewqs by this technology therefore costs $\$66 \times 120 = \$7920$. (Compare this with a total cost for 120 trewqs of $9360 using the old technology.)

(g) With the new technology (exclusively), marginal cost is $66, so marginal cost equals marginal revenue at

$$198 - 0.8x = 66 \quad \text{or} \quad x = \frac{132}{0.8} = 165 \text{ units,}$$

at which point the price is $198 - (165)(0.4) = \$132$. This gives a profit of $10,890. (Compare this with a profit of $8640 with the old technology.)

(h) If the firm could "mix" the two technologies, it would use the original technology up to the level of production where its marginal cost rises to $66, then use the second technology for all the rest. The joint marginal cost function (the horizontal sum of the two) traces out the first MC curve up to $66, then it is flat at $66.

To find the quantity at which the first technology has an MC of $66, we solve

$$54 + 0.4x = 66 \quad \text{or} \quad 0.4x = 12 \quad \text{or} \quad x = 30.$$

To find the profit-maximizing level of production, we note that, beyond 30 units, MC is the same as in part g. Since the intersection of MC and MR in part g was well beyond 30 units, the intersection in this case is in the same position (see Figure II.7). Therefore, the profit-maximizing level of production is 165 units, sold at a price of $132 apiece. The revenue side of the firm is the same. On the cost side, the firm saves a bit on the 30 units it makes with the old technology, relative to part g. Specifically, those 30 units cost $(54)(30) + 30^2/5 = \$1800$ if made with the old

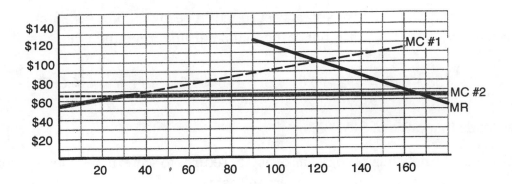

Figure II.7 Problem II.5(b), (g), and (h). In this figure, dashed lines represent the marginal cost functions for the original technology (large dashes) and the new technology (small dashes), labeled MC#1 and MC#2, respectively. Their horizontal sum, the marginal cost function of the "mix and match" technology (depicted in gray) follows the heavy dashes up to the quantity 30 and cost of $66, and then is flat at $66 for all quantities beyond 30. That is, with the ability to mix the two technologies, the firm produces the first 30 units with technology #1 and any other units with technology #2. The marginal revenue function is depicted by the downward-sloping solid line. To check your understanding, see if on this graph you can find the $180 that the firm saves in part h (relative to part g) by using both technologies. (Hint: It is an area.)

technology and $(66)(30) = \$1980$ if made with the new technology. This represents a savings (relative to part g) of $180, increasing profit to $11,070.

Solution to Problem II.6

(a) In the short run, the firm is stuck with 64 units of labor, so that its production function is $x = f(m, 64) = m^{1/3}64^{1/6} = 2m^{1/3}$. Hence, to produce x units in the short run, the firm must set m so that $x = 2m^{1/3}$ or $m = x^3/8$. Since material costs $1.20 per unit, this means short-run total cost becomes $\text{SRTC}(x) = 300+(4)(64)+1.20x^3/8 = 556+0.15x^3$. The short-run marginal cost is $0.45x^2$, so short-run marginal cost equals marginal revenue where

$$0.45x^2 = 160 - 4x,$$

which, by the quadratic formula, is where

$$x = \frac{-4 \pm \sqrt{4^2 - 4(-160)(0.45)}}{(2)(0.45)} = \frac{-4 \pm \sqrt{304}}{0.9}.$$

The positive root is apparently the one we are looking for, and we get

$$x = \frac{-4 + 17.4356}{.9} = 14.928.$$

This gives a price of $130.143 and material usage of 415.829 units.

(b) To work out what happens in the long run, we need to recompute the long-run total cost function. The old long-run total cost function would be fine if there were a shift of the demand function or any sort of change on the revenue side of the firm, but when an input price changes, we have to redo the cost function. Moreover, we can no longer assume that material and labor are used in an eight-to-one ratio as before, because that depended on the particular input prices.

Equating the ratios of input price to the input's marginal physical product gives us

$$\frac{1.20}{(1/3)m^{-2/3}l^{1/6}} = \frac{4}{(1/6)m^{1/3}l^{-5/6}}.$$

This simplifies to

$$3.6m = 24l \quad \text{or} \quad m = 6.6667l.$$

That is, instead of using materials to labor in an 8:1 ratio, the increased price of materials drives us to use relatively less material per unit of labor; we use 6.6667 units of material for each unit of labor. Substituting $6.6667l$ in for m in the production function, we get

$$x = (6.6667l)^{1/3}l^{1/6} = 1.8819l^{1/2},$$

so that, at the level of production x,

$$l = \left(\frac{x}{1.88191}\right)^2 \quad \text{and} \quad m = 6.6667\left(\frac{x}{1.88191}\right)^2.$$

Total cost, then, is

$$\text{TC}(x) = 300 + 4\left(\frac{x}{1.88191}\right)^2 + (1.20)(6.6667)\left(\frac{x}{1.88191}\right)^2 = 300 + 3.3883x^2.$$

Marginal cost is $MC(x) = 6.7766x$, and marginal cost equals marginal revenue when

$$160 - 4x = 6.7766x \quad \text{or} \quad 160 = 10.7766x \quad \text{or} \quad x = 14.847.$$

This gives a price of $130.306, labor usage of 62.24 units, and material usage of 414.94 units.

(It is interesting that, in the long run, when the cost of materials rises, the absolute level of labor usage falls. This happens, roughly, because while the relative level of labor to material rises, the rising cost causes the manufacturer to scale back output so much that the overall impact on labor usage is to decrease. This is not a general phenomenon; look at what happens to labor usage in Problem II.4, or consider a technology with constant marginal rates of substitution.)

Solution to Problem II.7

(a) The average and marginal cost functions are shown in Figure II.8(b). (The total cost function is reproduced in Figure II.8(a).) Note what we have here: Up to the quantity x^*, marginal and average cost are constant and equal to each other and equal to c^*/x^*. At x^*, marginal cost suddenly jumps up to a new (constant) level, which (according to my rough measurements) is approximately three times as high as the old marginal costs. Average costs move continuously (but with a kink) up toward the new level of marginal costs, and if we extended the graph out further and further, average costs would get closer and closer to this new level of marginal costs. (Although I do not indicate this on the picture, I can tell you the slope of average cost at x^* in terms of x^* and c^*, assuming the new marginal cost is $3c^*/x^*$. It is $2c^*/(x^*)^2$. How do I know this?)

(b) This is consistent with only decreasing (and not constant) returns to scale, because average costs are rising. If we had constant returns to scale, average costs would have to be constant; and with increasing returns to scale, average costs are nonincreasing.

Solution to Problem II.8

(a) Marginal cost at the first facility is $5 + x_1/1000$, so the firm can produce 10,000 units at that facility before its marginal cost rises above $15. And marginal cost at the second facility is $8 + x_2/2000$, so the firm can produce 14,000 units there before

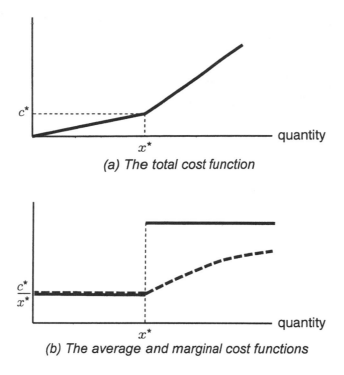

(a) The total cost function

(b) The average and marginal cost functions

Figure II.8. Problem II.7: Total, marginal, and average costs. In panel b, the average cost function is dashed and the marginal cost function is solid.

the marginal cost goes above $15. Therefore, the firm would produce up to 24,000 units domestically before going to the foreign supplier, but any quantity beyond 24,000 would be sourced from the foreign supplier.

(b) We follow the recipe for solving such problems from Chapter 9. Let $X_1^*(c)$ be the number of units that can made at the first facility at marginal cost c or less. This is the solution to $c = 5 + x_1/1000$ or $X_1^*(c) = 1000(c-5)$. Similarly, $X_2^*(c) = 2000(c-8)$. Thus the total number (up to 24,000, at a marginal cost of $15 or less) the firm can procure at for marginal cost c or less is

$$X^*(c) = \begin{cases} 0, & \text{if } c < 5, \\ 1000(c - 5), & \text{if } 5 \leq c < 8, \text{ and} \\ 1000(c - 5) + 2000(c - 8) = 3000c - 21{,}000, & \text{if } c \geq 8. \end{cases}$$

Let me reiterate that this is true only up to $c = \$15$; at that point, the firm can get as many as it wants, at a $15 marginal cost. The firm wishes to procure 15,000—below the 24,000 ceiling we computed in part a—so we solve $X^*(c) = 15{,}000$ for c. This gives $c = 12$. And thus the firm should source $X_1^*(12) = 7000$ from the first facility and $X_2^*(12) = 8000$ from the second.

(c) Marginal revenue is $MR(x) = 24 - x/3000$. This reaches $15 when $x = 27{,}000$, which is beyond the point (24,000) at which marginal cost has risen to $15. So the firm optimally produces 24,000 units domestically and procures another 3000 from the foreign supplier. The price will be $19.50, and the firm will source 10,000 units from facility #1 and 14,000 from facility #2.

Material for Chapter 11

Competitive Firms and Perfect Competition

Solution to Problem 11.1

The $1 million fixed cost is irrelevant, since it cannot be avoided. The firm's "relevant" total cost function is $\$4{,}000{,}000 + 5x + x^2/10{,}000$, and the firm will not supply at any price p that is less than the minimum average cost generated by this "relevant" cost function. To find minimum averge cost, equate marginal and average costs, or

$$\frac{4{,}000{,}000}{x} + 5 + \frac{x}{10{,}000} = 5 + \frac{2x}{10{,}000} \quad \text{or} \quad \frac{4{,}000{,}000}{x} = \frac{x}{10{,}000},$$

which gives $x^2 = 40$ billion or $x = 200{,}000$, for a minimum "relevant" average cost of $45. At prices above $45, the firm supplies along its marginal cost function, or $p = 5 + 2x/10{,}000$, or $x = 5000(p - 5)$. Therefore the overall supply function is

$$s(p) = \begin{cases} 0, & \text{if } p < \$45, \\ 0 \text{ or } 200{,}000, & \text{if } p = \$45, \text{ and} \\ 5000(p - 5), & \text{if } p > \$45. \end{cases}$$

Solution to Problem 11.2

I do not describe how to get the numbers, but in case you want to check your math, F_2, the avoidable portion of the fixed cost, is $40,000, and F_1, the rest of the fixed cost, is $50,000.

Solution to Problem 11.3

In case you do not recognize it, this is a case of a firm with marginal costs that fall and then rise.

With or without a fixed cost, this firm, being competitive, supplies nothing at prices below its minimum "relevant" average cost, where relevance here means ignoring all unavoidable fixed costs. At minimum average cost, it supplies 0 or efficient scale. At prices above minimum average cost, it produces along the *increasing* portion of its marginal cost function (really, at levels beyond efficient scale), which are solutions to

$$p = 8 - \frac{x}{10} + \frac{x^2}{2000}.$$

Solving for x in this quadratic equation and taking the greater root to be on the increasing part of marginal cost gives

$$s(p) = \frac{0.1 + \sqrt{0.01 - 4 \times (8 - p) \times 0.0005}}{2 \times 0.0005}$$

$$= 1000 \times [0.1 + 0.1\sqrt{1 + 0.02(p - 8)}] = 100[1 + \sqrt{1 + 0.02(p - 8)}].$$

Hence, in both the cases of no fixed cost and completely avoidable fixed cost,

$$s(p) = \begin{cases} 0, & \text{if } p < \min \text{ AC}, \\ 0 \text{ or efficient scale}, & \text{if } p = \min \text{ AC, and} \\ 100[1 + \sqrt{1 + 0.02(p - 8)}], & \text{if } p > \min \text{ AC}. \end{cases}$$

The final tasks are to find the minimum average cost and efficient scale for the two cases.

To do this, we equate marginal cost to average cost. If there is no fixed cost, we have to solve $8 - x/10 + x^2/2000 = 8 - x/20 + x^2/6000$, which is $x/20 = 2x^2/6000$, or $3000/20 = 150 = x$. That is, efficient scale in this case is 150. And to find min AC, we plug efficient scale back into the marginal cost function, getting $8 - 15 + 22500/2000 = \$4.25$.

If there is a fixed cost of \$10,000, we instead have to solve $8 - x/10 + x^2/2000 = 10,000/x + 8 - x/20 + x^2/6000$, which is a cubic equation, beyond my powers to do analytically. So I went to Solver and asked it to find the value of x that minimized average cost, and it returned: efficient scale = 396.6; and min AC = \$39.343.

Solution to Problem 11.4

I do not supply the answer to this question, but I give you a push in the right direction. The critical price level is $p^* = 10/101$. If the price of the good is more than this, the consumer is a supplier of the good: She sells out of her initial endowment of 100. (If prices get high enough, she sells all 100 units.) If prices are less than this, she enters the market on the demand side, purchasing more for her own consumption.

Solution to Problem 11.5

If $TC(x) = 4x + x^2/2$, $MC(x) = 4 + x$. This is an increasing function and the total cost function has no fixed costs, so the individual firm's supply function is this: At prices below 4, supply nothing; at prices 4 and above, supply $s(p)$ that solves $4 + s(p) = p$, or $s(p) = p - 4$. If 10 identical firms are in the industry, then industrywide supply is 10 times the supply from any single firm, which is

$$S(p) = \begin{cases} 0, & \text{if } p < 4, \text{ and} \\ 10p - 40, & \text{if } p \geq 4. \end{cases}$$

Equilibrium is where supply equals demand. For the demand function $D(p) = 10(20 - p)$, at $p = 4$, demand is 160, so the intersection must take place at a price larger than 4, and we can find that equilibrium price by setting

$$D(p) = 10(20 - p) = 10p - 40 = S(p)$$

which gives

$$240 = 20p \quad \text{or} \quad p = 12.$$

At this price, industrywide demand equals industrywide supply equals 80 units, so each firm supplies 8 units. This gives each firm revenue of $12 \times 8 = 96$, costs of $4 \times 8 + 8^2/2 = 32 + 32 = 64$, and a profit of $96 - 64 = 32$.

Solution to Problem 11.7

(a) Since the firms are identical and there is unlimited possibility of entry (and cost = 0 if a firm exits), in the long-run equilibrium, no firm can make a profit or take a loss. Therefore, the long-run equilibrium price must be the minimum average price of any firm, and firms that produce a positive amount must be producing at efficient scale. Total costs are given by

$$TC(x) = 100 + 3x + 0.04x^2,$$

and therefore average costs are

$$AC(x) = \frac{100}{x} + 3 + 0.04x.$$

To find minimum average cost and efficient scale, I set AC = MC getting

$$\frac{100}{x} + 3 + 0.04x = 3 + 0.08x \quad \text{or} \quad \frac{100}{0.04} = x^2 \quad \text{or} \quad x = \frac{10}{0.2} = 50.$$

So $x = 50$ is the efficient scale. And the minimum level of average cost is

$$MC(50) = 3 + 0.08 \times 50 = 3 + 4 = 7.$$

So, in a long-run equilibrium, the price must be $p = 7$. At this price, the total demand is

$$D(7) = 200(10 - 7) = 600,$$

which therefore must equal total supply. Since each firm (that is not producing 0) must produce 50 units at $p = 7$, this means that there must be 12 active firms. Of course, each of these active firms makes a profit of 0.

(b) To do the rest of this problem in a way that promotes understanding of the structure of these models, look at the table in Figure 11.10(a). The four columns describe the situation for the status quo, the new short-run equilibrium, the new intermediate-run equilibrium, and the new long-run equilibrium. Figure 11.10(a) has the answers for the status quo, taken from part a.

Now ask yourself, which cells in the other three columns can you fill in with no computation whatsoever? Figure 11.10(b) shows these "automatic" entries; please review why these entries are all "automatic."

Of course, this does not finish the problem. Figure 11.10(c) shows the rest of the table, based on the arguments that follow.

	status quo	new short run	new intermediate run	new long run
price	$7			
total quantity	600			
number of firms	12			
quantity per firm	50			
profit per firm	$0			

(a) The data from part a: the status quo.

	status quo	new short run	new intermediate run	new long run
price	$7			$7
total quantity	600	600		
number of firms	12	12	12	
quantity per firm	50	50		50
profit per firm	$0			$0

(b) Easy answers for part b.

	status quo	new short run	new intermediate run	new long run
price	$7	$9	$8.14	$7
total quantity	600	600	771.43	1000
number of firms	12	12	12	20
quantity per firm	50	50	64.29	50
profit per firm	$0	$100	$65.27	$0

(c) The full answer for part b.

Figure 11.10. Problem 11.7: Solving in stages. After finding the status-quo position and filling in the values into the first column, a number of entries for the new short-run, intermediate-run, and long-run equilibria are quite simple. These are shown in panel b, and the full answer is given in panel c.

Demand suddenly changes to $D(p) = 200(12 - p)$. If, in the short run, firms cannot change their production decisions, then each of the 12 active firms continues to produce 50 units, for a totally inelastic (vertical) supply of 600 units. Price must adjust so that demand is 600 units, or

$$D(p_{SR}) = 200(12 - p_{SR}) = 600,$$

which gives $p_{SR} = 9$. At this price, each of the 12 firms has a profit margin of 2 per unit produced, and since they produce 50 units each, this gives each firm a profit of 100.

In the intermediate-run, the firms supply along their marginal cost curve. (Even though they have fixed costs, they cannot exit and avoid those fixed costs, so the fixed costs are irrelevant.) Each firm's marginal cost function is $MC(x) = 3 + 0.08x$, and so (by the usual calculations) the intermediate-run supply function of each firm is

$$s(p) = \begin{cases} 0, & \text{if } p < 3, \text{ and} \\ 12.5(p - 3), & \text{if } p \geq 3. \end{cases}$$

Therefore, total intermediate-run supply $S_{\text{intermediate-run}}(p) = 12s(p)$, which is

$$S_{\text{intermediate-run}}(p) = \begin{cases} 0, & \text{if } p < 3, \text{ and} \\ 150(p - 3), & \text{if } p \geq 3. \end{cases}$$

Intermediate-run supply equals demand (clearly, at a price above 3) if

$$150p - 450 = 2400 - 200p \quad \text{or} \quad 350p = 2850 \quad \text{or} \quad p_{IR} = 8.14.$$

At this price, total supply (which is the same as total demand) is 771.43; each of the 12 firms supplies 64.29, for total revenue 523.47, total cost 458.19, and (therefore) profit equal to 65.27.

In the long run, firms, attracted by the profits in this industry, begin to enter. They continue to do so until price falls to $p_{LR} = 7$, so that profit for each active firm is 0. Price is 7 when total demand is $200(12 - 7) = 1000$. This, then, is also total supply. Since each active firm supplies 50 units, this gives us 20 active firms in total, or eight entrants. Profit, of course, is 0 per active firm.

Solution to Problem 11.8

I begin the solution by assuming that the fixed costs cannot be avoided by exiting the industry. Later I'll see if that assumption is relevant to my solution.

The four superior firms each have the marginal cost function $MC(x) = 1 + 0.08x$, so their (individual) supply functions are

$$s(p) = \begin{cases} 0, & \text{if } p < 1, \text{ and} \\ 12.5(p - 1), & \text{if } p \geq 1. \end{cases}$$

Each of the eight other firms supplies according to the supply function computed last problem, or

$$s(p) = \begin{cases} 0, & \text{if } p < 3, \text{ and} \\ 12.5(p-3), & \text{if } p \geq 3. \end{cases}$$

Overall supply is the sum of four of the first type and eight of the second, or

$$S(p) = \begin{cases} 0, & \text{if } p < 1, \\ 50(p-1), & \text{if } 1 \leq p < 3, \text{ and} \\ 50(p-1) + 100(p-3) = 150p - 350, & \text{if } p \geq 3. \end{cases}$$

We have to find where this supply function intersects the demand function

$$D(p) = 200(10 - p).$$

At this point, it is usually a good idea to move to a graph of supply and demand to get a sense of where supply and demand intersect. But let me instead be a bit clumsy and just try trial and error.

Does the intersection occur on the segment of the supply function where $S(p) = 50(p-1)$? If it does, then $50(p-1) = 2000 - 200p$ or $250p = 2050$. This gives $p = 8.2$, which is outside the range of prices for which $S(p) = 50(p-1)$.

So the intersection must take place at $p > 3$, where $S(p) = 150p - 350$. Equating supply and demand gives

$$150p - 350 = 2000 - 200p \quad \text{or} \quad 350p = 2350 \quad \text{or} \quad p = \$6.714.$$

At this price, total demand equals total supply, which is $D(6.714) = 657.2$, which is divided as follows: Each of the four superior firms produces $12.5(6.714 - 1) = 71.425$, and each of the eight other firms produces $12.5(6.714 - 3) = 46.425$. (If you check my math, you'll find that roundoff has produced a small discrepancy in total supply of 0.1 units.)

For each of the superior-technology firms, revenue is \$478.55, while cost is \$325.49, so that profit is \$154.06.

For each of the eight other firms, revenue is \$311.70, while cost is \$325.49, so that each of these firms sustains a loss of \$13.79.

In fact, we knew that these firms would sustain a loss as soon as we saw that the price was below 7, because in the previous problem, we saw minimum AC for firms with this technology is $7.

So the assumption that firms cannot avoid their fixed costs is relevant. If the less-efficient firms could avoid their fixed costs by exiting, they would choose to do so. As they exit, the price is pushed up, until it reaches $7. At that price, each of the four firms with the better technology produces $12.5(7 - 1) = 12.5 \times 6 = 75$ units, for a total supply from them of 300. This provides each with $175 in profit. Demand at $7 is for 600 units, so we need 300 units supplied by firms with the second technology. We know from the previous problem that their efficient scale is 50, so we need six of them producing. That is the equilibrium if firms can avoid their fixed cost by shutting down.

Solution to Problem 11.9

I do not give you the answer, but here is a big hint: It is somewhere very close by on this page.

On Industrywide Input Price Effects

In the text, I introduce the idea that, while individual firms might reasonably be supposed to be price takers when it comes to inputs to the production function, the industry as a whole might affect the price of inputs, which in turn would affect "industry supply." What follows is a simple model of this situation. Warning: This is somewhat subtle, and many readers will find this a bit hard to follow, at least at first.

Imagine a competitive industry with 40 firms. To keep matters simple, we assume for now that no fixed costs face the firms nor are entry or exit possible. Each of the 40 firms has a production technology given by the production function $f(k, l) = 20k^{1/4}l^{1/4}$, for two inputs, k and l. The price of k is a constant $100 per unit. The price of l depends on how much l is demanded by the industry as a whole; at the current equilibrium, this price is $100.

Each firm believes that it has very little impact on either the price p it gets for its output—this is the usual assumption of perfect competition—or the price r_l of the input l. So each firm chooses its production quantity and plan in a fashion that treats these prices as constant.

It the manner of Chapter 8, we conclude: If $r_l = 100 = r_k$, to make x units of output an individual firm will set $k = l = x^2/400$; therefore, for each firm, $\mathrm{TC}(x) = 200x^2/400 = x^2/2$, and $\mathrm{MC}(x) = x$. Each firm sets $p = \mathrm{MC}$, which gives individual firm supply functions $s(p) = p$. Industry supply is $S(p) = 40s(p) = 40p$. If we suppose that demand is given by $D(p) = 20(60 - p)$, then supply equals demand is $20(60 - p) = 40p$, or $p = 20$. Each firm produces 20 units of the product, taking 1 unit of k and 1 unit of l. Each firm's total cost is \$200 and its total revenue is \$400, so its profit is \$200.

Now the question arises, What would be the new equilibrium if demand shifts out to, say, $20(75 - p)$? Is it where supply intersects demand; that is, where $20(75 - p) = 40p$? For reference sake, the solution to this equation is $p = 25$.

The reason the answer is not a simple Yes, and the reason for this entire discussion, comes now. We supposed that the price of l is \$100. But suppose that this price holds when industry demand for l is 40 units. To be more specific, suppose that the inverse supply function of l to this industry is $\hat{r}_l(l) = 60 + l$. The concept of an inverse supply function is new, but I hope it is not mysterious: This says what price for this input is needed, as a function of industrywide supply of this input, to call out that level of supply from the industry that makes l.

Suppose that total supply by the first industry (the one that makes x) is X in total. Forty identical firms make this stuff, so each is necessarily producing $X/40$ units. This means that each firm requires $(X/40)^2/400 = X^2/640{,}000$ units of l, and the industry demand for l is 40 times this, or $X^2/16{,}000$. Therefore, the price of the input is $r_l = 60 + X^2/16{,}000$.

Now as the price r_l changes, holding p fixed, the supply from each of the firms changes, because their marginal costs change. We saw earlier that, if $r_l = 100$, then $\mathrm{MC}(x) = x$. But for a general r_l, the solution to each firm's cost minimization problem is $k = r_l l/100$, so $x = 20(r_l/100)^{1/4}l^{1/2}$, and $l = 10x^2/(400r_l^{1/2}) = x^2/(40r_l^{1/2})$ and $k = r_l^{1/2}x^2/4000$. Thus $\mathrm{TC}(x) = r_l^{1/2}x^2/20$, and $\mathrm{MC}(x) = r_l^{1/2}x/10$. Supply by a single firm is therefore $s(p) = 10p/r_l^{1/2}$, and industry supply is $S(p) = 400p/r_l^{1/2}$. Note that we have industry supply here as a function of r_l and p; earlier we had r_l as a function of industry supply X, so we can substitute to get the "real" supply function as the solution to

$$S(p) = \frac{400p}{\sqrt{60 + S(p)^2/16{,}000}}.$$

Solving for $S(p)$ is not easy, but solving for p is very simple, so instead of writing the supply function, I write the inverse supply function:

$$p_S(X) = \frac{X\sqrt{60 + X^2/16{,}000}}{400}.$$

How does this "inverse supply function" compare with the one we got using simple-minded summing of the individual firms' supply functions, at $r_l = 100$? Supply from that simple-minded procedure was $S(p) = 40p$, so inverse supply is $\hat{p}_S(X) = X/40$. In Table 11.1, I provide for a number of quantities the "inverse supply" values if supply is computed in the simple-minded fashion, as the horizontal sum of individual firm supply functions, assuming $r_l = 100$, and taking into account the impact the industry has on the price of l. I also provide the price of the l, as a function of x, taking into account industry effects on r_l.

Industrywide level of output	simple-minded inverse supply	"real" inverse supply taking industrywide input-price effects into account	price of the input
100	$2.50	$1.95	$60.63
200	$5.00	$3.95	$62.50
300	$7.50	$6.08	$65.63
400	$10.00	$8.37	$70.00
500	$12.50	$10.87	$75.63
600	$15.00	$13.62	$82.50
700	$17.50	$16.66	$90.63
800	$20.00	$20.00	$100.00
900	$22.50	$23.67	$110.63
1000	$25.00	$27.67	$122.50
1100	$27.50	$32.03	$135.63
1200	$30.00	$36.74	$150.00
1300	$32.50	$41.83	$165.63
1400	$35.00	$47.28	$182.50
1500	$37.50	$53.12	$200.63
1600	$40.00	$59.33	$220.00

Table 11.1. Industrywide input price effects: Two versions of inverse supply. In an industry in which the price of an input changes with the scale of the industry, supply is computed two ways: in a "simple-minded fashion," as the horizontal sum of individual firm supplies for a fixed price for the input; and taking into account the impact industry scale has on the price of the input. Inverting these two, we get the inverse supply function data in the table, together with the price of the input as a function of industry output.

Looking at the table, it is clear that, as industry output rises, the price of the input is driven up. Taking this into account, the real inverse supply varies more than does inverse supply computed assuming an unchanging price for the input.

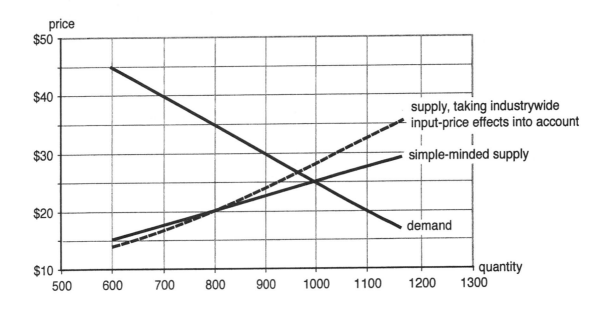

Figure 11.11. Industrywide input-price effects: Supply equals demand. The functions graphed here are the new demand function, simple-minded supply, and supply taking into account industrywide input price effects.

The question that drives all this is, What would be the equilibrium price if demand shifts from $D(p) = 20(60 - p)$ to $D(p) = 20(75 - p)$? This shift out in demand means the industry produces more. As it does so, the price of l rises. This ameliorates the supply response to higher prices. The new equilibrium would not be where simple-minded supply intersects demand but where demand intersects supply computed taking into account the impact on r_l of increased industry supply. A graph of the situation is given in Figure 11.11. Solving supply equals demand analytically is difficult, but with Excel and either Goal Seek or Solver you can solve this numerically: The equilibrium price is roughly $26.46.

As a final demonstration of how industrywide input price effects can affect the analysis of Chapter 11, let me change the assumptions about the industry a bit.

Suppose that, instead of 40 firms, the industry has an unlimited number of potential entrants, each with the same production technology as before but with an additional fixed cost, if they are active, of $200. This is now the situation that, in Chapter 11, gives a flat (long-run) supply function; the price must equal the minimum average cost of the firms. Suppose, to start, that r_l = $100, so that, as we computed earlier, total variable cost (without the fixed cost) is $x^2/2$. Total cost is now $200 + x^2/2$, and we find minimum average cost by equating marginal and average cost: $200/x + x/2 = x$ or $x = 20$, for a minimum average cost of $20. Assuming demand is where it originally was ($D(p) = 20(60 - p)$) this means total demand of 800 units, so we require 40 firms. This is the status quo.

But the "true" industry supply function is no longer flat. Let me first give you a picture of how it looks: Figure 11.12 graphs supply both under the simple-minded assumption that r_l is a constant $100 and taking into account that, as the industry increases its scale, r_l increases.

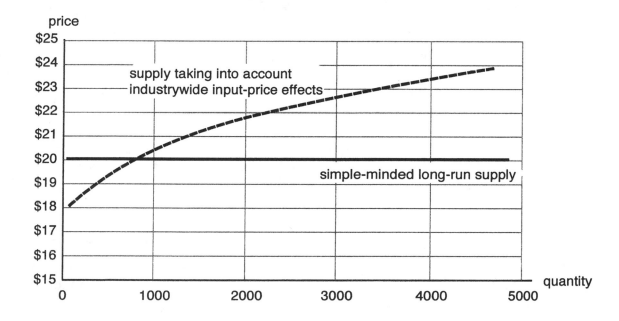

Figure 11.12. Industrywide input-price effects: Supply with free entry. The functions graphed here are simple-minded supply, assuming r_l is a fixed $100, and supply taking into account industrywide input price effects. Both functions assume free entry into and exit from the industry at the best available technology.

How did I get the "true" supply function? Warning: What follows involves fairly complex math.

Fix a level of total supply from the industry, X. Suppose that the corresponding price that elicits this supply is p. We know that p must be the minimum average cost for the firms in the industy. Each firm's total cost function is

$$200 + r_l^{1/2}x^2/20,$$

which means each firm's efficient scale is where

$$\frac{200}{x} + \frac{r_l^{1/2}x}{20} = \frac{r_l^{1/2}2x}{20} \quad \text{or} \quad \frac{4000}{r_l^{1/2}} = x^2 \quad \text{or} \quad x = \frac{20\sqrt{10}}{r_l^{1/4}}.$$

At this scale of production, each firm uses

$$l = \frac{10 \times 4000/r_l^{1/2}}{400r_l^{1/2}} = \frac{100}{r_l}$$

units of l. The number of firms is $X/[20\sqrt{10}/r_l^{1/4}] = Xr_l^{1/4}/[20\sqrt{10}]$, and so total demand by the industry for input l is

$$\frac{100Xr_l^{1/4}}{20\sqrt{10}r_l} = \frac{5X}{\sqrt{10}r_l^{3/4}},$$

and hence

$$r_l = 60 + \frac{5X}{\sqrt{10}r_l^{3/4}}.$$

Solving for X in terms of r_l,

$$X = [r_l - 60] \times \frac{\sqrt{10}r_l^{3/4}}{5}.$$

We also can compute the equilibrium price as a function of r_l: Each firm's efficient scale is $20\sqrt{10}/r_l^{1/4}$, which, plugged into marginal cost, gives

$$p = r_l^{1/2} \times 2 \times \frac{20\sqrt{10}/r_l^{1/4}}{20} = r_l^{1/4}2\sqrt{10}.$$

Now use Excel. For a range of values for r_l—I used \$65 to \$200—evaluate the corresponding values of quantity X and equilibrium price p, and put those in an

X-Y plot. The dashed line (supply taking into account industrywide input-price effects) in Figure 11.12 is what emerges.

Two comments about this:

- Chapter 11 concerns what economists call *partial equilibrium analysis*, studying one industry while assuming all other prices are fixed. This discussion and exercise have begun to discuss *general equilibrium effects*, where what happens in one market affects other markets and, in particular, affects prices in other markets. This is hard stuff. But, to the extent that real-life markets have these effects, to make accurate predictions about, for instance, how equilibrium price in one market would react to a shift in demand, you must consider several markets (in this case, two) simultaneously. (You'll get to do a few exercises of this sort in the next set of review problems, but we spend no more time on them in the text.)

- Looking at either Figure 11.11 or 11.12, there are two "supply functions," one based on a simple-minded hypothesis that the input price does not change and one based on recognition that, as the scale of the industry output changes, so does this input price. I tried to be careful and put quotes whenever I referred to the "true" supply curve, because both of these have their uses. If you want to make predictions about how prices would change if there were a shift in demand, then you want to take into account the impact of changes in r_l. In the next chapter, however, we discuss something called *producer surplus*; in that case, the simple-minded supply function is the right one to use. If you want to know why, consult a doctoral-level book on the subject: Be on the lookout for what is known as *Hotelling's lemma*.

Material for Chapter 12

Market Efficiency

Solution to Problem 12.1

The first step is to draw the picture of supply equals demand. See Figure 12.12. The market equilibrium is where

$$S(p) = 1000(p - 4) = 3000(20 - p) = D(p),$$

or $p - 4 = 3(20 - p)$, or $p - 4 = 60 - 3p$, or $4p = 64$, or $p = 16$. This corresponds to a quantity of $1000(16 - 4) = 12{,}000$. Therefore, consumer surplus is the area of a right triangle whose height is $20 - 16 = 4$ and whose base is 12,000, which is $24,000. And producer surplus is the area of a right triangle whose height is $16 - 4 = 12$ and whose base is 12,000, or $72,000.

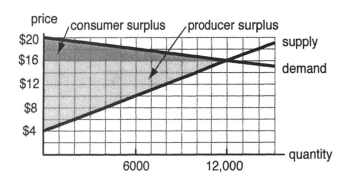

Figure 12.12. Solving Problem 12.1. Supply and demand are plotted and consumer and producer surpluses are the areas of the triangles indicated.

Solution to Problem 12.2

Consumer surplus is $900. Producer surplus is $700. But I do not tell you how I got those values, except to provide, in Figure 12.13, a substantial hint.

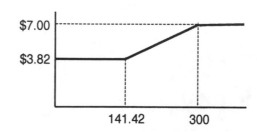

Figure 12.13. A hint for Problem 12.2.

Solution to Problem 12.3

Figure 12.14 recaps the solution from Problem 11.7: Long-run supply is flat, with as much quantity as needed at a price of $7. Hence, the initial equilibrium is where price is $7 and quantity is 600. Intermediate-run supply is shown as a medium gray line, and short-run supply, the light gray line, is vertical, fixed at 600 units. When demand shifts out,

- In the short run, the price rises to $9 and the quantity stays fixed at 600 units.

- In the intermediate run, the price falls to $8.14 and the quantity rises to 771.43 units.

- In the long run, the price falls back to $7 and the quantity rises to 1000 units.

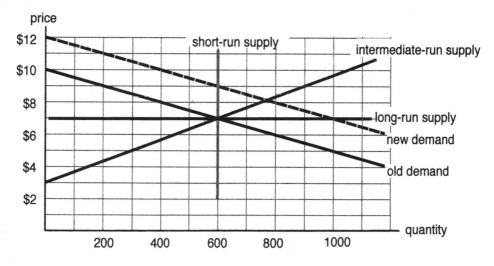

Figure 12.14. Problem 12.3: The big picture. This figure graphs the three supply curves (from the status-quo, old equilibrium), the old demand function, and the new demand function.

Consumer surpluses are computed next:

- At the old equilibrium, the consumer surplus is the area of a right triangle with height $3, from $7 to $10, and base 600 units, or $900.

- When demand shifts, the consumer surplus in the short run is the area of a right triangle with height $3, from $9 to $12, and a base of 600 units, or $900.

- In the intermediate run, the consumer surplus becomes the area of a right triangle with height $3.86, from $8.14 to $12, and a base of 771.43 units, or $1488.86.

- Finally, in the long run, consumer surplus becomes the area of a right triangle with height $5, from $7 to $12, and a base of 1000 units, or $2500.

Some care is needed is in the computation of producer surplus.

- At the status quo, in the long run, producer surplus is 0. Because the long-run supply curve is horizontal, the usual "triangle" is flattened down to a line, with no area. Of course, this corresponds to the idea that firms make profits of 0 in a long-run equilibrium in this sort of free-entry industry.

- Now the demand shifts. In the short run, short-run producer surplus is the area of a rectangle with sides of 600 units and $9, or $5400 (see Figure 12.15(a)). But this is not the sum of the profits of the firms involved: It is their profits gross of their short-run fixed costs. And, in the short-run, where they cannot vary their level of production, all their costs are fixed, so this is really just the sum of the revenues of the firms.

- In the intermediate run, intermediate-run producer surplus is the area of a right triangle with height $5.14, from $8.14 down to $3, and base 771.43 units, or $1982.57 (see Figure 12.15(c)). Note that this is profits gross of intermediate-run fixed costs; in the intermediate run, firms can neither enter nor leave, so each firm's fixed cost is the $100 that is tied to simply being in the market; industry fixed costs are thus $100 per firm times 12 firms or $1200 in total.

- Finally, in the long run, long-run producer surplus is again 0, as long-run supply is horizontal (see Figure 12.15(e)).

Suppose we wanted, on the graphs, to find out how the industry profits have shifted in the short run or intermediate run because of the shift in demand. The first paragraph on page 298 of the text tells us what to do. To find how much profits have gone up in the short run, we subtract the pre-shift short-run producer surplus from the post-shift short-run producer surplus. Since both of these figures are gross of short-run fixed costs, the fixed costs cancel out in the subtraction. In terms of the picture, we subtract the shaded area in panel b of Figure 12.15 from the shaded area in panel a. (If you do the math, the difference is $1200; profits rise by $1200 in the short run.) To find out how profits have shifted in the intermediate run, we subtract pre-shift intermediate-run producer surplus (panel d) from post-shift intermediate-run producer surplus (panel c). (Do the math and you should find

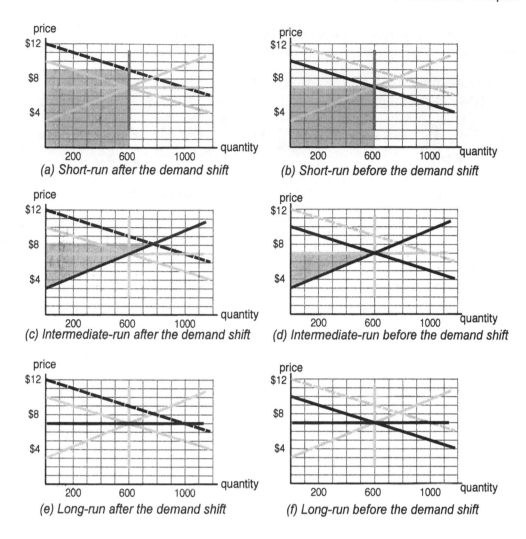

Figure 12.15. Problem 12.3. *Short-run, intermediate-run, and long-run producer surpluses before and after a shift in demand.* To find each run's producer surplus for a particular run, find the areas bounded by that run's supply curve and the equilibrium price, out to the equilibrium quantity. These are profits gross of any fixed costs for the particular run. Panels a and b show the short-run producer surpluses, after and before the demand shift; panels c and d show the pictures for the intermediate run. Panels e and f are for the long run; since long-run supply is horizontal, producer surplus is always zero.

a change in profit of $782.57.) We'd do the same thing for the long run, but since long-run supply is horizontal, long-run producer surplus is zero both before and after the shift in demand; profits start at $0 and end at $0.

Suppose, finally, we wanted to know the values of the short-run and intermediate-run fixed costs (at some given status quo point), and all we had were the graphs. Panels b, d, and f give the numbers. Panel f tells us that, at a long-run equilibrium, long-run producer surplus is $0. Panel d tells us that, at the same long-run equilibrium, intermediate-run producer surplus is $\frac{1}{2} \times (\$7 - \$3) \times 600 = \$1200$. So the difference, $1200 - \$0 = \$1200$, is intermediate-run fixed costs. And panel b tells us that, at this long-run equilibrium, short-run producer surplus is $7 \times 600 = \$4200$. So the difference between this and long-run producer surplus, $4200 - \$0 = \$4200$, is short-run fixed costs at this long-run equilibrium (or status quo point).

Solution to Problem 12.5

Inverse demand is given by $P(x) = 20 - x/3000$, so marginal revenue is given by $\text{MR}(x) = 20 - x/1500$. Marginal revenue equals marginal cost where

$$20 - \frac{x}{1500} = 4 + \frac{x}{1000} \quad \text{or} \quad 16 = \frac{5x}{3000} \quad \text{or} \quad x = 9600,$$

for a price of $16.80. (See Figure 12.16.)

- The consumer surplus is the area of a right triangle with height $3.20, from $16.80 to $20, and base 9600 units, or $15,360. (Compare this with consumer surplus of $24,000 in Problem 12.1.)

- The producer surplus is the area of a right quadrilateral, with base 9600 units, and parallel sides $12.80 (from $16.80 to $4) and $3.20 (from $16.80 to $13.60), or $9600(12.8 + 3.2)/2 = \$76,800$. (Compare this with producer surplus of $72,000 from Problem 12.1.)

Although you weren't asked to do this computation, note that total surplus in Problem 12.1 was $96,000, while here it is $92,160, a difference of $3840. This is the area of the deadweight loss triangle indicated in Figure 12.16: a base of $3.20 and a height of 2400 units, for an area of $3840.

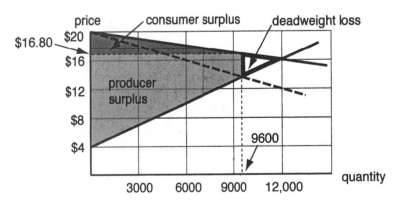

Figure 12.16. Solving Problem 12.5. Consumer surplus, producer surplus, and the deadweight loss are as marked.

Solution to Problem 12.6

(a) $400 million. (b) $700 million.

Solution to Problem 12.7

(a) If each firm has total cost function $TC(x) = 4x + x^2/200$, then the marginal cost function is $MC(x) = 4 + x/100$. Since the firms are perfectly competitive, the supply function for each is obtained by solving

$$p = 4 + x/100,$$

giving individual supply function

$$s(p) = 100(p - 4)$$

for prices above 4. There are 25 such firms, so total supply is

$$S(p) = 2500(p - 4),$$

and supply equals demand where

$$2500(p - 4) = 10{,}000(10 - p) \quad \text{or} \quad 2500p - 10{,}000 = 100{,}000 - 10{,}000p \quad \text{or}$$

$$12{,}500p = 110{,}000 \quad \text{or} \quad p = \$8.80.$$

Total supply at this point (equals demand, which) is

$$10{,}000(10 - 8.8) = 12{,}000.$$

See Figure 12.17(a). Consumer surplus is a triangle with base 12000 and height $1.2, or area = consumer surplus = $(1/2)(1.2)(12000) = \$7200$. Producer surplus is a triangle with base 12,000 and height $4.8, or area = producer surplus = $(1/2)(4.8)(12{,}000) = \$28{,}800$. Note that each of the 25 firms makes a profit of $28,800/25 = \$1152.

(b) Follow along on Figure 12.17(b). This $1 tax effectively raises the marginal cost of the firm by $1 per unit, to $MC(y) = 5 + y/100$. Therefore, supply equals demand where

$$2500(p - 5) = 10{,}000(10 - p) \quad \text{or} \quad 12{,}500p = 112{,}500 \quad \text{or} \quad p = \$9.$$

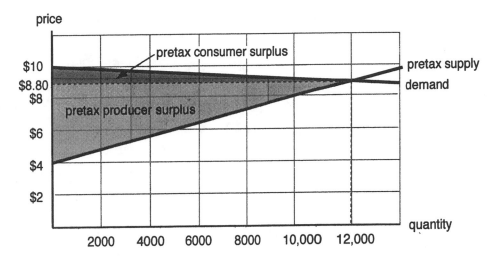

(a) *The pretax situation: equilibrium, consumer surplus, and producer surplus*

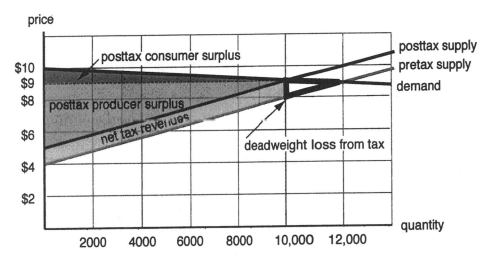

(b) *Posttax equilibrium, consumer surplus, producer surplus, tax revenues, and the deadweight loss in surplus from the tax*

Figure 12.17. Equilibrium and surpluses before and after a tax.

This reduces the amount supplied to $10,000(10 - 9) = 10,000$ units. Consumer surplus falls to

$$(1/2)(10,000)(1) = \$5000,$$

and producer surplus falls to

$$(1/2)(4)(10,000) = \$20,000,$$

or $800 per firm. In addition, the government collects $1 apiece on each of 10,000 units, for net revenues of $10,000.

(c) Note that the total surplus in part a is $28,800 + $7200 = $36,000, while in part b total surplus is $20,000 + $5000 + $10,000 = $35,000. The tax results in a $1000 loss in total surplus; firms lose $8800 of profit, consumers lose $2200 worth of utility, and the government gets back only $10,000. The lost $1000 of surplus can be seen in Figure 12.17(b), where the posttax consumer surplus, producer surplus, and government receipts from the tax are shaded in successively lighter shades. Comparing with the total surplus from before, what is missing is the little triangle that is heavily outlined. The surplus in this triangle is "lost" because the tax causes an inefficiently small amount of the good to be produced; firms stop short of the point where marginal cost gross of the tax equals marginal benefit.

Proving the Efficiency of Competitive Markets

The text proves that a competitive market equilibrium maximizes total surplus under fairly restrictive assumptions: Firms have rising marginal costs and no fixed costs, and consumers have utility functions of the form $u(x) + m$ for a concave u.

Proofs that work without these assumptions—that is, with somewhat weaker assumptions—are possible. I provide here a style of proof that is a good deal more general although a bit abstract.

Assume F firms produce the good in question, indexed by $f = 1, \ldots, F$. Each firm is characterized by a total cost function $\mathrm{TC}_f(z_f)$, where for this discussion, I use z_f to denote the amount of the good produced by firm f. I make no assumptions about these total cost functions.

Further assume I consumers can consume the good, indexed by $i = 1, \ldots I$. I cannot get away from assuming the consumers have *linear-in-money-left-over* utility functions of the form $v_i(x_i) + m_i$, where x_i is the amount of the good consumed by consumer i. (It is possible to deal with more general utility functions; see the following section.) I make no assumptions about the v_i functions.

I aim to prove the following: Suppose the economy is run by some mechanism: the market, a central planner, something. In the end, some total amount X of the good is produced. To produce X units of the good requires that the firms produce amounts z_f that sum to X. And the X units of the good must be split among the comsumers. Letting x^i be the share of consumer i, we need that

$$\sum_i x_i = X = \sum_f z_f.$$

Monetary transfers also are required: I let t_i be the amount of money consumer i gives up to get his x_i units, and I'll let s_f be the amount of money firm f takes in. These monetary transfers must balance:

$$\sum_i t_i = \sum_f s_f.$$

Under this sort of arrangement, consumer i's net benefit, measured in dollar terms, is $v_i(x_i) - t_i$, while firm f's net benefit, also measured in dollars, is $s_f - \text{TC}_f(z_f)$. Hence, the total benefit of such an arrangement is

$$\sum_i [v_i(x_i) - t_i] + \sum_f [s_f - \text{TC}_f(z_f)].$$

But, since the dollar transfers balance, this is

$$\sum_i v_i(x_i) - \sum_f \text{TC}_f(z_f). \tag{12.1}$$

I assert that a competitive market equilibrium allocation for this good maximizes the expression (12.1), over all arrangements for production and consumption of the good.

By a competitive market equilibrium, I mean levels of demand and supply that arise from supply equals demand: There is a price p for the good, consumption levels x_i^* for the consumers, and production levels z_f^* for the firms, where for each i, x_i^* maximizes the consumer's net utility $v_i(x_i) - px_i$ at the price p, for each f, z_f^* maximizes the firm's profit $pz_f - \text{TC}_f(z_f)$ at the price p, and supply equals demand, or $\sum_i x_i^* = \sum_f z_f^*$.

I prove this as follows. Let $\hat{x}_i$ and $\hat{z}_f$ be some other plan for consumption and production of the good that satisfies feasibility: $\sum_i \hat{x}_i = \sum_f \hat{z}_f$. Note that there is no reason to suppose that this sum is the same as $\sum_i x_i^*$; this alternative plan could involve some other total amount produced and consumed. We know that, for each consumer i,

$$v_i(x_i^*) - px_i^* \geq v_i(\hat{x}_i) - p\hat{x}_i,$$

since x_i^* is net utility maximizing at the price p for consumer i. And we know that, for each firm f,

$$pz_f^* - \text{TC}_f(z_f^*) \geq p\hat{z}_f - \text{TC}_f(\hat{z}_f),$$

since z_f^* maximizes the profit of firm f at price p. So, if we sum all these inequalities, for all consumers i and all firms f, we get

$$\sum_i [v_i(x_i^*) - px_i^*] + \sum_f [pz_f^* - \mathrm{TC}_f(z_f^*)] \geq \sum_i [v_i(\hat{x}_i) - p\hat{x}_i] + \sum_f [p\hat{z}_f - \mathrm{TC}_f(\hat{z}_f)].$$

But, since $\sum_i x_i^* = \sum_f z_f^*$, all the "money" terms on the left-hand side sum to a net 0. And, since $\sum_i \hat{x}_i = \sum_f \hat{z}_f$, all the "money" terms on the right-hand side sum to a net 0. Therefore, the inequality just written simplifies to

$$\sum_i v_i(x_i^*) - \sum_f \mathrm{TC}_f(z_f^*) \geq \sum_i v_i(\hat{x}_i) - \sum_f \mathrm{TC}_f(\hat{z}_f).$$

The market-equilibrium plan does at least as well as the alternative. But this is true of any alternative, so the market-equilibrium plan maxmizes the sum of the net benefits.

Competitive Markets Are Production Efficient

In the text, after proving (with some restrictive assumptions) that a competitive market equilibrium maximizes total surplus, this result was broken into three parts:

1. A competitive market equilibrium selects the right total quantity X to be produced and consumed.

2. A competitive market equilibrium arranges to have the total quantity X produced in a manner that minimizes the summed costs of the firms; it is production efficient.

3. A competitive market equilibrium arranges to have the total quantity X consumed in a manner that maximizes the total surplus generated from consumption; it is consumption efficient.

The manner of proof used in the preceding section is useful for proving these pieces separately. Let me illustrate with the second of these, production efficiency.

The question is the following: Suppose that, as commissar for the production of this good, you decide to produce X units in total. Your job as commissar for the production of the good is then to allocate this level of production among the F firms that can produce the good. You wish to do this to minimize the total cost of production. How do you do this?

This problem is, essentially, the problem from Section 9.3: How do you allocate production to F cost-independent production facilities or processes? Assuming that, if you are reading this, you have pretty good control of this stuff, I throw in a cryptic remark here: The assumption in Section 9.3 that the facilities or processes were cost independent is, in this context, an assumption that the firms do not generate any production externalities for one another; the total cost of production of a firm depends only on how much it produces.

Unlike in Section 9.3, I make no assumptions about the total cost functions TC_f of the different firms. With no assumptions, I assert the following:

Let $s_f(p)$ be the competitive-market supply function of firm f; that is, $s_f(p)$ is the solution to the problem of maximizing $pz - TC_f(z)$ for a fixed price p. Let $S(p)$ be the industry supply function, or $S(p) = \sum_f s_f(p)$. If the quantity X lies along the industry supply function (that is, if $X = S(p)$ for some price p), then the solution to the problem of procuring X units of the good as cheaply as possible is solved by having each firm produce its part of that supply; that is, have firm f produce $s_f(p)$ for the price p for which $X = S(p)$.

The proof is easy. Let $\hat{z}_f$ be some other production plan for firm f, such that $\sum_f \hat{z}_f = X$. Because each firm f maximizes its profit at the price p by producing $s_f(p)$, we know that

$$ps_f(p) - TC_f(s_f(p)) \geq p\hat{z}_f - TC_f(\hat{z}_f).$$

Sum this inequality over all the firms, and you get

$$\sum_f [ps_f(p) - TC_f(s_f(p))] \geq \sum_f [p\hat{z}_f - TC_f(\hat{z}_f)].$$

This inequality can be rewritten

$$p\left(\sum_f s_f(p)\right) - \sum_f TC_f(s_f(p)) \geq p\left(\sum_f \hat{z}_f\right) - \sum_f TC_f(\hat{z}_f).$$

The first terms on each side of inequality are both pX, since $X = \sum_f s_f(p) = \sum_f \hat{z}_f$. They cancel out. Multiply the inequality by -1, which flips the inequality sign, and you have precisely the inequality needed to verify the claim:

$$\sum_f TC_f(s_f(p)) \leq \sum_f TC_f(\hat{z}_f).$$

A Different Approach to the Invisible Hand: General Equilibrium

The method used in the previous two sections is also useful in proving that competitive markets are efficient in general. I italicized the *s* in markets because this subsection does something quite different from what we have done so far. So far, we looked at a single market in isolation. In this section, I show what is known as a *general equilibrium approach* to market efficiency, where we consider all markets in the economy at once. Warning: This is going to take a lot of setting up, and it becomes very abstract. It has nothing to do with anything that follows in the book. So read this section only for the sheer pleasure of it, and if you find what follows pleasing, you might wish to reconsider your career goals and think about getting a Ph.D. in economics.

The math that follows is not hard. But you must be comfortable with vector notation. Specifically, you must know that if p and x are two N-dimensional vectors, their "dot product," written $p \cdot x$, is $p_1 x_1 + p_2 x_2 + \ldots + p_N x_N$.

Rather than talk about the market in one product or another, we talk about the entire economy, all at once. In this economy, many products are made; let N be the number of products, and a vector $x = (x_1, \ldots, x_N)$ is a bundle giving quantities of each of these products. The economy is composed of a large number H of consumers, indexed by $h = 1, \ldots, H$, and a large number F of firms, indexed by $f = 1, \ldots, F$.

- Each consumer begins life with an initial endowment of goods and a utility function as in Chapter 5. Because this is general equilibrium, money left over is not an argument of anyone's utility function; we assume that all the consumer's purchases are being considered simultaneously. The symbol h might seem funny for consumer, but the tradition in this part of economics is to refer to *households* instead of consumers.

- Each firm is characterized by a technology for turning inputs into outputs.

Money in this model is used purely as an accounting device. It has no residual value to anyone except that it represents purchasing power. Firms are owned by consumers; if a firm earns a positive profit, that profit is distributed to its owners in proportion their shareholdings and, once distributed, is used to purchase consumption goods.

We let x^h (h here is a superscript and not a power) denote the final consumption bundle chosen by consumer h. The production plan of firm f is denoted by z^f, where negative components of z^f represent inputs and positive components denote outputs. The initial endowment of consumer h is denoted by e^h. (All these are

N-dimensional vectors.)

An *allocation* for this economy is a set of consumption bundles for all the households and production plans for all the firms. The allocation is *feasible* if each firm's production plan is technologically feasible for it and if the sum of goods consumed is less than the sum of initial endowments plus amounts produced (net of inputs to the production process), or

$$\sum_{n=1}^{H} x^h \le \sum_{h=1}^{H} e^h + \sum_{f=1}^{F} z^f.$$

The test of efficiency in this setting is not the maximization of total surplus but instead what economists call *Pareto efficiency*. A feasible allocation for this economy is *Pareto efficient* if there is no other feasible allocation such that, when it comes to consumption, every consumer gets as much utility in the alternative as in the original allocation and some single consumer gets more utility. In other words, we cannot improve the utility of any consumer without making someone else worse off. (Firm profits are not part of the measure of efficiency because profits are distributed to consumers; they are valuable only to the extent that consumers use them to improve their utility. We do not sum up consumer utilities because utilities are not measured on an equivalent "dollar-equals-utility" scale; utility functions are not of the money-left-over form.)

A market equilibrium for this economy is a feasible allocation (consumption and production plans) and a vector of nonnegative prices p for all the commodities such that (1) each firm is maximizing its profit at the prices p with its part of the allocation, and (2) each consumer is maximizing his or her uility, given prices p and given his or her resources, derived from the endowment the consumer starts with and profits paid out by the firms.

So far, no assumptions have been made about each firm's technology or each consumer's utility function. It is assumed that consumers maximize their utilities and that firms maximize profits. In addition, three other assumptions are made:

1. All consumers are *locally insatiable*. This is economic fancy talk for the property that each consumer, at each possible consumption bundle, can increase his or her utility if given a little more money to spend. If one of the goods always raises utility, that is more than adequate for this assumption. This assumption guarantees that a utility-maximizing consumer always spends all of his or her money. Since a consumer's wealth consists of his or her endowment and profits received from firms, this in turn ensures that, in a market equilibrium, with

prices p, consumption levels x^h, and firms' production plans z^f, the market value of all the consumption bundles equals the market value of consumer endowments plus the sum of firms' profits, or

$$\sum_h p \cdot x^h = \sum_h p \cdot e^h + \sum_f p \cdot z^f.$$

2. All markets are competitive or, in other words, all firms and all consumers are price takers.

3. Equilibrium prices are always nonnegative. This can be assumed directly or more primitive assumptions can be made that imply this. Examples of such more primitive assumptions are that at least one consumer has nondecreasing utility or at least one firm's technology permits free disposal of any commodity.

The big result, which is so important to economists that it is known as *the first theorem of welfare economics*, is that the allocation part of a market equilibrium is efficient. (This is the invisible hand at work, in a general equilibrium. In case you are comparing this with a more advanced textbook, you should know that general equilibria are often referred to as *Walrasian equilibria*.)

It is remarkably easy to prove this result. Suppose prices p, consumption bundles x^h for $h = 1, \ldots, H$, and production plans z^f for $f = 1, \ldots, F$ constitute a market equilibrium. If the allocation part is not efficient, some other feasible allocation, given by consumption bundles $\hat{x}^h$ and production plans $\hat{z}^f$, gives each consumer at least as much utility as the equilibrium allocation and gives one consumer more. Now, for the plan $(\hat{x}^h, \hat{z}^f)$ to be feasible, we must have

$$\sum_h \hat{x}^h \leq \sum_h e^h + \sum_f \hat{z}^f.$$

Since prices are nonnegative, we can multiply each side of this inequality by prices and keep the inequality, or

$$\sum_h p \cdot \hat{x}^h \leq \sum_h p \cdot e^h + \sum_f p \cdot \hat{z}^f.$$

Firm by firm, since z^f maximizes profits at the prices p, $p \cdot z^f \geq p \cdot \hat{z}^f$. Therefore,

$$\sum_f p \cdot \hat{z}^f \leq \sum_f p \cdot z^f.$$

And consumer by consumer, $p \cdot \hat{x}^h \geq p \cdot x^h$. This is true because x^h maximizes the consumer's utility subject to his (or her) budget constraint at the prices p. But $\hat{x}^h$ gives the consumer as much utility as x^h. If $\hat{x}^h$ gives much utility and is cheaper than x^h, then (by local insatiability) the consumer could do better than x^h at prices p. Moreover, for any consumer (and there is at least one) for whom $\hat{x}^h$ has higher utility than x^h, it must be that $p \cdot x^h < p \cdot \hat{x}^h$. Hence, summing over all consumers,

$$\sum_h p \cdot x^h < \sum_h p \cdot \hat{x}^h.$$

Now combine the three inequalities displayed in this paragraph:

$$\sum_h p \cdot x^h < \sum_h p \cdot \hat{x}^h \leq \sum_h p \cdot e^h + \sum_f p \cdot \hat{z}^f \leq \sum_h p \cdot e^h + \sum_f p \cdot z^f.$$

But, two paragraphs ago, we argued that the first and last terms in this progression must be equal. We have a contradiction to the assumption that the allocation part of a market equilibrium is not Pareto efficient.

Material for Chapter 13

Taxes, Subsidies, Administered Prices, and Quotas

Solution to Problem 13.1

The first step is to find the pretax equilibrium. This is where supply equals demand, or

$$2000(p-4) = 1000(10-p) \text{ or } 2p-8 = 10-p \text{ or } 3p = 18,$$

which is $p = \$6$. This gives an equilibrium quantity of 4000 units.

The slope of the demand function is -1000, so the absolute value of the slope of inverse demand is $1/1000 = 0.001$. The slope of the supply function is 2000, so the slope of inverse supply is $1/2000 = 0.0005$. Now we can use the formulas:

- The change in price is $[(0.001)/(0.001 + 0.0005)]\$0.30 = \$0.20$, so the new price is $\$6.20$.

- The change in quantity is $0.30/(0.001 + 0.0005) = 200$, so the new quantity is $4000 - 200 = 3800$.

- The deadweight cost is $(0.5)(0.3)^2/(0.001 + 0.0005) = \$30$.

- The relative burden on consumers is $0.001/0.0005$, or 2 to 1.

Lost consumer and producer surplus are, approximately, the change in the "effective" price times the number of units. For consumers, the effective price rises from $\$6$ to $\$6.20$, so this is approximately $\$0.20 \times 4000 = \$800$; for firms, their effective price falls from $\$6$ to $\$5.90$, so this is $\$0.10 \times 4000 = \$400$. To be exact, we have to take into account that the number of units changes with the tax: Precise consumer surplus loss, for instance, is a quadrilateral of height $\$0.20$ and parallel sides 3800 and 4000, for a precise area of $[(3800 + 4000)/2] \times \$0.20 = \$780$. Precise loss in producer surplus is, similarly, \$390.

All these calculations can be done without the formulas, just on first principles. For instance, with a tax of \$0.30, inverse supply increases by \$0.30. Inverse supply pretax is $P(x) = x/2000 + 4$, so posttax it is $x/2000 + 4.3$, and posttax supply is $S(p) = 2000(p - 4.3)$. Solving posttax supply equals demand gives

$$2000(p - 4.3) = 1000(10 - p) \text{ or } 2p - 8.6 = 10 - p \text{ or } 3p = 18.6,$$

giving $p = \$6.20$. Just for the exercise, let me also calculate the change in consumer surplus from "first principles": Pretax consumer surplus is a right triangle with height \$4 and base 4000 units, or \$8000. Posttax, it is a right triangle with height \$3.80 and base 3800 units, or \$7220, a net loss of \$780.

Solution to Problem 13.2

The key to deriving the formulas is to figure out the change in price and the change in quantity in terms of the size of the tax and the slopes of inverse supply and demand. Once you have those, the other formulas are easy. To derive these two, follow along on Figure 13.12.

The tax raises inverse supply by the amount of the tax, t. Hence, the fall off in quantity, or ΔX, must give an increase in inverse demand and a decrease in inverse supply that sum to t. In the figure, a denotes the increase in inverse demand; as a function of the slope of inverse demand, we have

$$a = |\text{Slope}_{\text{ID}}|\Delta X.$$

The decrease in inverse supply, denoted by b, is

$$b = \text{Slope}_{\text{IS}}\Delta X.$$

So $a + b = t$ is

$$|\text{Slope}_{\text{ID}}|\Delta X + \text{Slope}_{\text{IS}}\Delta X = t \text{ or } \Delta X = \frac{t}{|\text{Slope}_{\text{ID}}| + \text{Slope}_{\text{IS}}}.$$

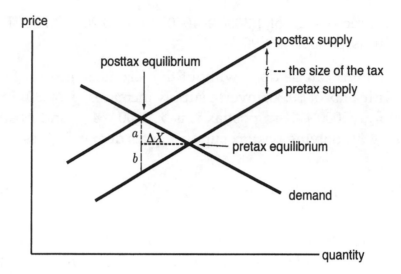

Figure 13.12. Deriving the formulas for ΔP and ΔX. (See the text for the derivation.)

The change in price, which is just a, it then

$$a = |\text{Slope}_{\text{ID}}|\Delta X = \frac{|\text{Slope}_{\text{ID}}|}{|\text{Slope}_{\text{ID}}| + \text{Slope}_{\text{IS}}}\, t.$$

From this point, the remaining formulas are relatively easy.

Solution to Problem 13.4

Refer to Figure 13.13. Without the tax, production is at the level y, where marginal cost equals marginal revenue. If the tax is imposed, this raises the marginal cost function by the amount of the tax. This causes the quantity chosen by the firm to fall somewhat. How big is Δy, the fall in quantity? If the tax is of size t, Δy must be set so that the gap between the old marginal cost curve and the marginal revenue curve opens up to size t. As long as t is small, the rate at which the gap grows is

$$\frac{d\text{MC}(y)}{dy} - \frac{d\text{MR}(y)}{dy}.$$

Therefore,

$$\Delta y \times \left(\frac{d\text{MC}(y)}{dy} - \frac{d\text{MR}(y)}{dy} \right) = t$$

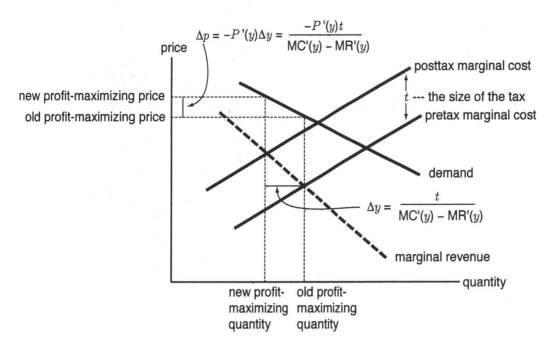

Figure 13.13. Problem 13.4: The incidence of a tax on a monopolist, in general.

or, using primes to denote derivatives,

$$\Delta y = \frac{t}{\mathrm{MC}'(y) - \mathrm{MR}'(y)}.$$

Letting $P(y)$ denote the inverse demand curve, this fall in quantity causes prices to rise by the amount

$$-P'(y)\Delta y = \frac{-P'(y)t}{\mathrm{MC}'(y) - \mathrm{MR}'(y)},$$

so the proportion of the tax that is passed on to the consumer is

$$\frac{-P'(y)}{\mathrm{MC}'(y) - \mathrm{MR}'(y)}.$$

Since I promised you some second derivatives, let me rewrite this a bit: $\mathrm{TR}(y) = yP(y)$, so that $\mathrm{MR}(y) = P(y) + yP'(y)$, and $\mathrm{MR}'(y) = P'(y) + P'(y) + yP''(y) = 2P'(y) + yP''(y)$. Therefore, the proportion of the tax passed on to the consumer is

$$\frac{-P'(y)}{\mathrm{MC}'(y) - 2P'(y) - yP''(y)}.$$

This offers little intuition, but let me note one consequence: The more steeply sloped is marginal cost, the more of the tax is borne by the producer.

Solution to Problem 13.6

Without the subsidy, the firm equates marginal cost to marginal revenue, or

$$100 - 0.002x = 20.$$

This give $x = 40,000$ and a price of $60. Consumer surplus is the area of a right triangle with height $40 (from $100 to $60) and a base of 40,000 units, which is $800,000. Producer surplus is just producer profit, a rectangle with height $40 and base 40,000 units, or $1.6 million. Hence, total surplus is $2.4 million (see Figure 13.14(a).)

The subsidy of $4 lowers the firm's marginal cost function by $4, to a constant $16. Now, marginal revenue equals marginal cost gives a quantity of 42,000 and a price of $58. Consumer surplus is the area of a right triangle with height $42 and base 42,000 units, which is $882,000. Producer surplus, or profit, is the area of a rectangle with height $42 and base 42,000 units, or $1.764 million. (See Figure 13.14(b).) The government spends $4 on each of 42,000 units, or $168,000. Therefore, the net surplus is

$$\$0.882 \text{ million } + \$1.764 \text{ million } - \$0.168 \text{ million } = \$2.478 \text{ million} .$$

Surplus has *risen* by $78,000. The reason is that the monopolist, presubsidy, stops short of the socially optimal level of production, which is 80,000 units, where the demand function intersects marginal cost. The subsidy increases the level of production, getting us 2000 units closer to the social optimum. The increase in total surplus is the "value" of those 2000 units in consumption less their cost of production, which is the heavily outlined quadrilateral in Figure 13.14(c).

(b) Once the concession is established, as long as the concessionaire's prices are not regulated, the concessionaire is a virtual monopolist on services inside the park. Assuming the concessionaire is a profit maximizer, it will set prices too high and produce too low a level of services, relative to the social optimum. As in part a, by subsidizing the concessionaire—more specifically, by lowering its marginal cost— the concessionaire is pushed toward the levels of service and prices that are socially optimal.

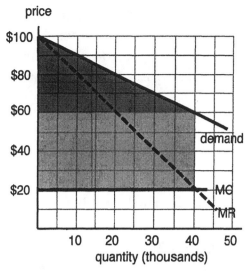

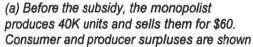

(a) Before the subsidy, the monopolist produces 40K units and sells them for $60. Consumer and producer surpluses are shown

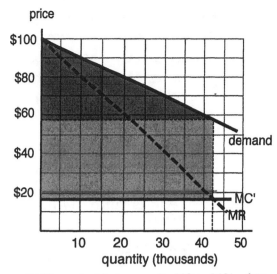

(b) The subsidy lowers its MC to MC' = $16. Production increases, and price falls to $58. Consumer and producer surplus both increase.

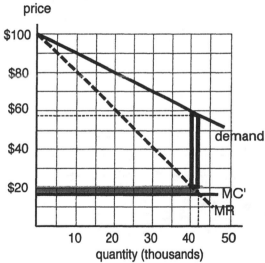

(c) The cost of the subsidy is the shaded rectangle, so the net impact of the subsidy is to **raise** surplus by the area of the heavily outlined quadrilateral.

Figure 13.14. A subsidized monopolist. A small subsidy on a monopolist increases the monopolist's output, compensating for the monopolist's tendency to underproduce relative to the socially efficient level of production and moving the outcome toward greater (net) efficiency.

But, does this mean a transfer of government funds to a monopoly concessionaire? Not necessarily, assuming the auction for the concession is competitive. Potential concessionaires, aware of these subsidies, increase their bids for the business. Although we do not quite have the tools (yet) to discuss how the auction process will go, it should not be too hard to imagine that the bids of prospective concessionaires will rise by the (effective) total subsidy they will receive, so the government gets back at least the concessionaire's share of increased surplus due to the subsidy.

Solution to Problem 13.7

So that it is easier to read, I use $ to denote the local currency.

(a) The current equilibrium is where supply equals demand, or where

$$25,000(p-4) = 5000(10-p) \quad \text{or} \quad 30,000p = 150,000 \quad \text{or} \quad p = \$5.$$

At this price, quantities are 25,000 kgs.

The equilibrium is depicted in Figure 13.15. Profits are given by the lightly shaded triangle, which has length 25,000 kgs and height $1 per kilogram, for a total area of $\frac{1}{2} \times 25,000 \times \$1 = \$12,500$. Consumer surplus is given by the heavily shaded triangle, which has length 25,000 kgs and height $5 per kilogram, for an area of $\frac{1}{2} \times 25,000 \times \$5 = \$62,500$.

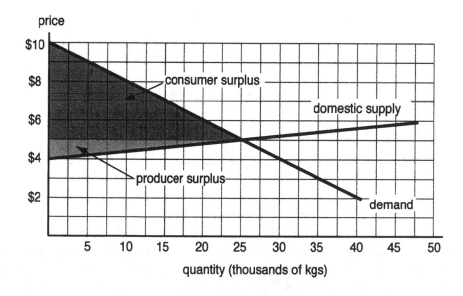

Figure 13.15. No importation allowed.

(b) If the free importation of sorghum were allowed, the picture would be as in Figure 13.16. Supply would be completely elastic (flat) at a price of $3; and the domestic sorghum industry would be put completely out of business. Equilibrium consumption of sorghum would be 35,000 kgs, so total consumer surplus would be the area of the shaded triangle in Figure 13.16. This has base 35,000 kgs and height $7 per kilogram, for a total of $\frac{1}{2} \times 35,000 \times \$7 = \$122,500$. Hence consumer surplus is increased by $60,000 if the free importation of sorghum is allowed. Note that the total impact on Freedonian society, measured as the sum of consumer and producer surplus, would be a net gain of $60,000 - \$12,500 = \$47,500$.

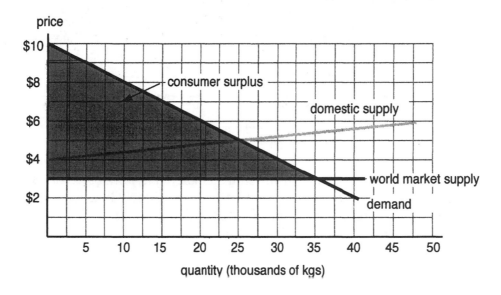

Figure 13.16. Free importation of sorghum.

(c) The subsidy has to lower the marginal costs of domestic growers enough that the subsidized marginal cost at 25,000 total output is $3. Since this is just a movement of the domestic inverse supply function downward by the amount of the subsidy, we can solve it algebraically or graphically. For the graphical solution, see Figure 13.17; the answer is a subsidy of $2 per kilogram. For an algebraic solution, let r be the amount of the subsidy, and we need to solve $25,000(p - 4 + r) = 25,000$ at $p = 3$. This is $3 - 4 + r = 1$,, which is $r = 2$.

Since the market price would be $3 per kilogram, demand and consumer surplus would be as in part b; demand is 35,000 kgs, and consumer surplus is $122,500. The domestic growers are in precisely the position of part a (except that they get $2 less per kilogram gross but the same amount net, once the subsidy is accounted for), so they sell 25,000 kgs and make $12,500 in profits. The government spends $2 per kilogram for each of the 25,000 kgs produced domestically, for a total subsidy bill of $50,000.

(d) The comparison of the three scenarios (the status quo, free importation of sorghum, and subsidized production plus free importation) is delayed until the

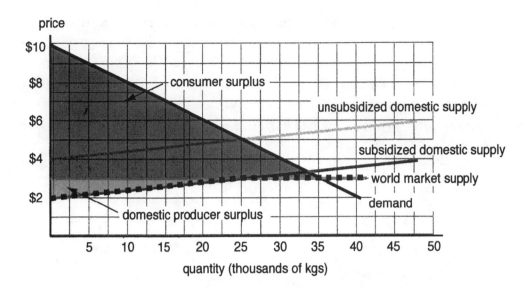

Figure 13.17. A subsidy for farmers. A subsidy of $2 per kilogram for the farmers lowers their inverse supply function by that amount so that, at the world price of $3 per kilogram, domestic supply is the 25,000 kgs from part a. The supply function follows the heavy dashes: domestic supply until the price reaches $3, and then unlimited supply from the world market at $3 per kilogram. Freedonian consumer and producter surpluses are as shown.

completion of Problem 13.8.

Solution to Problem 13.8

I do not provide the details of this scenario but I provide a summary of this scenario and those from Problem 13.7 in Table 13.1.

	no imports allowed	free importation of sorghum	$2 subsidy & free imports	licenses for 10 friends
consumer surplus	$62,500.00	$122,500.00	$122,500.00	$71,106.00
domestic farm profits	$12,500.00	$0.00	$12,500.00	$5,555.00
government net revenue	n/a	n/a	-$50,000.00	n/a
profits of political cronies	n/a	n/a	n/a	$16,667.00
total surplus	$75,000	$122,500	$85,000	$93,328
deadweight cost vs. free imports	$47,500	n/a	$37,500	$29,172

Table 13.1. Comparing the four regimes in Problems 13.7 and 13.8.

Solution to Problem 13.9

Hints: (1) In which scenario is total surplus, including the surplus of foreign producers, greater? (2) What are the profits of foreign producers, if the worldwide supply of rice is flat?

Solution to Problem 13.11

This problem can be done either graphically or algebraically. I give the answers both ways.

(a) Figure 13.18 shows supply and demand. Demand is obvious. For supply, I note that each firm's marginal costs are $4 + y$, so at prices below 4 the firms supply nothing, while at prices 4 and above, the supply from a single firm at price p is the solution to price equals marginal cost, or $p = 4 + y$, or $s(p) = p - 4$. Since there are 10 firms, this makes supply equal to $S(p) = 10(p - 4)$ (again, for prices above 4). The two intersect at a quantity of 80 and $p = 12$, which is the equilibrium.

If you want this algebraically, we equate supply to demand, getting

$$10(20 - p) = 10(p - 4) \quad \text{or} \quad 240 = 20p \quad \text{or} \quad p = 12,$$

and from that we compute that the equilibrium quantity is 80.

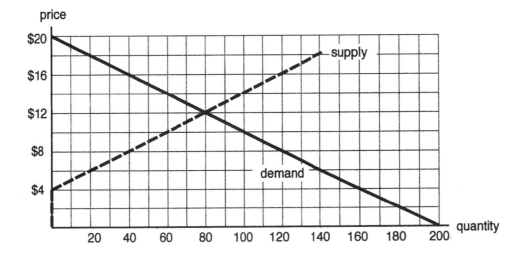

Figure 13.18. Problem 13.11(a): Supply equals demand.

(b) The five firms that receive a subsidy have their marginal costs lowered by $1. So, for each of them, supply at price p (now for $p \geq 3$) is the solution to $p = 3 + s(p)$, or $s(p) = p - 3$, and their supply in total (since there are five of them) is $S_1(p) = 5(p-3)$. (The subscript 1 denotes the first group of firms.) The five firms that must pay a tax have their marginal costs raised by $1. So for each of them, supply starts at a price of 5 and is the solution to $p = 5 + s(p)$, or $s(p) = p - 5$. There are five of them, so their supply is $S_2(p) = 5(p-5)$. This means that, at prices above 5, the total supply is

$$S(p) = S_1(p) + S_2(p) = 5(p - 3) + 5(p - 5) = 10p - 40,$$

or *precisely the same supply curve as before*. Note carefully, this is true only at prices above 5; at prices below 5 (and above 3), supply is only from the subsidized firms, and supply is $5(p - 3)$. All this drawn on Figure 13.19. Note that the supply from the five subsidized firms is drawn at all levels of price.

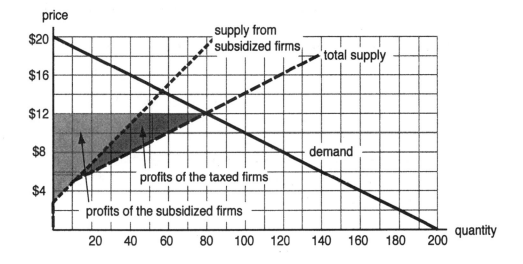

Figure 13.19 Problem 13.11(b): Supply equals demand.

Hence, supply equals demand just where it did before, at $p = 12$ and a quantity of 80. Note that the five subsidized firms provide $5(12 - 3) = 45$ units (or 9 units apiece), while the five taxed firms provide $5(12 - 5) = 35$ units (or 7 units apiece). So the government is paying out $10 more in subsidies than it is taking in from the tax.

(c) Consumer surplus does not change from one equilibrium to the other. In both cases, it is the area of a triangle with a base of 80 (units) and a height of $8, or $320.

In the original equilibrium, total profits of the firms is given by a triangle with a base of 80 units and a height of $8, or $320. In the new equilibrium, the profits of the five subsidized firms is the lightly shaded area in Figure 13.19, a triangle with a base of 45 units and a height of $9, or $202.50, while the profits of the five taxed firms is the more heavily shaded region in Figure 13.20, a triangle with a base of 35 units and a height of $7, or $122.50. So total profits are $325.

The government is a net 0 in the original equilibrium, and it comes up $10 in the red in the new equilibrium, as noted in part b. But in the old equilibrium, 40 units were being produced by the polluters, a cost to society of $80, while now only 35 units are being produced by the polluters, a cost of $70.

So the total surplus to society was $320 + $320 + $0 − $80 = $560, and now it is $320 + $325 − $10 − $70 = $565. Finally, we have a government policy that raises social surplus in a perfectly competitive market. Think back to the discussion in Chapter 12, in which we claimed that an unfettered competitive market would maximize social surplus. Here is a case where (apparently) it does not, so here is a case in which one of the implicit assumptions made in that argument fails. The key word here is *externalities*, of which pollution is a prime example; this is next on our agenda.

Material for Chapter 14

Externalities

Solution to Problem 14.1

Partial answers:

(a) $n_T = 40{,}000$ and $n_B = 360{,}000$.

(c) $n_T = 60{,}000$ and $n_B = 340{,}000$.

(d) $0.50 toll for the bridge.

Solution to Problem 14.2

(a) In part a, there is no possibility of entry or exit. Assuming X is the total catch, the marginal cost for any fisherman is

$$\text{MC}(x) = 10 + \frac{X}{1000} + \frac{2x}{100},$$

so supply by a single fisherman is where marginal cost equals price, or

$$p = 10 + \frac{X}{1000} + \frac{2s(p)}{100} \quad \text{or} \quad s(p) = 50\left(p - 10 - \frac{X}{1000}\right).$$

Total supply by 10 fishermen is

$$S(p) = 500\left(p - 10 - \frac{X}{1000}\right).$$

Supply equals demand is

$$500\left(p - 10 - \frac{X}{1000}\right) = 5000(60 - p),$$

or

$$p - 10 - \frac{X}{1000} = 10(60 - p) \quad \text{or} \quad 11p = 610 + \frac{X}{1000}.$$

But $X = 5000(60 - p)$, so this equation is

$$11p = 610 + 5(60 - p) \quad \text{or} \quad 16p = 910,$$

which is $p = \$56.875$, $X = 15{,}625$, and $x = 1562.5$.

(b) If there is free entry and exit from the market, the price falls until it equals the minimum average cost of fishermen. So first we find the efficient scale by equating marginal and average cost:

$$10 + \frac{X}{1000} + \frac{2x}{100} = \frac{10{,}000}{x} + 10 + \frac{X}{1000} + \frac{x}{100},$$

which gives 1000 for efficient scale and (therefore) minimum average cost ($=$ MC(1000)) of

$$10 + \frac{X}{1000} + \frac{2 \times 1000}{100} = 30 + \frac{X}{1000}.$$

This must equal p, the equilibrium price. But, if p is the equilibrium price, then $X = 5000(60 - p)$. So we have the equation that determines p:

$$30 + \frac{5000(60 - p)}{1000} = p \quad \text{or} \quad 330 = 6p \quad \text{or} \quad p = \$55.$$

This gives a total quantity of $5000(60 - 55) = 25{,}000$, which means 25 active fishermen.

Of course, each fisherman earns 0 profit. Consumer surplus is a triangle with height \$5 (per pound) and base 25,000 lbs, for the total consumer surplus of \$62,500.

(c) By imposing a tax of \$6 per lb of fish, both the marginal and average costs of fishermen are raised by \$6. This does not change the efficient scale of 1000, but it does change minimum average cost to

$$36 + \frac{X}{1000}.$$

This must be the new (posttax) price, and to find p, we have to solve

$$36 + \frac{5000(60 - p)}{1000} = p \quad \text{or} \quad 336 = 6p \quad \text{or} \quad p = \$56.$$

This gives a total quantity of 20,000 lbs of fish and 20 active fishermen. Producer surplus is 0, and consumer surplus is $\frac{1}{2} \times \$4 \times 20,000 = \$40,000$. But net government revenues are $\$6 \times 20,000 = \$120,000$. So total surplus rises, and substantially, by virtue of this tax.

Because of the externality in fishing costs and the free entry assumption, it is not easy to find the inefficiency on a graph. But, in general, the cause of the free-market inefficiency is clear: Each fisherman, by raising the costs of others, exerts a negative externality. By taxing fish to depress the level of fishing, the externality is reduced.

What level of output maximizes social surplus? We first note that the efficient scale is 1000, regardless of industry scale. So, if we are going to produce X units in total, it is most efficient to have $X/1000$ firms. Ignoring the problem of a noninteger number of firms, the total cost for providing X most cheaply is

$$10,000 \frac{X}{1000} + \left(10 + \frac{X}{1000}\right) X + \frac{X}{1000} \times \frac{1 \text{ million}}{100} = 10X + 10X + \frac{X^2}{1000} + 10X.$$

Hence, the true marginal cost is $30 + X/500$, and this equals marginal utility (which tracks inverse demand) where

$$30 + \frac{X}{500} = 60 - \frac{X}{5000} \quad \text{or} \quad 30 = \frac{11X}{5000} \quad \text{or} \quad X = 13,636.$$

Now, in fact, this does not quite work, because $X = 13,636$ implies 13.636 fishermen (if each catches 1000 lbs. of fish). But this indicates that the answer is probably to have 13 or 14 fishermen. At this point, if you go to a spreadsheet (sheet 2 of CHAP14), you can find that the social optimum, taking into account the integer nature of fishermen, is to have 14 fishermen and a total catch of 13,779 lbs of fish; I leave it to you to figure out how this spreadsheet works. And I leave it to you to see how close you can get to this social optimum with the optimal-sized tax on fish.

Solution to Problem 14.4

(a) If this is a private good, then the socially efficient outcome is where marginal utility (measured, with this sort of utility function, in dollars per unit) equals marginal cost. Since marginal cost is a constant $3, this occurs for the first sort of individual, with utility function $24\ln(x_i + 1) + m_i$, where $24/(x_i + 1) = 3$, or $x_i = 7$. For individuals with utility function $12\ln(x_i + 1) + m_i$, this is where $12/(x_i + 1) = 3$, or $x_i = 3$. For individuals with the utility function $6\ln(x_i + 1) + m_i$ this is where $6/(x_i+1) = 3$, or $x_i = 1$. And for individuals with the utility function $\ln(x_i+1)+m_i$ or $.5\ln(x_i + 1) + m_i$, this is at $x_i = 0$, since for these individuals, marginal utility at $x_i = 0$ is 1 or 0.5, which is less than marginal cost.

So the answer is to produce 11 million units of the good, giving 7 to each of the 1 million folks with the first utility function, 3 to each of the second 1 million folks, 1 to each of the 1 million folks with $k_i = 6$, and none to the last 2 million folks.

(b) If the good is a public good and if X units are produced in total, then the total surplus generated is

$$1 \text{ million} \times 24\ln(X + 1) + 1 \text{ million} \times 12\ln(X + 1) + 1 \text{ million} \times 6\ln(X + 1)+$$
$$1 \text{ million} \times \ln(X + 1) + 1 \text{ million} \times 0.5\ln(X + 1) - 3X = 43{,}500{,}000\ \ln(X + 1) - 3.$$

This is maximized where the derivative in X equals 0, or where

$$43{,}500{,}000\left[\frac{1}{X+1}\right] - 3 = 0, \quad \text{or} \quad X = 14{,}499{,}999.$$

It is interesting that the total amount of the good produced is more here than would be the case if the good were a private good. But it is much more than that: In part a, individuals consume 0 or 1 or 3 or 7 units of the good. Here, each consumes almost 14.5 million units. If consumption of, say, Yosemite National Park were a matter of private consumption, individuals would consume very little "park." But efficiency leads to the conclusion that, if millions of folks can consume this in the manner of a public good—and I hasten to add that, with Yosemite Park, there is some congestion that makes it less than a pure public good—then a *lot* more park is consumed by each individual.

(c) If a person with utility function $24\ln(x_i + 1)$ assumes that no one else makes any contribution, then she chooses the contribution c_i to maximize $24\ln(c_i/3 + 1) - c_i$, which gives $c_i = \$21$. And if everyone else anticipates that she would contribute this amount, then each chooses a contribution c_i to maximize

$$k_i \ln((21 + c_i)/3 + 1) - c_i,$$

where $k_i = 24, 12, 6, 1,$ or 0.5, depending on which of the five types of individual this person is. I let you do the checking, but with the constraint that the contribution c_i must be nonnegative (an individual can't withdraw funds from the collection plate), the answer in every case is $c_i = 0$. Once the total contributions from any source are expected to be $21 or more, no one has a further incentive to contribute voluntarily. With public goods, the free rider problem is ferocious.

(d) The person who obtains the least utility from this arrangement is a member of the fifth group, with utility function $0.5 \ln(X + 1) - m_i$. For $X = 14{,}499{,}999$, this person's utility is $\ln(14{,}499{,}999)$ less the tax contribution required, which is $3 \times 14{,}499{,}999/5{,}000{,}000 = \$8.70$. Excel computes $0.5 \ln(14{,}499{,}999) = \$8.24$, so this person is worse off for being taxed to provide this public good.

(e) Suppose the monopolist produces X units of the public good. It can then charge members of the first group up to $24 \ln(X + 1)$ dollars for the privilege of consuming the good, members of the second group up to $12 \ln(X + 1)$, and so forth. It charges one of those five prices or a penny or two less; it has no reason to charge any less.

If it charges $24 \ln(X + 1)$, the net take will be

$$1 \text{ million} \times 24 \ln(X + 1) - 3X,$$

which is maximized in X where

$$\frac{24{,}000{,}000}{X + 1} = 3 \quad \text{or} \quad X = 7{,}999{,}999.$$

If it charges $12 \ln(X + 1)$, 2 million citizens sign up, for a net take of

$$2 \text{ million} \times 12 \ln(X + 1) - 3X,$$

which is maximized in X where

$$\frac{24{,}000{,}000}{X + 1} = 3 \quad \text{or} \quad X = 7{,}999{,}999.$$

If it charges $6\ln(X + 1)$, 3 million citizens sign up, for a net take of

$$3 \text{ million} \times 6\ln(X + 1) - 3X,$$

which is maximized in X where

$$\frac{18,000,000}{X + 1} = 3 \quad \text{or} \quad X = 5,999,999.$$

If it charges $\ln(X + 1)$, 4 million citizens sign up, for a net take of

$$4 \text{ million} \times \ln(X + 1) - 3X,$$

which is maximized in X where

$$\frac{4,000,000}{X + 1} = 3 \quad \text{or} \quad X = 1,333,332.33.$$

And if it charges $0.5\ln(X + 1)$, all five million individuals sign up, for a net take of

$$5 \text{ million} \times 0.5\ln(X + 1) - 3X,$$

which is maximized in X where

$$\frac{2,500,000}{X + 1} = 3, \quad \text{or} \quad X = 833,332.33.$$

To find out which of these five gives the highest profit for the monopolist, we need to resort to a spreadsheet; Figure 14.7 shows you sheet 1 of PROB14.4. For each of the five "levels of service," we compute the price that would be charged, total revenue, and profit to the monopolist. We also compute the total amount of surplus generated by the arrangement. The numbers show that a monopolist is indifferent between serving only 1 million citizens or 2 million; the "tie" is because it gets twice the price with 1 million because the coefficients are 24 and 12, but twice as many people pay the lower price. In comparison with the efficient outcome, it

	C	D	E	F	G	H	
6	Number of Citizens Who Sign	1,000,000	2,000,000	3,000,000	4,000,000	5,000,000	
7	Level of X provided	7,999,999	7,999,999	5,999,999	1,333,332.33	833,332.33	
8	Gross utility = Price to enter	$381.48	$190.74	$93.64	$14.10	$6.82	
9	Gross revenue	$381,478,850	$381,478,850	$280,930,860	$56,412,771	$34,082,972	
10	Cost	$23,999,997	$23,999,997	$17,999,997	$3,999,997	$2,499,997	
11							
12	PROFIT	$357,478,853	$357,478,853	$262,930,863	$52,412,774	$31,582,976	
13	TOTAL SURPLUS PRODUCED	$357,478,853	$548,218,279	$637,505,344.14	$602,437,286	$590,543,724	

Sheet1 / Sheet2 / Sheet3 /

Figure 14.7. Problem 14.4(e): Finding the optimal price scheme for a public good with exclusion. Five different "entry prices" can be tried, each the best for pursuing a subset of the entire citizenry. In this case, the first two, which go after the smallest sets of citizens, are tied for optimal.

serves fewer people (for a public good, it is always efficient to serve everyone) and restricts the output level as well.

About Public Goods

With Problem 14.4 as background, a few general remarks about public goods are in order. Throughout this discussion, I imagine a society with N citizens, indexed $i = 1, \ldots, N$, who have linear-in-dollars-left-over style utility. Suppose that, if Y units of a particular public good is produced and if exclusion is either impossible or not practiced, then the gross gain of utility of consumer i, measured on a dollars-left-over scale, is $u_i(Y)$. If consumer i is excluded from the consumption of the public good, his gross gain in utility is $u_i(0)$. Therefore, if we charge consumer i the amount c_i for the public good and do not exclude him, his net benefit is $u_i(Y) - c_i$. To keep matters simple, I assume that it costs kY to supply Y units of the public good. Also suppose that $u_i(\cdot)$ is a nondecreasing function: No one prefers less of the public good to more, although we do not rule out the possibility that some people attach no (marginal) utility to more. (I also assume in what follows that $u_i(\cdot)$ is a concave function.)

How Much Public Good to Provide: The Ideal

If the objective is to maximize the sum of the (dollar-measured) net consumer utility, how much of this public good should be provided? If we want to maximize the sum of net consumer utility, there would be no reason to exclude anyone; if Y units are provided to a subset of the population, it costs nothing to extend this provision to everyone.

Hence, we want to find the value of Y that maximizes $\sum_{i=1}^{N} u_i(Y) - kY$, or the sum of gross gains in utility less the dollar cost of providing the good. To maximize this, set the derivative in Y equal to 0, getting the optimality condition

$$\sum_{i=1}^{n} \frac{du_i(Y)}{dY} = k.$$

In words, the sum of the marginal utilities for the public good, summed over all the citizens in the society, should equal the marginal cost of the public good.

Compare this with the level of private good provision that maximizes the sum of consumer surpluses. If Y units of a private good are produced, at a cost to society of $c(Y)$, and those Y units are divided among the citizens with citizen i getting y_i units of the good, the net gain to society is $\sum_{i=1}^{N} u_i(y_i) - kY = \sum_{i+1}^{N} u_i(y_i) - k(y_1 + \ldots + y_N)$. As we saw in Chapter 12, to maximize this we set $u_i'(y_i) = k$, or the marginal utility of each citizen's share of the private good should equal the marginal cost of producing all of the private good; hence, marginal utilities should be equal across citizens.

These are very different rules. To see how different they are, we can represent them graphically. We already know how to represent graphically the private-goods rule: We sum *horizontally* the marginal utility functions of each individual consumer, which is his or her inverse demand function, and see where this hits society's marginal-cost-of-provision function. But, with a public good, we want to equate marginal cost to the sum of the marginal utilities. So instead of summing individual marginal utilities horizontally, we have to sum them *vertically* (see Figure 14.8).

In Problem 14.4, consumers consumed more of the good if it were public than if it were private. Indeed, in the problem, if the good were a private good, the amount consumed by each consumer at the social optimum was on the order of a few units of the good, while the amount consumed by each consumer if the good is public was on the order of millions of units. And the total amount of the good produced if it were a public good was more than the total amount produced if the good were private. The first of these (that per capita consumption is more when the good is a public good than when it is private) is quite general, but the rest most certainly is not general. If you are unsure about this, consider the simple case in which all consumers are identical, with linear marginal utility $u_i'(y) = 10 - y$. Assume that k, the marginal cost of provision, is 1. Then, if the good is private, each consumer gets 9 units of the good at the efficient outcome. If there are 1 million citizens, 9 million units are produced. But if the good is a public good, then the amount produced

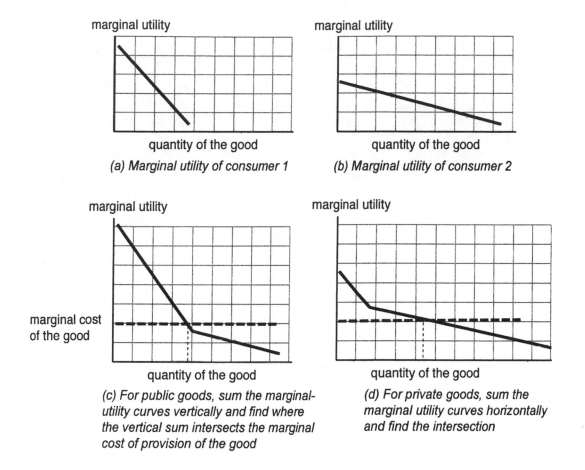

(a) Marginal utility of consumer 1

(b) Marginal utility of consumer 2

marginal cost of the good

(c) For public goods, sum the marginal-utility curves vertically and find where the vertical sum intersects the marginal cost of provision of the good

(d) For private goods, sum the marginal utility curves horizontally and find the intersection

Figure 14.8. The efficient level of production of a private good and a public good, for two consumers. In this case, more of the good is produced in total if it is a private good (panel d) than if it is a public good (panel c), but remember that the good must be divided between the two consumers if it is a private good; each consumer consumes the full amount of the good in panel c, while each gets only a share of the amount indicated in panel d. (In panel d, a bit more than 4 units of the good are provided. Slightly more than half of this goes to consumer 1. How do I know this?)

never exceeds 10 units, no matter how many citizens there are, because at 10 units, every citizen's marginal utility for the good is 0.

The Free-Rider Problem and Private Provision of Public Goods

Public goods are typically provided by collectives, such as governments, rather than privately. The reason is the one we saw in part c of Problem 14.4: Public goods suffer from a very strong free-rider problem. Specifically, suppose funds for the public good are provided by voluntary subscription. If enough funds have been contributed to give Y units of the public good, citizen i, deciding whether to contribute more for his own benefit, asks how $u_i'(Y)$ compares to k. Specifically, if $u_i'(Y) \leq k$, citizen i has no desire to contribute any more funds, while if $u_i'(Y) > k$ and citizen i believes that no one will contribute more, his incentives are to contribute up to the point where the funds collected are sufficient to finance Y_i^* units, where Y_i^* solves $u_i'(Y_i^*) = k$. In other words, for private reasons, citizens are ready to subscribe funds so that the total amount of the public good matches what they would choose for themselves if they were buying a private good for personal consumption.

This means that, once private contributions reach the level sufficient to finance the largest "private goods consumption level" (that is, $\max_i Y_i^*$), no one has any incentive to contribute more. Everyone wants a free ride on the contributions made by others.

So what does society do to get closer to the efficient level of public good provision? One possibility is to raise the marginal utility of donors for their donations. Societies can impose guilt on nongivers or provide esteem and public acclaim to those who make very large contributions. The first is a description of a norm of giving; the latter is why public benefactors get their names on buildings and other public goods they provide.

A second possibility, if the good is a public good with the possibility of exclusion, is to exclude those citizens who do not contribute an "entry" or "use" fee. Things might be arranged so that a private provider is given the right to provide this public good and exclude those who do not contribute. But, in such instances, society wants to be very careful in regulating the private provider. You saw some of this in part e of Problem 14.4; to learn more about this situation, an interesting exercise is to work through similar exercise if society consists of 1 million identical citizens, each with $u_i'(y_i) = 10 - y_i$, and if $k = 1$.

Most often, though, the government steps in, using its power to coerce contributions through the power to tax. In such circumstances, the government faces two basic problems:

First, the government must decide how much of the public good to provide. Interest-group politics makes this as much a political issue as an economic one, but suppose, taking a very idealistic perspective, that the government wishes to maximize total surplus. The government must try to ascertain the marginal values of each citizen for the public good at various levels of provision; then citizens have a positive incentive to misrepresent the value of the good to themselves.

Suppose the government goes to each citizen in turn and asks very directly *What is your marginal utility for the public good at various possible levels of provision?* The citizens understand that, in the end, the government will provide that level of the public good that equates the sum of the (reported) marginal utilities to the marginal cost of provision. Moreover, citizens understand that, to pay for the public good, some taxes will be imposed. To keep matters simple, citizens believe that they will be taxed equally for the public good. That is, Y is the amount of the public good provided, so that kY is the total cost of provision, then each citizen will be told to pay kY/N, where N is the number of citizens.

It should be intuitive that, in this case, citizens who have a relatively high marginal value for the public good have the incentive to overstate that marginal value, while those who have a relatively low marginal value have an incentive to understate the value. I do not subject you to a mathematical derivation of this, but the idea is simple: Those who attach a relatively high marginal value to the public good want the government to supply more of it, even if they pay an equal share of the cost, because they realize that their fellow citizens will pay for most of the good. At the same time, those who attach a relatively low marginal value want less of it provided, given that they pay an equal share of the cost. In part d of Problem 14.4, you saw at least some of this, in that the folks who got the least utility from the public good came out behind, if the socially optimal level of public good were provided and equal taxation used to finance provision of the good. They, at least, would like to see less of the public good provided, so they would report lower marginal utilities.

Perhaps, you might think, the answer is to have citizens who say they want more of the good pay a higher share of the cost. It is harder to see, so I do not bother with a demonstration, but this does not work either. In fact, it can be proven that there is *no* way for the government to elicit honest responses to the question *What is your marginal utility for the public good?* if the government plans to use the information provided to determine the efficient level of provision, with some form of taxation imposed to pay the cost. To prove this is quite difficult (see, for example, Section 18.3 in D. M. Kreps, *A Course in Microeconomic Theory*, Princeton, NJ: Princeton University Press, 1990). But common sense probably suggests that no matter what mechanism is used to try to elicit this information, someone in the population will try to take advantage of the elicitation scheme to influence unduly the social decision.

Despite this, government economists often engage in benefit–cost analyses in an attempt to measure the benefits and costs to society of certain types of public goods such as roads or dams for flood control. Decisions on how much of these goods to provide are rarely determined solely by these studies (political considerations play a rather large role), but a good deal of attention is paid to how best to estimate the social benefits and costs of public goods, as an aid in determining how much to provide. If you are interested in public sector economics, you will probably meet this topic again.

Paying for the Public Goods

Once it is determined how much of a public good to provide, funds must be found to pay for it. Governments usually rely on general tax revenues, such as revenues from income or sales or value-added or property taxes, to pay for these things.

In Chapters 12 and 13, many things are said, none of them very nice, about government interference in perfectly competitive markets. Every time the government places a tax on the good in the market, we wind up with a deadweight cost. In the calculations of those chapters, we valued \$1 of consumer surplus equal to \$1 of producer surplus equal to \$1 of government net revenue. Thus, financial transfers from a tax were a net wash; all that matters to efficiency is the impact on physical goods outcomes.

In cases of public goods, the story is not so simple. Suppose we decide to have public provision of a particular public good. The government needs to raise money to provide the good. One way is to impose a tax on the sale of some other good. This may cause a deadweight cost in the market for the second, taxed good, but the amount of this deadweight cost may be less than the gain in value that comes from the provision of the public good. This happens because, when government net receipts are used to provide public goods, \$1 in a consumer's or producer's pocket can generate less surplus than \$1 of government net receipts. In essence, \$1 spent on public goods can generate a lot more benefits than that \$1 spent on "private goods," which is where it goes if it winds up in the pockets of a producer or consumer. So a good reason for governments to impose taxes, even on goods for which there are no externalities, is to raise the funds needed to pay for public goods. In such a case, the government may wish to tax goods for which the deadweight cost is particularly small, with a very inelastic supply or demand, but still, when we consider where the money would go, even a moderate deadweight cost for the good may be a worthwhile sacrifice.

(If we could attach a deadweight price tag to revenue raised to pay for the public good, we could include that cost in the cost of provision of the public good when determining how much of the public good to provide. That is, the socially optimal level of public good is no longer where the sum of marginal utilities equals the direct marginal cost of the public good but where the sum of marginal utilities equals the direct marginal cost plus the marginal deadweight cost.)

For more on public goods and related topics, seek out a good textbook on public finance and public sector economics.

Review Problems III

This set of review problems covers the material in Chapters 11 through 14.

III.1 A particular perfectly competitive industry consists of 25 identical firms. There is no possibility of entry into the industry, because to produce, a firm needs a license, and only 25 licenses will ever be granted. There are no fixed costs, so you need not worry about exit from the industry. The long-run supply function of each of these 25 firms is upward sloping.

Making this product requires two inputs. In the short run, a period of about a month, firms cannot vary either of these inputs, so firms cannot change their production quantity. In the intermediate run, a period of about half a year, firms can vary one of the two inputs. This gives an intermediate-run supply curve that is steeper than the long-run supply curve. The good in question cannot be inventoried.

Imagine that this industry has reached equilibrium at a point where supply equals demand. Suddenly, the government imposes a tax on the good in question, which is less than 10% of the good's initial equilibrium price. This is a per-unit tax, collected from producers. Equilibrium prices are computed net of the tax. That is, if the tax is $1 per unit and the equilibrium price is $5 per unit, this means that $1 out of the $5 a consumer pays goes to the government, and the other $4 goes back to the firm. This tax has no effect on the demand schedule.

(a) In the short run, what is the impact of the tax, in terms of the (net of tax) price, the quantity sold, consumer surplus, and the profits of the firms? Be as specific as you can be.

(b) If we measure the "burden of the tax on consumers" by the amount the equilibrium price rises divided by the size of the tax, is the burden of the tax be highest in the short run, the intermediate run, or the long run? Justify your answer.

III.2 In Figure III.1, you see portions of the supply and demand curves in a particular perfectly competitive industry.

(a) If the government places a $2 per-unit tax on the good in question, by how much does its price rise?

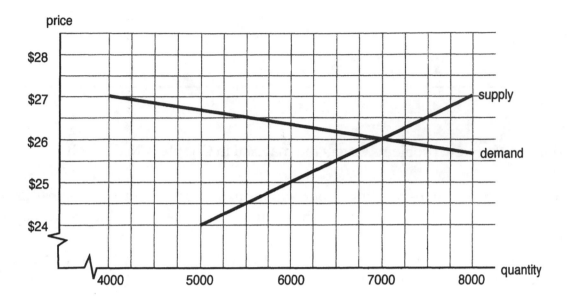

Figure III.1. Problem III.2: Supply and demand in a perfectly competitive industry.

(b) If the government places a $2 per-unit tax on the good in question, what is the magnitude of the deadweight cost to society?

III.3 In Figure III.2, you see demand, marginal revenue, and marginal cost for a monopolist.

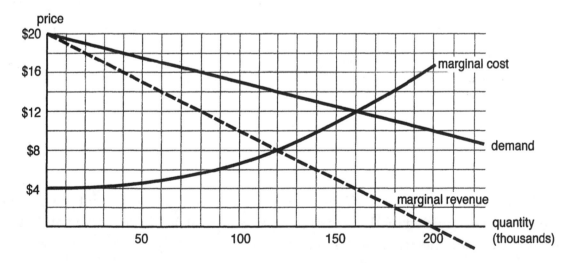

Figure III.2. Problem III.3: Demand, marginal revenue, and marginal cost for a monopolist.

(a) If the monopolist can charge any (single) price it wishes, what price would it charge? How much consumer surplus would consumers receive?

(b) Suppose the government could impose on the monopolist any price ceiling that it (the government) wants. What price ceiling would maximize the sum of consumer and producer surplus obtained in this market?

(c) Suppose the government imposed a price ceiling of $10 on the good. What would be the level of consumer surplus? Would consumer surplus be higher or lower than in part b? Would total surplus be higher or lower than in part a?

III.4 (a) In a competitive industry, demand is given by $D(p) = 1000(8 - 2p)$. Supply is given by $S(p) = 400p - 400$ for prices above 1; supply equals 0 at prices below 1. What are the equilibrium price and quantity in this industry?

(b) If a tax of $0.60 per unit is imposed on this good (say, imposed on manufacturers), what are the new equilibrium price and quantity?

(c) What is the deadweight cost of this tax?

III.5 A competitive firm has the long-run total cost function

$$900 + 10x + \frac{x^2}{16}.$$

In the long run, it finds itself producing 120 units of output, at a price of $25 apiece. In the short run, the firm cannot leave the industry and cannot avoid paying its fixed costs. Moreover, to change its level of output, it must incur higher short-run costs than long-run costs; its short-run total cost function is

$$\text{SRTC}(x) = \begin{cases} 300 + 15x + x^2/16, & \text{for } x \geq 120, \text{ and} \\ 1500 + 5x + x^2/16, & \text{for } x \leq 120. \end{cases}$$

In the short run, for what range of prices will this firm continue to produce precisely 120 units?

The Firefly Chronicles

The next few problems chronicle the further adventures of Rufus T. Firefly, prime minister of Freedonia, as he manages the economy of his nation. For purposes of exposition, you should assume that the dollar is the currency of Freedonia.

III.6 Qwarts are a good consumed only by the Sylvanian people. The demand function for qwarts in Sylvania is given by

$$D(p) = 1000(8 - p),$$

where $D(p)$ is the number of qwarts demanded at price p. Qwarts are produced both in the kingdom of Sylvania and in the neighboring republic of Freedonia. Ten firms in all make qwarts. No other firms can enter into this business. All 10 firms are identical, having total cost functions

$$TC(y) = y + \frac{y^2}{200}.$$

Five of the firms are Freedonian, and five are Sylvanian. All are price-taking or competitive firms.

(a) For many years, the kingdom of Sylvania imposed a tariff of $2 per qwart on qwarts imported from Freedonia. Under these conditions, what has been the equilibrium in the qwart market? You should compute the equilibrium price of qwarts, the amount consumed, the amount produced per Sylvanian firm and per Freedonian firm, the profit of each sort of firm, consumer surplus of the Sylvanian consumers, and the revenues generated by this tariff for the Sylvanian treasury.

(b) As part of a general trade liberalization policy, the Sylvanian government is about to drop the tariff on qwarts. The Sylvanians are concerned that this will mean a loss of revenue to their treasury, so they have decided to impose a tax of $0.80 per qwart. This tax will be imposed on both Sylvanian and Freedonian producers at the source; that is, the equilibrium price will be net of this tax. What will be the equilibrium in this case?

(c) If you answered parts a and b correctly, you will find that both consumer surplus and Sylvanian revenues increase when changing from the $2 tariff to the $0.80 tax. Also, total surplus increases. What are the sources of the gain in efficiency that accrues from moving from the tariff to the tax?

III.7 In Freedonia, the price of raw milk, purchased from farmers, is currently $0.50 per liter. The situation is as depicted in Figure III.3(a), where I've supplied both demand and the long-run supply curve.

In the short run, dairy farmers cannot change their production quantities. In the intermediate run of a year or so, they can change their production quantities by increasing the size of the herds. In the long run, the total supply of raw milk can be affected by changes in the size of herds and the addition of new pasture land. This gives the three supply curves (long-run, intermediate-run, and short-run) shown in Figure III.3(b).

In case you want the algebraic formulas for these functions, they are as follows:

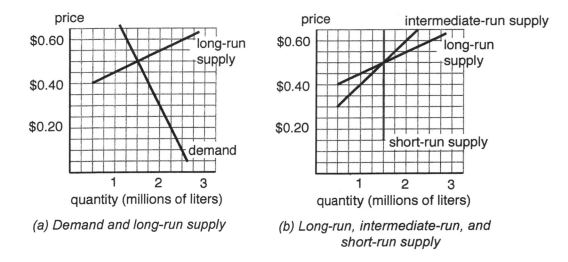

price
$0.60
$0.40
$0.20
long-run supply
demand
1   2   3
quantity (millions of liters)

(a) Demand and long-run supply

price
intermediate-run supply
$0.60
$0.40
$0.20
long-run supply
short-run supply
1   2   3
quantity (millions of liters)

(b) Long-run, intermediate-run, and short-run supply

Figure III.3. Problem III.7: The raw-milk market in Freedonia.

- Demand: $D(p) = 2.75 - 2.5p$.

- Short-run supply: $S_{\text{short-run}}(p) = 1.5$.

- Intermediate-run supply: $S_{\text{intermediate-run}}(p) = 5p - 1$.

- Long-run supply: $S_{\text{long-run}}(p) = 10p - 3.5$.

The dairy farmers' association, in return for a large contribution to the reelection fund for Prime Minister Firefly, has won Firefly's support for a program to raise their profits. Firefly is considering three separate programs.

1. In Program 1, his government would undertake to support the price of milk at $0.60 per liter, in the fashion of the EEC's program of agricultural price supports: The Freedonian government would buy up and destroy stocks of milk, sufficient to raise the price of milk to $0.60.

2. Program 2 would also result in a support price of $0.60 per liter paid to farmers: Farmers would sell as much as they want to the government at $0.60 per liter. The government would then take all the milk it purchases from farmers and sell it at the market clearing price to consumers. Of course, this means the price to consumers would be less than $0.60 per liter.

3. Program 3 is a simple subsidy to farmers of $0.15 per liter of milk they produce and sell.

(a) If the Freedonian government undertakes Program 1, what would be the short-run, intermediate-run, and long-run consequences? I want numbers for the price, quantity demanded by consumers, consumer surplus lost relative to the position in Figure III.3(a), quantity of milk destroyed by the government, cost to the government of the support program, gain in producer profits relative to the starting position. (Even though raw milk is probably demanded at least in part by other firms and not only by final consumers, compute consumer surplus changes in the usual fashion.)

(b) What would be the outcome of Program 2? I want the same quantities for each of the short run, intermediate run, and long run.

(c) And what would be the outcomes of Program 3?

(You can do this algebraically, but if you want to do it graphically, Figure III.4, blown up version of Figure III.3, may help with Program 3.)

(d) Another name for the deadweight cost of a program is the *net social cost of the program*, computed as the net cost to the government, plus any loss in consumer surplus (or minus any gain in consumer surplus), minus any gain in producer profits or less any loss in producer profits. For each of the three programs and each of the three time periods, compute the net social cost of the program.

III.8 The production of qwerty in Freedonia is done by 120 firms, each of which has the same production technology. (There is no possibility of entry, and no fixed costs, so there is nothing to be concerned about with regard to exit.) This technology uses two inputs, quinella and labor. To make n units of qwerty requires n^2 units of quinella and $2n$ units of labor. (There is no possibility of substituting quinella for labor or vice versa.) The cost of labor is $3 per unit, and the cost of quinella is $2 per unit. Just so there is no misunderstanding, let me be clear that the supplies of labor and quinella are completely flat at prices of $3 and $2 per unit, respectively. There are no fixed costs in the production of qwerty.

(a) What is the total cost to one of the qwerty manufacturers of producing n units of qwerty?

(b) What are the marginal costs of producing qwerty?

(c) Suppose that the demand for qwerty is given by $Q = 100 - 10P$, where Q is quantity and P is price. All the 120 firms that supply qwerty are price takers. What is the equilibrium in the qwerty market? I want to know the price of qwerty, the total amount of qwerty produced, and the amount of qwerty supplied by each of the 120 firms.

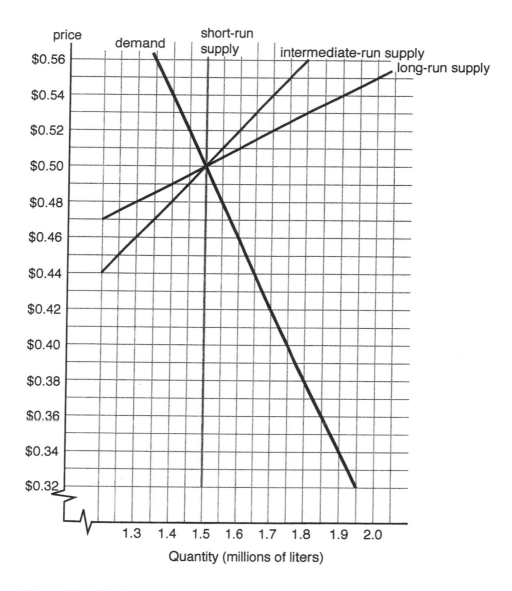

Figure III.4. Problem III.7: The Freedonian raw-milk market, magnified.

(d) Suppose that the government imposes a tax of $1 on quinella. For the sake of definiteness, imagine that quinella is supplied by many perfectly competitive firms, each of which has constant marginal costs of $2 per unit of quinella produced. What impact does this tax have on the price of qwerty?

III.9 Concerning this problem, you should have little problem with parts a, b, c, and (probably) d, but d is getting hard, and f takes a real leap of imagination.

Prime Minister Firefly has yet another problem. Freedonia is a very small country, and it is not able to sustain a domestic poiuyt manufacturing capability. All the poiuyts purchased by Freedonia come from a single manufacturer in Sylvania, which acts as a classic monopolist in the Freedonian market. This Sylvanian firm has constant marginal costs equal to 4 per unit (in local currency). Demand for poiuyts in Freedonia is given by the demand function $P = 20 - Q/1000$, where Q is the number of poiuyts sold and P is their price.

(a) If the Sylvanian poiuyt manufacturer can set any single price it wishes in the Freedonian market, what price maximizes its profit? (This manufacturer is unable to engage in price discrimination.) What corresponding quantity of poiuyts is sold in Freedonia, and what profit does the poiuyt manufacturer receive from Freedonian sales? (Assume that the poiuyt manufacturer has no fixed costs.)

(b) Suppose that Firefly considers either imposing a tax on the domestic sale of poiuyts or a subsidy for their sale in his country. The tax or subsidy would be levied on the Sylvanian producer and be a constant amount per unit sold. Consider both a tax and a subsidy of $1 per unit. How will the market equilibrium change in each case? What would be the effect on consumer surplus, on the Sylvanian firm's profit, and on tax revenues or subsidy expenses? Comparing with the equilibrium in part a, and taking into account only the consumer surplus of Freedonian consumers and the net impact on the Freedonian budget, which of the three (a tax of $1, a subsidy of $1, no interference) is best for Freedonia?

(c) Suppose that Firefly were able to enforce a price ceiling on poiuyts of $8 per poiuyt. That is, no poiuyt could be sold in Freedonia for more than $8. How would the monopolist respond to this?

(d) Suppose that, in addition to the price ceiling on poiuyts of $8 per poiuyt, Firefly is able to impose a tax of $2 per poiuyt on the importation of poiuyts. What would be the impact of this tax, in addition to the price ceiling?

(e) Suppose that Firefly were able to extract from the Sylvanian firm a lump-sum amount as an import license. That is, the Sylvanian firm, if it wishes to export at all to Freedonia, must pay for an import license, which has a price set by the Freedonian government. (Assume, as you should be assuming throughout, that the Sylvanian government is not retaliating to all these actions by Freedonia.) Assuming that Freedonia takes no actions except to issue this import license, what is the optimal fee it should set for the license (to make the welfare of its citizens, as measured by consumer surplus plus the revenues from this license, as large as possible)?

(f) Suppose that Firefly were able to charge the Sylvanian firm a fee for importing, as in part e, and in addition Freedonia can either tax or subsidize the import of poiuyts on a per-unit basis. Can you see what (from the point of view of Freedonian welfare) would be the ideal combination of import license fee plus tariff or subsidy to impose?

III.10 Roiuyts are produced by a large number of firms, all found in the country of Freedonia. These firms are price takers, and their supply function is given by

$$S(p) = 10(p - 4),$$

where p is the price to the manufacturer of roiuyts.

Roiuyts are consumed in Freedonia and in the neighboring country Sylvania. The demand for roiuyts in Freedonia is

$$D_F(p) = 5(46 - p),$$

where p is the price to consumers in Freedonia. Demand in Sylvania is given by

$$D_S(p) = 5(46 - p),$$

where p is the price to consumers in Sylvania.

Roiuyts can be shipped to Freedonian and Sylvanian markets at the same cost, 0. (You can think of there being 10 manufacurers of roiuyts, each of whom has no fixed costs and marginal costs of $MC(x) = x + 4$.)

(a) What is the equilibrium price for roiuyts, assuming there are no barriers to trade between Freedonia and Sylvania? What is the level of consumer surplus in Sylvania?

(b) The Sylvanian government, concerned with the profits Freedonian manufacturers are making from the sale of roiuyts, decides to put a tariff of $8 per roiuyt on every roiuyt brought into Sylvania. (Assume that roiuyts must be installed in one's home by the manufacturer, so Sylvanian citizens cannot purchase roiuyts in Freedonia and bring them into Sylvania. Also assume that roiuyts are very large objects, hence they cannot be smuggled into Sylvania.) What is the impact of this tariff on the price of roiuyts in Freedonia? What price would Sylvanian consumers pay for their roiuyts, and how many roiuyts would they consume? What would be their consumer surplus? What would be the tariff revenue of the Sylvanian government?

(c) What is the deadweight cost from this tariff program? Compute this two ways. First, compute surplus gains or losses for Sylvanians, Freedonian consumers, and Freedonian producers separately, then net them out. Second, considering the physical goods outcome only, identify the inefficiencies that result from the tariff and evaluate their cost.

III.11 *The final chapter of Rufus T. Firefly.* In Freedonia, the production of jhunks has always been managed by the Old Original Jhunk Company, which was established in 1576 and was given "the sole right to sell jhunks within Freedonia for all time." The Freedonian High Court of Justice has always maintained that this right cannot be abrogated, and so the Old Original Jhunk Company (or OOJC) has a monopoly on the sale and production of jhunks.

(a) Demand for jhunks is given by the inverse demand function $P(x) = 20 - (x/2000)$. The total cost to OOJC of producing x jhunks is $4x + (x^2/2000)$. Assuming that OOJC sets prices as a traditional profit-maximizing monopolist, what price does it set and how many jhunks does it produce and sell?

(b) The total cost function given in part a refers to domestic production of jhunks. Jhunks are also produced worldwide, in a competitive market, at a market price of \$8 per jhunk. (The worldwide market in jhunks is enormous relative to the Freedonian market, so this price does not change no matter how many jhunks are bought on the world market for Freedonian use.) The OOJC is seeking for the first time to obtain a license to import jhunks into Freedonia; the OOJC would maintain its monopoly to sell jhunks within Freedonia. If it obtains the license it desires, what would be the outcome? What would be the domestic price of jhunks charged by the OOJC? How many would be sold? Would any be made domestically? How many?

(c) Firefly is concerned that, if he allows the OOJC to import foreign-made jhunks, unemployment in Freedonia would rise as the domestic production of jhunks decreases. At the same time, he is aware that allowing the OOJC to import foreign-made jhunks would increase the supply of these items to his consumers, increasing consumer surplus. He has considered offering a subsidy to the OOJC for domestic production of jhunks, but his subsidies budget is already overdrawn, given his management of trade in sorghum and raw milk.

Accordingly, he has decided to make the following offer to the OOJC. As long as the OOJC maintains domestic production at its current (part a) level (or if it increases that level of production), it may then import into Freedonia as many additional jhunks as it wishes to.

Freedonia's minister of Consumer Affairs, Ciccolini, warns against this plan, claiming that it would harm the interests of Freedonian consumers, relative to what they can get if the OOJC is allowed free importation of jhunks without constraint. To what extent is this warning valid? How much of a loss in consumer surplus would Freedonian consumers suffer relative to the result of part b, if Firefly places this constraint on the ability of the OOJC to import jhunks?

III.12 A monopoly firm serves a market whose inverse demand curve is given by

$$P(x) = 20 - \frac{x}{2000}.$$

This firm has rising marginal costs given by

$$MC(x) = 2 + \frac{x}{1000}.$$

(This firm has no fixed costs, so its total cost function is $TC(x) = 2x + x^2/2000$.) Suppose the government passes legislation that accomplishes two things. (1) The firm, to remain in this business, must purchase a license from the goverment, which costs $18,000. (Think of the demand and marginal cost functions given previously as measured in quantities sold and produced per month and the $18,000 fee as a monthly licensing fee.) The firm, if it purchases this license, is guaranteed to remain a monopoly. (2) The firm is given a subsidy of $2 for every unit it sells.

In terms of the total surplus generated (sum of consumer surplus, producer surplus (= profits), and net government receipts), what is the combined impact of these two policies, measured as the change in total surplus? In terms of the distribution of that surplus (taking consumers of the product, the monopoly firm, and taxpayers), who gain and who lose by the combination of these two policies, and by how much?

III.13 Many local governments operate transportation agencies that provide bus transportation over set routes according to set schedules. In other cases, private firms operate the transport services but are regulated by the local government. One reason for providing bus service is to reduce congestion on city streets from privately owned automobiles.

The cost function for bus transportation service is, to a first approximation, a fixed cost plus a constant marginal cost per passenger mile. That is, if x is the amount of passenger miles provided by the bus company in a fixed period, then the total cost of operations is

$$TC(x) = F + cx$$

for constants F and c.

Suppose that, at price p per passenger mile, the demand for bus services is $x(p)$. Suppose that we wish to set p with a view toward maximizing social surplus. (Because the agency running the bus service is either an agency of the local government or a regulated firm, the local government has the ability to set this price, subject to the constraint that operations must be financed somehow.)

Some people argue that price should be set so that the bus operations are self-supporting: Find p so that $p \times x(p) = F + cx(p)$. Others argue that price should be set equal to the marginal cost of production: $p = c$. Since this involves a net loss in bus operations, the fixed cost would then be paid by a lump-sum subsidy, paid for out of general tax revenues. Still others argue that price should be set at a level below the marginal cost: A lump-sum subsidy should be given to cover the fixed cost and a further per-unit subsidy should be offered to pay the difference between marginal costs and the price charged.

You *do not* have enough information to say which of these is correct, but you should now be able to comment intelligently on the considerations that might allow one of these to be "socially optimal." What do you believe are the most important considerations that should go into deciding between these three options? Your answer should involve the terms *total surplus*, *deadweight cost*, and *externality*.

III.14 A New East Coast Business School (NECBUS) has been created to award MBA degrees. The distinctive feature of NECBUS is that it is run on a strictly for-profit basis; the school's motto is "Practice What You Preach," and the dean of NECBUS, Rob Berbaron, preaches profit maximization. An issue that arose immediately concerned the school's tuition policy; in particular, would it offer marked-down tuition (sometimes called *scholarships* or *fellowships*) for prospective students with below-average family income and resources? After consulting with the VP for Marketing who is also the dean of Admissions, Dean Berbaron announced that the school would mark down its tuition level for students with below-average family income and resources. Remember, this school maximizes profit. Provide one or more possible explanations for this policy.

Solution to Problem III.1

(a) Since, in the short run, firms cannot change the amount they produce, the quantity produced stays the same. As demand did not shift, the equilibrium price stays the same, and consumer surplus is unchanged. The firms, however, must pay the tax, so their profits decrease by the amount of the tax times the pretax quantity (which is the posttax quantity).

(b) In general, the burden on consumers is higher the more elastic is supply, so the burden is highest in the long run and smallest (actually, no burden) in the short run. If you want to see this in a picture, Figure III.5 is the appropriate diagram.

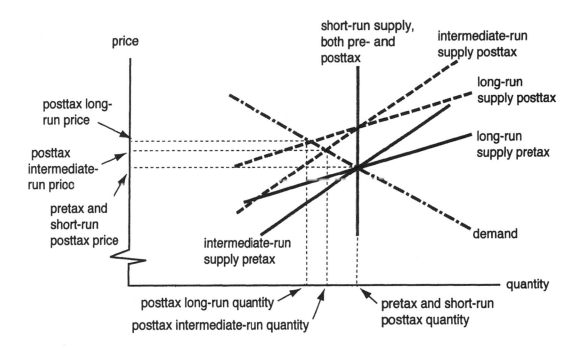

Figure III.5. Problem III.1: Imposing a tax on a perfectly competitive industry. Because short-run supply is completely inelastic (that is, the quantity supply is fixed), in the short run, the tax is borne entirely by producers. In the intermediate run, some of the tax is passed on to consumers; in the long run, more of the tax is borne by consumers.

Solution to Problem III.2

(a) A tax of $2 per unit raises the supply curve by $2. Doing this graphically (see Figure III.6) shows a new supply = demand of 5500 units, at a price of $26.50. Therefore, the $2 tax increases price by $0.50.

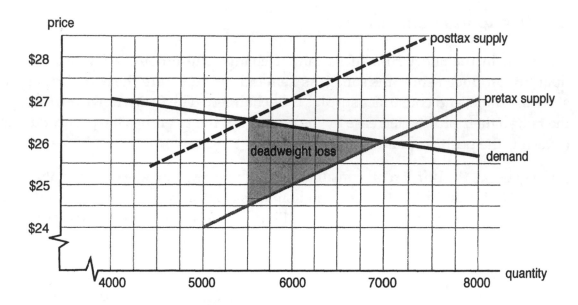

Figure III.6. Problem III.2: The effect of a $2 tax.

(b) The deadweight cost is represented by a triangle (shaded, in Figure III.6) with height $2 (the size of the tax) and, perpendicular to this height, a decrease in quantity of 1500 units, for a deadweight cost of

$$\tfrac{1}{2} \times \$2 \times 1500 = \$1500.$$

Solution to Problem III.3

(a) The monopolist equates marginal cost to marginal revenue, giving a quantity of 120,000 and a price of $14 (see Figure III.7(a)). The total consumer surplus is the area of a triangle with base 120,000 and height $20 − $14 = $6, which is $\tfrac{1}{2} \times \$6 \times 120{,}000 = \$360{,}000$. The deadweight loss from monopoly is (roughly, because marginal cost is not quite linear) the area of a triangle with a base of $6 and a perpendicular to that base of 40,000 units, or $\tfrac{1}{2} \times \$6 \times 40{,}000 = \$120{,}000$. (This is the deadweight loss relative to the surplus-maximizing outcome where 160,000 units are produced; see part b.

(b) To maximize total surplus, the government wants to equate marginal cost and demand. It does this by setting a price ceiling at the price where the two intersect, $12, for a quantity of 160,000 units. Note that this gives a consumer surplus equal to

$$\tfrac{1}{2} \times \$8 \times 160{,}000 = \$640{,}000.$$

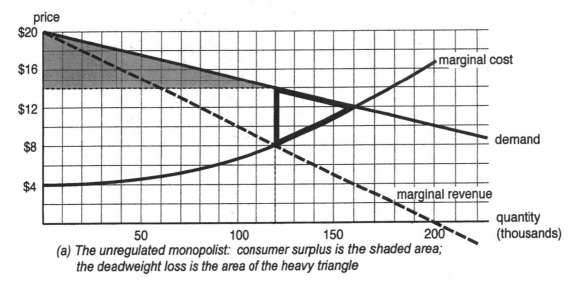

(a) The unregulated monopolist: consumer surplus is the shaded area;
the deadweight loss is the area of the heavy triangle

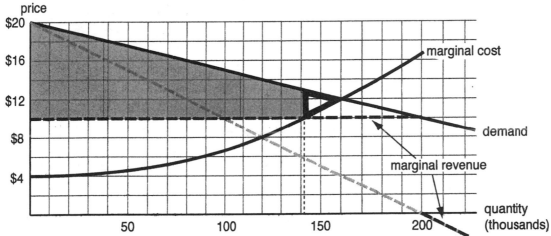

(b) The impact of a $10 price ceiling: marginal revenue is flat at $10 until the demand
function is reached, then jumps down to the original marginal revenue function. The
monopolist chooses a price of $10, giving the shaded area for consumer surplus and
the heavily outlined triangle for deadweight loss.

Figure III.7. Problem III.3: A monopolist, without and then with a price ceiling.

(c) A $10 price ceiling would change the monpolist's marginal revenue function;
it would be flat at $10 until the demand curve is hit and then rejoin the original
marginal revenue function (see Figure III.7(b)). In this case, the monopolist would
set its price at the ceiling price of $10, selling approximately 141,000 units. (Since
the price of $10 means demand of 200,000, some rationing is required. I assume
that the rationing scheme gets the 141,000 units into the "right" hands, in the sense
of maximizing the consumer surplus from these units.) Consumer surplus is the
area of a quadrilateral with a base of 141,000 and two sides (at right angles to the

base) of $10 and $2.95, which is

$$141,000 \times \frac{\$10 + \$2.95}{2} = \$912,975.$$

This is more than the consumer surplus in part b. As for total surplus, it is of course less than total surplus in part b (the ceiling price of $12 is selected to maximize total surplus), but it is a good deal better than total surplus in part a: The deadweight loss in this case (relative to the efficient ideal of part b) is (roughly) the area of a triangle with a base of $2.95 and a perpendicular to that base of 39,000 units, or $\frac{1}{2} \times \$2.95 \times 39,000 = \$57,525$.

Solution to Problem III.4

(a) Equate supply and demand:

$$1000(8 - 2p) = 400p - 400 \quad \text{or} \quad 8400 = 2400p \quad \text{or} \quad p = \frac{8400}{2400} = \$3.50.$$

This gives a quantity of $1000(8 - 2 \times 3.5) = 1000$.

(b) Solve this algebraically. The tax raises marginal costs, hence inverse supply, by 0.6. Inverse supply pretax is

$$\frac{x}{400} = p - 1 \quad \text{or} \quad p = \frac{x}{400} + 1,$$

so posttax is

$$p = \frac{x}{400} + 1.6,$$

and so posttax supply is

$$S(p) = 400(p - 1.6) = 400p - 640.$$

Supply equals demand is

$$400p - 640 = 8000 - 2000p \quad \text{or} \quad 2400p = 8640 \quad \text{or} \quad p = \frac{8640}{2400} = \$3.60,$$

which gives quantity of $1000(8 - 2 \times 3.6) = 800$.

(c) The deadweight cost triangle has height $0.60 and length (perpendicular to this height) 200 units, for an area of $\frac{1}{2} \times \$0.60 \times 200 = \$60$. The deadweight cost of the tax is $60.

Solution to Problem III.5

Since the firm cannot avoid its fixed costs, it will produce where price equals marginal cost. The marginal cost function is

$$\mathrm{MC}(x) = \begin{cases} 15 + 2x/16, & \text{for } x > 120, \text{ and} \\ 5 + 2x/16, & \text{for } x < 120. \end{cases}$$

This is graphed for you in Figure III.8: By inspection, production will be 120 for all prices between $20 and $30.

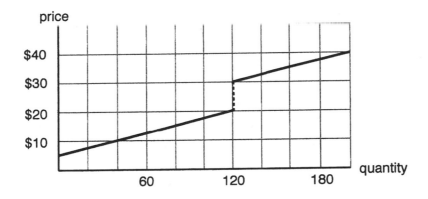

Figure III.8. Problem III.5: The short-run marginal cost function.

Solution to Problem III.6

(a) The marginal cost function of each of the five Sylvanian firms is $\mathrm{MC}(y) = 1 + y/100$, so at price p each one supplies the amount y that satisfies $p = 1 + y/100$ or $y(p) = 100(p - 1)$. (This is for prices p above $1.) Each of the five Freedonian firms pays a tariff of $2 per qwart, so its (net of tariff) marginal cost function is $\mathrm{MC}(y) = 3 + y/100$, and its supply function is $y(p) = 100(p - 3)$ for prices above $3.

Hence, the total supply function is

$$S(p) = \begin{cases} 0, & p < 1, \\ 500(p-1), & 1 \le p < 3, \text{and} \\ 500(p-1) + 500(p-3) = 1000p - 2000, & p \ge 3. \end{cases}$$

We want to find where price intersects demand. One way to proceed is to graph the two (which would be useful for answering later parts of this problem), but instead I work through the problem algebraically: At a price of $p = 3$, supply is 1000 units, all coming from the five Sylvanian firms, while demand is for $1000(8-3) = 5000$ units, so demand exceeds supply at this price. Hence, price must rise, and the equilibrium is where

$$1000(8-p) = 1000p - 2000 \quad \text{or} \quad 10{,}000 = 2000p \quad \text{or} \quad p = 5.$$

At this price, the quantity produced is 3000 units, or 400 from each of the Sylvanian firms (2000 total) and 200 from each of the Freedonian firms (1000 total).

- Consumer surplus is a triangle with base 3000 units and height $3 per unit, for a total area of $4500 of consumer surplus.

- The profit for each of the Sylvanian firms is revenue minus total cost, or $400 \times \$5 - 400 - (400^2)/200 = 2000 - 400 - 800 = \$800$ apiece.

- The profit for each of the Freedonian firms is revenue minus total cost of production and the tariff, or $200 \times \$5 - 200 - (200^2)/200 - 200 \times \$2 = 1000 - 200 - 200 - 400 = \$200$ apiece.

- The revenue to the Sylvanian treasury is $2 for each of the 1000 units imported, or $2000 in total.

(b) If a tax of $0.80 is imposed uniformly on all 10 producers, each supplies $100(p - 1.80)$ for prices above $1.80, so that total supply is $1000(p - 1.8)$. Supply equals demand where

$$1000(p - 1.8) = 1000(8 - p) \quad \text{or} \quad 2p = 9.8 \quad \text{or} \quad p = \$4.90.$$

At this price, the quantity is $1000(8 - 4.9) = 3100$ units, with 310 coming from each of the 10 firms.

- Consumer surplus is a triangle with base 3100 units and height $3.10 per unit, for a total consumer surplus of $4805, $305 more than before.

- The profit of each of the 10 firms is revenue (net of tax) less cost, or $4.10 \times 310 - 310 - (310^2)/200 = \$480.50$ apiece.

- The government's revenue is now $3100 \times \$0.80 = \$2480$.

(c) Consumer surplus has risen by $305 and tax revenue by $480. Total profits were $4000 + 1000 = \$5000$; now they are $4805, so they have decreased $195. Total surplus has therefore increased by $305 + \$480 - \$195 = \$590$. This increase in surplus comes about because production with the tariff was unevenly distributed among identical firms and so was being done inefficiently. Efficient production is at levels where the marginal cost to each producer is the same, which (in this case) means equal production amounts from each of the 10 firms. Of course, this change is bad news in particular for the domestic (Sylvanian) producers.

Solution to Problem III.7

The results for the three programs are shown in panels a, b, and c of Table III.1. You should have no difficulties with any of these numbers, as long as you remember that in comparing producer profits in any given run, you should look at the new producer surplus less the original producer surplus for that run. Finding the equilibrium in the third program (with a $0.15 per liter subsidy) is probably most easily done graphically, using the blown-up picture of supply and demand in Figure III.4; short-run supply does not move, while intermediate- and long-run supply are simply displaced vertically by $0.15. Do this, and you should find the intersection with demand at the locations indicated in Table III.1(c).

If we assume that Firefly's purpose is providing a payoff for milk producers without a major impact on his budget, he is not succeeding very well, at least in the long run. Program 1 costs his budget $750,000 to transfer $200,000 to milk producers. Program 2 does worse in this regard; to get the same $200,000 to milk producers, his budget expends $1.25 million. (Of course, Program 2 also provides consumers with milk at $0.10 per liter; there might be a few votes to be had there.) Finally, the subsidy doesn't have a huge impact on his budget—it costs him $270,000 in the long run. But it provides only $49,500 in benefits to milk producers in the long run, because competition among milk producers pushes the price of milk down to $0.38. Even with a $0.15 subsidy, that leaves milk producers not much better off than they were originally.

How do the three compare in terms of total surplus? What are the deadweight costs or net social costs of the three programs? The answers are recorded in Table III.2.

	short run	intermediate run	long run
price	$0.60	$0.60	$0.60
quantity consumed	1.25 million liters	1.25 million liters	1.25 million liters
lost consumer surplus relative to original equilibrium	$137,500	$137,500	$137,500
milk destroyed by government	0.25 million liters	0.75 million liters	1.25 million liters
cost to government of program	$150,000	$450,000	$750,000
gain in producer profits relative to original equilibrium	$150,000	$175,000	$200,000

(a) Program 1 results.

	short run	intermediate run	long run
quantity of milk supplied to the government	1.5 million liters	2 million liters	2.5 million liters
consumer price	$0.50	$0.30	$0.10
gain in consumer surplus relative to original equilibrium	$0	$0.20(2 + 1.5)/2 = $350,000	$0.40(2.5 + 1.5)/2 = $800,000
cost to government of program	1.5M(0.60 - 0.50) = $150,000	2M(0.60 - 0.30) = $600,000	2.5M(0.60 - 0.10) = $1,250,000

(b) Program 2 results. (The results for the producers are the same as in Program 1.)

	price	quantity consumed	long run
price	$0.50	$0.40	$0.38
quantity consumed	1.5 million liters	1.75 million liters	1.8 million liters
gain in consumer surplus relative to original equilibrium	$0	$162,500	$198,000
gain in producer profits relative to original equilibrium	$225,000	$81,250	$49,500
cost to government of program	$225,000	$262,500	$270,000

(c) Program 3 results.

Table III.1. Problem III.7: Results of the three programs.

In each case, we add the direct cost to the government plus any loss in consumer surplus (Program 1) or less any gain in consumer surplus (Programs 2 and 3) less the gains in milk producer profits. Program 1 is clearly the big loser—it makes no sense to pour all that milk down the drain—and Program 3 looks the best according to this measure. But Firefly probably has to worry: Will the meager benefits of the subsidy to milk producers in the long-run be adequate?

Could we have guessed that Program 3 would have the lowest net social cost? Perhaps not, but once we compute figures for the amount of milk produced, it is clear why Program 3 wins: Assuming any milk that is produced is consumed— that is, as long as we avoid the extraordinarily wasteful Program 1—the key to net social cost is, Which program keeps production levels as close as possible to the surplus-maximizing level of 1.5 million liters. The subsidy program results in some overproduction of milk, but not nearly as much as we get in Program 2, where the price-to-the-producer is held at $0.60.

	short run	intermediate run	long run
Program 1	$150,000 + $137,500 − $150,000 = $137,500	$450,000 + $137,500 − $175,000 = $412,500	$750,000 + $137,500 − $200,000 = $687,500
Program 2	$150,000 − $0 − $150,000 = $0	$600,000 − $350.000 − $175,000 = $75,000	$1,250,000 − $800.000 − $200,000 = $250,000
Program 3	$225,000 − $0 − $225,000 = $0	$262,500 − $162,500 − $81,250 = $18,750	$270,000 − $198,000 − $49,500 = $22,500

Table III.2. Problem III.7: The net social costs of the three programs. For each program and each run, we take the net cost to the Freedonian treasury, plus any loss in consumer surplus or less any gain in consumer surplus, less the gain in producer surplus. Remember that in this table, positive numbers are "bad" (costs) and negative numbers are "good" (benefits). Note that Programs 2 and 3 have net social cost $0 in the short run: Because the quantity of milk is fixed in the short run, no overproduction is possible, and in these two programs, no milk is poured down the drain.

Solution to Problem III.8

(a) $\mathrm{TC}(n) = 2n^2 + 3(2n) = \$(2n^2 + 6n)$.

(b) $\mathrm{MC}(n) = 4n + 6$.

(c) Each of the 120 firms has a supply function $s(p)$ given by

$$p = 4s(p) + 6 \quad \text{or} \quad s(p) = \frac{p-6}{4},$$

(for prices above $6), so that total supply is given by

$$S(p) = 120\frac{p-6}{4} = 30p - 180.$$

Supply equals demand where

$$100 - 10p = 30p - 180 \quad \text{or} \quad 280 = 40p \quad \text{or} \quad p = 7,$$

at which point the quantity demanded is 30, so each firm supplies 0.25 units of qwerty.

(d) A $1 tax on quinella, given that quinella is produced by many perfectly competitive firms, each having a constant marginal cost of $2 per unit, results in the price of quinella going up to $3 per unit. For qwerty manufacturers, $TC(n)$ becomes $3n^2 + 6n$, $MC(n) = 6n + 6$, $s(p) = (p - 6)/6$, and market supply becomes $S(p) = 20p - 120$. Supply equals demand where

$$20p - 120 = 100 - 10p \quad \text{or} \quad 30p = 220 \quad \text{or} \quad p = \$7.33,$$

at which point total supply = total demand is 26.666 and the amount supplied by each firm is 0.2222.

Solution to Problem III.9

(a) For the poiuyt manufacturer, marginal revenue is given by

$$MR(Q) = 20 - \frac{Q}{500},$$

so marginal cost equals marginal revenue where

$$20 - \frac{Q}{500} = 4 \quad \text{or} \quad \frac{Q}{500} = 16 \quad \text{or} \quad Q = 8000.$$

At this quantity, the price of a poiuyt is $P = 20 - 8000/1000 = \$12$, so that the poiuyt manufacturer earns a profit of $(12 - 4)(8000) = \$64{,}000$.

(b) A tax of \$1 per unit sold raises the monopolist's marginal cost by \$1 and so raises price by \$0.50, to \$12.50. This lowers the amount sold by 500, to 7500. Producer profit decreases to $(\$12.5 - \$5) \times 7500 = \$56{,}250$, tax revenue is \$7500, and consumer surplus is reduced by $\$0.50 \times (8000 + 7500)/2 = \$3875$. Therefore, the net effect of a tax on Freedonian interests is a net gain of $\$7500 - \$3875 = \$3625$. (Since profit falls by \$7750, the net impact, including the effect on the Sylvanian monopolist, is a loss of \$4125.)

A subsidy of \$1 per unit lowers the monopolist's marginal cost by \$1 and so lowers price by \$0.50 to \$11.50. Demand (and supply) rise to 8500. The Freedonian treasury expends \$8500, while Freedonian consumer surplus rises by $\$0.50 \times (8500 + 8000)/2 = \$4125$, so the net effect on Freedonian interests is a net loss of \$4375. Profit of the monopolist rises to $(\$11.50 - \$3) \times 8500 = \$72{,}250$, an increase of \$8250, hence the overall impact is a net increase in surplus of \$3875.

From the point of view of Freedonian interests alone, the tax is best.

(c) A price ceiling of \$8 causes the monopolist's marginal revenue curve to be a constant \$8 up to the quantity, 12,000, where the constraint no longer binds, at which point it jumps down to $-\$4$ and then falls along the old marginal revenue function $MR(Q) = 20 - Q/500$. Therefore, the monopolist chooses to produce 12,000 units, selling them for \$8 apiece.

(d) Imposing a tax of \$2 per unit raises the monopolist's marginal cost from \$4 to \$6. Given the marginal revenue function described in part c, the monopolist still chooses to produce 12,000 units, charging the price \$8 for each of them. So the impact of this tax is simply to transfer \$24,000 from the monopolist's pocket to the Freedonian treasury.

(e) The import license is a fixed cost of the monopolist, so as long as the monopolist agrees to pay it, its decision concerning price and quantity is unaffected. It agrees to pay for the import license as long as its net profit from operation exceeds 0, and since its gross profit (if it operates at all) is \$64,000, this (or a bit less) is the optimal import license fee to set.

(f) Since, with the import license fee, Firefly is able to capture all (but a bit of) the gross profit of the Sylvanian monopolist, he wants to give the Sylvanian monopolist the incentive to produce the quantity that makes total surplus as large as possible. This is where the amount produced is 16,000, because at this level of production, demand price equals marginal cost. To get the monopolist to produce 16,000, a subsidy of $16 per unit is required, which gives the monopolist a gross profit of $16 per unit times 16,000 units or $256,000. Therefore, the import license fee should be set just a bit below this level.

Solution to Problem III.10

(a) Total demand is

$$5(46 - p) + 5(46 - p) = 10(46 - p),$$

so supply equals demand where

$$10(46 - p) = 10(p - 4) \quad \text{or} \quad 46 - p = p - 4 \quad \text{or} \quad 50 = 2p,$$

which is $p = \$25$. At this price, Sylvanians consume $5(46 - 25) = 105$ roiuyts, for consumer surplus equal to the area of a triangle of height $46 - 25 = \$21$ and base 105 units; consumer surplus equals $\frac{1}{2} \times \$21 \times 105 = \$1102.50$.

(b) Let p_S be the price in Sylvania and let p_F be the price in Freedonia. Then $p_S = p_F + 8$. This must hold if there are to be sales in both countries, because if $p_S > p_F + 8$, then manufacturers would want to sell in Sylvania only, and if $p_F + 8 > p_S$, then manufacturers would want to sell in Freedonia only.

The total supply is $10(p_F - 4)$, since p_F is the effective price to manufacturers whether they sell in Freedonia or Sylvania.

The total demand is

$$5(46 - p_F) + 5(46 - p_S) = 5(46 - p_F) + 5(46 - (p_F + 8)) = 460 - 10p_F - 40 = 420 - 10p_F.$$

So supply equals demand where

$$420 - 10p_F = 10p_F - 40 \quad \text{or} \quad 20p_F = 460 \quad \text{or} \quad p_F = \$23,$$

which gives $p_S = \$31$. Sylvanians consume $5(46 - 31) = 75$ roiuyts, and the consumer surplus for Sylvanian consumers is the area of a triangle of height $(46 - 31) = \$15$ and length 75, or $\frac{1}{2} \times \$15 \times 75 = \$562.50$. The tariff revenue is $\$8 \times 75 = \$600$.

(c) Note that Sylvanian total surplus increases from \$1102.50 to \$1162.50, and Freedonian consumer surplus increases from \$1102.50 to $\frac{1}{2} \times 23 \times 115 = \$1322.50$. But producer profits are off: Whereas previously producer surplus was $\frac{1}{2} \times (\$25 - \$4) \times 210 = \$2205$, now the effective price to producers is only \$23 and their total production is 75 units for Sylvania and 115 units for Freedonia, or 190 units in total, for a producer surplus equal to $\frac{1}{2} \times (\$23 - \$4) \times 190 = \$1805$. In net, producer profits are off by \$400, Freedonian consumer surplus is up by \$220, and Sylvanian total surplus is up by \$60, a net deadweight cost of \$120.

This deadweight cost comprises two components. First, there is social underproduction of roiuyts by 20 units, which gives a deadweight cost equal to the area of a triangle with height \$4 and base 20 units, or \$40. Second, 190 units should be optimally shared: 95 for Sylvania and 95 for Freedonia. But Freedonians are getting 115 units and Sylvanians only 75. The surplus gain to the Freedonians of their last 20 units is a quadrilateral whose base is 20 units and whose two heights are \$27 and \$23, or \$500. If those 20 units were given to the Sylvanians instead, the surplus from them would be a quadrilateral whose base is 20 units and whose heights are \$31 and \$27, for surplus of \$580. Hence, there is a loss of \$80 of surplus, relative to what there could be, from this maldistribution of roiuyts.

Solution to Problem III.11

(a) $MR(x) = 20 - x/1000$ and $MC(x) = 4 + x/1000$, so MC = MR at $x = 8000$, for a price of \$16 per jhunk.

(b) If the OOJC could import jhunks at \$8 apiece, it would produce jhunks domestically up to the point where its marginal cost is \$8, which is where $4 + x/1000 = 8$ or $x = 4000$. After this, it would buy jhunks internationally and resell them (at a marked-up price). Therefore, its marginal cost above 4000 units would be \$8, so equating MC and MR gives $x = 12{,}000$ and price = \$14.

(c) Ciccolini should go back to business school; the consuming public would not be hurt by this. Beyond 8000 jhunks, the marginal cost to the OOJC falls to \$8, so the OOJC would still sell 12,000 in total (importing 4,000) at a price of \$14. Of course, the OOJC makes less profit, but it makes more profit than if it were not allowed to import at all.

If you want to see all this in a picture, have a look at Figure III.9. Panel a shows the situation with no imports. Panel b shows what happens with free imports. And panel c depicts what happens with the constraint that 8000 units must be produced domestically. Note that the MC curve in panel c rises linearly to 8000 units and $12, then falls discontinuously to $8 for all units above 8000. The lightly shaded area is the amount of profit the OOJC makes above what it makes with importation rights relative to none (relative to the situation in part a), while the darker triangle is what it would make above what it does in part c if it were allowed free importation; i.e., this is the difference in profits between b and c.

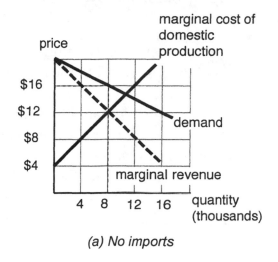

(a) No imports

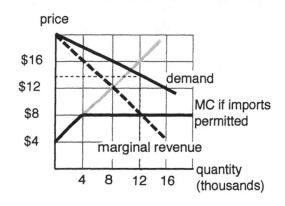

(b) Free importation permitted

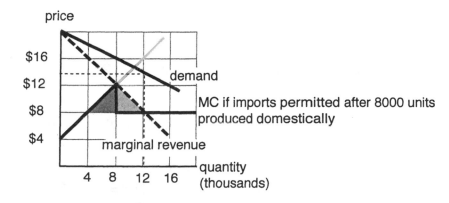

(c) Importation permitted after 8000 units produced domestically

Figure III.9. Problem III.11: Jhunks and the OOJC.

Solution to Problem III.12

The first step is to find the equilibrium before the policies go into effect. Inverse demand is given by $P(x) = 20 - x/2000$, so marginal revenue is $\mathrm{MR}(x) = 20 -$

$x/1000$, and marginal revenue equals marginal cost is

$$20 - \frac{x}{1000} = 2 + \frac{x}{1000} \quad \text{or} \quad 18 = \frac{2x}{1000} \quad \text{or} \quad x = 9000,$$

which gives $p = \$15.50$. Consumer surplus is therefore a triangle with height $20 - 15.5 = \$4.50$ and base 9000 units, for an area of $\frac{1}{2} \times \$4.50 \times 9000 = \$20,250$. Profit is total revenue less total cost, or

$$\$15.50 \times 9000 - \left[2 \times 9000 + \frac{9000^2}{2000}\right] = \$81,000.$$

The impact of the new policy is to raise the monopolist's fixed cost to $\$18,000$ and lower its marginal cost to $x/1000$. Hence, MC = MR becomes

$$20 - \frac{x}{1000} = \frac{x}{1000} \quad \text{or} \quad 20 = \frac{2x}{1000} \quad \text{or} \quad x = 10,000,$$

for a price of $\$15$. The new consumer surplus is $\frac{1}{2} \times (\$20 - \$15) \times 10,000 = \$25,000$, an increase of $\$4750$. And new profit, net of the fixed cost, is

$$\text{TR} - \text{TC} = 150,000 - \frac{10,000^2}{2000} - 18,000 = \$82,000;$$

that is, profit rises by $\$1,000$. Government net revenue is $\$18,000$ for the fee, less $\$2 \times 10,000 = \$20,000$ for the subsidy, or a net $-\$2000$. So the overall impact is a net gain of $\$4750 + \$1000 - \$2000 = \$3750$.

(The idea here is that, with the subsidy, the government pushes the firm closer to the socially optimal level of production, but it recoups much of the subsidy with the fixed fee. Note that, with the figures we gave, it does not recoup all of the subsidy. But consumers are enough better off to be willing to underwrite this policy.)

Solution to Problem III.13

Unless the supply of bus services has an external impact in some other part of the economy, production should be to the level where demand equals marginal cost. This maximizes total surplus. However,

1. This requires a subsidy from general tax revenues, which may cause a dead-weight cost in some other market. If there is a small deadweight cost in this market from "mispriced" bus services, coming nearer to self-supporting operations may be better.

2. The mention of congestion suggests that private automobiles exert a negative externality. If setting bus prices below marginal cost encourages the use of buses over cars, this may reduce those negative externalities and improve social welfare.

Solution to Problem III.14

This can be explained as an instance of price discrimination. If students with lower family incomes have more elastic demand on average, it will enhance profit, using discrimination by group, to charge them a lower price.

This can also be explained as an instance of an externality. If below-average income students generate positive externalities for other students, by increasing diversity and so enhancing student discussions in and out of class, the school may be able to charge above-average-income students more *if* it provides these positive externalities, and to do so it may need to charge below-average-income students less.

Material for Chapter 15
Risk Aversion and Expected Utility

Solution to Problem 15.1

Sheet 1 of the spreadsheet CHAP15, depicted in Figure 15.13, gives the answer. Jo would select gamble A, Professor Kreps would select gamble B, and Professor Patel would select gamble C.

		prizes	probs	Jo MBA	Prof. Kreps	Prof Patel
					Utilities of prizes	
	gamble A	$5,000	1	0.6	-0.9512294	-0.9048374
	gamble B	$40,000	0.4	1	-0.67032	-0.449329
		-$10,000	0.6	0	-1.1051709	-1.2214028
	gamble C	$21,000	0.3333	0.85	-0.8105842	-0.6570468
		$9,000	0.3333	0.68	-0.9139312	-0.8352702
		-$9,000	0.3333	0.1	-1.0941743	-1.1972174
				Jo MBA	Prof. Kreps	Prof Patel
					Expected utilities	
			gamble A	0.6	-0.9512294	-0.9048374
			gamble B	0.4	-0.9312306	-0.9125732
			gamble C	0.543279	-0.9394693	-0.8964218
				Jo MBA	Prof. Kreps	Prof Patel
					Certainty eqivalents	
			gamble A	$5,000	$5,000	$5,000
			gamble B	-$2,500	$7,125	$4,574
			gamble C	$2,500	$6,244	$5,467
				Jo MBA	Prof. Kreps	Prof Patel
					Risk premia	
			gamble A	$0	$0	$0
			gamble B	$12,500	$2,875	$5,426
			gamble C	$4,500	$756	$1,533

Figure 15.13. Sheet 1 of the spreadsheet CHAP15: The answer to Problem 15.1.

Solution to Problem 15.3

(a) The insurance company takes in $40,000 in premium from this policy, and its expected payout is $0.05 \times \$750,000 = \$37,500$, so its expected net from the policy is a gain of $2,500.

(b) If the individual is risk neutral, then without insurance he "owns" a gamble with prizes $1 million with probability 0.95 and $250,000 with probability 0.05, for an expected value of $962,500. If he buys insurance, he will have a net asset position of $960,000 regardless of whether there is a fire or not. So he is better off without insurance.

(c) But if the individual is a risk-averse expected utility maximizer with the utility function $\sqrt{x}$ where x is is net asset position, then with insurance, he has a net asset position of $960,000 with certainty. Without insurance, he "owns" the lottery shown in Figure 15.14, where I supply the utility levels and compute expected utility. His expected utility is [975]. We can either find the utility of $960,000 for sure (by evaluating $\sqrt{960,000} = [979.796]$) or, a bit more informative, we can find his certainty equivalent for the utility level [975] by squaring 975 (since utility is the square-root of the dollar value): $975^2 = \$950,625$, and the decision maker is about $10,000 better off with insurance than without.

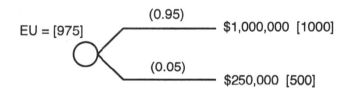

Figure 15.14. Problem 15.3: The lottery facing the decision maker if he does not buy insurance.

(d) To evaluate the possibility of fractional insurance, I build a simple spreadsheet; sheet 2 of the spreadsheet CHAP15, shown in Figure 15.15. In consecutive rows, I give the premium, probability of a loss, asset position if no loss, and the amount of the loss. Then comes the fraction of insurance taken. The next two rows compute the decision maker's net assets if he sustains no loss (assets if no loss less the fraction of the full premium paid) and his net assets if the loss occurs (assets, net of the loss, less the fraction of premium plus the fraction of the loss reimbursed). Then, using the square root function, utility levels, expected utility, and the certainty equivalent are computed.

	A	B	C	D	E	
2						
3			optimal			
4			fractional	full insurance	no insurance	
5		premium	$40,000	$40,000	$40,000	
6		prob loss	0.05	0.05	0.05	
7						
8		asset position no loss	$1,000,000	$1,000,000	$1,000,000	
9		amount of loss	$750,000	$750,000	$750,000	
10						
11		fraction insurance	83.60%	100.00%	0.00%	
12						
13		net if no loss	$966,560	$960,000	$1,000,000	
14		net if loss	$843,564	$960,000	$250,000	
15						
16		utility if no loss	983.14	979.80	1,000.00	
17		utility if loss	918.46	979.80	500.00	
18						
19		expeoted utility	979.9037032	979.7958971	975	
20		CE	$960,211	$960,000	$950,625	

Figure 15.15. Problem 15.3(d): Optimal fractional insurance. This spreadsheet, which is sheet 2 of the spreadsheet CHAP15, shows the computations leading to the conclusion that the optimal fraction of this insurance for this decision maker is 83 percent.

I then ask Solver to maximize expected utility, by varying the fraction of insurance taken. (Had I asked Solver to maximize the CE, I would have gotten the same answer.) The answer is shown in Figure 15.15: The optimal fraction of insurance for this individual is insurance of around 83%, which pushes his CE up a whole $211 over full insurance. (Just for comparison sake, I give the numbers for full insurance and no insurance in the following two columns.)

Solution to Problem 15.4

In Figures 15.16 and 15.17, you will find the calculations for Professors S. Patel and K. Patel, respectively. I hope that the numbers are self-explanatory. These come from sheet 3 of CHAP15, which you should consult if you have questions about how the numbers are computed. (In particular, the formula for turning Professor K. Patel's expected utilities back into CEs should be examined carefully.)

	A	B	C	D	E	F	G	H
4		PROFESSOR S. PATEL						
5					net if wealth =	net if wealth =	net if wealth =	
6			basic prizes	probs	$500,000	$1,000,000	$0	
7		gamble A	50,000	1	$550,000	$1,050,000	$50,000	
8								
9		gamble B	100,000	0.8	$600,000	$1,100,000	$100,000	
10			0	0.2	$500,000	$1,000,000	$0	
11								
12		gamble C	200,000	0.7	$700,000	$1,200,000	$200,000	
13			0	0.3	$500,000	$1,000,000	$0	
14								
15				utilities	-1.67017E-05	-7.58256E-10	-0.367879441	
16								
17					-6.14421E-06	-2.78947E-10	-0.135335283	
18					-4.53999E-05	-2.06115E-09	-1	
19								
20					-8.31529E-07	-3.77513E-11	-0.018315639	
21					-4.53999E-05	-2.06115E-09	-1	
22								
23				EXPECTED UTILITIES				
24				gamble A	-1.67017E-05	-7.58256E-10	-0.367879441	
25				gamble B	-1.39954E-05	-6.35388E-10	-0.308268227	
26				gamble C	-1.4202E-05	-6.44772E-10	-0.312820947	
27								
28				CERTAINTY EQUIVALENTS				
29				gamble A	$550,000	$1,050,000	$50,000	
30				gamble B	$558,839	$1,058,839	$58,839	
31				gamble C	$558,106	$1,058,106	$58,106	

Figure 15.16. Problem 15.4: Computations for Professor S. Patel.

	A	B	C	D	E	F	G	H
33								
34		PROFESSOR K. PATEL						
35					net if wealth =	net if wealth =	net if wealth =	
36			basic prizes	probs	$500,000	$1,000,000	$0	
37		gamble A	50,000	1	$550,000	$1,050,000	$50,000	
38								
39		gamble B	100,000	0.8	$600,000	$1,100,000	$100,000	
40			0	0.2	$500,000	$1,000,000	$0	
41								
42		gamble C	200,000	0.7	$700,000	$1,200,000	$200,000	
43			0	0.3	$500,000	$1,000,000	$0	
44								
45				utilities	99.9999665966	99.9999999985	99.2642411177	
46								
47					99.9999877116	99.9999999994	99.7293294335	
48					99.9999092001	99.9999999959	98.0000000000	
49								
50					99.9999983369	99.9999999999	99.9633687222	
51					99.9999092001	99.9999999959	98.0000000000	
52								
53				EXPECTED UTILITIES				
54				gamble A	99.9999665966	99.9999999985	99.2642411177	
55				gamble B	99.9999720093	99.9999999987	99.3834635468	
56				gamble C	99.9999715959	99.9999999987	99.3743581056	
57								
58				CERTAINTY EQUIVALENTS				
59				gamble A	$550,000	$1,050,000	$50,000	
60				gamble B	$558,839	$1,058,840	$58,839	
61				gamble C	$558,106	$1,058,106	$58,106	

Figure 15.17. Problem 15.4: Computations for Professor K. Patel.

Further Discussion: Exponential Utility Functions

Please note carefully the following from the solution to Problem 15.4:

- The ranking of the three gambles by either Professor Patel does not depend on his base level of wealth. In fact, the CE of each gamble simply moves up and down linearly with the twins' wealth; that is, Sanjay Patel's CE for gamble B is $558,839 if his base level of wealth is $500,000; it is $1,058,839 if his base level of wealth is $1 million; and it is $58,839 if his base level of wealth is $0. Indeed, with this utility function, if his initial net asset position were, say, −$100,000 (he is in debt), then his CE for gamble B superimposed on this initial net asset position would be $58,839 − $100,000 = −$41,161. Changing the base level of wealth changes the utility numbers but nothing else of economic significance.

- Notwithstanding the problem's remarks about how K. Patel is twice as excitable and 100 units more optimistic than S. Patel, their utility functions are simple "displacement plus uniform stretching or compression" of one another's. So they rank the gambles identically and, in fact, their certainty equivalents are identical. All that changes are the utility numbers themselves.

Exponential utility functions, which have constant absolute risk aversion, are particularly noteworthy for the first of these two properties: If you add or subtract a constant amount to all the prizes in a given gamble and the decision maker has exponential utility, then you shift the certainty equivalent by this amount. This makes certain calculations relatively easy, which is why exponential utility functions turn up a lot in examples and models.

Let me illustrate with a further example, the example from Problem 15.2. An uninsured individual faces a situation in which assets will be either $1,000,000 or $250,000, with probabilities 0.95 and 0.05, respectively. In Problem 15.2, we assumed that the individual had utility function $\sqrt{x}$, so that this individual's (uninsured) expected utility is $0.95 \times \sqrt{1,000,000} + 0.05 \times \sqrt{250,000} = [975]$. This meant a certainty equivalent of $950,625.

Change the problem as follows. First, assume that the only available insurance policy has a $100,000 deductible; that is, the individual who buys this insurance policy has a final asset position of $1,000,000 less the premium for this policy if there is no loss, and $900,000 less the premium for this policy if the loss is incurred. And then, instead of asking whether the individual would be willing to purchase the policy (if the alternative is no insurance), we ask, What is the largest premium this individual would pay, if the alternative is no insurance?

To solve this, note that with insurance, if the premium is P, the individual's expected utility is

$$0.95 \times \sqrt{1,000,000 - P} \; + \; 0.05 \times \sqrt{900,000 - P}.$$

To find the largest premium the individual would pay, we have to set this expression equal to the person's no-insurance expected utility level [975] and solve for P. This is not too difficult—you can do it with Excel and either Solver or Goal Seek—but you cannot solve this precisely using algebra.

Suppose instead we were doing this problem for an individual with a utility function that is exponential. Suppose, being specific, the individual has exponential utility function $U(x) = -e^{-0.00001x}$. You still need either Excel or a good calculator, but the following are straightforward computations:

1. If the individual goes without insurance, his expected utility is

$$0.95 \times [-e^{-0.00001 \times 1,000,000}] \; + \; 0.05 \times [-e^{-0.00001 \times 250,000}] = -0.00414738$$

Therefore, his certainty equivalent with no insurance is the solution to

$$-e^{-0.00001 \times \text{CE}} = -0.00414738 \quad \text{or} \quad \text{CE} = \frac{\ln(0.00414738)}{-0.00001} = \$548,527.85.$$

2. If the individual gets insurance with a deductible of \$100,000 *for free* (that is, with a premium of \$0), his expected utility is

$$0.95 \times [-e^{-0.00001 \times 1,000,000}] + 0.05 \times [-e^{-0.00001 \times 900,000}] = -0.0000493$$

Therefore, his certainty equivalent with free insurance is the solution to

$$-e^{-0.00001 \times \text{CE}} = -0.0000493 \quad \text{or} \quad \text{CE} = \frac{\ln(0.0000493)}{-0.00001} = \$991,757.79.$$

With these two calculations done, we reask, What is largest premium this individual would pay, if the alternative is no insurance? A premium of P lowers the two prizes in the second gamble (the gamble with insurance) by the premium P. Therefore, *because this individual has exponential utility*, a premium of P lowers the with-insurance certainty equivalent by precisely the amount of the premium, P.

In other words, if the premium for this insurance policy is P, the certainty equivalent for the with-insurance gamble is $\$991{,}757.79 - P$. The largest premium the individual would pay for this insurance is therefore the solution to

$$\$991{,}757.79 - P = \$548{,}527.85 \quad \text{or} \quad P = \$443{,}229.94.$$

The Mean–Variance Model

In courses and books in finance, you are likely to encounter the *mean–variance model* of choice under uncertainty. It is applied primarily in the context of selecting portfolios of risky assets, but in principle it can be used much more broadly, whenever prizes are monetary. It is quite simple: Since prizes are monetary, a measure of the "average prize" of each gamble is its expected monetary value, or EMV. A measure of the amount of risk in the gamble is its variance. The decision maker then is assumed to have preferences represented by indifference curves in mean–variance space; more mean is better, less variance is better.

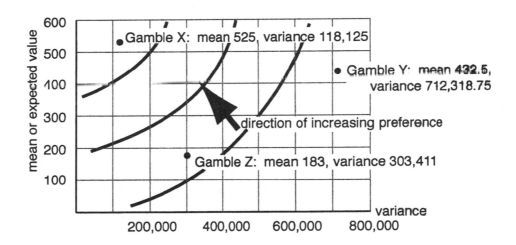

Figure 15.18. Mean-variance preferences. This figure shows "typical" indifference curves in mean–variance space and locates the three gambles from Figure 15.6 along these two dimensions. Gamble X is most preferred according to the preferences represented by these indifference curves, with Gamble Z coming second. (Since Gamble X has the highest mean and the lowest variance, it is ranked first by *every* set of mean–variance preferences.)

For instance, imagine that the decision maker has the preferences given by the indifference curves in Figure 15.18. And imagine that the decision maker has her choice of the three gambles in Figure 15.6. We compute the means and variances of the three gambles and locate them in mean variance space; they appear as the three heavy dots shown. Since the mean–variance pair for the first gamble is on the highest indifference curve for this individual, that is what she chooses according to this model of behavior.

Mean–variance preferences are analytically very convenient when the "gambles" the decision maker might choose are portfolios made from some finite list of securities. Your finance textbook or professor can show you why this is, but it is so; and this is the reason that finance courses and textbooks use the mean–variance model. But despite its analytical convenience, the model gives rise to some pretty strange behavior.

For instance, imagine two investment strategies. One gives a payoff of $100 for sure. The second is risky, with an expected payoff of $101 and with variance n. If a decision maker trades off mean against variance at all, it ought to be that, for n large enough, she prefers the sure thing. Suppose, for example, that a variance of $n = 10^{10}$ is "too much risk" to bear for the extra $1 in expected return. (If it takes a larger variance so this is true, simply adjust the numbers following.) Now suppose that the second, risky gamble has the following full distribution: With probability $(10^{11} - 1)/10^{11}$, it provides a payoff of $100. With probability $1/10^{11}$, it provides a payoff of $100 + 10^{11}$. The expected value of this gamble is $101 and its variance is $10^{11} - 1 > 10^{10}$. Therefore, if the decision maker took mean–variance preferences literally, they would tell her to choose $100 for sure, rather than this gamble, which, I assume, she would not do, since the gamble gives her $100 at least and a small chance for a lot more.

The problem is that mean and variance are roughly descriptive of the "average" and "risk" of a random variable, but it takes the whole distribution and not two summary statistics to figure out how individuals feel about the distribution. To the extent that mean and variance capture average and risk approximately, a mean–variance model based preferences give an approximation to "correct" preferences; but only an approximation.

In restricted cases, mean–variance preferences work perfectly well. The first is if the individual's utility function is quadratic; that is, of the form

$$U(x) = ax - bx^2 \text{ for } a, b > 0.$$

Then, for any gamble at all, if the expected value of the gamble is m and its variance is s^2, its expected utility is $am + bm^2 - bs^2$; the expected utility of the gamble is a simple function of gamble's expected value and variance, and so the mean–variance model works. But quadratic utility has a problem. For large values of

x ($x > a/(2b)$), this utility function is decreasing in x; someone with a quadratic utility function prefers less money to more when the amount of money gets large enough.

Alternatively, if all the gambles considered are from some restricted family of probability distributions, such as Normals, then mean–variance preferences work, whatever is the decision maker's utility function. The reason takes us more deeply into the subject than I want to go, so I do not explain why. But, as a partial explanation, note that two Normals with the same mean and variance have the same distribution; this is clearly going to be necessary for the family of distributions, if mean and variance adequately describe preferences for all utility functions. For more on this, ask your Finance instructor.

Material for Chapter 16

Expected Utility as a Normative Decision Aid

Solution to Problem 16.1

It is of course impossible to give a solution to this problem, since the problem involves your personal subjective judgments. Good luck!

Solution to Problem 16.2

In Figure 16.5, I show you numbers from the spreadsheet CHAP16, which tell you the certainty equivalents for the five gambles of Figure 16.1 for individuals having constant risk aversion and coefficients of risk aversion λ = 0.000005, 0.000008, 0.00001, 0.000012, and 0.000015. (Note that these progress from less risk averse to more.) If you are unsure how the spreadsheet does all these computations, it might be a good idea to download and examine it.

The place to direct your attention (once you see how this works) is the bottom, where the CEs for the five gambles are given for each of the five levels of risk aversion. For column F, the least risk averse, the order is Gamble B, then C, E, D, and A, with a substantial gap (almost $400 in value) between E and D, and a tiny gap between B and C. For the four other levels of risk aversion, gamble C is best, then B, E, D, and A.

The point should be clear. For levels of risk aversion over this wide range, gambles B and C are the best two of this set, with little separating them. To make this choice, I really need not know my precise level of risk aversion or, more precisely, if I got my level of risk aversion "wrong" in the sense that (say) I estimated it at 0.000005 when it was really 0.00001, I would pick B instead of C, an error of $37 in value ($6852 versus $6815). Big deal.

This is not to say that everyone with constant risk aversion would rank these gambles in this fashion. But it takes dramatically different coefficients of risk aversion to make a difference. In Figure 16.6, I give you the numbers for levels (coefficients) of risk aversion λ = 0.00005, 0.0001, and 0.005 (more and more risk averse). You

	A	B	C	D	E	F	G	H	I	J
1			coefficient of risk aversion			0.000005	0.000008	0.00001	0.000012	0.000015
2										
3			prizes	probs				UTILITY LEVELS		
4										
5		gamble A	$6,000	1		-0.9704455	-0.9531338	-0.9417645	-0.9305309	-0.9139312
6										
7		gamble B	$10,000	0.8		-0.9512294	-0.9231163	-0.9048374	-0.8869204	-0.860708
8			-$5,000	0.2		-1.0253151	-1.0408108	-1.0512711	-1.0618365	-1.0778842
9										
10		gamble C	$10,000	0.5		-0.9512294	-0.9231163	-0.9048374	-0.8869204	-0.860708
11			$3,800	0.5		-0.9811794	-0.9700574	-0.9627129	-0.9554241	-0.9445941
12										
13		gamble D	$13,000	0.3		-0.9370675	-0.9012253	-0.8780954	-0.8555592	-0.8228347
14			$4,000	0.5		-0.9801987	-0.9685066	-0.9607894	-0.9531338	-0.9417645
15			$2,000	0.2		-0.9900498	-0.9841273	-0.9801987	-0.9762857	-0.9704455
16										
17		gamble E	-$7,500	0.07		-1.038212	-1.0618365	-1.0778842	-1.0941743	-1.1190723
18			$1,000	0.23		-0.9950125	-0.9920319	-0.9900498	-0.9880717	-0.9851119
19			$6,000	0.38		-0.9704455	-0.9531338	-0.9417645	-0.9305309	-0.9139312
20			$15,000	0.32		-0.9277435	-0.8869204	-0.860708	-0.8352702	-0.7985162
21										
22		EXPECTED UTILITIES								
23				gamble A		-0.9704455	-0.9531338	-0.9417645	-0.9305309	-0.9139312
24				gamble B		-0.9660466	-0.9466552	-0.9341242	-0.9219037	-0.9041432
25				gamble C		-0.9662044	-0.9465869	-0.9337752	-0.9211722	-0.902651
26				gamble D		-0.9692295	-0.9514463	-0.9398631	-0.9284918	-0.9118218
27				gamble E		-0.9671749	-0.9485013	-0.9364604	-0.9247369	-0.9077298
28										
29		CERTAINTY EQUIVALENTS								
30				gamble A		$6,000	$6,000	$6,000	$6,000	$6,000
31				gamble B		$6,909	$6,853	$6,815	$6,776	$6,710
32				gamble C		$6,876	$6,862	$6,852	$6,842	$6,828
33				gamble D		$6,251	$6,221	$6,202	$6,183	$6,154
34				gamble E		$6,675	$6,609	$6,565	$6,521	$6,454

Figure 16.5. Problem 16.2: Ranking the five gambles for constant risk aversion, for five different levels of risk aversion.

see here that, while Gamble C remains the most attractive for the first two levels, the risks of Gambles B and E begin to make those look very unattractive, and by the time we get to $\lambda = 0.005$ (which is very risk averse), the sure-thing Gamble A takes first place. Please note how risk averse is $\lambda = 0.005$: For this level of risk aversion, a gamble with prizes $0 and $6200, each equally likely, would have a certainty equivalent of $139. Now that's risk averse!

	L	M	N	O	P	
1		coef risk aver	0.00005	0.0001	0.005	
2						
3						
4						
5			-0.7408182	-0.5488116	-9.358E-14	
6						
7			-0.6065307	-0.3678794	-1.929E-22	
8			-1.2840254	-1.6487213	-7.2E+10	
9						
10			-0.6065307	-0.3678794	-1.929E-22	
11			-0.8269591	-0.6838614	-5.603E-09	
12						
13			-0.5220458	-0.2725318	-5.9E-29	
14			-0.8187308	-0.67032	-2.061E-09	
15			-0.9048374	-0.8187308	-4.54E-05	
16						
17			-1.4549914	-2.117	-1.932E+16	
18			-0.9512294	-0.9048374	-0.0067379	
19			-0.7408182	-0.5488116	-9.358E-14	
20			-0.4723666	-0.2231302	-2.679E-33	
21						
22						
23			-0.7408182	-0.5488116	-9.358E-14	
24			-0.7420296	-0.6240478	-1.44E+10	
25			-0.7167449	-0.5258704	-2.801E-09	
26			-0.7469466	-0.5806657	-9.081E-06	
27			-0.7533004	-0.6362527	-1.353E+15	
28						
29						
30		Gamble A	$6,000	$6,000	$6,000	
31		Gamble B	$5,967	$4,715	-$4,678	
32		Gamble C	$6,661	$6,427	$3,939	
33		Gamble D	$5,835	$5,436	$2,322	
34		Gamble E	$5,666	$4,522	-$6,968	

Figure 16.6. Problem 16.2: More analysis, for more risk averse people.

Material for Chapter 17

Risk Sharing and Spreading:

Securities and Insurance Markets

Solution to Problem 17.1

(a) Figure 17.2 displays sheet 1 of the spreadsheet PROB17.1, which gives the basic calculations: The two prizes and their probabilities are specified, then Jan MBA's expected utility and certainty equivalent are calculated for a given percentage share retained. Note that, at 100% retained, Jan MBA's CE is −$1005.44

	A	B	C	D	E	F	G
1							
2		prize #1	$50,000				
3		prize #2	-$25,000				
4							
5		probability #1	0.5				
6		probability #2	0.5				
7							
8		percent retained	utility #1	utility #2	Exepected U	Certainty Eq	
9							
10		100%	9.9999793	-0.0000563	4.9999615	-$1,005.44	
11							

Figure 17.2. Problem 17.1: Basic calculations. In this spreadsheet, sheet 1 of PROB17.1, the basic calculations for this problem are performed.

In Figure 17.3, you find the upper portion of sheet 2. Row 10 of sheet 1 is copied 51 times, and the percentage retained is set successively at 100, 98, 96, and so forth, down to 0. The corresponding CEs are graphed, giving the shape shown.

(b) Take any row of spreadsheet and ask Solver to maximize the expected utility (or certainty equivalent), changing the percentage retained. Solver comes back with a maximizing percentage to retain of 43.80077, and a corresponding CE of $2684.03. (I copied a row of the basic spreadsheet into row 66 of sheet 2 and did the analysis there, with the results shown in Figure 17.4.)

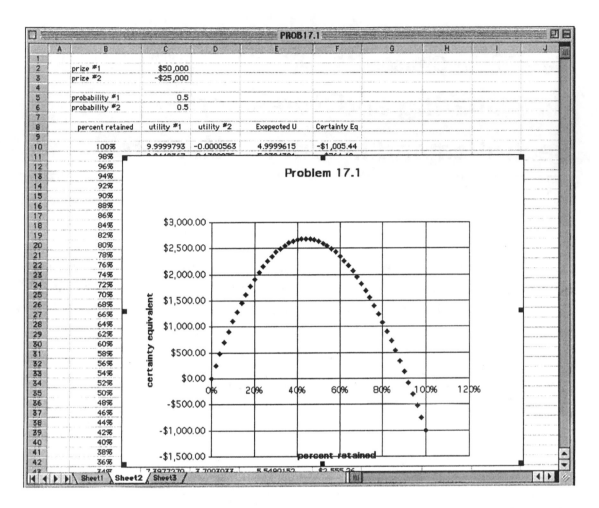

Figure 17.3. Problem 17.1: CE versus percentage retained. The percentage Jan retains is set at 100, 98, and so forth, and her corresponding CE is computed. Then, the percentage retained versus CE is graphed.

(c) In theory, since this is the (limit of) the ratio of CE to percentage retained as the percentage retained approaches 0, the slope should be the expected value of the gamble, $12,500. And this is what happens: I copied the basic row of the spreadsheet one more time, into row 71 of sheet 2, and had EXCEL calculate the CE and so forth for 0.0001 percent retained. I took the corresponding CE, in cell F71, and divided it by 0.0001 percent, with the result shown in cell G71: The ratio is $12,499.99 (see Figure 17.4).

PROB17.1

	A	B	C	D	E	F	G
62							
63							
64		FINDING THE MAXIMIZING SHARE TO RETAIN					
65							
66		43.80077%	7.9073722	3.2288443	5.5681083	$2,684.03	
67							
68							
69		FINDING THE SLOPE AT ZERO RETAINED					
70							RATIO
71		0.0001%	5.1592078	5.1591961	5.1592020	$0.01250	$12,499.99
72							

Sheet1 Sheet2 Sheet3

Figure 17.4. Problem 17.1: Further calculations. In row 66 of sheet 2 of the spreadsheet, I had Solver find the share retained that maximizes Jan's EU (or CE). In row 71, results are given if she retains a tiny share (0.0001%), then the ratio of her CE for this share to the size of the share is computed. Per theory, the ratio is (practically) the EMV of the gamble.

Solution to Problem 17.2

The spreadsheet PROB17.2 is a how-to manual on this problem. The bottom lines are these:

(a) The buyer would not take a 10% share on these terms.

(b) 4.21%.

(c) 1.69%, 8.89%, and 3.56%.

(d) For $U(x) = \sqrt{x}$, $-U''(x)/U'(x) = 0.00001$ at $x = 0$, so the answers you come up with will look a lot like the second two pieces of part c. If you are this far, you can probably untangle what is going on.

Solution to Problem 17.3

Sheet 1 of the spreadsheet PROB17.3/4 gives the basic setup for this problem and the next. After recording basic facts about the gamble (including the probability of the $50,000 outcome according to Jan MBA), figures for price per 1% and the percentage share retained by Jan are recorded. With these, we compute the net outcomes for Jan in the two different outcomes (percentage retained times overall outcome, plus percentage sold times the price), Jan's utility levels, her expected utility, and finally her CE. All this is depicted in Figure 17.5.

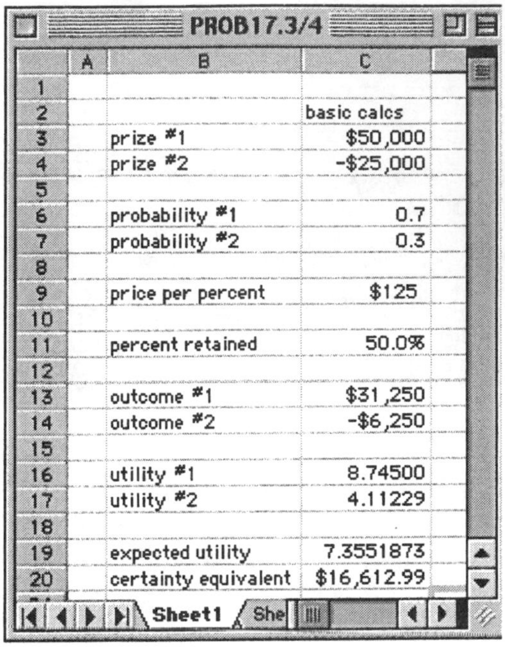

PROB17.3/4

	A	B	C
1			
2			basic calcs
3		prize #1	$50,000
4		prize #2	-$25,000
5			
6		probability #1	0.7
7		probability #2	0.3
8			
9		price per percent	$125
10			
11		percent retained	50.0%
12			
13		outcome #1	$31,250
14		outcome #2	-$6,250
15			
16		utility #1	8.74500
17		utility #2	4.11229
18			
19		expected utility	7.3551873
20		certainty equivalent	$16,612.99

Sheet1 / She

Figure 17.5. Problems 17.3 and 17.4: Basic calculations. Sheet 1 of the spreadsheet PROB17.3/4 performs the basic calculations for these two problems: Taking the data of the problem, including the price per percent sold and as a function of the percent Jan MBA retains, it calculates her net outcomes, their utility, her expected utility, then her certainty equivalent.

Now, we optimize the share sold. Solver is asked to maximize Jan's EU, varying the percentage she retains. The result is given in Column C of sheet 2 of this spreadsheet (shown in Figure 17.6); the optimal share for Jan to retain in these circumstances is 53.5417%.

Solution to Problem 17.4

Jan's best course of action is to sell off 30% of the venture (retain 70%). (Columns E through H of Sheet 2 of PROB17.3/4 should be consulted. There is one column for each of the ranges of percentage sold; when Solver optimizes the percentage sold in each column, it does so subject to the appropriate constraint.)

Real-life applications of this basic phenomenon add another level of complication. To get investors to trust in your venture, an entrepreneur may have to reveal critical details that lower the probability of success, as in this problem. But the "leakage" of information (which degrades the chances of success) is not a simple function of how much is sold; it depends on the number and character of the investors. In

		Problem 17.3		Problem 17.4.1	Problem 17.4.2	Problem 17.4.3	Problem 17.4.4
prize #1		$50,000		$50,000	$50,000	$50,000	$50,000
prize #2		-$25,000		-$25,000	-$25,000	-$25,000	-$25,000
probability #1		0.7		0.7	0.65	0.6	0.5
probability #2		0.3		0.3	0.35	0.4	0.5
price per percent		$125		$261	$226	$190	$119
percent retained		53.5417%		90.0000%	70.0000%	50.0000%	2.1066%
outcome #1		$32,578		$47,613	$41,769	$34,500	$12,678
outcome #2		-$7,578		-$19,888	-$10,731	-$3,000	$11,098
utility #1		8.85114		9.86637	9.50950	8.99956	6.90237
utility #2		3.87147		1.28697	3.27197	4.67389	6.70970
expected utility		7.357240575		7.29255286	7.326363139	7.269293995	6.806035616
certainty equivalent		$16,631.60		$16,048.85	$16,352.54	$15,841.07	$11,881.58

Figure 17.6. Problems 17.3 and 17.4: Analysis. In column C, we have the Solver-optimized share to retain if Jan believes the chances of success are 0.7, but she can sell shares only for $125 per 1%. In columns E, F, G, and H, we find the SOLVER-optimized shares for her to sell in Problem 17.4, where the more she sells, the lower are her chances of the successful, $50,000 outcome. The overall optimum is in column G: retain 70%, for a CE of $16,352.54.

information-sensitive cases, entrepreneurs may be motivated to seek out only a few outside investors, those who are less likely to leak information or who are more willing to invest on more or less blind faith. Therefore we observe both: investors who are family or friends of the entrepreneur; and investors (venture capitalists or angels) who cultivate a reputation for preserving confidentiality.

Solution to Problem 17.5

We spend a lot of time on the issue raised by this problem in the next chapter, so I do not go into a lot of detail here. But the explanation is not hard to give: At a price of $120 per 1%, MBA students who own a gamble that pays off $50,000 with probability 0.6, if they have the risk attitude of Jan MBA, want to sell only 83% of their gamble. But MBA students who own a gamble that pays $50,000 with probability 0.4 want to sell all 100% of their shares at this price per 1%. (To replicate my numbers, you can use the spreadsheets PROB17.3/4.) Therefore, assuming a market price of $120 per 1%, more shares are in circulation from the less good gambles; the numbers work out so that the chances of the $50,000 for a randomly selected share offered for sale in these circumstances is the 0.484 number mentioned in the problem.

If you think about it, there is a way around this problem: When an MBA offers you a 1% share in a gamble, ask: "How much of your own gamble are you retaining?" Students with good gambles want to retain more of their gambles, so it makes sense for you to invest only in MBA gambles where the student involved retains more of that gamble. Then the price per 1% of gambles from students who are retaining more should be higher than the price per 1% of gambles from students who are retaining less. This is going to get very complex very quickly, which is why Chapter 18 is devoted entirely to this subject.

Solution to Problem 17.7

(a) This requires, conceptually, a simple application of Solver. Taking the basic spreadsheet, we ask it to maximize Ringo's CE (or expected utility), subject to holding John, Paul, and George's CEs (or EUs) at their initial levels, varying the sharing rule amounts for John, Paul, and George, and giving Ringo whatever is left over after giving John, Paul, and George their shares.

As noted in the statement of the problem, to get Solver to work on this, I needed to choose the option of automatic scaling. Once that was done, I got back the answers shown in Figure 17.7.

It is perhaps worth noting the general nature of the "answer." Paul is the least risk averse, so his shares show the widest dispersion. There is little difference in George, John, and Ringo, although George seems the most risk averse.

(Optional: I can check that this is the answer, by looking across the Fab Four at the ratios of their marginal utilities in various states. See Figure 17.8, which should be self-explanatory to anyone reading this far into a parenthetical remark marked "optional.")

(b) This is easy. Ringo is risk neutral, so efficient risk sharing means he gets all the risk, and John, Paul, and George get sure things. Since we want the three to have CEs of $50,000 each, we give them sure-thing payments of $50,000 each, and Ringo sucks up what is left: If the overall outcome is $100,000, Ringo has to lay out $50,000. If the overall outcome is $200,000, Ringo takes home $50,000. If the overall outcome is $300,000, Ringo takes home $150,000. And if the overall outcome is $400,000, Ringo makes the big bucks: He gets $250,000. Given the probabilities of the four outcomes, this gives Ringo an EMV (= CE) of $50,000. In other words, this efficient sharing rule is also the rule that equilibrates the CEs for the Fab Four.

PROB17.7

	A	B	C	D	E	F
1						
2						
3			state 1	state 2	state 3	state 4
4		Total	$100,000.00	$200,000.00	$300,000.00	$400,000.00
5						
6		John	$31,725.77	$47,799.90	$65,109.31	$83,249.03
7		Paul	$645.26	$51,600.56	$106,567.78	$164,117.50
8		George	$34,632.01	$47,106.04	$59,378.77	$71,396.83
9		Ringo	$32,996.96	$53,493.50	$68,944.14	$81,236.64
10						
11		probs	0.4	0.3	0.2	0.1
12						
13		John's utility	178.1172967	218.6318798	255.1652602	288.5290766
14		Paul's utility	317.2463735	389.3591652	454.4972844	513.923628
15		George's utilit	32.58426347	36.10242924	38.99880344	41.46972868
16		Ringo's utility	-0.718945595	-0.58570734	-0.501856344	-0.443806584
17						
18			EU	CE		
19		John	216.7224423	$46,968.62		
20		Paul	385.9981186	$48,994.55		
21		George	35.81116771	$45,925.66		
22		Ringo	-0.608042368	$49,751.07		
23						

Sheet1 | Sheet2 | Sheet3

Figure 17.7 Problem 17.7: The answer according to Solver.

PROB17.7

	A	B	C	D	E	F	G	H	I	J
1										
2										
3			state 1	state 2	state 3	state 4				
4		Total	$100,000.00	$200,000.00	$300,000.00	$400,000.00				
5										
6		John	$31,725.77	$47,799.90	$65,109.31	$83,249.03				
7		Paul	$645.26	$51,600.56	$106,567.78	$164,117.50				
8		George	$34,632.01	$47,106.04	$59,378.77	$71,396.83				
9		Ringo	$32,996.96	$53,493.50	$68,944.14	$81,236.64				
10										
11		probs	0.4	0.3	0.2	0.1				
12										
13		John's utility	178.1172967	218.6318798	255.1652602	288.5290766				
14		Paul's utility	317.2463735	389.3591652	454.4972844	513.923628				
15		George's utilit	32.58426347	36.10242924	38.99880344	41.46972868				
16		Ringo's utility	-0.718945595	-0.585707342	-0.501856344	-0.443806584				
17										
18			EU	CE						
19		John	216.7224423	$46,968.62						
20		Paul	385.9981186	$48,994.55						
21		George	35.81116771	$45,925.66						
22		Ringo	-0.608042368	$49,751.07						
23								ratio 1:2	ratio 1:3	ratio 1:4
24										
25		John's MUs	0.002807	0.002287	0.001960	0.001733		1.22746013	1.43256868	1.61988241
26		Paul's MUs	0.001576	0.001284	0.001100	0.000973		1.22730848	1.43263193	1.61995115
27		George's MUs	0.000314	0.000256	0.000219	0.000194		1.22762687	1.43252806	1.61982674
28		Ringo's Mus	0.000007	0.000006	0.000005	0.000004		1.22748264	1.4325725	1.61995252

Sheet1 | Sheet2 | Sheet3

Figure 17.8. Problem 17.7: I know Figure 17.7 is the answer because . . . the ratios of marginal utilities across states are equalized across the Fab Four.

How Do Insurance Companies Defeat Risk Aversion?
Risk Spreading or the Law of Averages?

Although it is a special excursion, having introduced risk spreading and sharing as the raison d'être for insurance companies, it may be useful to say a few more words about how insurance companies defeat risk aversion.

Think of an insurance company as a body that combines many independent risks and then spreads the risk out among a large number of shareholders. Most popular accounts of the insurance business invoke the law of averages or of large numbers to explain why this arrangement leads to risk neutrality. The idea is that, when insurance companies put together a lot of risks in a portfolio, the good outcomes cancel out the bad and, if the "average" payout is less than the premium paid on the policy, the good outcomes (policies where the premium more than covers any payout) outweigh the bad, where the payout exceeds the premium.

This is *not* the story told in Chapter 17. Chapter 17 says that insurance companies are close to risk neutral because they spread the risk over a large number of individuals, each of whom is therefore nearly risk neutral for his or her share of the risk.

Notwithstanding all those popular accounts, the second story captures the truth. If the first story is right (if the portfolio of many risks does the trick), then insurance companies with a single shareholder, bearing all the risk of the portfolio, would work. If the second story is right (if the explanation for why insurance companies work is risk spread over a large number of individuals), then an insurance company with many small shareholders that insures a single risk would work.

Of course, we already know that the second story works. If you take a single risk and parcel it out in many small shares to many individuals, its value rises to its expected monetary value, because each of the small shares represents a very small amount of risk. This is true even if it is a single risk; if no "law of averages" is at work at all.

As for the first story, when we sum up the risks in an insurance company's portfolio, it is certainly true that some good outcomes cancel out some bad outcomes. But there is a lot of risk in the sum, more than any single investor would be comfortable taking on. The law of averages (that the good outcomes almost surely outweigh the bad outcomes, assuming the expected value of each risk is positive) applies not to the sum of a collection of risks but to their average. And we are looking at average outcomes only if we take the insurance company's large portfolio and divide it into pieces; that is, if we share the risk.

Hidden Information, Signaling, and Screening

Job Market Signaling, or Why Are MBA Programs So Painful?

The theory of equilibrium signaling was developed by A. Michael Spence (for which he shared the Nobel Prize in 2001). Spence developed the theory in the context of job-market signaling; he explained how able young men and women might use an otherwise useless education to signal that they are relatively able, if the cost to them of surviving higher education is lower than the cost to individuals who are relatively less able. Especially since Spence was later dean of the Stanford Graduate School of Business, it is appropriate to retell his original analysis in the context of MBA programs. But a warning is in order: My experiences telling this entirely fanciful tale—it is good theory, but not empirically valid, I hope—have been that a nonnegligible fraction of Stanford Business School students, struggling in their first term, do not find this at all humorous.

Imagine a completely fictitious world in which investment bakeries seek to hire individuals who possess a single skill; the ability to work at all hours of day and night, even in a state of advanced sleep deprivation. Such individuals are invaluable to investment bakeries, which are willing to pay a large amount of money to lure such people into their employ. The amount of money is so large that everyone in society wishes to get one of these jobs, even though only 1% of the population is really qualified to do so. For reasons I do not get into, bakeries must know in advance that the people they hire are from the 1% that can stand up to the physical demands of the job, and bakeries are unable to ascertain this through direct observation or medical examination.

In this society, there is a Famous East Coast Bakery School (hereafter called FECBAS), which specializes in providing MBAs (Masters of Bakery Administration) to its students while giving them absolutely no useful knowledge. None of the education imparted at FECBAS is of any use in a productive sense. But FECBAS does provide a signaling device. The heart of the FECBAS MBA program is the core, a full-year trip into the pits of hell, in which students must work all hours of the day and night, even in a state of advanced sleep deprivation. Since the FECBAS core curriculum is only a year long, any member of the population can survive it. But it is extremely distasteful to everyone.

The key is that, while this program is distasteful to everyone, it is comparatively less distasteful to the 1% of the population that investment bakeries would like to identify. That is, for any member of that 1% of the population, two years at FECBAS (including a year in the core) followed by a job with an investment bakery is preferable to a more normal job; while for the other 99% of the population, the job with an investment bakery is insufficient compensation for two years at FECBAS. Hence, the 1% of the population that can stand the FECBAS program go there as a signal that they are in this 1%; and they get jobs as investment bakers in consequence. "Education" at FECBAS is a pure signal sent by the 1% to distinguish themselves from the masses, and the signal works because while everyone dislikes the FECBAS program, this 1% dislikes it relatively less.

Solution to Problem 18.1

(a) Suppose Drake does not buy insurance. If he lands a summer job, his utility is $\sqrt{50,000 + 40,000} = 300$. If he fails to land a summer job, his utility is $\sqrt{40,000} = 200$. Since he has probability 0.7 of landing a job, this gives him expected utility (without insurance) of 270, for a certainty equivalent of $270^2 - 40,000 = \$32,900$. On the other hand, if he buys this insurance policy, his utility if he lands a summer job is $\sqrt{80,000} = 282.84$, and if he fails to land a summer job, his utility is $\sqrt{60,000} = 244.94$, for an expected utility of 271.47 and a certainty equivalent of $33,698. Therefore, Drake will buy this insurance policy.

You can do the calculations in the preceding paragraph by hand (if your calculator gives you square roots). But I used an Excel spreadsheet, PROB18.1. Sheet 1 of this spreadsheet is reproduced in Figure 18.1. Note that this spreadsheet calculates EUs and CEs for all five types of FECBUS students (categorized by their chances of landing a job), both for no insurance and for this policy. Note in particular the CE values for no insurance for the five types; these numbers are used a lot in what follows.

(b) If Beantown is risk neutral, since Drake is risk averse, efficient risk sharing mandates that Drake should be completely shielded from risk, which means (in this context) a full insurance policy, or one that has a payout of $50,000. If the

				prob of job	0.9	0.8	0.7	0.6	0.5
NO	premium	$0							
INSURANCE	payout if no job	$0							
	outcome if job	$50,000							
	outcome if no job	$0							
	utility if job	300							
	utility if no job	200							
	expected utilities				290	280	270	260	250
	certainty equivalents				$44,100.00	$38,400.00	$32,900.00	$27,600.00	$22,500.00
PART (a)	premium	$10,000							
	payout if no job	$30,000							
	outcome if job	$40,000							
	outcome if no job	$20,000							
	utility if job	282.842712							
	utility if no job	244.948974							
	expected utilities				279.053339	275.263965	271.474591	267.685217	263.895843
	certainty equivalents				$37,870.77	$35,770.25	$33,698.45	$31,655.38	$29,641.02

Figure 18.1. Problem 18.1: The basic spreadsheet. This is sheet 1 of the spreadsheet PROB18.1, which computes EUs and CEs for the five categories of students from FECBUS, for policies specified by a premium and payout amount if the student fails to land a job.

premium is P, Drake's outcome with such a policy is $50,000 - P$ for sure, and since going without insurance gives him a certainty equivalent of $32,900, the largest premium he would be willing to pay for full insurance is $50,000 - $32,900 = $17,100. On the other hand, to break even, Beantown must charge a premium of at least $0.3 \times $50,000 = $15,000$. So the answer is this: full insurance and any premium between $15,000 and $17,100.

(c) If Beantown offers an insurance policy that gives full insurance ($Q = $50,000$) for a premium of $15,000, it gives any student who buys it a sure outcome of $35,000. Compared with going without, this turns out to be a worthwhile deal for students for whom the chance of a summer job is 0.7 (like Drake), 0.6, or 0.5. But students whose chance of a summer job is 0.9 and 0.8, respectively, have certainty equivalents without insurance of $44,100 and $38,400, respectively, (see Figure 18.1). So they would not buy this insurance policy. Then, the "average payout probability" on the policy for students who buy this policy would be 0.4; this is the average of 100 students with a payout probability of 0.3, 100 with a payout probability of 0.4, and 100 with a payout probability of 0.5. Therefore, the expected payout per policy is $0.4) \times $50,000 = $20,000$, and Beantown would lose money (on average) on these policies.

Of course, this is adverse selection at work: While the average odds of a job are 0.7, for those willing to buy this policy, the average odds are only 0.6.

(d) If Beantown offers a full insurance policy, it has to worry what groups would buy it. Since students with 0.9 probability of a job have a certainty equivalent of $44,100 without insurance, to get their business, Beantown would have to charge a premium no higher than $5900. With such a small premium, Beantown would get all 500 students to buy, and the average payout probability would be 0.3, for an expected payout per policy of $15,000. The premium ($5900 or less) does not cover the expected payout.

Beantown could get the 400 students with a job probability of 0.8 or less if it charged a premium of $11,600 or less. (The no-insurance CE of the 0.8-chance students is $38,400.) For these 400 students, the average probability of a payout is 0.35, hence the average payout per policy is $17,500. The premium does not cover the expected payout.

Beantown could shoot for the 300 students with a probability of 0.7 of less of getting a summer job, with a premium of $17,100 or less. The average probability of a payout for these 300 is 0.4, for an expected payout per policy of $20,000. This is not going to work.

Beantown could charge a premium of up to $22,400 and get the 200 students with a probability of 0.6 or 0.5, since students with probability 0.6 of a job have a certainty equivalent without insurance of $27,600. The average payout probability for these 200 students is 0.45, so the expected payout per policy is $22,500. This is only $100 more than the premium, but this is not horseshoes, and close does not count.

So, the only way Beantown could offer a full-insurance policy where the premium covers the expected payout is if it tailors the policy for the 100 students with a job probability of 0.5. The expected payout per policy is $25,000, so the premium has to be at least that large. Since these students have a no-insurance certainty equivalent of $22,500, Beantown can charge them a premium of up to $27,500 and get them to buy. So for premiums in this range, Beantown makes a positive expected profit.

(e) The drill here is to compute the certainty equivalent for each type of Beantown student, for this partial insurance policy, and compare it with no-insurance CEs. You can do this by hand, but since I have the spreadsheet PROB18.1, it is easiest for me to change the terms of the insurance policy. See sheet 2 of the spreadsheet, reproduced here as Figure 18.2. It is evident from the numbers that the 200 students with job-prospect probabilities of 0.6 or 0.5 would purchase this policy, so the average probability of payout would be 0.45 and the expected payout per policy would be

$0.45 \times \$30{,}000 = \$13{,}500$. Beantown would make an expected \$500 per policy, and it would (partially) insure 200 FECBUS students.

PROB18.1

	A	B	C	D	E	F	G	H	I	J
3				prob of job		0.9	0.8	0.7	0.6	0.5
4										
5	NO	premium	$0							
6	INSURANCE	payout if no job	$0							
7		outcome if job	$50,000							
8		outcome if no job	$0							
9		utility if job	300							
10		utility if no job	200							
11		expected utilities				290	280	270	260	250
12		certainty equivalents				$44,100.00	$38,400.00	$32,900.00	$27,600.00	$22,500.00
13										
14	PART (a)	premium	$14,000							
15		payout if no job	$30,000							
16		outcome if job	$36,000							
17		outcome if no job	$16,000							
18		utility if job	275.680975							
19		utility if no job	236.643191							
20		expected utilities				271.777197	267.873418	263.96964	260.065862	256.162083
21		certainty equivalents				$33,862.84	$31,756.17	$29,679.97	$27,634.25	$25,619.01

Sheet1 Sheet2 Sheet3

Figure 18.2. Problem 18.1(e): Calculating EUs and CEs, with and without insurance.

(f) Go to sheet 3 of the spreadsheet PROB18.1 (Figure 18.3). I economized a bit on the calculations to save space: What we have here are EUs and CEs as functions of the terms of the various insurance policies on offer, for each of the five groups. So for each of the five groups, look at which option gives the highest EU or, equivalently, the highest CE.

PROB18.1

	B	C	D	E	F	G	H	I	J
3			prob of job		0.9	0.8	0.7	0.6	0.5
4									
5	premium	$0		EU	290.0000	280.0000	270.0000	260.0000	250.0000
6	payout if no job	$0		CE	$44,100	$38,400	$32,900	$27,600	$22,500
7									
8	premium	$25,000		EU	254.9510	254.9510	254.9510	254.9510	254.9510
9	payout if no job	$50,000		CE	$25,000	$25,000	$25,000	$25,000	$25,000
10									
11	premium	$3,500		EU	286.2618	278.4148	270.5678	262.7207	254.8737
12	payout if no job	$10,000		CE	$41,946	$37,515	$33,207	$29,022	$24,961
13									
14	premium	$500		EU	289.6205	280.0755	270.5305	260.9855	251.4405
15	payout if no job	$2,000		CE	$43,880	$38,442	$33,187	$28,113	$23,222
16									
17	premium	$20		EU	290.0149	280.0632	270.1115	260.1598	250.2081
18	payout if no job	$200		CE	$44,109	$38,435	$32,960	$27,683	$22,604

Sheet1 Sheet2 Sheet3

Figure 18.3. Problem 18.1(f): Calculating EUs and CEs for a variety of options.

We see that students whose probability of getting a job is 0.5 take the full insurance policy. Since this means the average probability of payout on this policy is 0.5, the expected payout is $25,000, which just matches the premium.

Students whose probability of getting a job is either 0.6 or 0.7 take the $10,000 insurance policy with a premium of $3500. The average probability of a payout on this policy is therefore 0.35, so the expected payout matches the premium.

Students whose probability of getting a job is 0.8 take the $2000 policy with a premium of $500. The average probability of a payout on this policy is 0.2, for an expected payout of $400. Beantown Casualty makes a little money on this one.[1] And students whose probability of getting a job is 0.9 take the $200 policy, whose expected payout ($20) just matches the premium.

Altogether, Beantown's expected profit is 100 times $100, or $10,000. This should just about cover the costs of writing and administering all those policies. (Of course, Beantown could raise its profits by increasing the premiums. If you want to give Solver a task that it isn't very good at, see what you can come up with if you assume that Beantown wishes to maximize its profits.)

The point to be made here is that partial insurance or, equivalently, deductible provisions in insurance policies, can be used as screening devices: High-risk clients opt for lower deductibles and higher premia (because they need the insurance more), while lower-risk clients go for higher deductibles, if it means a lower premium.

Solution to Problem 18.3

While seniors may have information that they are in failing health, it is fairly rare that this information takes this form: You have two (or more) years to live, or you will require extensive care in two years but not before. By essentially having the seniors commit to purchase the insurance two years in advance, the adverse selection problem is enormously reduced if not entirely eliminated.

Solution to Problem 18.5

People sell cars for a variety of reasons. They may be able to afford a better or more expensive car. They may move to a location to which is it impractical to bring their

---

[1] Why not cut the premium to $400? Because if we do this, the 0.7 group will head for this policy, screwing up the $10,000 insurance policy.

car. Or they may have a lemon on their hands, which they want to unload. Hence, used cars sell at a discount relative to new cars; it is well known that driving a brand new car "off the lot" immediately lowers its market value significantly.

Still, because a used car might be sold for a variety of reasons, seeing that a car is being sold as used is not a certain signal that the car is a lemon. But, holding age fixed, a car that has made its way through, say, three owners, is a lot more likely to be a lemon (something constant about the car) than a car being sold by its original owner. Hence, as a signal of hidden information about the quality of the car, the more hands it has passed through, the lower is its value in the market.

Solution to Problem 18.7: RE/MAX

Why does RE/MAX attract more aggressive agents? This is pure signaling or screening. More aggressive, better agents are more confident of their ability to make sales, hence more willing to take a higher fraction of their compensation in the form of risky commissions. (Is this screening or signaling? To the extent that the uninformed party (the agency) has set the terms of the "signal," it is screening. But the semantic distinction is entirely unimportant.)

There is probably also a second-order, reinforcing effect, that aggressive folks like to be around aggressive folks, and the more laid back prefer to be around people like them. So, once RE/MAX gets a reputation, in the local community of realtors, for being filled with aggressive types, it becomes increasingly attractive to those types and unattractive to the less aggressive.

RE/MAX makes its money by charging its agents more for the services it provides than it costs to provide those services. Why are aggressive agents willing to pay RE/MAX more for these services than if they procured them independently? This is the genius of the whole scheme. RE/MAX charges aggressive agents for the reputation that its brand provides them. A new, aggressive agent, who knows she is talented and aggressive, has a hard time (as an independent) convincing potential clients of this. I never met an agent who was not ready to claim superior skills. But an agent who signs with RE/MAX signals her skills and aggressiveness to potential clients. Clients who want this kind of agent go to RE/MAX to find them. (It is doubtful that people who go to RE/MAX know why RE/MAX has aggressive, talented agents; the signaling mechanism is not well known to the general public. But that is unimportant. What is important is that the general public is aware that RE/MAX, for some reason or another, has a stable of this sort of agents.) An agent with these skills, to be matched with clients who want these skills, pays RE/MAX in the form of higher-than-market fees for the clerical services provided. In effect, RE/MAX, having developed the brand image, can and does milk the image, by charging those realtors who want to signal their aggressiveness for their use of its brand.

In addition to joining RE/MAX or a more traditional firm, realtors can go independent. How does this third option affect RE/MAX? How does it affect the more traditional firms? An independent agent bears all the risk for his or her own compensation, just like a RE/MAX agent. So why is the decision to be an independent agent not an equally good signal of aggressiveness? I think the answer to this combines a few things. First, some independent agents are independent because real estate is a bit of a hobby, or they are in semi-retirement but want to maintain their license. How does a potential client screen out these sorts of independents? A RE/MAX agent, on the other hand, has to make those monthly service payments to the agency, which is relatively expensive for the semi-retired and hobbyist. Moreover, RE/MAX is a brand name for aggressive agents, and my guess is that, to maintain that brand imagine, RE/MAX will do some internal monitoring of its agents, shedding those who do not perform.

An agent who is well established in a local community, with a strong local reputation for aggressiveness, may not need the signaling services RE/MAX provides, at least to the extent that this agent's local contacts generate sufficient business. Of course, national agencies like RE/MAX provide their realtors other services (networking etc.). But on a comparative basis, as they establish themselves in a market, agents originally attracted to RE/MAX are probably less needful of the things they go to RE/MAX for than agents attracted to more traditional agencies. So I predict that tenures at RE/MAX are shorter than at traditional agencies—agents who go to RE/MAX are more likely to move to being independent after they are established.

The nature of the local real estate market plays a role here. For newcomers in a local market, RE/MAX is a national brand image. So, in a market with a lot of transients moving in and out, like Silicon Valley, a strong local reputation may be of less comparative value than the sort of instant image RE/MAX gives. My guess is that the depart-to-go-independent phenomenon, if it does exist, is relatively more pronounced in a market where local reputation is more important (the county seat in rural South Carolina) than in a market where people move in and out, like Silicon Valley. (I do not know if these hypotheses have been tested, so I am just guessing.)

Solution to Problem 18.8

I use a decision tree to solve this problem.[2] In Figure 18.4, you see my first cut at the decision tree facing Ace. It must decide whether to "bid" for the job. If it does, then there is a chance node for whether it gets the job or not, and another chance node for whether the job's true cost is $100,000 or $200,000.

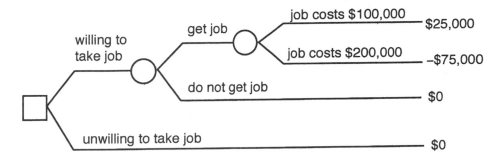

Figure 18.4. Problem 18.8: A first cut at a decision tree.

This decision tree captures the natural temporal order of things, but the chance nodes in it are not presented in an order that makes it easy to assess the required probabilities. So switch the order of the two chance nodes, putting the chance node for the project cost first. Then add chance nodes for whether Base and Case learn the true cost or not (if the true cost is $100,000). We can add these chance nodes and put the chance nodes in any order we choose because they all come after the one and last choice node for Ace. The end product is the decision tree you see in Figure 18.5. Note that, when the true cost is $200,000, I have not put in chance nodes for whether Base and Case learn the true cost. I explain why momentarily.

---

[2] A decision tree depicts a strategic situation from the perspective of one party. Chance nodes, depicted by circles, represent events outside the control of this party; nature or some other party chooses a branch of the node, with probabilities on the branches giving the probabilities assessed by the first party of the various possibilities. Choice nodes, depicted by boxes, represent the options facing the original party at a given point in time. The rules for constructing decision trees are these: (1) Branches should never "grow back together"; the tree should open up, so that each complete branch represents a particular sequence of events. (2) A chance node should precede a choice node in the tree if and only if the uncertainty of that chance node resolves for the original party before the time that the party has to make that choice. (3) Probabilities placed on the branches of chance nodes should be conditional probabilities, conditional on everything that "occurred" earlier in the tree. (4) Endpoints of the tree are evaluated in whatever fashion is most relevant to the original party. After constructing a tree, a procedure called *rolling back the tree* is used to analyze the decision problem facing the original party. Textbooks in decision analysis and managerial economics usually have detailed discussions of decision trees; see, for instance, W. F. Samuelson and S. G. Marks, *Managerial Economics*, New York: John Wiley and Sons, 2003.

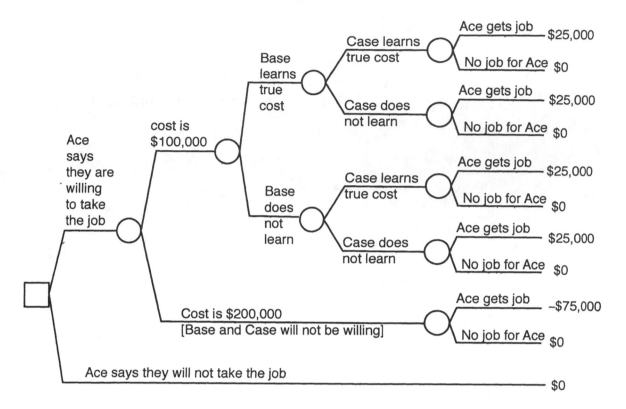

Figure 18.5. Problem 18.8: A second cut at a decision tree.

Now to assess probabilities in the rest of the tree. The rule is that probabilities in a decision tree should be conditional on everything that occurs earlier. Ace knows that it does not know the true cost, so at the first chance node, we must enter the conditional probability that the cost of the project is $100,000, given that Ace did not learn this. But the problem statement says that Ace's learning the true cost is independent of the value of that cost—Ace is no more likely to learn the true cost if the cost is $100,000—so the conditional probabilities are the marginal probabilities of 0.8 and 0.2.

Next, we need probabilities that Base and Case learn the true cost. These are 0.75, even after we condition on whether the true cost is $100,000 or $200,000, and even conditional on Ace's having not learned the cost, per the problem statement.

Finally we need probabilties that Ace gets the job, if it signals its willingness to take the job. This depends on whether Base or Case said it would take the job: the probability is 1 if both said no; $\frac{1}{2}$ if one said yes and the other no; and $\frac{1}{3}$ if both said yes. We are conditioning on whether Base or Case learned the true cost, and we are assuming their decision rule is, Say yes only if the true cost is known to be $100,000. Therefore, we know (once we condition on whether each got the information) whether they say Yes or No, and the probabilities for whether Ace gets the job are easy to assign.

We do not need to know whether Base and Case got the information if the true cost is $200,000. If one of these firms got the information, they do not volunteer for the job. And if they did not get the information, they do not volunteer for the job. If the true cost is $200,000 and Ace has said it would take the job, Ace is certain to get the job.

The probabilities are supplied on the tree in Figure 18.6 and an expected monetary value rollback is performed. Ace would expect to lose $6250 if it were to say that it is willing to take the job. Having failed to learn the true cost of the project, Ace should decline to participate.

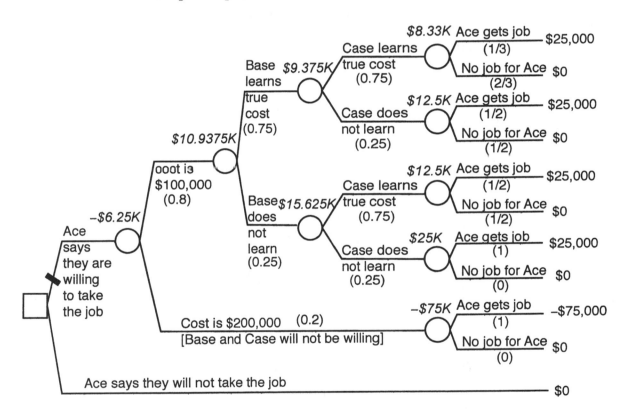

Figure 18.6. Problem 18.8: Probabilities and rollback.

What is going on here? If the true cost of the job is $200,000, Ace faces no competition for it; it is certain to get the job if it says it is willing to do it. But if the true cost of the job is $100,000, it is not certain to get the job; Base and Case might also indicate their willingness to do the job. This is a classic (if somewhat simple) winner's curse; the fact that Ace wins the job means that Base and Case are less likely to have bid for it, which in turn means that the job is more likely to have a true cost of $200,000. In fact, if you compute the conditional probability that the true cost of the job is $100,000, conditional on Ace's getting the job (assuming it is willing to take it), you should find that this conditional probability is 0.68, less than the 0.8 marginal probability of the cost being $100,000.

Solution to Problem 18.9

Good luck with this one. If you want to try it, let me make some suggestions. First, think of the problem as a decision tree in which Bidder 1 decides how much to bid, and then chance nodes ensue: The true values of X and V are resolved, the signals s_2 and s_3 are resolved (and the bids of bidders 2 and 3 are determined), and then it is determined if bidder 1 wins the auction or not.

Note that, in that lineup of chance nodes, the last is determined by the others. Once you know how much each party is bidding, you know whether 1 will win or lose the auction.

You need to find the conditional distribution of X given $s_1 = 15.3$. This takes a bit of Bayesian inference with Normal priors and likelihoods. If you do this right, you'll find that the conditional distribution of X is Normal with mean 15.14 and variance 0.5.

The distributions of s_2 and s_3 given X and s_1 are easy, given the assumptions of conditional independence.

Once you have values for s_2 and s_3, you'll need to engage in Bayesian inference again to determine the expected value of V (not X) given s_2 and then s_3. First, find the distribution of X given s_2 (or s_3), then use the formula for the mean of a lognormally distributed random variable.

Since your decision tree has three generations of continuous chance nodes, you cannot really roll back. You could try discrete approximations, but I suggest instead Monte Carlo simulation. And, at this point, I reiterate my initial comment. Good luck!

Material for Chapter 19

Incentives

Solution to Problem 19.1

First is the solution via a spreadsheet. We learned in the problem assignment that, if the incentive scheme is constrained to elicit the effort choice *tries but not hard*, the best the firm can do (in terms of expected net profit, or minimizing expected compensation) is a base wage of $9506 and a bonus of $12,250, giving an expected net profit of $2341 (and an expected compensation package of $12,568.50).

We need to redo this analysis for the other three effort levels. First comes *loafing*. It turns out that we can quickly reason our way to the answer here: If the firm chooses to elicit *loafing* as the effort choice, there is no motivation problem at all. Hence, the firm can be entirely concerned with efficient risk sharing, which in this problem, means giving the salesperson a constant wage. We worked out (back on page 452 of the text) that, if the firm aims to sign up the worker and get loafing, the (constant) wage must be $10,000. Which yields for the firm a net expected profit of $0.05 \times \$60,000 - \$10,000 = -\$7000$.

In case you do not trust my logic, it is easy enough to get Solver to confirm this. Get sheet 1 of CHAP19 and ask Solver to maximize E8, varying B1 and B2, subject to the constraints that D8 should be at least as large as D9, D10, D11, and D12. Figure 19.8 shows what Solver returns—close enough, I suppose, for a numerical solution.

Next comes *works hard*. Maximize F10 by varying B1 and B2, subject to the constraints that E10 is at least as large as E8, E9, E11, and E12. Solver reports back the numbers shown in Figure 19.9. (Actually, I have to admit here that Solver did not do this quite as smoothly as I would have liked. It bombed on me, depending on the starting values I gave it. I figured out how to fix this, and I discuss the fix in a couple of paragraphs.)

Finally, we have *kills self*. Maximize F11, varying B1 and B2, subject to the constraints that E11 exceeds E8, E9, E10, and E12. Solver responds as in Figure 19.10. Net profit maximization while eliciting *kills self* takes a base wage of $1600 and a bonus of $56,000, for expected net profit equal to $400.

	A	B	C	D	E	F
1	base wage	$10,000				
2	bonus	$0				
3						
4	gross utility if sale	99.99999993				
5	gross utility if no sale	99.99999993				
6						
7		EFFORT CHOICE	DISUTILITY	PROB SALE	EU	Expected net profit
8		loafing	0	0.05	99.9999999	-$7,000
9		tries but not hard	10	0.25	89.9999999	$5,000
10		works hard	20	0.4	79.9999999	$14,000
11		kills self	40	0.5	59.9999999	$20,000
12		reservation level			100	
13						

Sheet1 / Sheet2 / Sheet3 /

Figure 19.8. The optimal loafing incentive scheme.

	A	B	C	D	E	F
1	base wage	$8,711				
2	bonus	$16,889				
3						
4	gross utility if sale	159.9999985				
5	gross utility if no sale	93.33333507				
6						
7		EFFORT CHOICE	DISUTILITY	PROB SALE	EU	Expected net profit
8		loafing	0	0.05	96.6666682	-$6,556
9		tries but not hard	10	0.25	100.000001	$2,067
10		works hard	20	0.4	100	$8,533
11		kills self	40	0.5	86.6666668	$12,844
12		reservation level			100	
13						

Sheet1 / Sheet2 / Sheet3 /

Figure 19.9. The optimal works hard incentive scheme.

	A	B	C	D	E	F
1	base wage	$1,600				
2	bonus	$56,000				
3						
4	gross utility if sale	240				
5	gross utility if no sale	40.00000178				
6						
7		EFFORT CHOICE	DISUTILITY	PROB SALE	EU	Expected net profit
8		loafing	0	0.05	50.0000017	-$1,400
9		tries but not hard	10	0.25	80.0000013	-$600
10		works hard	20	0.4	100.000001	$0
11		kills self	40	0.5	100.000001	$400
12		reservation level			100	
13						

Sheet1 / Sheet2 / Sheet3 /

Figure 19.10. The optimal kills self incentive scheme.

Comparing the four possible effort levels, the firm gets the highest expected net profit for itself if it aims to elicit *works hard*. So the answer to the overall question is the incentive scheme in Figure 19.9, in which the base wage is $8,711, the bonus is $16,889, and the expected net profit for the firm is $8533.

(Read this paragraph only if you are vastly interested in things that can go wrong with Solver and how to fix them.) The problems I encountered with Solver go back to problems we encountered in Chapter 5, when we were maximizing logarithmic utility. If you ask Excel to evaluate the square root of a negative number, it simply quits on you. And Solver, while it is searching for an answer, might try a negative base wage. If cell B5 reads = SQRT(B1), the bomb explodes and Solver quits. So, to make things work, I write the formula for B5 as = SQRT(MAX(B1,0)). And B4 is = SQRT(MAX(B1 + B2,0)). Now Excel is never going to be asked to evaluate a negative square root. But now, to keep things honest, I have to constrain the values of B1 and B2 to be nonnegative. Put these constraints in, and Solver seems to work fine.

To do this by hand, we simply replicate the maximizations of Solver, where we can do this because we "know" what the answer will look like. For instance, suppose we look at the least expected compensation (= largest expected profit) scheme for eliciting *works hard*. Using the same variables x and b as in the problem assignment, we need to set x and b so that: (1) the salesperson will take the job (if he or she is going to work hard), or

$$0.4x + 0.6b - 20 = 100,$$

and (2) the salesperson is motivated to take this level of effort, with as small an amount of risk transferred onto the salesperson as possible, which means the expected utility (net of effort aversion) for *works hard* should equal the expected utility (net of effort) of *tries but not hard*, or

$$0.4x + 0.6b - 20 = 0.25x + 0.75b - 10.$$

This is two equations in two unknowns, and we solve it as follows: The second equation is

$$0.15x = 0.15b + 10, \quad \text{or} \quad x = b + (10/0.15).$$

Substitute for x in the first equation, $.4x + .6b = 120$, to get

$$0.4\left(b + \frac{10}{0.15}\right) + 0.6b = 120.$$

This is $b = 120 - 4/0.15 = 93.333$; therefore, $x = b + 10/0.15 = 160$. The base wage B is $b^2 = 93.333^2 = \$8711.11$, and the bonus is $x^2 - B = \$16,888.88$. Now compute by hand the net expected profit. If the salesperson is working hard, the gross expected profit from the sale is $0.4 \times \$60,000 = \$24,000$, from which must be subtracted the expected compensation: \$8711.11 for sure, plus \$16,888.88 with probability 0.4, for an expected compensation of \$15,466.67. Netted against the gross \$24,000, this means an expected profit of \$8533.33.

Now, we do it again but aiming to elicit *kills self*. The equations are

$$0.5x + 0.5b - 40 = 100, \quad \text{and}$$
$$0.5x + 0.5b - 40 = 0.4x + 0.6b - 20.$$

Solving for x and b, this yields $b = 40$ and $x = 240$, which gives the incentive scheme shown in Figure 19.10. You then calculate that this means an expected net profit to the employer of \$400.

The problem assignment already had you do by hand the case of *tries but not hard*. As for *loafing*, use the logic that there is no incentive problem if you aim for the lowest level of effort, so you pay a constant wage just high enough to get the salesperson to sign on. Compare expected net profits in the four cases, and we are done.

Warning: In doing this by hand, we have assumed that to elicit one level of effort, the binding constraint is that the expected utility from that level is equal to the expected utility from the next lower level. The logic is that the salesperson should be shielded from risk to the greatest extent possible, and if he is going to move from the desired lack of effort because of a lack of incentive, it will be to move down one notch. The logic is good, but for some parameterizations of this sort of problem, things can get a bit more complex. Since you'll never solve real incentive problems this way in practice (you would lack information about precise probabilities and utility functions) you need not worry about this as far as the postexam portion of your life is concerned. And as far as exams are concerned, you might ask your instructor to give you a guarantee that all the problems you are asked to work out will be "okay" as far as this assumption goes.

Solution to Problem 19.2

(a) If we suppose the factory owner cannot get any insurance, he must choose between taking due care and facing the gamble depicted in Figure 19.11(a), or not doing so and facing the gamble depicted in Figure 19.11(b). The first, as shown, has a net expected utility (net of the cost of due care) of 2930. The second has a net expected utility of 2900. So taking due care is better, without insurance.

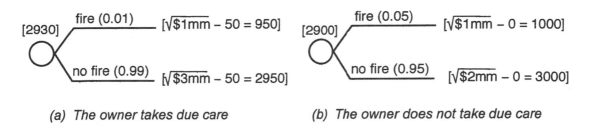

(a) *The owner takes due care*   (b) *The owner does not take due care*

Figure 19.11. The two no-insurance options. If the factory owner does not buy insurance, he either takes due care and faces the gamble shown in panel a, or he does not take due care and faces the gamble in panel b. Panel a, taking due care, has a higher net expected utility.

(b) If the insurance company can specify contractually that the owner must take due care, then there is no incentive problem and the best thing to do (efficient risk sharing) is to insure the building fully. Since the owner can obtain net expected utility 2930 without insurance, this is his reservation (net) expected utility; if the contract specifies due care and the owner faces no financial risk, then his gross utility (whether there is a fire or not) must be 2980. But this corresponds to a dollar outcome of $\$2980^2 - \$8,000,000 = \$7,880,400$, which means that the premium charged can be no larger than $\$8,000,000 - \$7,880,400 = \$119,600$. If the owner takes due care, the expected payout on a full insurance policy is $0.01 \times \$8,000,000 = \$80,000$, so the net expected profit from the best "take due care" full-insurance policy the firm can write (that is, the policy with the highest acceptable premium) is $\$119,600 - \$80,000 = \$39,600$.

On the other hand, the insurance company could think of writing a contract that specifies no due care (or that makes no specification at all). It is still efficient from a risk-sharing perspective for the policy to be for full insurance, so that owner faces no risk. And in this case, the gross utility of the owner's final financial position (which is certain) must be at least 2930. This corresponds to a dollar outcome of $\$2830^2 - \$1,000,000 = \$7,584,900$, or a maximum premium of $\$415,100$. But, if the owner is not taking due care, the expected payout on the (full-insurance) policy is

$0.05 \times \$8,000,000 = \$400,000$, for a net expected profit to the insurance company of $\$15,100$.

The best contract the insurance company can write (in terms of maximizing its expected profit) is a full-insurance contract that specifies that the owner will take due care, for a premium of $\$119,600$.

(c) If the insurance company cannot contractually specify the level of care taken, and if it provides full insurance, the factory owner has no incentive to take care and suffer the utility loss of 50 that due care entails. So the factory owner will not take due care. The best full-insurance policy that the insurance company can write in this circumstance is the second policy of part b, a full-insurance policy with a premium of $\$415,100$, giving a net expected profit of $\$15,100$.

(d) The point of a deductible in the policy is that this subjects the factory owner to the threat of some loss, and if the threat is big enough, the owner may be motivated to take due care. If this doesn't happen (if the factory owner is not going to take due care), then we might as well go in for efficient risk sharing, and we get the full-insurance policy (and net expected profit) from part c.

But, suppose the insurance company writes and sells a policy with the premium P and a payback to the owner of Z. (The size of the deductible is $\$8,000,000 - Z$.) The owner then faces the financial outcome $\$8,000,000 - P$ if there is no fire, and the outcome $Z - P$ if there is a fire.

Let the variable x be $\sqrt{8,000,000 - P + 1,000,000}$, or the gross utility of the owner if there is no fire. And let $y = \sqrt{Z - P + 1,000,000}$, or the gross utility if there is a fire. Then, as a function of x and y, if the owner takes due care, his net expected utility is

$$0.99x + 0.01y - 50,$$

while if he does not take due care, his net expected utility is

$$0.95x + 0.05y.$$

He is motivated to take due care as long as x and y are such that

$$0.99x + 0.01y - 50 \geq 0.95x + 0.05y, \quad \text{or} \quad 0.04x \geq 0.04y + 50,$$

which is

$$x \geq y + 125.$$

And he signs up for this insurance (if his option is to go without) as long as

$$0.99x + 0.01y - 50 \geq 2930.$$

To maximize its profit in this ideal world, the insurance company wants to set x and y so these two inequalities are equalities: The insurance company wants $0.99x + 0.01y - 50 = 2930$, so that it extracts as much as it can from the factory owner, and it wants $0.99x + 0.01y - 50 = 0.95x + 0.05y$, so that it goes as far in risk sharing as it can while maintaining sufficient incentive for the factory owner to take care. Therefore, we have to solve simultaneously

$$x = y + 1250 \quad \text{and} \quad 0.99x + 0.01y - 50 = 2930.$$

Substituting $y + 1250$ for x in the second equation, we get

$$0.99(y + 1250) + 0.01y - 50 = 2930, \quad \text{or} \quad y = 2930 + 50 - 0.99 \times 1250 = 1742.5,$$

and therefore $x = y + 1250 = 2992.5$. But if $x = 2992.5$, then

$$\sqrt{9{,}000{,}000 \text{ - } P} = x = 2992.5 \quad \text{or} \quad P = \$9{,}000{,}000 - \$2992.5^2 = \$44{,}943.75,$$

and if $y = 1742.5$, then

$$\sqrt{Z - P + 1{,}000{,}000} = 1742.5 \quad \text{or} \quad Z = \$1742.5^2 + P - \$1{,}000{,}000 = \$2{,}081{,}250.$$

The expected payout on this policy (since it induces taking due care) is $0.01 \times \$2{,}081{,}250 = \$20{,}812.50$, hence, the insurance company's net expected profit is $\$44{,}943.75 - \$20{,}812.50 = \$24{,}131.25$.

(e) We redo the problem supposing that due care carries a dollar cost of $100,000 rather than a utility cost of 50. Without insurance, the owner can choose not to take due care, which (as we computed earlier) has an expected utility of 2900. Or he can choose to take due care, which has an expected utility of

$$0.99\sqrt{8{,}000{,}000 - 100{,}000 + 1{,}000{,}000} + .01\sqrt{-100{,}000 + 1{,}000{,}000} = 2962.94.$$

So he will choose to take due care. Note that the certainty equivalent corresponding to utility level 2962.94 is $2962.94^2 - 1,000,000 = \$7,779,018$.

If we suppose that the insurance company can specify due care contractually, there is no incentive problem, so full insurance is profit maximizing. The premium must be such that the factory owner nets \$7,779,018. This includes the out-of-pocket cost of \$100,000 for due care, so the maximum premium that can be charged is $\$8,000,000 - \$7,779,018 - \$100,000 = \$120,982$. The insurance company's expected net from this policy is \$120,982 less the expected payout of $0.01 \times \$8,000,000 = \$80,000$, or \$40,982.

If the insurance company specifies no due care contractually, it will write a full-insurance contract. The largest premium it can charge (since, with no due care, the owner has no out-of-pocket expense other than the premium) is \$220,982. At this premium, its expected net is \$220,982 less the expected payout on the policy of $0.05 \times \$8,000,000 = \$400,000$; in other words, the insurance company loses an expected \$179,018 on this policy. Hence, if the insurance company can specify care level, it will definitely want to specify due care.

Now if it cannot specify due care (if that is a moral-hazard decision by the owner) and writes a full-insurance policy, the owner has no incentive to take due care. As we just saw, with a full-insurance policy and no due care, the insurance company takes a loss.

So we look at partial insurance. Here is where the change in formulation causes difficulties. Let Z be the payback on the policy and P the premium. The owner's expected utility, if he takes due care, is

$$0.99\sqrt{9,000,000 - P - 100,000} + 0.01\sqrt{1,000,000 + Z - P - 100,000}.$$

His expected utility if he does not take due care is

$$0.95\sqrt{9,000,000 - P} + 0.05\sqrt{1,000,000 + Z - P}.$$

We want to find Z and P so that these two are equal (just enough incentive to take due care) and each equals the reservation expected utility of 2962.94. Now, with the "cost" of due care under the square-root sign, you cannot solve these equations analytically. You must either solve them numerically or put the entire problem in a spreadsheet and ask Solver to do it. That is what I did. The spreadsheet is sheet 2 of PROB19.2, shown in Figure 19.12. I leave it to you to discover how this spreadsheet works, except to point out that column D gives the no-insurance computations, E gives the specify-due-care numbers, F the specify-no-due-care numbers, and G the best-partial-insurance numbers. (Also, if you get this spreadsheet, in sheet 1 you find an analysis of parts a through d in a spreadsheet; that is, with the problem formulated so the cost of due care is a utility cost rather than a dollar cost.)

	B		D	E	F	G
			NO INSURANCE	FULL INSURANCE FOR DUE CARE	FULL INSURANCE FOR NO DUE CARE	BEST PART INSURANCE
4	Insurance premium		$0	$120,982	$220,982	$95,865
5	insurance payback if fire		$0	$8,000,000	$8,000,000	$5,665,853
6						
7	outcome if fire and due care		-$100,000	$7,779,018	$7,679,018	$5,469,988
8	outcome if no fire and due care		$7,900,000	$7,779,018	$7,679,018	$7,804,135
9						
10	expected utility if due care		2962.94	2962.94	2946.02	2962.94
11						
12	outcome if fire and no due care		$0		$7,779,018	$5,569,988
13	outcome if no fire and no due care		$8,000,000		$7,779,018	$7,904,135
14						
15	expected utility if no due care		2900.00		2962.94	2962.94
16						
17	max utilility		2962.94			
18	CE		$7,779,018			
19						
20	Inurance company Expected net, due care		$0	$40,982		$39,206
21	Insurance company Expected net, no due care		$0		-$179,018	

Figure 19.12. A spreadsheet for Problem 19.2(e). This spreadsheet was used to find the best partial insurance for part e of Problem 19.2, in which the cost of due care is a dollar cost. Columns D, E, and F give computations that are doable by hand; column G is where Solver was used: Solver was asked to maximize G20, changing G4 and G5, with G10 constrained to be greater or equal to G15 and D17.

A Stylized Model with More Than One Agent

In the text, tournament and comparative incentives systems are discussed informally. One reason we do nothing more formal on this topic is that stylized models of such systems require a few tools and concepts that are developed only in Chapters 21 and 22. This is the appropriate place contextually for a stylized model with more than one agent, and so I develop one here. You may, however, choose to put off reading through this until you complete Chapter 22.

Imagine a manager in charge of two workers. Each worker (or agent) is asked to perform a particular task, and each can either work hard at the task or loaf. The value to the manager of each task is either $10,000 or $0. Whether the value is $10,000 or $0 depends in part on how hard the worker works and in part on factors outside the worker's control. The following data apply:

If the worker works hard, the probability that the task has value $10,000 is 0.7 and the probability that its value is $0 is 0.3. If the worker loafs, these probabilities reverse; the probability that the task has value $10,000 is 0.3 and the probability of a $0 value is 0.7.

Moreover, the outcomes of the two tasks are correlated:

- If both workers work hard, the joint probability that both produce $10,000 outcomes is 0.6.

- If both loaf, the joint probability that both produce $10,000 outcomes is 0.2.

- If one loafs and the other works, the joint probability that both produce $10,000 outcomes is 0.25.

(You should use these data to prepare joint probability tables of the possible outcomes, as functions of the effort levels of the two workers.)

Each worker has a utility function that depends on the amount of money received and the amount of effort expended. The form of the utility function is

$$U(w, a) = \sqrt{\frac{w}{1000}} - a,$$

where w is the amount of money received, and $a = 0$ for loafing and $a = 0.8$ for working hard. The two workers have the same utility function, and each has a reservation utility level of 1; that is, the worker's expected utility must be 1 to get the worker to take the job.

The manager is risk neutral and seeks to maximize the expected net profit from these two workers. Can you answer the following questions?

(a) Suppose that the manager could, at no cost, monitor the efforts of the two workers and can make the choice of effort level an enforceable part of their employment agreement. Would the manager want to make them work hard, or is it better to have them loaf? What payments would the manager offer them?

(b) Suppose that the manager cannot monitor the efforts of the two workers, so cannot enforce their effort level. The manager can, however, sign a contract of the form: The worker is paid $X if the task he or she performs has value $10,000, and $Y if the task has value $0. Subject to the constraints that the worker must be willing to sign, and the worker, seeing what is being paid, will choose how hard to work, what is the best contract of this form for the manager to offer? (The worker resolves all ties in his or her utility in the manager's favor.)

Now suppose that the manager cannot monitor the two but can offer more complex contracts, of the following form: The worker is paid $X if both workers produce $10,000 outcomes, $Y if the worker produces a $10,000 outcome and his or her fellow worker produces $0, $Z if the worker produces $0 and his or her fellow worker produces a $10,000 outcome, and $W if both produce $0.

(c) What contracts of this form are optimal if the manager wants to induce both workers to loaf?

(d) Suppose that the manager wishes to offer contracts that induce both to work hard. Imagine that this means the contract offered must meet the following constraints: Each worker must be induced to take the contract; and each worker, assuming that the fellow worker is going to work hard, must be induced to work hard. What is the optimal contract to offer in this case?

(e) The manager is worried that the contract offered in d might induce loafing by each worker. The manager would worry less about this possibility if each worker would prefer to work hard, even if he or she assumes the other worker is loafing. If you add this constraint to part d, is the old solution still valid? If not, what is the new solution?

(f) Worried that the two might collude, the manager wishes to add to the solution of part e the constraint that each worker prefers working hard (given that the other worker works hard) to their payoffs if both loaf. If you add this constraint to part e, what happens?

As a first step, I put together the three joint probability tables. They are in Figure 19.13. Then the answers to the questions above can be given.

(a) If the manager can monitor the two workers and make their choice of effort an enforceable part of their contracts, the manager would shield them from risk entirely. (The usual argument about efficient risk sharing applies.) To get either to loaf takes a payment of $1000, for a net profit of $0.3 \times \$10000 - \$1000 = \$2000$ per if both work hard

	$10K outcome	$0 outcome	
$10K outcome	0.6	0.01	0.7
$0 outcome	0.1	0.2	0.3
	0.7	0.3	

if one works hard (outcome given in the row) and the other loafs

	$10K outcome	$0 outcome	
$10K outcome	0.25	0.45	0.7
$0 outcome	0.05	0.25	0.3
	0.3	0.7	

if both loaf

	$10K outcome	$0 outcome	
$10K outcome	0.2	0.01	0.3
$0 outcome	0.1	0.6	0.7
	0.3	0.7	

Figure 19.13. Probability tables for the two-agent problem.

worker. To get either to work hard takes a payment that solves

$$\sqrt{\frac{w}{1000}} - 0.8 = 1 \quad \text{or} \quad \sqrt{\frac{w}{1000}} = 1.8 \quad \text{or} \quad w = \$3240,$$

for a net profit of $0.7 \times \$10,000 - \$3240 = \$3760$ per worker. So the manager would elect to have them try hard.

(b) This problem is similar to Problems 19.1 and 19.2. To get them to loaf takes no motivation, so the manager might as well engage in efficient risk sharing. From part a, we know that the net from such an arrangement is $2000 per worker.

To get them to try hard, let $x = \sqrt{X/1000}$ and $y = \sqrt{Y/1000}$, so the constraints that must be satisfied are

$$0.7x + 0.3y - 0.8 \geq 0.3x + 0.7y$$
$$0.7x + 0.3y - 0.8 \geq 1$$

In fact, the optimal solution is where both these are equalities. The first one gives $0.4x = 0.4y + 0.8$ or $x = y + 2$; and substituting into the second, we get $0.7y + 1.4 +$

$0.3y - 0.8 = 1$ or $y = 0.4$, or $Y = \$160$, and $x = 2.4$, or $X = 5760$, for a net profit of

$$0.7 \times \$10,000 - 0.7 \times \$5760 - 0.3 \times \$160 = \$2920 \text{ per worker.}$$

So, the best thing to do is to get them to try hard, motivating them with a payment of \$5760 if they get the \$10,000 outcome but only \$640 if they do not.

(c) We look at contracts where the workers get \$X apiece if both produce the \$10,000 outcome, \$Y to A and \$Z to B if A gets \$10,000 and B gets \$0, and \$W to each if each produces \$0. If we aim to get each one to loaf, we need not motivate them. Paying them the same amount (X = Y = Z = W) regardless of outcome is risk-sharing efficient, and both would loaf. We need to guarantee them a wage of \$1000 apiece, so just as in the first part of b, we can net \$2000 per worker with this scheme.

(d, e, and f) To answer these three questions, I use the spreadsheet TWO-AGENTS shown in Figure 19.14. This one takes a bit of staring.

PROBABILITIES

	both hard	A loafs, B tries	B loafs, A tries	both loaf
both \$1000	0.6	0.25	0.25	0.2
\$1000 for A	0.1	0.05	0.45	0.1
\$1000 for B	0.1	0.45	0.05	0.1
both \$0	0.2	0.25	0.25	0.6

PAYMENTS

	A's payments	sqrt A's pay	B's payments	sqrt B's pay
both \$1000	\$6,250	2.5	\$6,250	2.5
\$1000 for A	\$6,250	2.5	\$0	0
\$1000 for B	\$0	0	\$6,250	2.5
both \$0	\$2,250	1.5	\$2,250	1.5

OUTCOMES

	B tries hard		B loafs	
A tries hard	A's EU\	1.25		1.125
	1.25	\B's EU	1.325	
A loafs		1.325		1.65
	1.125		1.65	

PROFITS

	B tries hard	B loafs
A tries hard	\$4,350	\$2,625
A loafs	\$2,625	(\$450)

Figure 19.14. The spreadsheet TWO-AGENTS.

The first block of the spreadsheet gives the probability distributions for the four possible outcomes, for each of the four (2 × 2) possible choices of effort level. For instance, if A loafs and B tries hard (column F), the probability of $1000 for B (and, implicitly, $0 for A) is 0.45 (cell F6). (These probability distributions come from the joint probability tables in Figure 19.13.)

Next come payment schedules. I dispense with the notation X, Y, Z, and W, and simply record how much money goes to agent A and how much to agent B in each of the four possible outcomes. Actually, I do not do this. The variables are the square roots of these payment levels divided by 1000—that is, the entries in the cells F11 through F14 and in H11 through H14—with the payments (in E11 through E14 and G11 through G14) calculated from the entries in columns F and H. For instance, cell F11 contains the number 2.5; the formula for cell E11 is $= F11 \char`^ 2*1000$, and so forth.

The next block of the spreadsheet is a 2 × 2 table, with each cell having two entries. The two rows in the table give A's effort choice and the two columns give B's choice. Then, for each pair of effort level choices, I use the probabilities of the four outcomes and the utilities from the payments to compute the expected utilities of A and B, as a function of their own effort choice and that of the other person; A's number is in the southwest quadrant, and B's is in the northeast. So, to give two examples, for the case where A loafs and B tries hard, A's expected utility, found in cell E24, is given by the formula = SUMPRODUCT(F4:F7,F11:F14); B's expected utility, found in cell F23, is computed as = SUMPRODUCT(F4:F7,H11:H14) − 0.8. Please note that 0.8 is subtracted from B's entry because B is trying hard; A is loafing, so there is no 0.8 term for cell E24. (If you do not know about the Excel function SUMPRODUCT, this is a good time to learn.)

Looking at the data in Figure 19.14: I've set payments to agents A and B so each gets $6250 if he or she gets the $10,000 outcome, regardless of what the other person gets; each gets $0 if he or she gets the $0 outcome while the other person gets the $10,000 outcome; and each gets $2250 if both get the $0 outcome. This has the following consequences in terms of expected utility for, say, A: If both try hard, A's expected utility is 1.25 (net of the disutility of trying hard). If A loafs while B tries hard, A's expected utility is 1.125. If A tries hard and B loafs, A's expected utility is 1.325. And if both loaf, A's expected utility is 1.65. (B's expected utilities are symmetric.)

What do you think would happen if we set up this pair of compensation schemes? The point of presenting the data in this 2 × 2 bimatrix form is, We have a game between A and B. (This is where the concepts and language of Chapters 21 and 22 come into play. If you have yet to read those chapters and know nothing about

Figure 19.16. Part d with a gap built in.

of \$3240, which in turn is equivalent to \$1000 for sure, together with loafing; and a utility of .95 if they are loafing is equivalent to a for-sure dollar payment of \$902.50. So (calculated assuming a base of loafing), the 0.05 utility difference translates to around \$100 in compensation. Is this enough of a gap? That is a judgment call that economics will not help you make.

Second, you might have thought that to get the most efficient incentive effect, you would pay agents the most when they get the good outcome and the other person gets the bad outcome, since that is the strongest evidence that the first is trying hard. But Solver tells us that this is not right. Why is it incorrect? Let me answer this question two ways. (1) When we move from two outcomes to four, we move into problems for which intuitive explanations are rarely possible. The general principle is to reward outcomes that indicate the desired level of effort. But beyond that general principle, these things are hard to disentangle. (2) While they are hard to disentangle, it is possible. The key is to look at the ratios of the probabilities of outcomes given the action you want versus given the action you do not want. (And life is simple here because, at least, each agent has only two effort level choices.) Assuming B is going to try hard, the outcome that both get $10,000 outcomes has probability 0.6 if A tries hard and 0.1 if A loafs, a 6:1 ratio. The outcome that B gets the $10000 outcome and A gets the $0 outcome has probability 0.1 if A tries hard and 0.05 if A loafs, a 2:1 ratio. The bigger reward should go with the bigger of these ratios; and, Solver tells us, it does. (But just wait, it will not be so easy in a minute.)

Third, and this takes us to part e, for these numbers, while both trying hard is a Nash equilibrium, so is both loafing. And both loafing is a lot better Nash equilibrium for them. Indeed, without the built-in gap, loafing is just as good as trying if the other side is trying. In other words, for the numbers in Figure 19.15, trying hard is weakly dominated by loafing.

The weak dominance problem is solved by putting in a gap, as discussed several paragraphs ago. But, even if you put in a gap, both loafing can be a better Nash equilibrium than both trying; see, for instance, the numbers in Figure 19.16. So I rerun Solver, adding two constraints: If B loafs, A should prefer trying hard to loafing; if A loafs, B should prefer trying to loafing. (In terms of the spreadsheet, G20 >= G24, and F23 >= H23.) (I also remove the 0.05 utility gap.) Figure 19.17 is the result.

The scheme now is to give both $4350 if both achieve the $10,000 outcome and $1284 if both get the $0 outcome. If one succeeds and the other fails, they get $9818 and $7, respectively, for a net profit to the manager of $6301. Again I have three remarks.

First, the added constraints make trying a dominant strategy for both agents. That's a good strong solution concept. However, Solver, in trying to economize, sets things up so neither agent cares which effort level he or she takes, although each agent is very anxious to have the other loaf. If this massive bit of indifference worries you, rerun Solver with some gaps stuck in; that is, replace G20 >= G24 with G20 >= G24 + .1, and so forth, where you can choose what size gaps you want (perhaps converting back to certainty equivalents, so the size of the gaps is measured in meaningful terms).

Now, despite what I said before about likelihood ratios, the big bucks go with the outcome where one agent succeeds and the other fails. Adding the extra constraint makes this problem a level more complex, and my first (non)explanation of the results—this is too hard to explain intuitively—is now entirely appropriate.

We still have a problem to worry about. Even if you open up some gaps, so trying

		TWO-AGENTS				
	C	D	E	F	G	H	I

PROBABILITIES

	both hard	A loafs, B tries	B loafs, A tries	both loaf
both $1000	0.6	0.25	0.25	0.2
$1000 for A	0.1	0.05	0.45	0.1
$1000 for B	0.1	0.45	0.05	0.1
both $0	0.2	0.25	0.25	0.6

PAYMENTS

	A's payments	sqrt A's pay	B's payments	sqrt B's pay
both $1000	$4,350	2.08571429	$4,350	2.08571416
$1000 for A	$9,818	3.13333335	$7	0.08571429
$1000 for B	$7	0.08571428	$9,818	3.13333431
both $0	$1,284	1.133333336	$1,284	1.13333325

OUTCOMES

	B tries hard		B loafs	
A tries hard	A's EU\ 1.000000006		0.999999999	
	1.000000004 \B's EU	1.419047628		
A loafs	1.419048007		1.419047642	
	1	1.419047623		

PROFITS

	B tries hard	B loafs
A tries hard	$6,301	$2,270
A loafs	$2,270	$754

Figure 19.17. Part e answer.

hard is strictly dominant for both sides, unless you make the gaps very big, you wind up with a situation that is strategically the prisoners' dilemma game. Both have unilateral interests to try hard, but if both loaf, they are better off than if both try hard. If these are two employees, you might worry that they might collude, somehow guaranteeing that each loafs. (If this is a repeated situation and each can monitor the other's choice of action, the discussion of implicit collusion in Chapter 22 becomes disturbingly relevant to the manager.)

So—time for part f—we throw in two more constraints: The outcome for A if both try should be at least as good as if both loaf (or, E20 >= G24) and similarly for B (F19 >= H23). Solver does its stuff again, and Figure 19.18 is the result.

Look familiar? It should. We threw in so many constraints that the best Solver can do is hold each agent to an expected utility (net of the cost of effort) of 1 for each of the four outcomes. Which, if you think about it, means that each gets expected utility 1 *on the margin* from either action. This is the "nontournament" solution

		both hard	A loafs, B tries	B loafs, A tries	both loaf
		PROBABILITIES			
	both $1000	0.6	0.25	0.25	0.2
	$1000 for A	0.1	0.05	0.45	0.1
	$1000 for B	0.1	0.45	0.05	0.1
	both $0	0.2	0.25	0.25	0.6

		A's payments	sqrt A's pay	B's payments	sqrt B's pay
		PAYMENTS			
	both $1000	$5,760	2.40000001	$5,760	2.40000001
	$1000 for A	$5,760	2.4	$160	0.4
	$1000 for B	$160	0.4	$5,760	2.4
	both $0	$160	0.4	$160	0.4

OUTCOMES

	B tries hard		B loafs	
A tries hard	A's EU\ 1.000000006			1.000000003
	1.000000006	\B's EU 1.000000003		
A loafs		1.000000003		1.000000002
	1.000000003		1.000000002	

PROFITS

	B tries hard	B loafs
A tries hard	$5,840	$4,080
A loafs	$4,080	$2,320

Figure 19.18. Part f answer.

computed back in part b. Each gets $5760 if he or she is successful and $160 for a failure, regardless of what the other person does.

Although I have answered all the questions originally posed, I want to do one thing more. We looked at optimal compensation to induce both to loaf and the optimal (incentive) compensation to induce both to try hard. How about the optimal way to get A to try hard and B to loaf? Fire up Solver. This time we want to maximize cell G29 subject to the constraints that G20 (what A gets by trying hard when B is loafing) is as good as G24 (A's expected utility if both loaf) and is at least 1. I could throw in the constraint that B prefers loafing, but if B wants to try hard, that is fine with me. Solver returns Figure 19.19.

Note first of all that we give B a flat $1000 payment. No reason to put any uncertainty into B's life, if he or she is going to loaf. But, for A, there are lots of incentives: $3978 if both succeed, $6537 if A succeeds when B fails, $684 if both fail, and $192 if B

	TWO-AGENTS						
	C	D	E	F	G	H	I

PROBABILITIES

	both hard	A loafs, B tries	B loafs, A tries	both loaf
both $1000	0.6	0.25	0.25	0.2
$1000 for A	0.1	0.05	0.45	0.1
$1000 for B	0.1	0.45	0.05	0.1
both $0	0.2	0.25	0.25	0.6

PAYMENTS

	A's payments	sqrt A's pay	B's payments	sqrt B's pay
both $1000	$3,978	1.99459453	$1,000	1
$1000 for A	$6,537	2.55675678	$1,000	1
$1000 for B	$684	0.82702731	$1,000	1
both $0	$192	0.43783781	$1,000	1

OUTCOMES

	B tries hard		B loafs	
A tries hard	A's EU\	0.2		1
	0.822702689	\B's EU	1.000000002	
A loafs		0.2		1
	1.108108214		1.000000001	

PROFITS

	B tries hard	B loafs
A tries hard	$9,853	$4,982
A loafs	$7,323	$3,367

Figure 19.19. Two-agent problem: A tries, B loafs.

succeeds and A fails.[1] Expected profits are $4982, which is $2000 from B and $2982 from A.

This is no better than inducing both to try hard, even if we go with the no-comparisons scheme where each is rewarded on his or her own. But there are still a couple of nice points to make about this.

Suppose that the manager employs two agents, A and B, who are working at their respective tasks. All the story stays the same but with one change: B really hates trying hard. Instead of a disutility of 0.8, trying hard has a disutility of, say, 6 for B. That is so much disutility, that there is no point in trying to motivate B to try hard. And the manager, offering B a flat $1000 compensation package, makes

---

[1] Since this is a single incentive constraint problem, my characterization about relative likelihoods works. Check it if you want.

$2000 out of B's paltry efforts. Even so, B's existence helps the manager deal with A. We can still tie A's compensation to how he or she does relative to B; we use the compensation scheme Solver supplies in Figure 19.19. And the manager nets $2982 from A's efforts, compared to the $2920 made with the no-comparisons incentive scheme of part b. The $62 isn't a ton of money, but it's something.

Second, things like the disutility of effort are often psychological. Suppose we are in the story of the previous paragraph and B suddenly gets a pang of conscience and decides, despite no extrinsic incentive to do so (B is being paid a flat $1000, remember), to try hard. Suppose A notices that B is trying hard. Look at Figure 19.19. If A assumes B is trying hard, and if A remains crassly materialistic, with a 0.8 disutility for trying hard, A is going to loaf. You can't win 'em all. (Although look at the net impact this has on profits. Maybe you can win some of them.)

Review Problems IV

IV.1   Ford Frick owns the rights to a gamble that is unfavorable: It may generate $20,000 in income for him, but this happens with probability 0.2; with probability 0.8, Frick will lose $10,000. Frick's utility function for this gamble is

$$U(z) = \sqrt{z + 10{,}000}\,,$$

where z is his winnings from the gamble (that is, z = either $20,000 or −$10,000.)

(a) What is Frick's expected utility for this gamble? What is his certainty equivalent?

(b) Francesca Frack has utility function

$$V(z) = 100 + 3\sqrt{z + 10{,}000}$$

for gambles with prizes in the range from $100,000 gained to $10,000 lost. Note that for every level of prize, Frack's utility function is greater than Frick's. Does this mean that Frack is less risk averse than Frick?

(c) Frick is thinking of "selling" this gamble to Frack. Since it is unfavorable, this means that Frick will give Frack some amount of money, if Frack assumes the gamble in its entirety. What is the least amount of money Frick could give Frack and still have Frack be willing to assume the gamble, if Frack's alternative is no payment and no gamble? (If you cannot provide a number, at least give an equation that, when solved, would provide the answer.)

(d) Rather than give Frack the entire gamble, Frick has decided to investigate giving her half the gamble and keeping half for himself. Of course, he must compensate her up front for taking on half the gamble. What is the range of up-front payment Frick can give Frack so that (1) she will assume 50% of the gamble for this payment and (2) he would rather make this payment and be left with 50% of the gamble than be left with 100% of the gamble? (Give either numbers or one or more equations, the solutions to which answer the question.)

IV.2 Jo MBA, a second-year student who is a risk averse expected utility maximizer, is in the fortunate position of owning a can't-lose gamble: With probability 0.9

she will win $10,000 and with probability 0.1 she will win $50,000. Her certainty equivalent for this gamble is $13,000. Recalling a course she took in her first year of studies based on this book, she thinks about "securitizing" this gamble: breaking it into 100 equal shares and selling some or all of those shares to her fellow students, all of whom just happen to be exactly as risk averse as she. But a friend tells her not to bother, saying, "Because you can't lose with this gamble—you win money no matter what—there can be no gain from breaking the gamble into pieces." Is Jo's friend correct, or should Jo's friend go back and review, because this just is not so?

IV.3 The Wizzywig Manufacturing Company (WMC) signed a government contract to provide the U.S. Army with 10,000 two-handled grudonzas. There are two possible production processes, each of which is either high cost or low. The probability that either is high cost is 0.5, and these are independent events; that is, the probability that both are high cost is 0.25. The choice between the two production processes will be made by Will B. Donne, the production manager at WMC. Donne can, at the cost of some personal exertion, discover beforehand whether either or both processes are low cost. But unless motivated to do so, he would not; instead he would choose one of the two at random. Specifically, Donne's utility function on the job depends on the wages he is paid W and whether he exerts himself to discover whether either or both processes are low cost: The function is

$$\sqrt{W} - \text{disutility of investigating,}$$

where the disutility of investigating is 0 if he does not try to find out, and 20 if he does. (He either investigates both processes or neither; he cannot check just one.) Donne will work for WMC as long as his expected (net) utility is 100 or more.

Donne is risk averse, and WMC is risk neutral. WMC to this point has been paying Mr. Donne a fixed salary of $10,000. Top management at WMC knows, however, that if they pay him a fixed salary, he has no incentive to investigate. Accordingly, WMC is determined to pay him a fixed base salary S and a bonus B, which he gets if the technology he chooses is low cost.

(a) If $S = \$6400$ and $B = \$13,200$, would Donne have adequate incentive to investigate which technology is low cost (if either is)?

(b) What combination of S and B provides Donne sufficient motivation to investigate which technology is low cost, provides him enough expected utility so he stays on the job, and minimizes the expected wages that WMC must pay him?

IV.4 You are in the market for a very particular boat, a Spinnaker 72. You found the owner of such a boat who claims to be willing to consider a sale. This is a very rare occurrence—these boats rarely come to market—and you figure that if you do not buy this boat, you will probably never get one.

Spinnaker 72's were manufactured by Spence Enterprises in the late 1960s and by Baron's Knockoffs in the early 1970s. To make the problem interesting, we assume it is impossible to tell whether a particular boat was manufactured by Spence Enterprises or Baron's Knockoffs. To you, the buyer, however, this is very important: The boats originally made by Spence Enterprises were made by hand in Portugal and are much more reliable than the machine-manufactured boats made later by Baron's Knockoffs in Key West. Sellers of these boats know which sort of boat they have, an original Spence or a Baron Knockoff, and those who own a Baron Knockoff are much more eager to sell: Specifically, the owner of the boat you might buy will sell her boat only if offered at least $75,000 if it is a Spence original, while she will be willing to sell her boat for $50,000 if it is a Baron Knockoff. A Spence original is worth $85,000 to you, while a Baron Knockoff is worth only $60,000. Equal numbers of Spence originals and Baron Knockoffs were manufactured, so any single Spinnaker 72, absent other information, is equally likely to be one or the other.

The owner of the Spinnaker 72 you might purchase maintains that her boat really is a Spence-built original. This individual, though, is very opportunisitic; she would say exactly the same thing if her boat were a Baron Knockoff.

Throughout the problem, assume you are risk neutral concerning any randomness that you face.

(a) Without any further information, what is the most you should be willing to pay for this boat?

(b) Because of the difficulties of buying and selling these boats, you and the potential seller have decided to obtain the services of a boat-sales mediator. This individual will propose a "deal" to the two of you, and you either consummate this deal or walk away with no deal.

Spence originals are virtually maintenance free, so a warranty offered by the seller of a Spence original costs the seller nothing and is worth nothing to the buyer. But Baron Knockoffs require constant expensive maintenance; the cost to the seller of a Baron Knockoff of a warranty is $3000 per month of the warranty, which must be netted against the sales price, and is worth $2000 per month to the buyer over and above the value of the boat itself.

Suppose the boat-sales mediator proposes the following deal. You pay the seller of the boat $80,000 for her boat if she offers it with a 10 month warranty, and you will pay her $55,000 for her boat if she insists on selling it with no warranty. The seller indicates that she will go ahead with this deal, but she has not indicated whether she plans to offer the warranty. From your point of view, does it make sense to go ahead with this deal? Why?

(c) Suppose that instead of the deal suggested in part b, the boat-sale mediator proposes that the seller provide a six-month warranty and you should purchase the boat for $80,000. The seller has indicated that she is willing to go ahead with this deal. Should you go along with this proposal? Why or why not?

(d) Suppose that the boat-sale mediator is willing to propose only deals that take the form of the deal in part c: a single sales price and a single duration of warranty. Suppose further that this boat-sale mediator is in cohoots with you and will try to structure the deal that gives you the largest expected (mean) level of benefit as possible. What deal should he propose?

IV.5 Imagine a savings and loan bank, newly formed, that holds $210 million dollars in cash. Of this cash, $200 million was generated from 12-month certificates of deposit (CDs), which pay a 5% per year rate of interest. The remaining $10 million comes from the initial capitalization of the bank; that is, it is the equity holder's equity.

These $210 million can be invested in one of two ways. One course, more risky, would leave the bank with $300 million in assets in a year's time with probability $\frac{1}{2}$, and it would leave the bank with $100 million in assets with probability $\frac{1}{2}$. The second course would leave the bank with either $220 million or $240 million in assets, each with probability $\frac{1}{2}$. (Note that the the EMV of the first investment is $200 million, while the second is $230 million.)

The decision of which investment to make is made by the CEO of the bank, who is also the sole equity holder. He plans to liquidate the bank after this year, and he will choose whichever investment gives him the highest expected return on his equity. His ending equity is determined as follows: If the assets of the bank in a year exceed $210 million, the CDs are paid off ($200 million in face value plus $10 million in accrued interest) and whatever remains is the CEO's. If the assets of the bank fall below $210 million but are above $200 million, the bank is declared bankrupt: Depositors are paid their pro-rata shares of the assets and the CEO is left with nothing. If the assets of the bank are $200 million or less, the bank is bankrupt and the CEO is left with nothing. Depositors get back the face value of their CDs (a total of $200 million), with any short-fall from the $200 million needed to pay off the depositors provided by the FSLIC (the Federal Savings and Loan Insurance Corporation). (The FSLIC guarantees the face value of CDs but not interest payments. If the bank goes bankrupt, depositors may lose some or all of the interest they expected.)

Provide the following: the investment choice of the CEO, the expected value of his equity at the end of the year for this investment choice, the expected value of paybacks to depositors from their $200 million in initial deposits, and the expected amount to be paid out by the FSLIC.

IV.6 (a) Imagine you have just turned in an exam for a course that uses this book as a text, and your instructor hands you and all your classmates a sheet of paper that reads:

> You have two options for a grade in this course. If you do nothing, you will be graded on the basis of your exam performance. But if you sign this sheet of paper and hand it to your instructor, your course (letter) grade will be based instead on the average (mean) of the exam scores received by all students who sign and turn in this sheet of paper. That is, if five students sign and turn in this piece of paper, and their exam scores are 100, 90, 80, 80, and 70, then all five of these students will be graded on the basis of having scored $(100 + 90 + 80 + 80 + 70)/5 = 84$. You must decide in the next 5 minutes whether to accept this generous offer.

This offer is completely unexpected. What are the most salient considerations about whether you should take up this offer?

(b) Suppose this offer were made to all students in this supposed course one week before the exam, with the stipulation that the decision whether to take up the offer had to be made prior to the start of the exam. How does this change (from an unexpected offer after the exam is over, to an offer made a week before the exam that must be taken up prior to the exam) affect your considerations?

(c) Suppose this offer were made to all students after the exam has been graded and grades have been distributed to students, together with the full distribution of grades received. How does this affect your considerations?

In 1997, in a course based on a draft of this book, I put this problem as the final problem on the final exam and then added:

(d) *Not graded. Not for real. Just for the amusement and information of the instructors.* Suppose the option outlined in part a were open to you, to be decided at this moment (that is, before you turn in the exam, but (presumably) fairly far into it). Would you take this option? *We reiterate that the information you provide in answer to this part of the question in no way will affect your grade.*

How do you think the 1997 students responded?

IV.7 (In Problem 18.1, a story about catastrophic summer income insurance for students at FECBUS was used to illustrate adverse selection. Here is very different sort of story, based on similar "details.")

(a) Consider the following variation on the catastrophic summer income insurance problem. Students at FECBUS either get summer jobs at high-powered investment banks or they do not. If they do not, they refuse any other summer job, and earn no wages. A summer job is worth $80,000.

Students at FECBUS are risk-averse, expected-utility maximizers when it comes to their summer job income (and income related to this), with utility function

$$U(Y) = \sqrt{Y + 10,000},$$

where Y is the level of wages earned; that is, Y is either $80,000 or $0.

(a) Consider a student at FECBUS who has a 0.8 chance of getting a summer job. What is this student's expected utility of summer income? What is the student's certainty equivalent? Imagine that Beantown Casualty offers complete summer income insurance, where for a premium payment of P, the company would pay out $80,000 if the student does not land a job. What is the maximum premium this student would be willing to pay?

(b) It turns out that students, by their efforts, can influence the probability that they get a summer job. Students can either *make an effort* or *coast through the interview*. Suppose that the student in part a has a 0.8 chance of getting the job if he makes an effort, but the chances of landing a job are 0.4 if the student coasts through the interview. Moreover, in trying to determine whether to make an effort or coast, the student reckons as follows: He computes his expected utility if he makes an effort, subtracts 50 (on the utility scale), and compares this with his expected utility if he coasts. If the former is as large or larger than the latter, he makes an effort. (In other words, making an effort "costs" 50 units of utility. And, the students at FECBUS are shameless in one respect at least: Except for what it might cost them in wages, they are just as happy to sit on the banks of the Chuckie River and work on their tans as they are to land a plum summer job in New York City.) If there is no possibility of insurance, will the student coast or make an effort?

(c) Suppose that Beantown offers the student in part b full summer income insurance for a premium of P. That is, in return for a payment of P, Beantown will give the student $80,000 if he fails to land a summer job. What is the maximum premium P that can be charged for this sort of insurance (maximum in the sense that the student would accept the policy)? What are Beantown's expected profits with this policy? (Hint: What would the student do if offered full insurance?)

(d) Beantown considers the possibility of offering only partial insurance; that is, for a payment of P, Beantown would pay X back to the student if he does not land a summer job. From the perspective of Beantown (maximizing the premium less the expected payback to the student), what is the best combination of P and X to offer?

IV.8 Problem 18.1 analyzes catastrophic summer income insurance in a context that involves adverse selection, and Problem IV.7 looks at a context of moral hazard and incentives. This problem concerns a formulation combining both phenomena.

All the students at FECBUS, the Famous East Coast Business School, try to get summer jobs at New York investment banks. If a student lands a job, the income derived is $90,000. If the student does not land a job, the student (on grounds of pride) refuses to take any other employment, giving net wages of $0.

Students at FECBUS, by their efforts, can affect the odds with which they land a job. Specifically, students at FECBUS can either *try hard* to get a job or just *go through the motions*. Of the FECBUS students, 90% are *smooth operators* who have probability 0.5 of landing a summer job even if they go through the motions, but these students can improve that probability to 0.9 if they try hard to get a job. Ten percent of the FECBUS students are *less smooth*; if they go through the motions, they have probability 0.4 of getting a summer job, while if they try hard, this probability rises to 0.7.

FECBUS students decide on whether to try hard or go through the motions based on the expected utility of their wages and the disutility they incur by trying hard. Specifically, each has the utility function

$$\sqrt{\text{summer wages}} - \text{disutility of effort},$$

where the disutility of effort is 0 if he or she goes through the motions and it is 40 if he or she tries hard.

(a) Take one of the students who is a smooth operator; that is, this student has a 0.5 probability of landing a summer job if she goes through the motions, and a 0.9 probability of landing a summer job if she tries hard. What is her expected utility (net of the disutility of effort) if she tries hard? What is her expected utility (net of the disutility of effort) if she goes through the motions? What would she do?

(b) Take any student who is not so smooth; that is, this student has a 0.4 probability of landing a summer job if he goes through the motions and a 0.7 probability if he tries hard. Would he try hard or go through the motions?

(c) Suppose an insurance company, Beantown Casualty, offers catastrophic summer income insurance: This insurance has a premium of $17,000 and pays back $90,000 if the student fails to land a summer job. Suppose that the insurance company can discriminate between smooth operators and students who are not so smooth, and it is able to offer this insurance only to smooth operators. Will the insurance company make or lose money on each policy of this sort that it writes (for smooth operators, only)? (Evaluate policies by premium less expected payout.)

(d) What insurance policy, offered only to smooth operators, maximizes the expected profits made by the insurance company?

(e) Suppose the insurance company cannot distinguish between smooth operators and students who are not so smooth. Any policy that the company offers must be offered to all the students. Imagine that the company offers two policies to the students: The first has a payback (if the student does not get a job) of $90,000 and a premium of $44,000; while the second has a premium of $10,600 and a payback of $38,000. Students may have one policy or the other (or none), but they are not allowed to "overinsure" by buying both. How much money (in terms of its premium income less expected payouts) does the insurance company make or lose by offering this menu of choices? For simplicity, assume there are 1000 FECBUS first-year students, 900 smooth operators and 100 students who are not so smooth.

(f) (This part of the problem probably takes a spreadsheet.) You are put on the FECBUS Exploitation Team of Beantown Casualty, with the mandate to come up with the best scheme for making (expected) profits out of the 1000 FECBUS students. You are unable to tell a student's type, and any offer you make to one student, you must make to all. How well can you do in terms of expected profits?

Solution to Problem IV.1

(a) Frick holds a gamble that pays $20,000 with probability 0.2 and $ − 10,000 with probability 0.8. The first outcome has utility $\sqrt{20,000 + 10,000} = [173.205]$, while the second has utility $\sqrt{-10,000 + 10,000} = [0]$. So the gamble has an expected utility of

$$0.2 \times [173.23] + 0.8 \times [0] = [34.64].$$

The certainty equivalent is the value that solves

$$\sqrt{10,000 + \text{CE}} = 34.64,$$

which is (approximately) CE = −$8800.

(b) No, this does not mean that Frack is less risk averse than Frick. In fact, because Frack's utility function is a positive affine transformation of Frick's (fancy talk for, take Frick's, multiply by a positive number (3) and add a constant (100) and you have Frack's), they hold identical attitudes toward risk.

In parts c and c, I use the (equivalent) utility function $\sqrt{z + 10,000}$ for Frack as well as Frick, just to keep the notation in bounds.

(c) If Frack does not participate in the gamble, her utility is $\sqrt{10,000 + 0}$ for sure, or [100]. If Frick pays her P for taking on the gamble, she has an expected utility of

$$0.2\sqrt{30,000 + P} + 0.8\sqrt{P}.$$

So she would accept the payment to assume the gamble, as long as

$$0.2\sqrt{30,000 + P} + 0.8\sqrt{P} \geq [100],$$

and the least amount of money P that would induce her to do this is the value of P for which

$$.02\sqrt{30,000 + P} + 0.8\sqrt{P} = [100].$$

You cannot solve for P algebraically, but P can be found numerically; the answer is (approximately) $P = \$6015$.

(d) Frack would take on half the gamble in return for a payment of P only if

$$0.2\sqrt{20{,}000 + P} + 0.8\sqrt{5000 + P} \geq [100],$$

which gives $P \geq \$2636.4$. And Frick would be willing to pay P to get rid of half his risk, as long as

$$0.2\sqrt{20{,}000 - P} + 0.8\sqrt{5000 - P} \geq [34.64],$$

which is $P \leq \$4776.4$

Solution to Problem IV.2

Jo's friend needs to go back and review; this just isn't so. If you break the gamble into, say, 100 pieces, each piece is a gamble with a 0.9 chance at $100 and a 0.1 chance at $500. The risk is not very great, and with an expected value of $140, my guess is that most folks would be willing to pay at least $135 for a share. Then, 100 shares could be sold for $13,500 or more, which exceeds Jo's CE if she holds the entire gamble.

Solution to Problem IV.3

(a) Mr. Donne lacks adequate incentive to investigate for those values of S and B:

- If he doesn't investigate, he gets $19,600 (utility [140]) with probability 0.5, and $6400 (utility [80]) with probability 0.5, for an expected utility of [110].

- If he does investigate, he gets $19,600 (utility [140]) with probability 0.75, and $6400 (utility [80]) with probability 0.25, for an expected utility of [125], less [20] for exerting the effort, or a net [105].

The key here is to note that even if he does not investigate but picks a technology at random, he has a 50% chance of being right by luck, while if he does investigate, he improves this to only 75%, since there is probability 25% that neither technology is low cost.

(b) To get Mr. Donne to take the job at all, we need that

$$0.75\sqrt{S + B} + 0.25\sqrt{S} - 20 \geq 100.$$

And to get him to investigate instead of picking without investigating, we need

$$0.75\sqrt{S+B}+0.25\sqrt{S}-20 \geq 0.5\sqrt{S+B}+0.5\sqrt{S}.$$

To do this as cheaply as possible, we need equalities in both places. Turn the two inequalities into equations and solve. You should find that

$$B = \$16{,}000 \quad \text{and} \quad S = \$3600,$$

where you may want to increase B a bit, to make the two equations into inequalities that slightly favor the actions you want.

Solution to Problem IV.4

(a) At prices above $75,000, you are as likely to get a Spence as a Baron, so the value to you would be

$$0.5 \times \$85{,}000 \ + \ 0.5 \times \$60{,}000 \ = \ \$72{,}500,$$

and so you are unwilling to pay any price over $75,000. At prices below $75,000, only Barons are for sale, worth $60,000. So the most you should be willing to pay for a boat (with no further information) is $60,000.

(b) Yes, this deal does make sense for you, because if the seller owns a Spence, the warranty costs her nothing, so of course she would offer to sell the boat for $80,000. If she owns a Baron, the 10-month warranty costs her $30,000, so $55,000 without the warranty is a better deal than $80,000 with a 10-month warranty. Therefore, you are paying $80,000 for a Spence (if that is the offer) and $55,000 for a Baron, both of which are acceptable prices for what you are getting.

(c) No, this deal makes no sense for you. We already know that a Spence owner would sell to you on these terms. A Baron owner would net $80,000 less six times $3000 = $62,000 if she takes this deal, above her reservation price of $50,000. So she would say yes. Therefore, this boat is equally likely to be a Spence or a Baron, worth either $85,000 or $60,000 plus six times $2000 = $72,000, respectively, for an average value of $78,500K, below the $80,000 price.

(d) Let P be the price (in thousands of dollars) and N be the length of the warranty. Four sorts of "deals" could be offered: (1) a deal acceptable to Spence owners but not to Baron owners; (2) a deal that is acceptable only to Baron owners; (3) a deal acceptable to both; or (4) a deal acceptable to neither. The last type gives you no boat, hence no surplus. We can ignore this.

For type 1, we need that $P \geq 75$ but $P - 3N < 50$. This gives you the expected surplus $0.5 \times (85 - P) + 0.5 \times 0$, since there is a 50% chance you get no boat. Maximizing your expected surplus subject to the two constraints gives $P = \$75,000$ and N anything bigger than 8.333, for an expected surplus of $5000.

For type 2, we need that $P < 75$ but $P - 3N \geq 50$. Your expected surplus is $0.5 \times 0 + 0.5 \times (60 + 2N - P) = 30 + N - P/2$. To increase N by 1 month requires an increase of P by $3000, which decreases your expected surplus, so the best deal of this sort is $P = \$50,000$, $N = 0$, and your expected surplus equals $5000.

For type 3, we need that $P \geq 75$ and $P - 3N \geq 50$. Your expected surplus is

$$0.5 \times (85 - P) \; + \; 0.5 \times (60 + 2N - P) \; = \; 72.5 - P + N.$$

Increasing N takes a $3000 increase in P as long as P is above $75,000, which is not worth it. So the best deal of this sort involves $P = \$75,000$ and $N = 8.333$, giving you an expected surplus of $5833.33. This is the best deal and the answer to part d.

(Please note that while $5833.33 is the best you can do with a single price–warranty package, you can do better with packages that involve two price–warranty pairs, one intended for Spence owners and the other for Baron owners.)

Solution to Problem IV.5

(This problem is relatively easy, if you take it a step at a time.)

With the more risky investment, if the outcome is $300 million, the owner takes out $90 million, depositers get $210 million, and the FSLIC pays out nothing. If the outcome is $100 million, the owner gets $0, depositors get $200 million, and the FSLIC pays out $100 million. Since the two outcomes are equally likely, the owner's expected value is $45 million, the depositors get $205 million (expected value), and the expected payout by the FSLIC is $50 million. (Note these add up to $200M, as they should, since this is the overall expected value.)

In the less risky investment, if the outcome is $240 million, the owner takes out $30 million, depositors get $210 million, and the FSLIC pays out nothing. If the outcome is $220 million, the owner takes out $10 million, depositors get $210 million, and the FSLIC pays out nothing. So the owner has an expected value of $20 million, depositors get $210 million for sure, and the FSLIC pays out nothing.

Of course, since the owner controls the investment decision, he takes the more risky course of action, to the detriment of depositors and the FSLIC.

(Are the owner's and depositor's interests always opposed? No. Suppose the more risky course of action had the outcomes as indicated, and the safer course of action gave $204 million for sure. Then, the owner and the depositors both prefer the risky course of action, while the FSLIC prefers the safer course of action.)

Solution to Problem IV.6

(a) The basic two considerations are these: How well can students guess how they have done on the exam, and how risk averse are they against getting a low grade vs. getting a high grade.

Suppose no student knows how well he or she has done. Suppose each would accept a middling grade, rather than running the chance of getting a low grade for the chance of a high grade. Then, everyone would sign up for the option. In fact, if no student knows how well he or she has done, and if tastes for the different grades are not correlated with exam performance, students who would rather accept the middling grade than the gamble would sign up, since the students who sign up would be a representative sample of the class as a whole.

Suppose, at the other extreme, each student can guess exactly what grade he or she is about to receive. Students expecting the highest possible grade will opt out of the deal—why average in and have the chance of some lesser grade, when you have the highest possible grade in the bag? Then those who know they have a second-tier grade will opt out, since they cannot improve their grade by averaging in. The third-tier grades opt out next, and so on, leaving only the folks who expect to fail the course in the pool (and since they get nothing for being in the pool, they may as well opt out, as well). This is an extreme example of adverse selection, like people opting out of the self-insurance pool for earthquake insurance region by region, starting with the least earthquake prone, until we get to the most.

Of course, neither of these extreme conditions pertains. On leaving the exam, most people have a fairly good idea, but not a perfect idea, how they fared. You have to imagine that those who opt into the pool will be those who think they did relatively poorly, and those who are very adverse to the chances of a relatively poor grade.

Therefore, the pool is an adverse selection of the class in terms of scores.

(b) This adds a layer of moral hazard. If you sign up for the pool, you will not affect your grade much at all by studying. Hence, you probably will spend all your time studying for some other exam. Therefore, the performance of those in the pool will tend to be low. That would not be a problem as long as enough folks are in the pool that the pool gets a passing grade. But, assuming grades are assigned on a relative and not absolute basis, since the people in the pool would not study, by staying out and studying even somewhat, you have a better shot at a relatively good grade. Countervailing this is that you probably have less sense, in advance, of how well you will do, which ought to incline you to pool and be safe. (Another countervailing force is peer pressure to join the pool.) My guess is that, at some schools where peer pressure to act "cooperatively" is strong, only people at the top end of the distribution would opt out. But at schools where the culture is more competitive, a lot more people would opt out.

(c) This is like the case from part a where people know precisely how well they did. No one would join the pool (at least, based on own-score considerations alone; there might be substantial peer pressure for folks to join).

About the last, ungraded part of the question, around 40% of the students checked the "I would take this option" box, representing an adverse selection (average score a standard deviation or so below the mean) of the class as a whole, but not a uniformly adverse selection. (That is, some people who did quite well joined, and some who did poorly did not. Of course, for those who did poorly and did not join, we have the explanation that they did not understand the ideas behind this analysis, and they confirmed their confusion by opting out when they "ought" to be in.)

Solution to Problem IV.7

(a) The student gets $80,000 = utility 300 with probability 0.8 and $0 = utility 100 with probability 0.2, for an expected utility of 260 and a certainty equivalent that is the solution to

$$\sqrt{CE + 10,000} = 260$$

or $CE + 10,000 = 67,600$ or $CE = \$57,600$.

If Beantown gives complete insurance at a premium P, the student gets $\$80,000 - P$ with certainty. So the largest premium that could be charged and still entice the student is the solution to $80,000 - P = 57,600$ or $P = \$22,400$.

(b) In this case, if the student makes an effort, he has a 0.8 chance of landing the job, for an expected utility of 260 gross of the "cost of effort." If he coasts, his chances of landing the job are only 0.4, so his gross expected utility is

$$0.4 \times [300] \ + \ 0.6 \times [100] \ = \ [180].$$

The utility cost of making an effort, according to the problem, is 50, so since 260 is more than 50 greater than 180, he will make the effort.

(c) If full insurance is offered, the student has no incentive to make an effort. To be pedantic about it, if he makes the effort, his net expected utility (if the premium is P) would be

$$0.8 \times \sqrt{90,000 - P} \ + \ 0.2 \times \sqrt{90,000 - P} \ - \ 50 \ = \ \sqrt{90,000 - P} - 50,$$

while if he coasts, his net expected utility would be

$$0.4 \times \sqrt{90,000 - P} \ + \ 0.6 \times \sqrt{90,000 - P} \ = \ \sqrt{90,000 - P}.$$

Since his best alternative without insurance gives him a net utility of 210 (see part b), he would purchase the insurance only if

$$\sqrt{90,000 - P} \geq 210 \quad \text{or} \quad 90,000 - P \geq 44,100,$$

or $P \leq \$45,900$.

Even at the premium \$45,900, since the student is going to coast, Beantown must pay back \$80,000 with probability 0.6, for an expected payback of \$48,000. Therefore, at best, Beantown would lose an expected \$2100 on a full-insurance policy.

(d) Given a premium P and payback amount X, the student has the net utility

$$0.8 \times \sqrt{90,000 - P} \ + \ 0.2 \times \sqrt{10,000 + X - P} \ - \ 50$$

if he makes an effort and

$$0.4 \times \sqrt{90,000 - P} \ + \ 0.6 \times \sqrt{10,000 + X - P}$$

if he does not. Let A be the variable $\sqrt{10,000 + X - P}$ and let B be $\sqrt{90,000 - P}$, and to find the best partial insurance contract for Beantown that induces an effort, we must solve

$$0.8B + 0.2A - 50 = 0.4B + 0.6A \quad \text{and}$$
$$0.8B + 0.2A - 50 = 210,$$

where the second equality ensures that the student would take the contract and the first ensures that just enough incentive is built in so that the student would be willing to make an effort. If you solve for A and B, then for P and X, you find that the optimal contract has

$$P = \$8775 \quad \text{and} \quad X = \$24,375,$$

which gives Beantown an expected profit of \$3900.

Solution to Problem IV.8

If you could do this problem start to finish, you are doing very well.

(a) If a smooth operator goes through the motions, she has expected utility

$$0.5 \times \sqrt{90,000} + 0.5 \times \sqrt{0} = 150.$$

If she tries hard, she nets an expected utility (net of the disutility of effort) of

$$0.9 \times \sqrt{90,000} + 0.1 \times \sqrt{0} - 40 = 230.$$

So she would try hard.

(b) If a not-so-smooth student goes through the motions, he has an expected utility of

$$0.4 \times \sqrt{90,000} + 0.7 \times \sqrt{0} = 120.$$

If he tries hard, he nets an expected utility (net of the disutility of effort) of

$$0.7 \times \sqrt{90,000} + 0.3 \times \sqrt{0} - 40 = 170.$$

So he would try hard.

(c) If a smooth operator takes this full-insurance policy, she has income $73,000 for sure. She will go through the motions (no incentive to try hard), netting expected utility $\sqrt{73,000} = 270.185$. Since the best she can do without insurance is an expected utility of 230, she buys this insurance. But since she loafs, the expected payout per policy is $0.5 \times 90,000 = \$45,000$, far in excess of the premium income of $17,000. So the insurance company would lose money—$28,000 on average—on each policy.

(d) This question is very similar to the salesperson compensation problem. I work it out by hand, rather than relying on Excel and Solver.

To answer this question, we look at two subproblems. First, what is the best policy for the insurance company to offer, if it is going to induce the smooth operators to go through the motions? This takes no incentive contract, so the firm might as well go for efficient risk sharing, which means full insurance. The question is, then, how high a premium can it charge? Without insurance, the smooth operators have utility 230, which is equivalent to an income of $52,900, or a maximum premium of $37,100. Since the expected payout on this policy (the student goes through the motions) is $45,000, this is a loser; the company would rather offer no insurance.

In the second subproblem, we look for the best policy that induces the student to try hard. Let X be the student's total income if she gets a job, and let $x = \sqrt{X}$. Let Y be the student's total income if she does not get a job, and let $y = \sqrt{Y}$. Then the constraints to be satisfied are

$$0.9x + 0.1y - 40 \geq 0.5x + 0.5y,$$

or she prefers to try hard instead of going through the motions, and

$$0.9x + 0.1y - 40 \geq 230,$$

or she takes the insurance. As usual in these simple models, the solution is where the two inequalities are equations (load as little risk as possible on the student but still induce her to try hard and leave her just indifferent between buying insurance or not), so we have to solve

$$0.9x + 0.1y - 40 = 0.5x + 0.5y \quad \text{or} \quad 0.4x = 0.4y + 40 \quad \text{or} \quad x = y + 100,$$
$$\text{and} \quad 0.9x + 0.1y - 40 = 230 \quad \text{or} \quad 0.9x + 0.1y = 270.$$

Substituting $y + 100$ for x in the second equation, we get

$$y + 90 = 270 \quad \text{or} \quad y = 180,$$

hence $x = 280$. Therefore,

$$X = x^2 = 78{,}400 \quad \text{and} \quad Y = y^2 = 32{,}400.$$

Since $X = \$90{,}000 - P$, where P is the premium, this gives a premium of \$11,600, and since $Y = Z - P$, where Z is the payback, we see that the payback on the policy (if the student fails to land a job) is \$44,000. The insurance company pays back an expected $0.1 \times 44{,}000 = \$4{,}400$ per policy. Netting this against the premium income of \$11,600 gives a per policy expected profit of \$7200. That is the answer.

(e) The spreadsheet I use to solve this is depicted in Figure IV.1. (This is sheet 1 of the spreadsheet FECBUS EXPLOITER.) The smooth operators choose policy 1 and try hard. The not-so-smooth students choose the second policy and (of course, since this is full insurance) loaf. The company makes \$6.12 million out of the smooth folks but loses \$1 million on the not so smooth.

		policy 1	policy 2	no insurance	
	premium	\$10,600	\$44,000	0	
	payback	\$38,000	\$90,000	0	max utility
	smooth tries	230.1549958	174.4761059	230	230.1549958
	smooth loafs	223.6547548	214.4761059	150	
utilities					
	not smooth, tries	206.9048753	174.4761059	170	214.4761059
	not smooth, loafs	212.0296946	214.4761059	120	
	smooth tries	1	0	0	
	smooth loafs	0	0	0	
choices					
	not smooth, tries	0	0	0	
	not smooth, loafs	0	1	0	
	smooth tries	\$6,120,000	\$0		
	smooth loafs	\$0	\$0	smooth sum	\$6,120,000
profits					
	not smooth, tries	\$0	\$0		
	not smooth, loafs	\$0	(\$1,000,000)	not smooth sum	(\$1,000,000)
				GRAND TOTAL	\$5,120,000

Figure IV.1. A spreadsheet for Problem IV.8.

(f) We basically have two choices for how to proceed if we are trying to find the overall best policy or menu of policies. We can just hunt around or we can try to use Solver.

Let me warn you that this is a fairly hard problem, because there are so many possibilities to run down. I give the complete story, but I move quickly.

Let me try a little hunting, first. My first idea was to take the policy that is optimal for the smooth operators and suffer whatever happens if that policy is taken by the not so smooth. The "logic" here is that there are so many more smooth students, I might as well tailor the insurance contract I offer to them. To do this, I put in the premium and payback from part d into policy 1 in the spreadsheet; and for policy 2, I put in a premium and payback of $90,000, so no one chooses this. I had to play a bit with the payback and premium, since the spreadsheet does not handle the exact ties in utility very well. The results are shown in Figure IV.2. Profit falls to $5 million, so this is not the answer.

		policy 1	policy 2	no insurance	
	premium	$11,599	$90,000	0	
	payback	$43,999	$90,000	0	max utility
	smooth tries	230.0016071	-40	230	230.0016071
	smooth loafs	230.0008929	0	150	
utilities					
	not smooth, tries	210.00125	-40	170	220.0007143
	not smooth, loafs	220.0007143	0	120	
	smooth tries	1	0	0	
	smooth loafs	0	0	0	
choices					
	not smooth, tries	0	0	0	
	not smooth, loafs	1	0	0	
	smooth tries	$6,479,190	$0		
	smooth loafs	$0	$0	smooth sum	$6,479,190
profits					
	not smooth, tries	$0	$0		
	not smooth, loafs	($1,480,040)	$0	not smooth sum	($1,480,040)
				GRAND TOTAL	$4,999,150

Figure IV.2. One policy, optimized for the smooth students but offered to both

I sustain a fairly sizeable loss on the not so smooth. Maybe I should try a contract tuned to maximizing profits out of them, then see how that contract does on the smooth operators. This means redoing part d for the not so smooth. I will save you the math and tell you that the answer is a premium of $27,500 for a payback of $41,111. But, because the smooth operators choose not to insure on these terms, profits are terrible.

So I try to find figures where both groups would insure and both would try hard. It took some hunting, but I finally found numbers that worked: If you make the payback $30,000 and the premium $9000, both insure and both try hard, and the total profit is $5.4 million. See Figure IV.3 (and note that this policy just breaks even on the not so smooth).

		FECBUS EXPLOITER2			
	B	**C**	**D**	**E**	**F**
		policy 1	policy 2	no insurance	
	premium	$9,000	$90,000	0	
	payback	$30,000	$90,000	0	max utility
	smooth tries	230.6358672	-40	230	230.6358672
	smooth loafs	214.7593784	0	150	
utilities					
	not smooth, tries	202.6976228	-40	170	202.6976228
	not smooth, loafs	200.7902562	0	120	
	smooth tries	1	0	0	
	smooth loafs	0	0	0	
choices					
	not smooth, tries	1	0	0	
	not smooth, loafs	0	0	0	
	smooth tries	$5,400,000	$0		
	smooth loafs	$0	$0	smooth sum	$5,400,000
profits					
	not smooth, tries	$0	$0		
	not smooth, loafs	$0	$0	not smooth sum	$0
				GRAND TOTAL	$5,400,000

Figure IV.3. One policy, both types try

At this point, I will be systematic. There are nine possible configurations:

1. All students buy insurance, and all students try hard.

2. All students buy insurance, and all students go through the motions.

3. All students buy. Smooth students try, not so smooth do not.

4. All students buy. Smooth students do not try, not so smooth do.

5. Only the smooth buy, and they try hard.

6. Only the smooth buy, and they do not try.

7. Only the not so smooth buy, and they try hard.

8. Only the not so smooth buy, and they do not try.

9. No one buys insurance.

We can deal with most of these possibilities quickly. If no one buys insurance, the insurance company makes no profit. We know already it can do better than that.

In scenario 8, we might as well offer the not so smooth full insurance. There is no motivational issue here, so go for ideal risk sharing. The biggest premium the not so smooth would pay for full insurance is $90,000 − $28,900 = $61,100$, since this leaves them with $28,900 for sure, for utility $\sqrt{28,900} = 170$. The not so smooth would not buy insurance on these terms, and the average payout per contract is $0.6 \times 90,000 = \$54,000$, for a net per policy of $7100, or $710,000 in total. Not close to the $5 million and change we already saw is possible.

As for scenario 7, we already answered the question, What is the best policy to offer the not so smooth to get them to try. It is a policy with a premium of $27,500 and a payback of $41,111. This is best without the added constraint that the smooth students would not take it, and still they do not, so it must be the best contract to offer that meets the conditions of scenario 7. It generates only $1.5 million and change in profit—not the answer.

Scenarios 2, 4, and 6 can't be optimal. (I am sure, in fact, that 6 is infeasible and I suspect 4 is as well, but I can dispose of those cases in any case, as follows.) All these scenarios have the smooth folks not trying. The best you could possibly do with a smooth student who does not try is the profit you get if you offer full insurance and take all the student's surplus away with a high premium. But the most you can charge a smooth student for full insurance is $37,100. If the student does not try, the payout on this policy is $0.5 \times 90,000 = \$45,000$. So, at best, you lose $7900 per smooth student. (Please note, selling this person less than full insurance, as long as he or she buys and goes through the motions, is only going to increase your losses per student.) For 900 students, this means losses of at least $7.11 million. Can you make it back on the not so smooth? Fat chance. Scenarios 7 and 8 together establish that the most money that can ever be made from the not so smooth is around $1.5 million.

Scenario 5 is essentially infeasible. By *essentially infeasible* I mean the only way it can come about is if the insurance company offers a $0 premium, $0 payback policy. The argument is not that hard: Let X be the net income of a smooth student who lands a job, and Y the net income of one who does not. For the smooth student to take the contract and try hard, we need that $0.9\sqrt{X}+0.1\sqrt{Y}-40 \geq 230$, or $0.9\sqrt{X}+0.1\sqrt{Y} \geq 270$. Multiply this inequality by $\frac{7}{9}$, and you get $0.7\sqrt{X} + 0.0777\sqrt{Y} \geq 210$, or $0.7\sqrt{X} + 0.0777\sqrt{Y} - 40 \geq 170$. But, if the not so smooth are to turn this contract down, it has to be that $0.7\sqrt{X} + 0.3\sqrt{Y} - 40 \leq 170$, and since $\sqrt{Y} \geq 0$, these two inequalities imply that $Y = 0$. Then $X = \$90{,}000$ must hold. This is the $\$0$ premium, $\$0$ payback policy, which generates no profit. This is not the answer.

This leaves us with scenarios 1 and 3 to investigate. Given the hunting around (*groping* might be a better term) we did above, my money is on 1. But we can settle this fairly easily with Solver.

Let me take you through the analysis of possibility 1: All students buy insurance and try hard. I have four decision variables x, y, z, and w, defined as follows:

- Let X be the net amount left to smooth operators if they get a job, so that $X = 90{,}000 - P_1$, where P_1 is their premium. And, let $x = \sqrt{X}$.

- Let Y be the smooth operators' net if they fail to land a job, so that $Y = B_1 - P_1$, where B_1 is the amount they get back. And, let $y = \sqrt{Y}$.

- Let Z be the net amount left to the not so smooth if they get a job, so that $Z = 90{,}000 - P_2$, where P_2 is their premium. And, let $z = \sqrt{Z}$.

- Let W be the not-so-smooth students' net if they fail to land a job, so that $Y = B_2 - P_2$, where B_2 is the amount they get back. And, let $w = \sqrt{W}$

You might worry that I assume there will be different contracts for the smooth and not so smooth. But I do not assume that. If Solver wants to set $x = z$ and $y = w$ (same contract for both groups), that is fine with me.

Now, to formulate my objective function, from each of the 900 smooth operators, I net $P_1 - 0.1B_1 = 90{,}000 - X - 0.1(Y + 90{,}000 - X) = 81{,}000 - 0.9x^2 - 0.1y^2$. And, from each of the 100 not-so-smooth students, I net $P_2 - 0.3B_2 = 90{,}000 - Z - 0.3(W + 90{,}000 - Z) = 63{,}000 - 0.7z^2 - 0.3w^2$. So my overall objective is to maximize

$$900 \times [81{,}000 - 0.9x^2 - 0.1y^2] + 100 \times [63{,}000 - 0.7z^2 - 0.3w^2].$$

Next I have a bunch of constraints. The smooth should prefer contract 1 and trying hard to contract 1 and going through the motions, to contract 2 and trying hard, to contract 2 and going through the motions, and to no insurance (and trying hard). This is four constraints:

$$0.9x + 0.1y - 40 \geq 0.5x + 0.5y,$$
$$0.9x + 0.1y - 40 \geq 0.9z + 0.1w - 40,$$
$$0.9x + 0.1y - 40 \geq 0.5z + 0.5w, \text{ and}$$
$$0.9x + 0.1y - 40 \geq 230.$$

For the not so smooth, we get four similar constraints:

$$0.7z + 0.3w - 40 \geq 0.4z + 0.6w,$$
$$0.7z + 0.3w - 40 \geq 0.7x + 0.3y - 40,$$
$$0.7z + 0.3w - 40 \geq 0.4x + 0.6y, \text{ and}$$
$$0.7z + 0.3w - 40 \geq 170.$$

Now is the time to use Solver. First I set up a new spreadsheet. (This is the second sheet for FECBUS EXPLOITER.) You see the spreadsheet with some starting values in Figure IV.4. The basic variables are in cells E5, E6, E8 and E9; these being x, y, z, and w. From these I calculate the values of X, and so forth, in cells D5, and so on, then work out the size of the premium and the payback amounts. The objective function is easy enough to write using the entries in column F. Then, in cells D14 to D17 I compute a smooth student's utility if he or she takes the contract intended for smooth students and tries hard, takes the contract intended for smooths and loafs, takes the contract intended for not-so-smooth students and tries hard, and takes the contract intended for not so smooths and loafs. Finally, I do these computations for a not-so-smooth student.

Then I call up Solver. We want to maximize the objective, F12, by changing the basic variables, subject to the constraints just written: D14 has to be at least as large as D15, D16, D17, and 230. And D19 has to be as large as D20, D21, D22, and 170. Solver has no problem with this and gives me the answer in Figure IV.5. I offer the same (single) contract to all the students, namely a payback of $32,222 for a premium of $9722, giving the company an expected net profit of $5.8555 million.

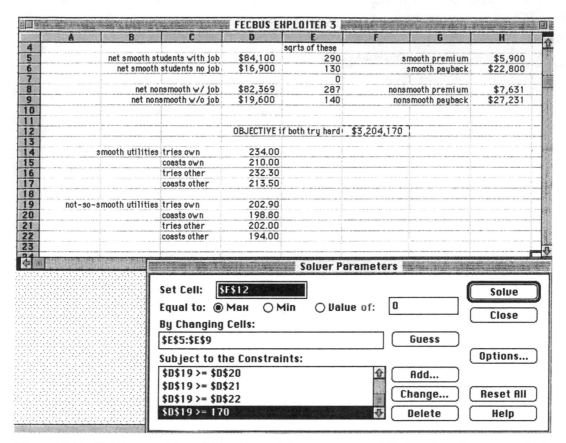

Figure IV.4. Solving problem IV.8: Spreadsheet setup and Solver box for scenario 1

	A	B	C	D	E	F	G	H
4					sqrts of these			
5		net smooth students with job		$80,278	283.333334		smooth premium	$9,722
6		net smooth students no job		$22,500	149.999997		smooth payback	$32,222
7					0			
8		net nonsmooth w/ job		$80,278	283.333333		nonsmooth premium	$9,722
9		net nonsmooth w/o job		$22,500	150		nonsmooth payback	$32,222
10								
11								
12				OBJECTIVE if both try hard	$5,855,555			
13								
14		smooth utilities	tries own	230.00				
15			coasts own	216.67				
16			tries other	230.00				
17			coasts other	216.67				
18								
19		not-so-smooth utilities	tries own	203.33				
20			coasts own	203.33				
21			tries other	203.33				
22			coasts other	203.33				
23								

Figure IV.5. Problem IV.8: Getting both to try

Please note that this is just the best contract, assuming we want both sorts of students to work hard. I still have scenario 3 to try: Both groups buy insurance, but only the smooth try. This takes rewriting the objective function and the constraints; I did what was necessary and ran Solver, which returned the values shown in Figure IV.6. The overall best outcome is from scenario 1 and the values in Figure IV.5.

	A	B	C	D	E	F	G	H
4					sqrts of these			
5		net smooth students with job		$79,940	282.735849		smooth premium	$10,060
6		net smooth students no job		$24,142	155.377362		smooth payback	$34,203
7					0			
8		net nonsmooth w/ job		$42,568	206.320797		nonsmooth premium	$47,432
9		net nonsmooth w/o job		$42,568	206.320732		nonsmooth payback	$90,000
10								
11								
12				OBJECTIVE if smooth tries	$5,319,339			
13								
14		smooth utilities	tries own	230.00				
15			coasts own	219.06				
16			tries other	166.32				
17			coasts other	206.32				
18								
19		not-so-smooth utilities	tries own	166.32				
20			coasts own	206.32				
21			tries other	204.53				
22			coasts other	206.32				
23								

Figure IV.6. Problem IV.8: Only the smooth try

Do not overprocess this example and, especially, the technique used to solve it. Real-life data do not come in anything like this form, so real-life problems that mix moral hazard and adverse selection (or just hidden information) are solved—to the extent that they are really solved at all—by very different techniques. What I hope you take away from this numerical exercise is a healthy respect for the difficulties of this sort of problem, where you are simultaneously worrying about the incentives you provide single individuals and the screening that those incentives engenders among the population of all individuals with whom you might contract.

Material for Chapter 21

Noncooperative Game Theory

Solution to Problem 21.1

(a) Row 1–column 2 is *not* a Nash equilibrium. If Column is choosing column 2, then Row's best response is row 2. (Although you were not asked for this, row 2–column 1 is a Nash equilibrium in this game.)

(b) Row 1–column 2, row 2–column 1, and row 3–column 3 are the three Nash equilibria of this game. (To be very precise, these are the three pure-strategy Nash equilibria of this game. Can you find any mixed-strategy equilibria?)

Solution to Problem 21.3

The following sequence of deletions leads to row 1–column 4:

- Column 4 dominates column 2. Delete column 2.

- Once column 2 is deleted, row 1 dominates row 3. Delete row 3. (Row 2 weakly dominates row 3 even without the deletion of column 2.)

- Once row 3 is deleted, column 3 (or 4) dominates column 1. Delete column 1.

- Once columns 1 and 2 are deleted, row 1 dominates row 2. Delete row 2. Only row 1 is left.

- Once rows 2 and 3 are deleted, column 4 dominates column 3. Delete column 3.

This leaves only row 1 and column 4, which is then the prediction of iterated dominance. (Since the iterated dominance was strict at each step, we know as well that row 1–column 4 is the unique Nash equilibrium of this game.)

Solution to Problem 21.5

Throughout this solution, I am sloppy and ignore the cases in which there is a tie for the highest bid. If you like precise arguments, repair my sloppiness.

(a) Suppose the auction is a first-price auction. If you bid $2000, then the two possible outcomes for you are that you win the auction, giving a payoff of 0, or you lose the auction, giving you a payoff of 0. Therefore, by bidding $2000, you guarantee yourself a payoff of 0 no matter what happens. But if you bid $1950 *and if the highest bid from all the others is less than $1950*, then your payoff is 50. Your payoff cannot be worse than 0, so this strategy (of bidding $1950) weakly dominates bidding $2000; it is just as good (giving a payoff of 0) in some cases and strictly better in others.

The strategies of bidding $1950 and bidding $1960 cannot be compared using dominance. The former does better (payoff of 50 vs. payoff of 40) if the highest bid among all the others is less than $1950, but it does worse (payoff of 0 vs. payoff of 40) if the highest bid among all the others is between $1950 and $1960. (The two are equally good, giving a payoff of 0, in all cases where the highest other bid is above $1960.)

The strategies of bidding any amount over $2000 are weakly dominated by the strategy of bidding $2000 since by bidding more than $2000 your possible payoffs are either 0 (if you lose) or negative (if you "win").

(b) For a second-price auction, bidding $2000 weakly dominates all other possible strategies. I show this by considering two cases.

First, bidding $2000 weakly dominates any bid X less than $2000:

1. If the highest bid among all the others, say, Y, is less than X, bidding X gives the same payoff as bidding 2000; namely, $2000 - Y$.

2. If the highest other bid Y exceeds 2000, then bidding X and $2000 give the same payoff; namely, 0.

3. If the highest other bid Y is between X and 2000, bidding X gives a payoff of 0 (you lose the auction), while bidding $2000 gives a payoff of $2000 - Y$. Since $Y < 2000, it is better to have bid $2000.

Second, bidding $2000 weakly dominates any bid X that exceeds $2000:

1. If the highest other bid Y is less than 2000, bidding X gives the same payoff as bidding 2000; namely, $2000 - Y$.

2. If the highest other bid Y exceeds X, then bidding X and $2000 give the same

payoff; namely, 0.

3. If the highest other bid X is between X and \$2000, bidding X gives a payoff of
   \$2000 $- Y < 0$, while bidding \$2000 gives a payoff of 0. Bidding \$2000 is better.

Solution to Problem 21.7

(a) See Figure 21.17. If Jan chooses to go to Old Pros, Sam's best response is to go to
Old Pros. If Jan chooses to go to the art museum, Sam's response is the art museum.
And if Jan chooses to go to Cafeen, Sam responds by going to Old Pros. Therefore,
Jan's best initial choice is the art museum.

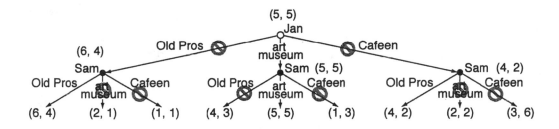

Figure 21.17. *A rollback of Sam and Jan, if Jan moves first.* Sam's payoffs are given
first.

(b and c) See Figure 21.18. Sam's 27 strategies are listed in the rows of the table,
while Jan's 3 strategies are listed as columns. Payoffs within the tables are given for
Sam first, then for Jan; ignore the bold-face and italics for a while. Jan's strategies—
the three main columns—should be clear, but I must explain Sam's. Sam must
make a choice of location (Old Pros, the art museum, or Cafeen) in each of three
information states, if she learns that he has gone to Old Pros, to the art museum, or
Cafeen. Therefore, in listing Sam's strategies, we have three items, in each of three
columns in the margin: How she responds if he goes to Old Pros, how she responds
to if he goes to the art museum; and how she responds if he goes to Cafeen. So,
for instance, the strategy labeled Sam #5 specifies that Sam goes to Old Pros if Jan
goes there, but she goes to the art museum if he goes to either the art museum or
Cafeen.

Putting in all the payoffs takes time and care. Take, for instance, the cell where
Sam plays her strategy #5 (just described) and Jan chooses Cafeen, his #3. Look at
the row and column so labeled. Since Sam's strategy #5 calls for her to respond to
Cafeen with art museum, this strategy profile ends up with Sam at the art museum

	if Jan goes to:	Old Pros	Art Museum	Cafeen	JAN'S STRATEGY					
	Sam responds with:				Jan #1 Old Pros		**Jan #2** **Art Museum**		Jan #3 Cafeen	
SAM'S STRATEGY	Sam #1	Old Pros	Old Pros	Old Pros	*6*	*4*	4	3	4	2
	Sam #2	Old Pros	Old Pros	Art Museum	*6*	*4*	4	3	2	2
	Sam #3	Old Pros	Old Pros	Cafeen	6	4	4	3	3	6
	Sam #4	**Old Pros**	**Art Museum**	**Old Pros**	6	4	*5*	*5*	4	2
	Sam #5	Old Pros	Art Museum	Art Museum	6	4	*5*	*5*	2	2
	Sam #6	Old Pros	Art Museum	Cafeen	6	4	5	5	3	6
	Sam #7	Old Pros	Cafeen	Old Pros	*6*	*4*	1	3	4	2
	Sam #8	Old Pros	Cafeen	Art Museum	*6*	*4*	1	3	2	2
	Sam #9	Old Pros	Cafeen	Cafeen	6	4	1	3	3	6
	Sam #10	Art Museum	Old Pros	Old Pros	2	1	4	3	4	2
	Sam #11	Art Museum	Old Pros	Art Museum	2	1	4	3	2	2
	Sam #12	Art Museum	Old Pros	Cafeen	2	1	4	3	3	6
	Sam #13	Art Museum	Art Museum	Old Pros	2	1	*5*	*5*	4	2
	Sam #14	Art Museum	Art Museum	Art Museum	2	1	*5*	*5*	2	2
	Sam #15	Art Museum	Art Museum	Cafeen	2	1	5	5	3	6
	Sam #16	Art Museum	Cafeen	Old Pros	2	1	1	3	4	2
	Sam #17	Art Museum	Cafeen	Art Museum	2	1	1	3	2	2
	Sam #18	Art Museum	Cafeen	Cafeen	2	1	1	3	3	6
	Sam #19	Cafeen	Old Pros	Old Pros	1	1	4	3	4	2
	Sam #20	Cafeen	Old Pros	Art Museum	1	1	4	3	2	2
	Sam #21	Cafeen	Old Pros	Cafeen	1	1	4	3	3	6
	Sam #22	Cafeen	Art Museum	Old Pros	1	1	*5*	*5*	4	2
	Sam #23	Cafeen	Art Museum	Art Museum	1	1	*5*	*5*	2	2
	Sam #24	Cafeen	Art Museum	Cafeen	1	1	5	5	3	6
	Sam #25	Cafeen	Cafeen	Old Pros	1	1	1	3	4	2
	Sam #26	Cafeen	Cafeen	Art Museum	1	1	1	3	2	2
	Sam #27	Cafeen	Cafeen	Cafeen	1	1	1	3	3	6

Figure 21.18. A strategic-form representation of Sam and Jan, if Sam responds to Jan's choice. Jan chooses one of three places to go, and Sam responds with one of three to Jan's choice. This gives Sam 27 strategies.

and Jan at Cafeen. Being alone at the art museum is second worst for Sam (Sam's payoff is therefore 2) while being alone at Cafeen is second worse for Jan, so he gets a payoff of 2.

The rollback performed in part a led to the following predictions: If Jan goes to Old Pros, Sam responds with Old Pros. If Jan goes to the art museum, Sam responds with the art museum. And if Jan goes to Cafeen, Sam responds by going to Old Pros. This is Sam's strategy #4, which I put in bold face. And the rollback predicted that Jan, in light of this, would choose to go to the art museum, his strategy #2, also depicted bold face. The corresponding cell, giving each party a payoff of 5, is highlighted with bold italic.

This is indeed a Nash equilibrium. Given that Jan is going to the art museum (his strategy #2), Sam does best with any strategy that has her choosing the art museum in response. And Jan's best response to Sam's strategy is (uniquely) to go to the art museum.

(d) But there are other Nash equilibria about. In fact, there are nine other (pure) Nash equilibria. I mark them by putting their corresponding payoffs in Figure 21.18 in italic. There are two types of them:

- First, in four strategy profiles Sam responds to Old Pros with Old Pros, to the art museum with either Old Pros or Cafeen, and to Cafeen with either Old Pros or the art museum. You can think of these four as "threats" by Sam of the sort: "I [Sam] wish to go to Old Pros. So, if you go there, so will I. But, if you [Jan] go somewhere else, I will punish you, and myself, by going to a locale where you are not." Jan's best response to this threat is to go to Old Pros, which renders the threat costless to Sam. But are such threats credible? If Jan in fact goes to the art museum, would Sam ignore the fact that she does best for herself with the art museum? At the cost of punishing herself, would she go to either Old Pros or Cafeen?

- And then, five strategy profiles have Jan going to the art museum and Sam responding to the art museum with the art museum and to Cafeen with anything other than Cafeen. (The response to Old Pros is free.) This general rule for forming Sam's strategy gives six possibilities, but one of those (where Sam responds to both Old Pros and Cafeen with Old Pros) is the original Nash equilibrium. You can think of these five as Sam being somewhat careless about how she responds to Old Pros and Cafeen: It does not affect her how she responds to Old Pros and Cafeen, if Jan indeed chooses the art museum. And, as long as she does not respond to Cafeen with Cafeen, she provides Jan with no incentive to go to Cafeen.

(e) You can verify that each of these nine alternative equilibria has Sam playing a weakly dominated strategy. In fact, the only one of Sam's strategies that is not weakly dominated is her strategy #4. Any strategy by Sam that has her responding to Old Pros with something other than Old Pros is weakly dominated by the same strategy, but with Old Pros as the response to Old Pros. Any strategy that has her responding to the art museum with something other than the art museum is weakly dominated by the same strategy, but with with art museum the response to the art museum. And, any strategy that has her responding to Cafeen with something other than Old Pros is weakly dominated by the same strategy, but with Old Pros the response to Cafeen. This, you should recognize, corresponds to the three parts of the backward induction. And once we have eliminated all Sam's strategies except her #4, Jan's best response of art museum "solves" the game, just as in the backward induction.

It is noteworthy that we could have applied some strict dominance first: For instance, Sam's #12 is strictly dominated by her #4. But the application of strict dominance alone does not get us to the solution of this game.

(f) See Figure 21.19. We begin with Figure 21.2, but join Sam's three nodes there into a single information set, since in this case, Sam doesn't know how Jan has moved when Sam must make her choice. It is worth noting that we could equally well put Sam's choice first and use a three-node information set for Jan.

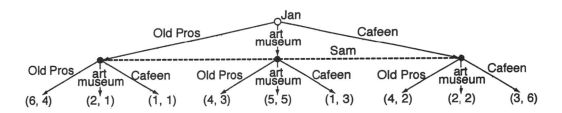

Figure 21.19. Sam and Jan, if Sam and Jan must each move without knowing what the other has done, in extensive form. The use of the dashed line, denoting an information set for Sam, accomplishes what we want. (Sam's payoffs are given first.)

Solution to Problem 21.9

Problem 21.9 asks you to recreate the classic models of oligopoly, which are known to economists as the Cournot model (and equilibrium), the Bertrand model (and equilibrium), and the von Stackelberg model (and equilibria). I present the problem without a lot of commentary here, reserving the commentary for the end of the companion material to Chapter 22; the economic content of this problem is best explained after you read Chapter 22.

Note that parts a and b involve *simultaneous strategy choices*, although the strategies in the two parts are different, while parts c and d involve *sequential strategy choices*, with firm A going first and firm B responding. Therefore, in parts a and b, we look for Nash equilibria; while in parts c and d, the style of analysis is backward induction. It turns out that parts a and b have a unique Nash equilibrium; and (of course) in parts c and d backward induction produces a unique answer, which is a Nash equilibrium. But, in parts c and d other Nash equilibria exist beyond those produced by backward induction; I say something about this at the end of part c (with similar comments appropriate but unstated for part d).

(a) In part a, the strategies for the players are their quantity choices, x_A and x_B. An equilibrium is a pair of quantities (x_A^*, x_B^*) such that each is a best response to the choice by the other firm. Suppose, for instance, that firm B chooses x_B. Firm A's profit, if it chooses x_A, is

$$(p_A - c)x_A = (a - x_A - bx_B - c)x_A = (a - bx_B - c)x_A - x_A^2,$$

which is maximized for a given x_B when the derivative in x_A is 0, or when

$$x_A = \frac{a - bx_B - c}{2}.$$

(To be a bit more precise, this is true when $a - bx_B - c \geq 0$. Firm A's optimal choice is $x_A = 0$ when $a - c \leq bx_B$.) By a symmetric argument, if firm A chooses x_A, firm B's best response is

$$x_B = \frac{a - bx_A - c}{2}.$$

So a Nash equilibrium is where these two equations hold simultaneously:

$$x_A^* = \frac{a - bx_B^* - c}{2} \quad \text{and} \quad x_B^* = \frac{a - bx_A^* - c}{2}.$$

This is two equations in two unknowns; the unique solution is

$$x_A^* = x_B^* = \frac{a - c}{2 + b}.$$

Figure 21.20 depicts the solution, with a graph of pairs (x_A, x_B). For each value of x_A, we graph the *best-response function for firm* B, $x_B(x_A) = (a - bx_A - c)/2$ as a solid line (with the extension $x_B(x_A) = 0$ if $bx_A \geq a - c$), and we graph the *best-response function for firm* A, $x_A(x_B) = (a - bx_B - c)/2$ as a dashed line. Where the two intersect, where each firm chooses the best response to what the other firm has

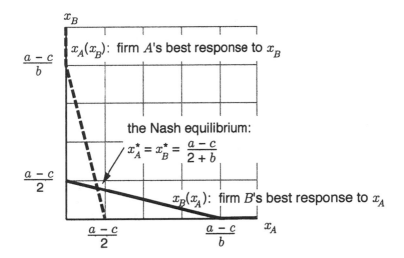

Figure 21.20. Problem 21.9(a) in a picture. For each level of x_A, the function $x_B(x_A)$, drawn with a solid line, gives B's best response to A's choice of quantity. For each level of x_B, the function $x_A(x_B)$, drawn with dashes, gives A's best response to B's choice of quantity. Where they intersect, at $x_A^* = x_B^* = (a-c)/(2+b)$, is the unique Nash equilibrium, the solution to part a.

chosen, is the Nash equilibrium. (The graph is drawn for the values $a = 10, b = 0.5$, and $c = 2$.)

(b) To solve part b, we first must invert the two inverse demand functions to get the corresponding pair of demand functions. It takes a bit of algebra, but these are

$$x_A = \frac{a(1-b) - p_A + bp_B}{1 - b^2} \quad \text{and} \quad x_B = \frac{a(1-b) - p_B + bp_A}{1 - b^2}.$$

The strategies for the two firms are now their price choices, and a Nash equilibrium is a pair of prices (p_A^*, p_B^*) where each firm chooses the best response to the price choice of the other firm. As in part a, for each price choice p_B by firm B, we can find firm A's best response, which I denote by $p_A(p_B)$: If firm A chooses p_A, and given firm B's choice p_B, firm A's profit is

$$(p_A - c) \times \left[\frac{a(1-b) - p_A + bp_B}{1 - b^2} \right] = \frac{[a(b-1) - bp_B]c + p_A[a(1-b) + bp_B + c] - p_A^2}{1 - b^2}.$$

Set the derivative in p_A to 0, to get

$$p_A(p_B) = \frac{a(1-b) + bp_B + c}{2}.$$

Similarly and symmetrically,

$$p_B(p_A) = \frac{a(1-b) + bp_A + c}{2}.$$

The Nash equilibrium occurs where each firm chooses the best response to each other, or where

$$p_A^* = \frac{a(1-b) + bp_B^* + c}{2} \quad \text{and} \quad p_B^* = \frac{a(1-b) + bp_A^* + c}{2},$$

the solution of which is

$$p_A^* = p_B^* = \frac{a(1-b) + c}{2-b}.$$

Once again, we can draw a picture of the equilibrium as in Figure 21.21. This time the graph is of pairs of prices. Firm A's best response function $p_A(p_B)$ once again is the dashed line and firm B's best response function $p_B(p_A)$ is the solid line. Where they intersect is the Nash equilibrium.

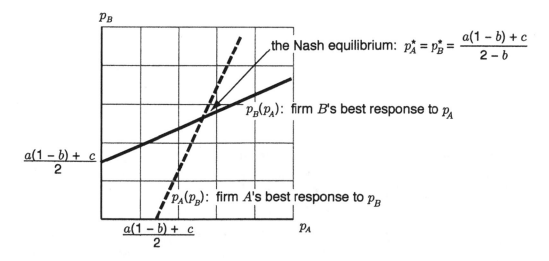

Figure 21.21. *Problem 21.9(b) in a picture.* For each level of p_A, the function $p_B(p_A)$, drawn with a solid line, gives B's best response to A's choice of price. For each level of p_B, the function $p_A(p_B)$, drawn with dashes, gives A's best response to B's choice of price. Where they intersect, at $p_A^* = p_B^* = [a(1-b) + c]/(2-b)$, is the unique Nash equilibrium, the solution to part b.

(c) If firm A chooses its quantity x_A, then firm B responds, a backward-induction analysis is in order. Firm B, faced with x_A, optimally responds with the choice $x_B(x_A)$ that we found in part a, namely $x_B(x_A) = (a - bx_A - c)/2$. Firm A understands that firm B will respond in this fashion, so it chooses its initial quantity to maximize its profit given this: If it chooses x_A, its profit will be

$$[a - x_A - bx_B(x_A) - c]x_A = \left[a - x_A - \frac{b(a - bx_A - c)}{2} - c\right]x_A =$$

$$\left[\left(a - c\right)\left(1 - \frac{b}{2}\right)\right]x_A - \left(1 - \frac{b^2}{2}\right)x_A^2.$$

This is maximized in x_A at

$$x_A^\sharp = \frac{(a - c)(1 - b/2)}{2 - b^2} = \frac{(a - c)(2 - b)}{2(2 - b^2)}.$$

You can work out the corresponding response by firm B by plugging $x_A^\sharp$ into the response function $x_B(x_A)$.

Although it is a bit confusing for some readers, let me draw some pictures that illustrate this backward-induction solution and compare it to the Nash equilibrium computed in part a. These pictures are all for the values $a = 10, b = 0.5$, and $c = 2$.

We begin with Figure 21.22(a). This figure shows firm A's *iso-profit curves*, curves of the form

$$(a - x_A - bx_B - c)x_A = K$$

for various constants K. (The four iso-profit curves are for $K = 4, 6, 8$, and 10. Firm A's profit increases unambiguously as x_B decreases, so the curve the furthest "south" is for $K = 10$.

Suppose firm B is committed to $x_B = 8$. What is the best response for firm A? Looking across the horizontal line $x_B = 8$, we can see that the largest profit that A can achieve is where $x_A = 2$, where the iso-profit curve is tangent to the horizontal line, which just says that, for this set of parameter values, the general function $x_A(x_B) = (a - bx_B - c)/2$ has the specific value $x_A(8) = (10 - 0.5 \times 8 - 2)/2 = 2$. In this figure, and more generally, if you connect the "tops" of the isoprofit curves,

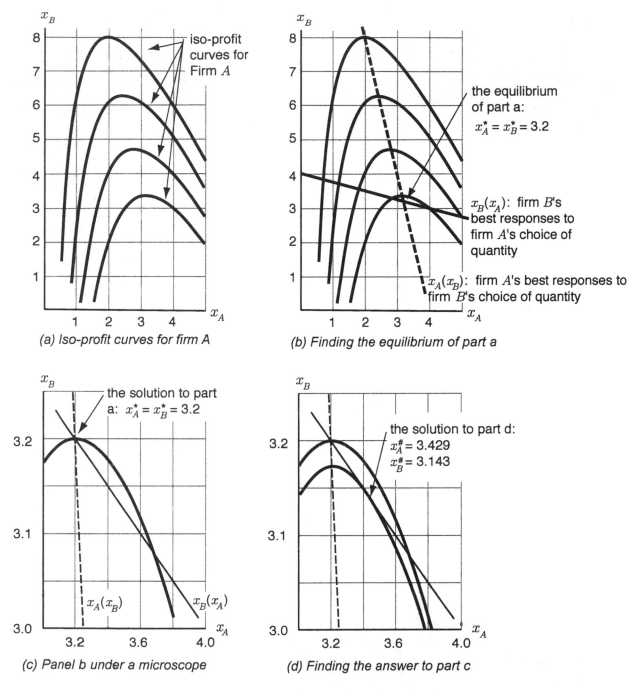

(a) *Iso-profit curves for firm A*

(b) *Finding the equilibrium of part a*

(c) *Panel b under a microscope*

(d) *Finding the answer to part c*

Figure 21.22. Comparing parts a and c. Panel a shows the iso-profit curves for firm A. In panel b, the (dashed-line) function $x_A(x_B)$ is constructed from the iso-profit curves and the (solid-line) function $x_B(x_A)$ is added. Where they intersect is the Nash equilibrium of part a. Panel c shows a close-up of the equilibrium, with the iso-profit curve of firm A at the equilibrium drawn in. If firm A moves first and firm B responds, firm B responds to x_A with $x_B(x_A)$, so firm A can choose any pair $(x_A, x_B(x_A))$ that it wants, and the choice that maximizes firm A's profit is shown in panel d.

you get the full function $x_A(x_B)$, shown in Figure 21.22(b) with the usual dashed line.

The answer to part a, the Nash equilibrium (x_A^*, x_B^*), occurs where $x_A(x_B)$ intersects $x_B(x_A)$. For these parameter values, this occurs at $x_A^* = x_B^* = 3.2$. I supply $x_B(x_A)$ as a solid line as well in panel b.

In panel c, you get a close-up view of the Nash equilibrium, together with firm A's iso-profit curve passing through the equilibrium. (For these parameter values, this profit level is 10.24.) Now we turn from part a of the problem, where the two firms choose quantities simultaneously, to part c, where firm A goes first. If firm A goes first, then firm B responds to x_A with $x_B(x_A)$. Firm A, recognizing this, knows that it can select whichever pair $(x_A, x_B(x_A))$ gives it the highest profit. It is apparent from panel c that firm A can increase its profit to some extent by increasing x_A from x_A^*, since the response of firm B to decrease x_B benefits firm A. How much should firm A increase x_A? It should do so until it attains the highest possible profit level along the line $(x_A, x_B(x_A))$. In panel d of Figure 21.22, you see this level of x_A, which is $x_A^\sharp$, and the corresponding iso-profit curve for firm A, which for these parameter values is a profit level of 10.28571429.

Note that $x_B(x_A)$ is a decreasing function of x_A (until x_B hits and stays at 0). This means that *the more aggressive is firm A in its choice of quantity, the less aggressive is the optimal response of firm B.* From firm A's perspective, less aggressive responses by firm B are always in its (firm A's) favor. So, relative to the equilibrium we found in part a, in this part of the problem, firm A is going to be more aggressive, or $x_A^\sharp > x_A^*$. The picture makes this clear; to verify it algebraically, note first that (since $b > 0$) $4 - b^2 > 4 - 2b^2$, therefore $(2 - b)(2 + b)(a - c) > 2(2 - b^2)(a - c)$ and hence

$$x_A^\sharp = \frac{(a - c)(2 - b)}{2(2 - b^2)} > \frac{(a - c)}{(b + 2)} = x_A^*.$$

A final thing to note about this part of the problem is that, while we have produced a Nash equilibrium for the game where firm A chooses its quantity first and firm B responds, there are other Nash equilibria to this game. We know that this is a Nash equilibrium because we produced it via backward induction and a general result tells us that the result of backward induction always is a Nash equilibrium. But imagine that firm B issued the following threat.

If you, firm A, choose the quantity $x_A = (a - c)/10$, I will respond with $9(a - c)/20$. If you choose any other quantity x_A, I plan to respond with $(a - c - x_A)/b$.

More to the point, suppose firm B adopts the strategy implicit in this threat. How should firm A respond? If firm A believes that B would carry out the threatened strategy, A can respond with $x_A = (a - c)/20$, which will result in a positive profit when B chooses $x_B = 9(a - c)/20$. On the other hand, if A chooses any other quantity, B's response of $(a - c - x_A)/b$ means firm A's profit is 0. So firm A's best response is $(a - c)/20$. And, if A chooses $(a - c)/20$, firm B's best response is $x_B((a - c)/20)$ which is, in fact, $9(a - c)/20$. Firm B's threatened responses to all other choices by A are costless, because firm A chooses $(a - c)/20$. This is indeed a Nash equilibrium.

But, suppose firm A chooses some quantity other than $(a - c)/20$. In particular, suppose firm A chooses $x_A^\sharp$. Would firm B carry out its threat to produce $(a - c - x_A^\sharp)/b$? This is not firm B's best response, given the *fait accompli* choice of $x_A^\sharp$ by firm A. This is indeed a Nash equilibrium but one based on incredible threats by firm B. As such, it is not a very credible prediction for this game.

(d) The answer to part d parallels the answer to part c, so I do this more quickly. Following a choice of p_A by firm A, firm B chooses $p_B(p_A) = [a(1 - b) + bp_A + c]/2$. Hence, if firm A chooses p_A, its profit is

$$(p_A - c)\left[\frac{a(1 - b) - p_A + bp_B(p_A)}{1 - b^2}\right] =$$

$$(p_A - c)\left[\frac{a(1 - b) - p_A + b[a(1 - b) + bp_A + c]/2}{1 - b^2}\right].$$

Since the denominator is a constant, we can drop it: Firm A chooses p_A to maximize

$$(p_A - c)\left(a(1 - b) - p_A + \frac{ab(1 - b)}{2} + \frac{b^2 p_A}{2} + \frac{bc}{2}\right).$$

Taking the derivative, setting it equal to 0, and denoting the solution by p_A^b gives

$$0 = a(1 - b) - p_A^b + \frac{ab(1 - b)}{2} + \frac{b^2 p_A^b}{2} + \frac{bc}{2} + c - p_A^b + \frac{b^2(p_A^b - c)}{2} \quad \text{or}$$

$$p_A^b(2 - b^2) = a(1 - b) + \frac{ab(1 - b)}{2} + \frac{bc}{2} + c - \frac{b^2 c}{2},$$

which is

$$p_A^b = \frac{2a - ab - ab^2 + bc + 2c - b^2 c}{2(2 - b^2)}.$$

The corresponding level of p_B is obtained by computing $p_B(p_A^b)$.

As in part c, it is instructive to compare p_A^* with p_A^b. The algebra is quite messy, and I leave it to you to verify that $p_A^b > p_A^*$. By moving first in selecting a price, firm A is less aggressive (chooses a higher price) than when it moves simultaneously. We see why by looking at the function $p_B(p_A) = [a(1 - b) + bp_A + c]/2$ in Figure 21.21, which is increasing in p_A: firm B responds less agressively if firm A is less aggressive. Since firm A always prefers a less aggressive firm B (that is the same as in part c), firm A raises the price it charges, to engender a less aggressive response by firm B (which is different from part c).

Remarks about how this is a Nash equilibrium, not the only Nash equilibrium but the only Nash equilibrium not based on noncredible threats by firm B, are all just as in part c. For the rest of the story connected to this problem, see the end of the companion material for Chapter 22.

Material for Chapter 22

Reciprocity and Collusion

Solution to Problem 22.1

The 6% commission is maintained by implicit collusion among brokers. If one broker charges a smaller commission, other brokers fail to cooperate with the deviator. In real estate sales, cooperation among brokers is essential to each; brokers rely on each other for information about available houses or prospective purchasers. If brokers as a group wish to punish a deviator, they can do so actively by failing to arrive for appointments or by providing nonserious buyers or sellers for the clients of the deviator, they could advise their own clients to make low offers or high asks when dealing with the clients of the deviators or simply fail to share information in a timely fashion with the deviator. All these things substantially punish the deviator. So, if deviations from the 6% commission "standard" can be detected, it is not hard to see how collusion could be sustained.

This collusive scheme is vulnerable in three ways: (1) Entrants into the business could increase competition and make collusion harder to sustain. (2) Home owners and potential buyers can try to sell and buy without the services of a broker. (3) The scheme requires that brokers be able to observe the actions of other brokers, so that deviations from the 6% rule can be observed. Brokers control entrants into their business by their control of the licensing of new brokers; they control the substitution of direct sales or purchases by their monopoly on information about available homes and prospective buyers; and they maintain observability by their collection and dissemination of the terms of sale, including commissions and other fees, on a transaction-by-transaction basis.

Therefore, to break the cartel, I would advise the state legislator to take three actions:

1. Remove the licensing function from the Board of Realtors. Put it under the control of a state agency, instead. I am not very strong on this recommendation, because there is every possibility that the state agency will be "captured" and controlled by the cartel; it will then have greater coercive powers by virtue of being an agency of the government. But, in conjunction with my other two

recommendations, this recommendation may have some impact.

2. Mandate that multiple listings be made available to the public on an at-cost basis and carry information about no-agent houses for sale. That is, any individual who wishes to sell a house may submit a listing to the multiple listings, for a nominal fee, which would be designated as a listing by a private buyer, who would not cooperate with agents or pay any commission. And a private individual who wishes to obtain the multiple listings book must be allowed to purchase it at cost.

3. Do not allow the collection or dissemination of information on fees by the Board of Realtors on a case-by-case basis. When local boards complain that this denies information to consumers, allow the collection and dissemination of anonymous grouped data; that is, report means and perhaps standard deviations of commissions and fees on both an absolute and percentage basis.

The first two actions should generate pressure on brokers to lower commissions; the third should remove the possibility of punishment of those who deviate from the cartel, effectively breaking the cartel. If forced to pick only one of the three, I would choose the third as the most important.

Note that the state legislator is likely going to commit political suicide with this campaign. Realtors are very easily and well organized, while the house buying and selling public is dispersed. If this legislator runs for office again, she can expect her opponent to get lots of contributions from real estate agents.

The Classic Models of Oligopoly: Four Fables

Problem 21.9 and its solution provide the mechanics of the classic models of oligopoly: the Cournot, Bertrand, and von Stackelberg models. For many years and for many economists today, those models constitute the economic theory of oligopoly. Chapter 21 is supposed to be about the theory of oligopoly, yet the classic models are not mentioned in the text. I rectify that omission here.

This discussion has three parts. First, I provide "stories" that support the game structures of the classic models. Then, while exploring the appropriateness of Nash equilibrium analysis of these games (what happens in the solution to Problem 21.9), I explain why I have little faith a priori in these models. Finally, I indicate why, despite my lack of faith, if you continue to study economics relevant to management, you are quite likely to encounter these models.

The Cournot Model and Equilibrium

Imagine two firms, A and B, that sell their product in a marketplace some distance from where they produce. Think in terms of a marketplace in the 19th century. The marketplace is the central square in the local market town. One day each week, people with stuff to sell load their carts, travel to the marketplace, and set up to sell what they brought. Customers also come into town this one day each week to buy.

The critical assumption in this story is that the two producers of this particular good (call it cheese) must decide each week how much of their cheese to bring with them, to sell that day. Their quantity decisions are made simultaneously and are irrevocable (each week)—unsold cheese spoils—so if the first duopolist arrives with x_A units of cheese and the second with x_B units, the prices p_A and p_B that the two set are the prices that clear the market. Assume that the market for these two varieties of cheese is symmetric and that market-clearing prices are given by the pair of inverse demand equations

$$p_A = a - x_A - bx_B \quad \text{and} \quad p_B = a - x_B - bx_B,$$

where a and $0 < b < 1$ are constants. Because $b > 0$, the two types of cheese are substitutes: The more firm B brings the market, the lower is the market-clearing price for firm A. Because $b < 1$, the two types of cheese are not perfect substitutes, although if firm B brings enough of its cheese to the market, it can drive the price of firm A's cheese to 0. (Its own price would have hit 0 at a lower quantity, so it is unlikely to do this.) The marginal cost of production for each firm is a constant c, and both firms have fixed costs of 0.

Assume this market reconvenes week after week and the two firms do not discount their weekly profits too heavily. Then, we have an ideal setting for folk-theorem-style collusion. Each firm brings to the market the same amount of cheese x^M that maximizes the joint profits of the two firms—I leave it to you to verify that this is $x^M = (a - c)/(2 + 2b)$, so the market-clearing prices are $p_A = p_B = (a + c)/2$—where each firm sticks to this quantity out of fear of a price war if it tries to take short-run advantage by bringing more cheese to the market in any given week. Please note that this is the symmetric collusive "solution"; the folk theorem, in the usual way, provides us with many equilibria, some collusive and asymmetric and some not very collusive at all.

But, nothing guarantees that the two firms arrive at a collusive solution at all. The cheese makers might not trust each other. It might never occur to them that they can trade off short-run profits for larger long-run profits, if they act with mutual restraint. So, the French economist Augustin Cournot asked (in 1838), What would happen in this market, if each firm attempts, each week, to maximize its own profit that week, given the actions of the other firm?

Although Cournot wrote long before game theory was developed, in modern terminology, he found the Nash equilibrium of the one-time, one-week game, in which firms A and B simultaneously choose x_A and x_B, each seeking the maximal one-week's profit, given the choice of the other firm. From Problem 21.9(a), we know that the Nash equilibrium of this game, known in the literature as the Cournot equilibrium, is

$$x_A^* = x_B^* = \frac{a-c}{2+b},$$

which means higher quantities, lower prices, and lower profits than if the two firm managed the symmetric collusive scheme. (At this point, if you have not consumed Problem 21.9 and its solution, do so. Much of the discussion that follows is based on the solution to that problem.)

Two special cases are worthy of note. If $b = 0$, the two types of cheese are not substitutes at all; the market-clearing price of one depends only on how much of it was brought to market that week and not at all on how much of the other type is being sold. And, in this case, the Cournot-equilibrium quantities are the monopoly quantities. At the other end of the spectrum, if $b = 1$, the two types of cheese are perfect substitutes, and the Cournot-equilibrium prices are significantly lower than the collusive prices, although not so low that the two firms make profits of 0.

Cournot–Von Stackelberg Equilibrium

Now change the story. Imagine that firm A can somehow commit to its quantity of cheese before firm B produces, and firm B sees how much cheese firm A has produced before choosing its own level of production. In game-theoretic terms, this is the game described and analyzed in Problem 21.9(c), and we know that, in this case, backward induction leads to the prediction that firm A chooses the quantity

$$x_A^\sharp = \frac{(a-c)(2-b)}{2(2-b^2)} > x_A^*,$$

and firm B responds with a quantity smaller than x_B^*. In the borderline case $b = 0$, both firms choose the monopoly quantities. In the other borderline case $b = 1$ of perfect substitutes, firm A chooses its monopoly quantity, but firm B produces a positive amount, so that firm A does not make its monopoly profit. This is known in the literature as the *Von Stackelberg* or *Cournot–Von Stackelberg* equilibrium, after the German economist Heinrich Von Stackelberg, who suggested in 1938 that one firm might take a first-mover or leadership position of this sort.

Bertrand Equilibrium

Another change to the story is to assume, as in the original, that the two firms move simultaneously but choose the prices they charge rather than the quantities they sell. To make a parable out of this, imagine the firms advertise the prices they will charge on market day (Saturday) in the local newspaper on Friday. The two firms phone in the prices they will charge on Wednesday afternoon, see what prices their rival picked when the paper arrives on Friday, and bring to the market as much as they are able to sell, given the pair of prices in the newspaper and the demand functions derived from the inverse demand functions given earlier, which are

$$x_A = \frac{a(1-b) - p_A + bp_B}{1 - b^2} \quad \text{and} \quad x_B = \frac{a(1-b) - p_B + bp_A}{1 - b^2}.$$

That price announcements are phoned in on Wednesdays is not quite consistent with this being an 19th century town-square market, but this is (just) a parable.

With this latest story, we look for a Nash equilibrium in the name-the-prices-simultaneously game, which is the Nash equilibrium computed in Problem 21.9(b),

$$p_A^* = p_B^* = \frac{a(1-b) + c}{2 - b}.$$

Although it is not obvious until you do the algebra, these prices are lower than the prices one gets in the Cournot equilibrium, and profits are correspondingly diminished; price competition of this sort is "more competitive" than quantity competition. As for the two extreme cases, if $b = 0$, this is once again the monopoly outcome. But for $b = 1$, well, that story takes another paragraph at least.

For the case $b = 1$, where the goods are perfect substitutes, the demand functions are not well defined; there is a 0 in the denominator. But the equilibrium prices are quite well defined; substitute $b = 1$ into $[a(1-b) + c]/(2-b)$ and out pops c. The story that goes with $b = 1$, which gives equilibrium prices of c, runs as follows. If the two goods are perfect substitutes, then the firm that names a lower price than the other gets all the demand. If the two name the same price, we assume, they split the entire demand 50–50. In such a situation, the only possible simultaneous-price equilibrium is $p = c$, for the following reasons:

- It is not an equilibrium for the two firms to name different prices if the lower of the two prices is less than c, because the firm naming the lower price takes a loss, which it can turn into 0 profit by naming price c.

- It is not an equilibrium for the two firms to name different prices if the lower of the two prices is c, because the firm naming the lower price of c makes profit 0 but would make a strictly positive profit by naming a price halfway between c and the price its rival names.

- It is not an equilibrium for the two firms to name different prices if the lower of the two prices strictly exceeds c, because the firm naming the higher price makes profit 0 but would make a strictly positive profit by naming a price halfway between c and the price named by its rival.

- It is not an equilibrium for the two firms to name the same price less than c, because then each firm takes a loss but would make 0 profit by naming price c instead.

- It is not an equilibrium for the two firms to name the same price more than c. In this case, let p be the price each firm names, and X the total demand at that price. Each firm gets half the demand, for a profit of $(p - c)X/2$. If one firm instead names the price $(3p + c)/4$, it has demand at least X (it gets all the old demand and more) and its profit per unit is $(3p + c)/4 - c = 3(p - c)/4$, for a profit of more than $3(p - c)X/4 > (p - c)X/2$.

This rules out everything except each firm naming the price c. And this is an equilibrium: Each firm makes profit 0, but if a firm raises the price it names, it gets no demand so continues to make profit 0; if it lowers the price it names, it loses money.

Whether in the extreme case of $b = 1$ or not, the simultaneous-price equilibrium is called the *Bertrand equilibrium*, named for Joseph Louis Francois Bertrand, who wrote (in 1883) that simultaneous-price competition was a more reasonable parable for real-life competition than Cournot's story of simultaneous choices of quantity.

Bertrand–Von Stackelberg and Comparisons

A final variation is if firm A names its price p_A and firm B responds. This is known as *Bertrand–von Stackelberg*, because it mixes price or Bertrand competition with one firm moving first, Von Stackelberg style. This is part d of Problem 21.9, and the backward induction analysis gives firm A naming the price

$$p_A^b = \frac{2a - ab - ab^2 + bc + 2c - b^2c}{2(2 - b^2)} > p_B^*,$$

and firm B responding with its best response price.

This gives us four different "predictions"–five if you count the prediction that the firms settle on the symmetric collusive outcome. To compare them, in Table 22.1 I provide quantities, prices, and profit levels for both firms, for each of the five predictions. In panel a, these values are given for $a = 10$, $b = 0.5$, and $c = 2$; panel b gives the values for $a = 10$, $b = 1$, and $c = 2$. (For Bertrand–Von Stackelberg and the case $b = 1$, I provide no data. If you evaluate p_A^b for $b = 1$, you get c, and it is a Nash equilibrium for firm A to name the price c and for firm B to respond with that price, but this is a very degenerate situation, and one should not put too much credence in this as the solution.)

	firm A quantity	firm B quantity	firm A price	firm B price	firm A profit	firm B profit
collusive	2.667	2.667	$6.000	$6.000	$10.667	$10.667
Cournot	3.200	3.200	$5.200	$5.200	$10.240	$10.240
Bertrand	3.556	3.556	$4.667	$4.667	$9.481	$9.481
Cournot–von Stackelberg	3.429	3.143	$5.000	$5.143	$10.286	$9.878
Bertrand–von Stackelberg	3.333	3.619	$4.857	$4.714	$9.524	$9.651

(a) Parameter values $a = 10$, $b = 0.5$, and $c = 2$

	firm A quantity	firm B quantity	firm A price	firm B price	firm A profit	firm B profit
collusive	2.000	2.000	$6.000	$6.000	$8.000	$8.000
Cournot	2.667	2.667	$4.667	$4.667	$7.111	$7.111
Bertrand	4.000	4.000	$2.000	$2.000	$0.000	$0.000
Cournot–von Stackelberg	4.000	2.000	$4.000	$4.000	$8.000	$4.000

(b) Parameter values $a = 10$, $b = 1$, and $c = 2$

Table 22.1. *Comparing the different predictions.* For two sets of parameter values, this table gives the quantities, prices, and profit levels of the two firms, assuming (symmetric) collusion, Cournot equilibrium, Betrand equilibrium, Cournot–Von Stackelberg, and (for the first set of parameter values) Bertrand–Von Stackelberg equilibrium.

Is Nash Equilibrium Analysis Appropriate? Repeated Play

It is hard to think of any real-life industries that mimic the conditions of these four parable settings. But suspend your disbelief a bit longer and imagine an industry that conforms to one of these stories. The question remains, Is Nash equilibrium analysis appropriate? In this imagined situation, would we expect the two firms to behave in accordance with the Nash equilibrium highlighted?

Recall from Chapter 21 that, to apply Nash equilibrium analysis, there should be some reason to suspect that the firms would find their way to the Nash equilibrium. It could be a matter of logic, general experience with this sort of situation, or experience with the specific opponent. In the context of these models, experience with the specific rival is generally the story told. Indeed, the literature concerning the Cournot model and equilibrium contains a sizeable subliterature on what is called the *stability of Cournot tâtonnement*, which is fancy talk for suppose that, at date t (think week t in an infinite sequence of weeks in which the two suppliers bring their product to the market square), each firm chooses its best response to what its rival did at date $t - 1$. Does this process converge to the Cournot equilibrium? (The answer in the context of the specific linear example of Problem 21.9 is yes.)

But, if the two duopolists compete with one another week after week, if they do not discount the future too heavily, and if they can observe what the other party brings to the market each week, then the folk theorem kicks in and they can do a lot better (jointly) than by playing the static Cournot–Nash equilibrium quantities prescribed by our analysis.

If the two compete repeatedly, each forms beliefs about how the other side responds to moves the first makes. They can sustain the cartel outcome as a Nash equilibrium, they can sustain repeated play of the Cournot quantities, and they can sustain a lot besides. (The literature on oligopoly contains concepts such as "conjectural response" and "kinked demand" equilibria, which explore how the conjectures each side has about how the other responds affects the long-run equilibrium they reach.)

My point is that the natural rationale for looking at Nash equilibria in this context— that the two firms interact repeatedly—contains a potential internal contradiction. If the firms interact repeatedly, the sorts of ideas encountered in Chapter 22 apply and much more than the specific equilibria identified in Problem 21.9 pass the test of being Nash equilibria.

The Use of These Models by Economists

Notwithstanding what I just said, economists continue to use the classic models in at least two ways.

1. They are used as building blocks in models that tackle more complex problems, such as the proliferation of product variety, the value of excess capacity, and the adoption of new technology. Ultimately, if one believes (as economists do) that product variety, capacity, and adoption decisions are taken by firms on a "rational" basis, then one needs a model of what would happen (what would be the profit levels of firms) if a new product were introduced, capacity were added, or a new technology were adopted. The classic models satisfy the need for such models. Moreover, they give some flexibility in these models: The Cournot model provides an example of so-called strategic substitutes, where a more aggressive stance by one firm engenders a less aggressive stance by its rivals; while the Bertrand model has so-called strategic complements, where more aggressive behavior by one firm provokes more aggressive behavior by its competitors. This fundamental difference in the nature of actions and reactions permits economists to see how that difference affects things like product variety, capacity, and technology adoption.

2. Empirical economists use the models as concrete parametric specifications to estimate what goes on in specific industries. The analogy here is to linear and constant-elasticity demand functions. No one seriously contends that the demand in a given industry is precisely linear or has constant elasticity, but it may be approximately so; these parametric models are used for statistical estimation, where the test of the model is how well the model fits the data. The data from a real-life industry can be fitted to a model that assumes, say, a Cournot equilibrium; whether this is a helpful exercise or not is an empirical question.

Speaking personally, I do not regard these models as likely to be descriptive of real-life industries. I believe that the discussion of collusion in Chapter 22 tells you more about the real world of oligopoly than the classic models. That is why, in the text, I have no chapter on oligopoly per se but instead one on collusion and cooperation. My own bottom line is that economics is unlikely to reach a point where we have the sort of precision in our predictions about oligopolies that we have about competitive markets; this is simply the nature of this particular beast. But my opinion is nothing like the "median" opinion of economists, and in your continued study of economics and related subjects, especially business strategy and corporate finance, you are likely to encounter these classic models.

Material for Chapter 23

Credibility and Reputation

Solution to Problem 23.1

(a) The extensive-form game played by Yaki and Zenith is depicted in Figure 23.5. Rolled back, it tells us that, notwithstanding its promise, Zenith would be likely to invade Yaki's territory, so that Yaki cannot affort to make this agreement. This is the trust game pure and simple, with the scale of one unit of utility equals $1 million.

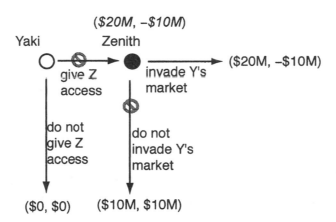

Figure 23.5. *Problem 23.1(a): Yaki vs. Zenith.* Yaki must decide whether to make its technology available to Zenith and, if it does, Zenith must decide whether to abide by its promise not to invade Yaki's market. Zenith's payoffs are listed first, in this figure and in those that follow; payoffs are in millions of dollars. A rollback indicates that, once Zenith has the technology, it would invade Yaki's market—Zenith's promise not to do so is not credible—and so Yaki cannot agree to this deal.

(b) The possibility of a court-enforceable agreement changes the game from that depicted in Figure 23.5 to the game in Figure 23.6. Yaki must decide whether to sign the contract. Zenith must decide whether to breach or honor the contract. If Zenith breaches it, Yaki must decide whether to go to court. Roll this back and you see that, since the damage award more than covers Yaki's court costs, Yaki would go to court if Zenith breached. This then makes breach an unattractive option for Zenith. And thus Yaki can sign the agreement.

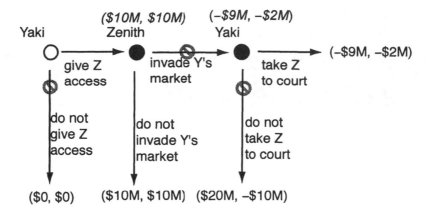

Figure 23.6. Problem 23.1(b): Yaki vs. Zenith. If we add the possibility that Yaki can take Zenith to court if Zenith breaches an agreement and Yaki stands to gain more than it loses (in court costs) if it goes to court, then the contract lends credibility to Zenith's promise and Yaki can sign the deal.

Note: If it comes to a court case, Yaki's final net position is a loss of $2 million. Yaki would be worse off than if it had not signed the contract. But the loss of $2 million is to be compared with a loss of $10 million if Yaki did not take Zenith to court. Yaki would take Zenith to court. And that keeps Zenith from breaching. Which means that Yaki can sign the contract.

(c) If there is only a 0.3 chance that, in the event of breach, the courts would find in Yaki's favor, then the court-enforced contract fails on two grounds. If Zenith breached, Yaki would not take Zenith to court, and even if Yaki did sue, the expected penalty imposed on Zenith is insufficient to keep Zenith from breaching. The deal is in trouble again.

For the analysis that supports this, see Figure 23.7. To explain the rollback through the final node, this node represents the chance that the Yaki would win or lose its suit. This is not a choice by one player or the other, but instead a chance node and, under the assumption of risk neutrality, we compute the expected payoffs (monetary values) of the two parties if this position is reached. Zenith, for instance, would lose a net $9 million if Yaki won the suit, but it would be ahead $11 million (its $20 million less $9 million in court costs) if it won the suit, so its EMV is $0.3 \times (-9) + 0.7 \times 11 = \$5$ million.

(d) If there is a chance of triple punitive damages added to compensatory damages, Yaki would take Zenith to court and Zenith would be deterred by the prospect. Back in business (see Figure 23.8). Note that the expected values are computed two nodes from the end, taking into account the three possible outcomes: Yaki

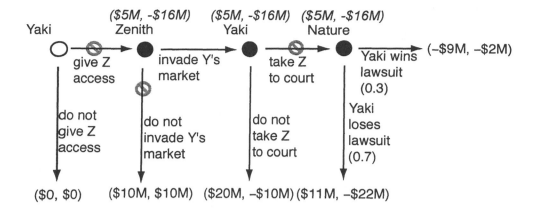

Figure 23.7. Problem 23.1(c): Yaki vs. Zenith, with an uncertain outcome in court. If the chance of Yaki winning its suit is too low, Yaki would have insufficient incentive to take Zenith to court, and even if it did, the threat of a suit is insufficient to deter Zenith.

loses the case, with probability 0.7. It wins and is awarded punitive damages, with probability $0.3 \times \frac{2}{3} = 0.2$. It wins but is not awarded punitive damages, with probability $0.3 \times \frac{1}{3} = 0.1$.

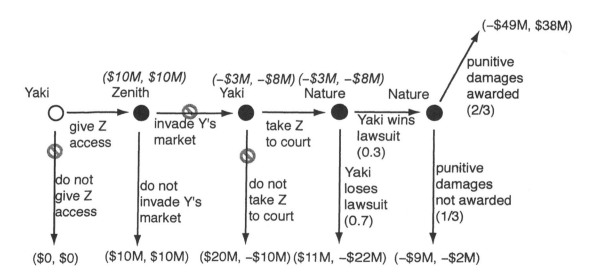

Figure 23.8. Problem 23.1(d): Yaki vs. Zenith, with an uncertain outcome in court and the chance of punitive damages. By adding in the chance of punitive damages, we both increase Yaki's motivation to go to court and Zenith's fears if it breaches the contract.

(e) If the punitive damages were not awarded to Yaki, while the prospect of a lawsuit would keep Zenith honest, Yaki has insufficient motivation to sue. The threat to sue Zenith, if it breaches, is not credible, so Zenith would breach. Therefore, Yaki cannot sign the agreement (see Figure 23.9).

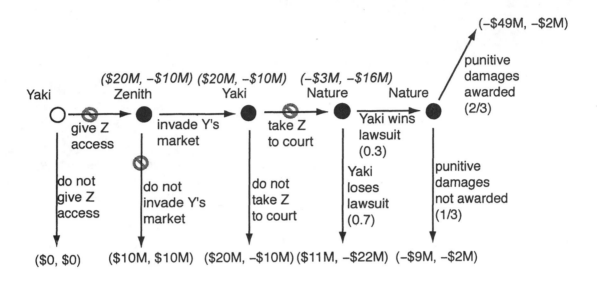

Figure 23.9. Problem 23.1(e): Yaki vs. Zenith, with an uncertain outcome in court and punitive damages that do not go to Yaki. Although the punitive damages would be sufficient to keep Zenith honest if it knew it would be sued, without them going to Yaki, Yaki has insufficient motivation to sue. Therefore, Zenith would breach. So, Yaki should not sign the agreement.

(f) Reputation could help us out of the dilemma of part e in two ways. First, if Zenith cultivated a reputation for never breaching contracts of this sort and that reputation was worth (in terms of the future payoffs) more than $20 million to Zenith, that would forestall Zenith from breaching in this case. Second, if Yaki cultivated a reputation of taking contractual partners to court even if the prospect of net gains from the suit were negative and if that reputation was worth at least $6 million to Yaki, a threat by it to take Zenith to court would become credible and Zenith would be forestalled from breach.

Final note: Although the problem did not mention this, in things like damages and punitive damage awards, another thing to worry about is whether punitive damages motivate plaintiffs to file nuisance suits or suits based on a small chance of winning even though the case is weak.

Review Problems V

V.1 (a) In the strategic form game depicted in Figure V.1(a), find two strategy profiles that are Nash equilibria. (There are more than two.)

	Left	Center Left	Center Right	Right
Top	10,1	1,1	3,2	0,0
Mid	7,1	2,2	0,1	1,1
Bot	5,2	−1,−1	1,2	2,3

(a)

	Left	Center Left	Center Right	Right
Top	10,1	2,1	3,2	0,0
Mid	7,1	1,2	0,1	−1,6
Bot	5,3	−1,−1	1,2	2,2

(b)

Figure V.1. Problem V.1: Two strategic form games.

(b) In the strategic form game depicted in Figure V.1(b), what does the application of iterated dominance tell you?

(c) In the extensive form game depicted in Figure V.2, what does the application of backward induction tell you?

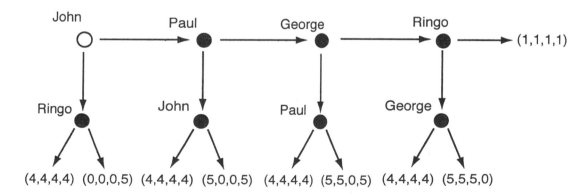

Figure V.2. Problem V.1: An extensive form game. John's payoff is listed first, Paul's second, George's third, and Ringo's last.

V.2 Imagine a three-player game in which each player (Mae, Larry, and Curley) picks either 1, 2, or 3. This is done independently. Each player is then given a reward equal to four times the smallest number chosen, less the number chosen by the player. So if Mae chooses 2, Larry 3, and Curley 3, Mae gets $4 \times 2 - 2 = 6$, and Larry and Curley each get $4 \times 2 - 3 = 5$. This game has three Nash equilibria: What are they?

V.3 Two firms, Ace Camera and Zenith Optics, are the sole suppliers of a certain type of specialty camera used in scientific research. Each is aware of development effort that could be undertaken to improve the quality of the camera but at substantial cost. Ace, because of its larger market share, does better to undertake this development than not, regardless of whether Zenith undertakes the development. But if Zenith undertakes development as well, then Ace is worse off than if both choose to forgo development. Zenith, on the other hand, would prefer to forgo development if Ace did likewise, but if Ace develops the new product, then Zenith must as well, to remain competitive.

(a) Translating all this into the language of game theory and supposing that the two firms must choose simultaneously and independently whether to undertake development of the innovation, we get the strategic form representation of the game shown in Figure IV.3.

Assuming this representation captures the situation and that both firms see the situation in this way, what prediction do you think a game theorist would make about the outcome of this competitive situation? Why?

		Zenith Optics	
		develop new product	do not develop new product
Ace Camera	develop new product	10, 2	15, 0
	do not develop new product	3, 3	12, 5

Figure V.3. Problem V.3: A strategic form game.

(b) Suppose Ace Camera could somehow commit to its action before Zenith must choose its action. (A commitment to undertake development is not difficult. Ace could start spending money on the development process, announce that it will sell the enhanced product shortly, perhaps back up this promise with guarantees to customers, and so on. A commitment not to undertake development is more difficult, but among actions that have this character is to invest heavily in capacity for the technologically less-advanced product. For the purposes of this problem, simply assume that Ace has a commitment technology available to it.) This changes the stategic form game of part a into an extensive form game, depicted in Figure V.4. Note that, in this game, Ace chooses whether to develop the product or not, then Zenith responds, having seen Ace's choice.

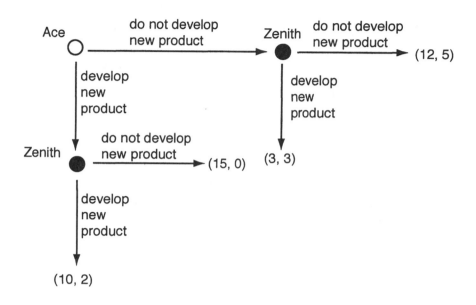

Figure V.4. Problem V.3: An extensive form game. Ace's payoffs are listed first.

Assuming this representation captures the situation and that both firms see the situation in this way, what prediction do you think a game theorist would make about the outcome of this competitive situation? Why?

Solution to Problem V.1

(a) Three Nash equilibria are Top–Center Right, Mid–Center Left, and Bot–Right.

(b) Top dominates Mid. Once Mid is removed, Center Right dominates Center Left and Left dominates Right. Then, Top dominates Bot (it was necessary only to remove Right on the previous step to get this far). And once Top is all that is left for the person picking the row, the person picking the column chooses Center Right.

(c) At each of the four nodes along the bottom row, the player whose turn it is would choose to go to the right. Thus along the top row: Ringo chooses to go straight right, getting (1,1,1,1); then George chooses to go straight right; then Paul chooses to go straight right; and so John chooses to begin with straight right.

Solution to Problem V.2

The three Nash equilibria are these: All three choose 1, netting payoffs of 3 apiece; all choose 2, netting payoffs of 6 apiece; and all choose 3, netting payoffs of 9 apiece. Note why these are Nash equilibria: Any single player, by increasing the number chosen does not affect the minimum, hence decreases her own payoff; by decreasing the number chosen, she decreases the minimum and thus decreases her own payoff. And there are no other Nash equilibria: If the three do not name the same number, any player who chooses a number other than the lowest among the three does better to decrease her number to equal the lowest.

Solution to Problem V.3

(a) For Ace, developing the new product dominates not doing it, so Ace certainly develops the new product. Zenith, anticipating this, chooses to develop the new product itself, giving payoffs of 10 to Ace and 2 to Zenith. The logic of iterated dominance applies here.

(b) In this case we use rollback. If Ace develops the new product, Zenith will respond by developing the new product, with payoffs 10 and 2, respectively. But, if Ace commits not to develop, then Zenith is better off if it does not develop, giving payoffs of 12 and 5. So Ace chooses not to develop.

Comparing parts a and b, this is a case in which one firm would like to be able to commit to a particular action, so as to guide its rival into a corresponding response that makes *both* of them better off. Ace, if it cannot affect Zenith's action, sees development as the better (dominant) strategy. Zenith, realizing that Ace sees no way to influence its (Zenith's) actions and so will develop the new product, must develop the new product itself. But if Ace could commit in advance, it chooses the strategy that is (otherwise) dominated, because this elicits from Zenith a response (no development) that makes each side better off.

Appendix: Calculus Cookbook

This appendix provides a very fast review of those parts of calculus that are used in the text and the *Companion*.

A.1. Why Calculus?

Calculus is one of the fundamental tools of mathematical analysis. It comes in two closely related pieces, differential calculus and integral calculus.

Differential calculus provides answers to questions like, Given the position of car traveling along a highway as a function of time, what is the speed that the car is traveling, also as a function of time? It takes a function and tells you the *rate of change* of the function.

Integral calculus provides answers to questions like, Given the speed of a car as a function of time, what is its position as a function of time? It takes a rate of change and tells you the value of the function (sort of).

Engineers, scientists, and motorists—all are interested in these types of questions, so calculus is of interest to them. Economists find calculus interesting and useful because of its close tie to marginal analysis and optimization. Economic models of consumers and firms typically assume that the individual consumer or firm acts in a purposeful fashion, maximizing some numerical objective function. For firms, this objective function typically is profit; for consumers, it is something called utility. (See Chapters 3 and 5 of the text. To reiterate, the idea is not that firms and consumers maximize these objective functions consciously, but they act *as if* they do.) Calculus comes in handy because it gives us the ability, in a mathematical model, to express the rate of increase or decrease in this objective function, as marginal changes are made in production quantities by firms or in amounts of goods consumed by consumers. It allows us to find levels of production and consumption that maximize profit and utility.

Calculus is not necessary for the study of economics, especially in this age of spreadsheets and Solver. Moreover, because it is scary to some people, it can be pedagogically counterproductive. But calculus is often more efficient than searching, and it gives a convenient and simple way to express simple ideas. For this reason, you should conquer any fears you may have and use calculus; it is not hard and it is awfully useful.

A.2. The Derivative

In calculus, the key concept is that of the *derivative* of a function. Imagine a function f that associates to every number x another number $f(x)$, in the way that functions do. To carry around a concrete example, I use the function

$$f(x) = x^2 - x + 2.$$

In the usual fashion, we can graph the function f. In Figure A.1, I graph four functions: In panel a, I graph $f(x) = x^2 - x + 2$; the other three panels show functions for which formulas do not exist. Those other three functions are there to illustrate what functions might look like; in particular, focus on the behavior of these functions around the value $x = 2$. The function in panel b is discontinuous at $x = 2$ (it jumps there); the function in panel c is continuous but kinked at $x = 2$; the function in panel d is both continuous and smooth (neither jumps nor kinks). (If you are not quite sure what I mean by a kink, wait a bit; it becomes clearer.)

For any function f, I can ask, *What is the rate of change in the function over some discrete interval?* For example, what is the rate of change in the function $f(x) = x^2 - x + 2$, over the interval from 2 to 4? Since we have a formula for this function, this is easy to answer:

$$\frac{f(4) - f(2)}{4 - 2} = \frac{(4^2 - 4 + 2) - (2^2 - 2 + 2)}{4 - 2} = \frac{14 - 4}{2} = 5.$$

Over this interval, the function increases at a rate of 5 units per 1 unit increase in the variable. Over the interval from 2 to 0, the function increases at a rate $(4 - 2)/(2 - 0) = 1$. Over the interval from 2 to 2.5, it increases at a rate

$$\frac{f(2.5) - f(2)}{2.5 - 2} = \frac{5.75 - 4}{2.5 - 2} = \frac{1.75}{0.5} = 3.5.$$

Over the interval from 2 to 2.1, it increases at a rate

$$\frac{f(2.1) - f(2)}{2.1 - 2} = \frac{4.31 - 4}{2.1 - 2} = \frac{0.31}{0.1} = 3.1.$$

Over the interval from 1.99 to 2, it increases at the rate

$$\frac{f(2) - f(1.99)}{2 - 1.99} = \frac{4 - 3.9701}{2 - 1.99} = \frac{0.0299}{0.01} = 2.99.$$

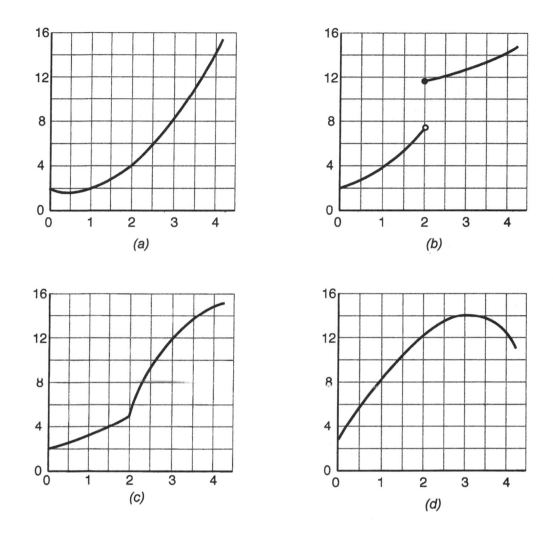

Figure A.1. Graphs of four functions.

These are all *rates of change* in the function over some discrete interval. In all the examples, the function increases over the interval in question, so the answer is always a positive number. But, if we consider the interval from 0 to 0.5, we get a negative rate of change, because the function decreases over this interval.[1]

Suppose I ask instead for the "instantaneous rate of change" of the function f at the point 2. The function is rising at 2, so the rate of change at 2 is a positive number. We find the instantaneous rate of change at 2 by taking smaller and smaller discrete intervals starting or ending at 2 or simply bracketing 2, measuring the rates of increase over those discrete intervals, and seeing what is the limit as the intervals get smaller. We actually did this to some extent in the examples:

---

[1] To be precise, we get $[f(0.5) - f(0)]/(0.5 - 0) = (1.75 - 2)/(0.5 - 0) = -0.25/0.5 = -0.5$.

1. Over the interval from 2 to 4, the rate of increase was 5.

2. Over the interval from 2 to 2.5, the rate of increase was 3.5.

3. Over the interval from 2 to 2.1, the rate of increase was 3.1.

4. Over the interval from 1.99 to 2, the rate of increase was 2.99.

The trend is clear. As the intervals get smaller, the rates of increase get closer and closer to 3.

Alternatively, lay a ruler along the function f at the value 2 and measure the slope of the *tangent line*. This is illustrated for you in Figure A.2. The slope of this tangent line is 3, to the limits of our measurement abilities.

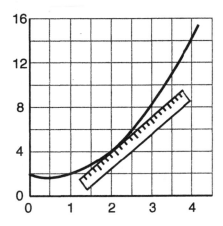

Figure A.2. *Measuring the slope of a function at a point.* To find the slope or instantaneous rate of change of a function at a point, you place a ruler tangent to the function at that point and calculate the slope of the line described by the ruler's edge.

This instantaneous rate of increase (or decrease) of the function is the *derivative* of the function. It is defined formally, mathematically, as the limit of the rates of increase (or decrease) over smaller and smaller discrete intervals encompassing the point at which you wish to find the derivative. Do not worry too much about that; it is just the slope of the tangent line to the function at the point you are interested in.

Note that the derivative changes as we change the point we are looking at. In the function $f(x) = x^2 - x + 2$, the tangent line has slope 3 at $x = 2$; but at $x = 3$ the tangent line has slope 5 (get your ruler out if you do not believe me); at $x = 0$, the slope is -1 (the function is decreasing); and at $x = 0.5$, the slope is 0. In Figure A.3, I graph the function f in panel a and directly below it I graph its derivative function.

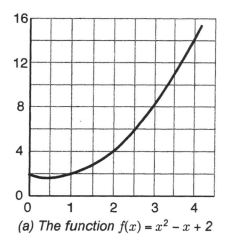

(a) The function $f(x) = x^2 - x + 2$

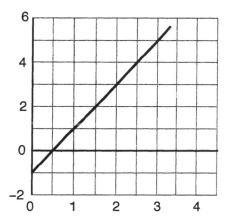

(b) The derivative of the function f

Figure A.3. The function and its derivative. Panel a shows the function $f(x) = x^2 - x + 2$, and panel b shows its derivative.

Note that the derivative is negative for $x < 0.5$, the function f decreases below $x = 0.5$, but the derivative is getting closer and closer to 0, the function is decreasing more and more slowly. The derivative is 0 at $x = 0.5$ (the function has bottomed out), then the derivative is positive and increasingly so for $x > 0.5$ (the function now increases and at an increasing rate). We see why I drew the derivative as a linear function in a bit.)

Not every function has a derivative at every point. If the function jumps discountinuously at a point, it cannot have a derivative there. And, even if it is continuous, if its slope changes at a point, as in Figure A.1(c) at $x = 2$, then the function has no derivative there. Note that the function in Figure A.1(c) has an identifiable rate of increase just to the left of $x = 2$ and a different rate of increase just to the right, but since these rates are not the same, the function kinks there: its slope changes discontinuously; it has no derivative at $x = 2$.

The function in Figure A.1(c) does have nice slopes at all points except for $x = 2$. In other words, this function has a derivative everywhere but at $x = 2$. In Figure A.4(a), I graph the function from Figure A.1(c) again, and below it, in Figure A.4(b), I graph its "derivative function," where the jump at $x = 2$ is meant to indicate that the function has no derivative at that one point. In fancy math-talk, we would say that the function from Figure A.1(c) is not differentiable at $x = 2$, but it is differentiable everywhere else. In less fancy talk, we say that this function is *kinked* at $x = 2$, but is *smooth* everywhere else.

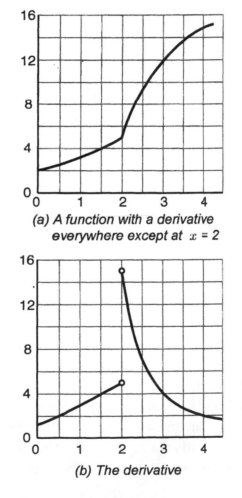

(a) A function with a derivative
everywhere except at $x = 2$

(b) The derivative

Figure A.4. A function with a derivative except at $x = 2$, and that derivative.

It should be clear that the shape of a function and that of its derivative are closely related. Where the function is increasing, its derivative is positive. If the function is decreasing and at an increasing rate, its derivative is negative and is decreasing. In Figure A.5, panels a, b, and c, I draw three functions. In panels x, y, and z, I draw three more functions, which are meant to be the derivatives of the first three functions, where the functions have derivatives. Can you match the functions to their derivatives? (The answer is at the end of this appendix.)

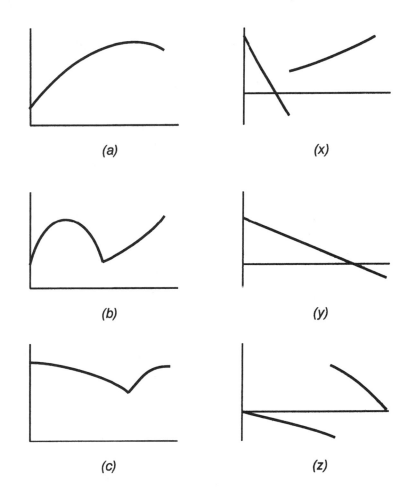

(a) *(x)*

(b) *(y)*

(c) *(z)*

Figure A.5. Three functions and three derivatives. Match each function in the left-hand column with its derivative (from the right-hand column). The answers are given at the end of the appendix.

For a function f that has a derivative, we write both f' and df/dx for that derivative. The f' notation is quite convenient in that it allows us to write $f'(x)$ to denote the derivative at the value x.

A.3. Maximization and Minimization

Suppose we want to find where a function f is maximized or minimized. Since the function cannot be at either a maximum or a minimum where it is either rising (has positive slope) or falling (has negative slope), if the function has a derivative at its max or min, that derivative must be 0. In other words, a *necessary* condition for a max or a min, if the function has a derivative there, is that the derivative is 0.

Turning this around, if you have a function f that has derivatives at all points, to find its maxes and mins, you look at places where its derivative is 0.

This procedure is not free of problems. For a max or a min, it is *necessary* that the derivative is 0. But, just because the derivative is 0 does not mean we are at a max or a min. For example, the function $f(x) = x^3$ has derivative $f'(x) = 3x^2$. (Trust me on this for now.) This derivative is 0 at $x = 0$. But the function $f(x) = x^3$ is neither maximized nor minimized at $x = 0$, it is rising for all values of x. The derivative of 0 at $x = 0$ simply means (for this function) that the instantaneous rate of change in the function is 0 at $x = 0$; it is momentarily flat at $x = 0$. But the function has positive slope everywhere else (the function $f'(x) = 3x^2$ is strictly positive for x different from 0), and so the function never achieves either max or min.

Also, the necessity of a zero derivative at a max or min depends on the function having a derivative there. For functions with kinks, you have to worry about the kink. This can be difficult, but there are easy cases; for example, suppose that a function f is kinked at the value x_0 but has a derivative everywhere else, moreover, $f'(x) > 0$ for $x < x_0$ and $f'(x) < 0$ for $x > x_0$. Because $f'(x) > 0$ for $x < x_0$, we know the function is increasing for $x < x_0$. And because $f'(x) < 0$ for $x > x_0$, we know it is falling for $x > x_0$. As long as f is continuous (it does not jump itself), this means it must achieve a maximum at x_0 precisely.

Second-Order Conditions

Are you at a max or a min (or something else) at a point where $f'(x) = 0$? One way to tell is to look at what are called the *second-order conditions*. These involve the second derivative of f, denoted f'', which is just the derivative of the derivative. You need not know about these things to read the text, but it seems a shame not to indicate how simple they really are.

Before starting the explanation, I should be clear on some terminology. We say that the function f (with argument x) achieves a *global maximum* at the point x^* if $f(x^*) \geq f(x)$ for every other argument x. And we say that the function f has a *local maximum* at x° if $f(x^\circ) \geq f(x)$ for every x that is "close" to x°. How close? As close as you want, as long as closeness is measured as, some strictly positive distance.[2] The concept is not as hard as the symbols make it seem: Think of x as coordinates (in latitude and longitude) on the Earth, and $f(x)$ as the height of the land mass over that point, measured in meters. Then, the global max of the function f is achieved at the coordinates of the peak of Mt. Everest, while there

---

[2] Formally, you need $f(x^\circ) \geq f(x)$ for all x within δ of x°, for some strictly positive distance δ.

are local maxes galore: at the coordinates of the peak of Mt. McKinley (the highest point in the United States), Mt. Blanc, and even the top of a hill in your backyard, if your backyard has a hill.[3]

Needless to say, when you are seeking to maximize a function, your aim is to find *the* global maximum. (There can be ties, so the *the* is not entirely appropriate.) Derivatives tell you only about local conditions, however, so the second-order conditions are about local maxima. Now for the explanation:

A function f achieves a local maximum at x_0 if $f'(x_0) = 0$ and $f''(x_0) < 0$. (The second-order condition for a maximum is that the second derivative is negative at the point where the first derivative is zero.) Why? If $f''(x_0) < 0$, this means that f' is decreasing at x_0. If $f'(x_0) = 0$, this (in addition) means that $f'(x) > 0$ for x a bit less than x_0, so f rises as we approach x_0 from below; and $f'(x) < 0$ for x a bit more than x_0, which means that f falls as we go beyond x_0. Thus, f achieves a (local) max at x_0.[4]

A.4. Derivatives of Some Functions

Functions that are expressed algebraically often have their derivatives worked out by formulas developed by mathematicians. Three important and useful examples of this are given here.

$$\text{For } f(x) = x^k, f'(x) = kx^{k-1}.$$

This works if k is an integer, so (for example), if $f(x) = x^3$, then $f'(x) = 3x^2$. But it works equally well for fractional powers of x; for instance, if $f(x) = x^{1/2}$, then $f'(x) = (1/2)x^{-1/2}$. And it works for negative powers of x: if $f(x) = x^{-2.76}, then f'(x) = -2.76x^{-3.76}$.

(Do you know about negative and fractional powers? Let me remind you: $x^{1/2}$ means the square root of x; $x^{2/3}$ means the square of the cube-root of x; $x^{5.76}$ means x^5 times the 100th root of x raised to the 76th power; x^{-5} means $1/x^5$; and so on.)

$$\text{For } f(x) = e^x, f'(x) = e^x.$$

---

[3] I hope you are not put off because, in this specific example, the argument x of the function, the latitudinal–longitudinal coordinates of a point, is a two-variable argument. If this confuses you, see Figure A.5(b). The top of the first "hump" is a local maximum of this function; since the function seems to continue rising to the right, we cannot be sure whether it has a global maximum.

[4] Let me remind those of you who have seen this before: The second-order condition is sufficient for a local max; it is not necessary; for instance, consider $f(x) = -x^4$ at $x = 0$.

This is purely for cultural enrichment. The exponential function is used in places in the text, but we do not take its derivative.

$$\text{For } f(x) = \ln(x), f'(x) = 1/x = x^{-1}.$$

Here $\ln(x)$ means the natural logarithm of x, which is sometimes written $\log(x)$ or $\log_e(x)$. We use the natural logarithm function in the text and exercises, and I expect you to know at least what it looks like and how to get your calculator (or EXCEL) to compute it for you. (For more about the natural logarithm function, see page 53 of this *Companion*.)

A.5. Five Important Rules

In addition to these formulas, derivatives of complicated functions like $f(x) = x^2 - x + 3$ are computed by using the following five rules.

Adding a Constant

If $f(x) = g(x) + c$, where c is some constant, then $f'(x) = g'(x)$. If you just want to memorize the rule, be my guest, but this is really quite sensible. If we add (or subtract) a constant to a function for every value of x, we certainly do not change its rate of increase or decrease at any point.

   To see this rule in action, consider $f(x) = x^2 - x + 3$. Since 3 is a constant, $f'(x) =$ the derivative of $x^2 - x$; we can forget about the 3.

The Addition Rule

If $f(x) = g(x) + h(x)$, then $f'(x) = g'(x) + h'(x)$. Hence, for the function $x^2 - x$, its derivative is the sum of the derivatives of x^2, which we know is $2x$, and the derivative of the function $-x$, for which we need the next rule.

Multiplication by a Constant

If $f(x) = kg(x)$ for some constant k, then $f'(x) = kg'(x)$. Intuitively, suppose $g(x)$ is the profit earned by a firm that produces and sells x units of output, measured in dollars. Suppose 110 yen equal 1 dollar; so if $f(x)$ is the profit measured in yen, $f(x) = 110g(x)$. Since $g'(x)$ is the rate of change in profit, measured in dollars, at production level x, the rate of change in yen, $f'(x)$, is just 110 times $g'(x)$. Which is just what the rule says.

   Hence the function $-x$, which is $-1 \times x$, has derivative -1 times the derivative of x, which is 1. Therefore, for $f(x) = x^2 - x + 2$, $f'(x) = 2x - 1$. (Now you know why I draw the derivative of $x^2 - x + 2$ as a linear function in Figure A.3(b).)

The Product Rule

If $f(x) = g(x)h(x)$, then $f'(x) = g'(x)h(x) + h'(x)g(x)$. The most intuitive explanation for this I know of runs as follows.[5] Think in terms of changing x a little bit, to $x+\delta$. Then, approximately, $f(x + \delta) = f(x) + \delta f'(x)$. And $g(x + \delta) = g(x) + \delta g'(x)$. So, approximately,

$$f(x + \delta)g(x + \delta) = [f(x) + \delta f'(x)][g(x) + \delta g'(x)]$$
$$= f(x)g(x) + \delta f'(x)g(x) + \delta g'(x)f(x) + \delta^2 f'(x)g'(x)]$$
$$= f(x)g(x) + \delta[f'(x)g(x) + g'(x)f(x)] + \delta^2 f'(x)g'(x).$$

The last term is very, very small if δ is small; so the "slope" of $f(x)g(x)$ for small changes δ in x is $f'(x)g(x) + g(x)f'(x)$, just as the product rule says.

The Chain Rule

If $f(x) = g[h(x)]$, then $f'(x) = g'[h(x)]h'(x)$. Think of a firm that transforms raw material into a saleable product. Let x be the amount of raw material the firm uses, and suppose $Q(x)$ tells us the amount of final product that can be produced from x units of raw material. Suppose as well that, if the firm produces and sells q units of final output, its total revenues are given by the function TR(q). Then, the total revenues of the firm *as a function of the amount of raw material it uses* is given by the composite function TR$[Q(x)]$.

What is the rate of change in total revenue as a function of x? First we ask, what is the rate of change in final output as a function of x, what is $Q'(x)$? Suppose that, at some level of raw material input x_0, we get (on the margin) two units more of output for every unit of input we use, or $Q'(x_0) = 2$.

Suppose as well that, at x_0 units of input, we have $Q(x_0) = q_0$ units of final product, and total revenues for the marginal extra unit of final product rise by \$3. That is, TR$'(q_0) = 3$.

Now, at x_0 units of input, what is the impact on total revenue of a marginal additional unit of input? On the margin, one more unit of input raises output by two units. Each of those two (marginal) units raises total revenues by approximately \$3. Hence, the marginal impact of an extra unit of input is \$6 in revenue, which is just what the chain rule tells us.

---

[5] This explanation may make a bit more sense to you after you read the next section. And it may not make sense at all, if you are seeing calculus for the first time or for the first time in a long time.

A.6. Derivatives and Discrete Changes

We said earlier that the derivative of the function f at a point x is the limit of the rates of change in the function over smaller and smaller intervals that encompass the point x. In a sense then, the rates of change over intervals give an *approximation* to the derivative of the function, an approximation that is better the smaller is the interval.

Turning this around, if we can compute derivatives analytically, we can use them to approximate discrete changes over intervals of positive length, approximations that improve the smaller is the interval.

To give an example, consider the function

$$f(x) = 4x^2 - x^{-3} + 5\ln(x).$$

Suppose for some reason I want to know what are $f(13) - f(10)$ and then $f(10.3) - f(10)$. One way to get these discrete differences would be to compute f for the arguments 13, 10.3, and 10 and subtract. But, if I am in a hurry, I can get an approximation by (a) computing the derivative of f at $x = 10$, and then (b) multiply this by the length of the interval.

The derivative of $f(x)$ is

$$f'(x) = 4 \times 2x - (-3) \times x^{-4} + \frac{5}{x} = 8x + 3x^{-4} + \frac{5}{x}.$$

Evaluated at $x = 10$, this is

$$f'(10) = 80 + \frac{3}{10^4} + \frac{5}{10} = 80.5003.$$

Therefore, my estimate of $f(13) - f(10)$ is $80.5003 \times 3 = 241.5009$, and my estimate of $f(10.3) - f(10)$ is $80.5003 \times .3 = 24.15009$. In fact, according to EXCEL, $f(13) - f(10) = 277.312$, and $f(10.3) - f(10) = 24.507$. The error is around 15% on the larger interval and 1.5% on the smaller interval. We have a fairly good quick approximation in both cases, but the approximation is a lot better on the smaller interval.

A.7. Integrals and Integration

For a function $f(x)$, its derivative $f'(x)$ is the slope of f at x, for each x. The *integral* of $f(x)$, on the other hand, is "the" function whose derivative is $f(x)$.

Why are there quotes around "the"? Because many functions have the derivative $f(x)$. Suppose that $g(x)$ is a function whose derivative is $f(x)$. The rules about derivatives tell us that for any constant k, $h(x) = g(x) + k$ is another function whose derivative is $f(x)$.

For example, consider $f(x) = 3x^2 - 4x + 3$ and $g(x) = x^3 - 2x^2 + 3x$. By the rules and formulas for derivatives, $g'(x) = f(x)$. But $f(x)$ is the derivative as well of $h(x) = x^3 - 2x^2 + 3x + 101$ and of $x^3 - 2x^2 + 3x - 101010101$.

Because of this, when we speak of the integral of $f(x)$, we either mean the entire class of functions whose derivatives are $f(x)$, all of which are constant translates of one another,[6] or we specify some single value of the integral we are interested in. For instance, we might say something like this: Let $g(x)$ be that function whose derivative is $f(x) = x^2 - x + 3$ and that takes on the value 10 at $x = 1$. If I am looking for this function, I proceed as follows: First, I note that integrals of $f(x)$ are functions of form $x^3 - 2x^2 + 3x + k$, for a constant k. Thus, at $x = 1$, the function has the value $1 - 2 + 3 + k = 2 + k$. If I want this to equal 10, then $k = 8$.

Actually, it is rare that one specifies an integral g of f with $g(1) = 10$ or $g(x) =$ anything except 0. That is, when we pin down an integral, normally we specify some argument x_0 and say that we want an integral whose value at x_0 is 0. We write this as

$$g(x) = \int_{x_0}^{x} f(x)\,dx.$$

This brings us to the characterization of integrals with which you are probably most familiar (if you have any familiarity with integrals). Suppose I want

$$g(x) = \int_{x_0}^{x} f(x)\,dx.$$

That is, I want a function whose derivative is $f(x)$ and value 0 at x_0. Graph the function f.

For $x > x_0$, the integral $g(x)$ is the area under the function f over the range from x_0 to x; for $x < x_0$, it is the negative of this area.

---

[6] Might two functions $g(x)$ and $h(x)$ both have the derivative f yet not be constant translates of one another? The answer is no. Suppose g and h both have f as their derivative. Look at the function $D(x) = g(x) - h(x)$. The rules for finding derivatives tell us that the derivative of D is $g'(x) - h'(x)$, which, by our hypothesis that $g'(x) = f(x) = h'(x)$, is the constant 0. But this means that $D(x)$ never increases or decreases; it is a constant k. This implies that $g(x) = h(x) + k$, just as we claim.

Consider Figure A.6, the function f graphed there, and the point x_0. We claim that $g(x) = \int_{x_0}^{x} f(x)\,dx$ is the shaded area, for $x > x_0$. This is not simply a definition, instead it is a mathematical, logical assertion that the function $g(x)$ constructed in this fashion satisfies $g(x_0) = 0$ (which should be obvious) and $g'(x) = f(x)$ (which is anything but obvious).

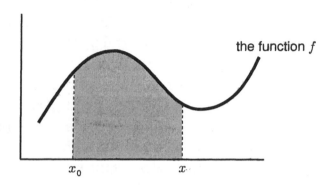

Figure A.6. The integral of f.

Why is $g'(x) = f(x)$? Recall that $g'(x)$ is the limit of the discrete rates of change of g over smaller and smaller intervals that begin, or end, or bracket x. Suppose we look at an interval from x to $x + \delta$, for small values of δ. The difference between $g(x)$ and $g(x + \delta)$ is the difference in the areas that define these two, which is the shaded "rectangular sliver" in Figure A.7. This is almost a rectangle whose base is δ and whose height is $f(x)$. It is only almost a rectangle because the height of the rectangle varies between $f(x)$ and $f(x + \delta)$. Suppose the function f is continuous (no jumps) and δ is small. Then, the height of f over this interval does not vary too much and the area of the shaded region is approximately $f(x) \times \delta$. Therefore, the rate of increase of the area function at x is $f(x)$; the derivative of the "area" function is f.

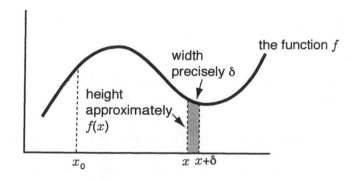

Figure A.7. Why the area under f is the integral of f.

Textbooks on calculus go on from this point to do several things, such as the following:

1. They give formulas for various important integrals, such as

$$\int_{x_0}^{x} x^k \, \mathrm{d}x = \frac{x^{k+1}}{k+1} - \frac{x_0^{k+1}}{k+1} \text{ for } k \neq -1.$$

2. They give rules, such as

$$\int_{x_0}^{x} [f(x) + g(x)] \, \mathrm{d}x = \int_{x_0}^{x} f(x) \, \mathrm{d}x + \int_{x_0}^{x} g(x) \, \mathrm{d}x.$$

3. They do all manner of other fancy stuff.

I do not bother you with any of this. Indeed, we do not actually evaluate any integrals anywhere in the text or in the exercises. But, for now, you should be clear on three things:

1. The integral of the function f is a function whose derivative is f.

2. You have to pin down the value of an integral at some point before you are sure what it is, and the usual thing is to specify some point x_0 and say that the integral should have the value 0 at x_0.

3. In which case, the integral of f is the area under the curve f, from x_0 up to (or, with a negative sign, down to) the argument x of the integral.

A.8. Partial Derivatives

So far we have dealt with functions of a single variable; the argument of the function is a number, and the value of the function is another number. We continue with functions whose values are numbers, but in many places we need to discuss functions whose arguments are vectors of numbers. Such functions are called *multivariate functions*.

For example, consider the function $F(x, y) = x^2 + 3xy - 2y^2 + 7x - y \ln(x) + 3$. If I give you values for x and y (where $x > 0$ is required, so that $\ln(x)$ makes sense), you can plug them in (or use EXCEL or your calculator) to evaluate the function.

Multivariate functions come up in economics because decision makers in economic problems often control more than one variable. Multiproduct firms have to decide how much of each sort of product to produce and sell. Even if the firm has a single product, this product can often be produced with varying combinations of several inputs. Consumers have to decide how much milk, bread, cheese, beef, beer, wine, and the like to consume. Hence, we have functions to be maximized or minimized that have more than one variable. How do we deal with these using calculus?

The first step involves the concept of a *partial derivative*. This gives the instantaneous rate of change of the function as we vary one of its arguments, leaving the other arguments at some fixed level.

For example, consider the function $F(x,y) = x^2 + 3xy - 2y^2 + 7x - y\ln(x) + 3$. Suppose we are interested in how this function changes as we vary x around the value $x = 2$, with y fixed at 4. If y is fixed at 4, the function, as a function of x alone, is $F(x,4) = x^2 + 12x - 32 + 7x - 4\ln(x) + 3$. And the instantaneous rate of change of this function in x is just its derivative with respect to x, which is

$$\frac{dF(x,4)}{dx} = 2x + 12 + 7 - \frac{4}{x} = 2x + 19 - \frac{4}{x}.$$

At $x = 2$, this is 21. For small increases in x (at $x = 2$, $y = 4$), the function rises at a rate of approximately 21 times the amount that x is increased. For example,

$$F(2.001,4) - F(2,4) \approx 21 \times 0.001 = 0.021.$$

At the same time, if we fix $x = 2$ and vary y slightly, we are looking at the function (in y) $4 + 6y - 2y^2 + 14 - y\ln(2) + 3$, whose derivative in y is $6 - 4y - \ln(2)$. At $y = 4$, this is $-10 - \ln(2)$. Thus, if we increase y from 4 to 4.01, keeping x fixed at 2, the function *decreases* by approximately $0.01 \times [10 + \ln(2)]$.

What we have done is to fix one of the variables and look at the derivative in the other. More generally, when we have functions of more than two variables, we fix all but one variable and look at the derivative or instantaneous rate of change in the one not fixed.

If we do this in general, we have what is known as the *partial derivative* of the function. For our two-variable function F, we would write for the partial derivative of F with respect to x the symbols

$$\frac{\partial F(x,y)}{\partial x},$$

where a curly d indicates that this is a partial derivative. This is just the derivative of F with respect to x, treating y as a constant. All the rules you know from differentiation of a function of a single variable apply, so that

$$\frac{\partial F(x,y)}{\partial x} = \frac{\partial [x^2 + 3xy - 2y^2 + 7x - y\ln(x) + 3]}{\partial x} =$$

$$\frac{\partial x^2}{\partial x} + \frac{\partial(3xy)}{\partial x} + \frac{\partial(-2y^2)}{\partial x} + \frac{\partial(7x)}{\partial x} + \frac{\partial[-y\ln(x)]}{\partial x}$$

by the addition rule for derivatives, which term by term is

$$= 2x + 3y + 0 + 7 - \frac{y}{x},$$

applying the rules and formulas for differentiation, *always treating y as a constant.* That is

$$\frac{\partial F(x,y)}{\partial x} = 2x + 3y + 7 - \frac{y}{x}.$$

At $x = 2$ and $y = 4$, this is just $2 \times 2 + 3 \times 4 + 7 - (4/2) = 21$. (This is the same 21 we computed three paragraphs ago.)

Just to check, what is

$$\frac{\partial F(x,y)}{\partial y}?$$

The answer is given at the end of this appendix.

We use partial derivatives in much the same way we use regular derivatives. For one thing, they can be handy for computing approximate discrete changes in a function. Suppose, for example, we want to know, for the function $F(x,y)$, what is

$$F(2.2, 4.1) - F(2, 4).$$

This amounts to an increase in x by 0.2 and an increase in y by 0.1. Hence, the discrete difference we are looking for is approximately

$$\left.\frac{\partial F(x,y)}{\partial x}\right|_{(x,y)=(2,4)} \times 0.2 \quad + \quad \left.\frac{\partial F(x,y)}{\partial y}\right|_{(x,y)=(2,4)} \times 0.1 =$$

$$21 \times 0.2 \quad + \quad [-10 + \ln(2)] \times 0.1 \quad = \quad 4.2 - 1 - 0.1\ln(2) = 3.13,$$

where I evaluated $\ln(2)$ on my calculator. (The term

$$\left.\frac{\partial F(x, y)}{\partial x}\right|_{(x, y)=(2, 4)}$$

means the partial derivative of F with respect to x, evaluated at the values $x = 2$ and $y = 4$.) I asked EXCEL to compute this difference by evaluating $F(2.2, 4.1)$ and $F(2, 4)$, and EXCEL told me that the precise difference is 3.22. This is around a 3% error, which is not too bad.

A.9. Maximization and Minimization of Multivariate Functions

The main way in which we use partial derivatives is in maximization and minimization problems. Suppose we are looking for values of x, y, and z that maximize the function $G(x, y, z)$. At any maximum, all three partial derivatives of G must be 0. Why? If, say $\partial G / \partial z < 0$, then a small decrease in z, leaving x and y fixed, increases the value of the function. If $\partial G / \partial x > 0$, then a small increase in x, leaving y and z fixed increases the value of the function. If the function is maximized at some point, it must be (instantaneously) flat in all three directions.

As with regular derivatives of functions of a single variable, having partial derivatives equal to 0 is only necessary for finding a max or a min (as long as the function is differentiable in all its arguments); it is not sufficient. There are generalizations of the second-order conditions for multivariate optimization problems, involving second-partial derivatives of the function to be maxed or minned, but we have no occasion to bother with those, so I do not "review" them here.

Exercises

Following are some problems that review some of the important ideas in this appendix. Some are a bit tricky, but to understand the use of calculus in the text, at least in terms of differentiation, you should be able to do problems A.1, A.3(a), A.4(a), A.5(a), and A.6.

A.1 Evaluate the derivatives of the following functions:

(a) $f(x) = x^7 - 4.5x^{3.2} + 7\ln(x) + 100$

(b) $g(x) = x^{-3}$

(c) $h(x) = 1/x^3$ (Do not look for tricks that are not there.)

(d) $F(z) = (z - 5)^2 z + 3.14159$

(e) $A(r) = 3.14159 r^2$ (This is a famous formula, if 3.14159 is replaced by the mathematical constant π. If you remember what it is the famous formula for and want a challenge, try to draw a picture that "explains" the answer you are getting. If you can do that, here is a hard question. You may remember from high school geometry that the formula for the volume of a sphere of radius r is $4\pi r^3/3$. A much less well-known formula is the formula for the surface area of a sphere. What is this formula? If you can work this out, you are way ahead of the game.)

A.2 Two more derivatives to take (these are harder than anything we use in the book, so do not worry if you have some problems with them):

(a) $G(y) = y^2 \ln(y)$

(b) $H(y) = \ln(y^6 + 2y^3 + 10)$

A.3 Part a should be fairly easy. Part b is tougher.

(a) Suppose $F(x) = x^3 + 2x^2 + 3x + 4$. Using calculus, compute (approximately) $F(2.08) - F(2)$.

(b) The answer to Problem A.2(b) is

$$\frac{1}{y^6 + 2y^3 + 10} \times (6y^5 + 6y^2)$$

(in case you did not get it). What then is $H(1.05) - H(0.95)$, for this function H? (I obviously want an approximate answer, calculated using calculus.)

A.4 Once again, part b may strain your capabilities, if you are not used to this stuff.

(a) If $M(x, y) = x^4 + x^2 y^2 + y^4$, what is the partial derivative of M in the variable x?

(b) If $H(a, b) = (a^2 + b^2)^{1/2}$, what is the partial derivative of H in the variable a?

A.5 You should have no problems with part a, but part b might be hard.

(a) If $M(x, y) = x^3 + 3x^2 y + 2xy^2 + y^2$, approximately what is $M(2.1, 0.9) - M(2, 1)$?

(b) Suppose we have a right triangle whose "short" sides have lengths 3 and 4, respectively. If we enlarge each of these sides by 0.01, how much longer (approximately, using calculus) is the hypotenuse. (I should add that this is a problem where using the calculus approximation is harder than computing the difference directly. But do not let that stop you from using the calculus approximation, and please look at the answer to A.4(b) if you need to before doing this one.)

A.6 Is it possible that the function $F(x, y, z) = 2x^2 - 2xy + yz + y^2 - 3xz + 3z^2$ hits a (local) minimum at the point $(x = 2, y = 1, z = 2)$? If yes, why? If not, can you find a point nearby this point for which F is smaller?

Solutions

Concerning Figure A.5

Panel a goes with panel y, b with x, and c with z.

Concerning the Exercise on Page 359

$$\frac{\partial F(x, y)}{\partial y} = 3x - 4y - \ln(x).$$

Solution to Problem A.1

(a) $7x^6 - 14.4x^{2.2} + 7/x$; (b) $-3x^{-4}$; (c) same as (b), which can be written $-3/x^4$; (d) You can use the product rule to get $2(z - 5)z + (z - 5)^2 = 2z^2 - 10z + z^2 - 10z + 25 = 3z^2 - 20z + 25$, or you can expand this polynomial into $z^3 - 10z^2 + 25z + 3.14159$ and take the derivative of that, getting the same $3z^2 - 20z + 25$; (e) I use the symbol π for 3.14159 (which is not quite accurate), and the derivative is $2\pi r$. Then πr^2 is the formula for the area of a circle with radius r, while $2\pi r$ is its circumference, and you just learned that the rate of change of the area of a circle, as you change its radius, is the circumference of the circle. Now, draw a picture. If you want to know, the formula for the surface area of a sphere, it is $4\pi r^2$. Why?

Solution to Problem A.2

(a) This one needs the product rule. The answer is

$$2y \ln(y) + y^2/y = 2y \ln(y) + y.$$

(b) Here you need the rule for taking the derivative of a composition of two functions. The answer is

$$\frac{1}{y^6 + 2y^3 + 10} \times (6y^5 + 6y^2).$$

Solution to Problem A.3

(a) The derivative of F is $3x^2+4x+3$, which at the value of $x = 2$ is $3\times4 + 4\times2 + 3 = 23$. Over this range, x changes by 0.08, so the approximate change in the function is $0.08 \times 23 = 1.84$. (In fact, the exact change, calculated using Excel, is 1.891712.)

(b) This is a change of 0.1 in the argument, in a range where the argument of the function is around 1. The derivative of H at the value of 1 (determined by plugging in the formula) is $\frac{12}{13}$, so the answer is $\frac{12}{13} \times 0.1 = 0.0923077$. Note that, if I use Excel to evaluate the function H at 1.05 and then at 0.95 and subtract, I get a difference of 0.09242314, so the calculus-based approximation is pretty good.

Solution to Problem A.4

(a) $4x^3 + 2xy^2$

(b)

$$(1/2)(a^2 + b^2)^{-1/2} \times 2a \quad = \quad \frac{a}{(a^2 + b^2)^{1/2}}$$

Solution to Problem A.5

(a) First we calculate the two partial derivatives and evaluate them at the point $(2,1)$:

$$\frac{\partial M}{\partial x} = 3x^2 + 6xy + 2y^2,$$

which is 26 at $(x = 2, y = 1)$. And

$$\frac{\partial M}{\partial y} = 3x^2 + 4xy + 2y,$$

which is 22 at $(2, 1)$. So if we increase x by 0.1 and simultaneously decrease y by 0.1, we should see a net change in the value of the function of $26 \times 0.1 + 22 \times (-0.1) = 0.4$. (In fact, the exact change is 0.38.)

(b) The formula for the length of the hypotenuse of a right triangle is $(a^2 + b^2)^{1/2}$, where a and b are the lengths of the two short sides, so that the two partial derivatives of the length of the hypotenuse as functions of a and b are, respectively, $a/(a^2 + b^2)^{1/2}$ and $b/(a^2 + b^2)^{1/2}$. At the point $a = 3$ and $b = 4$, these are $\frac{3}{5}$ and $\frac{4}{5}$, respectively, so if you enlarge each side by 0.01, the length of the hypotenuse will increase by (approximately) $\frac{3}{5} \times 0.01 + \frac{4}{5} \times 0.01 = 0.014$. (In fact, the exact answer is .014000399..., so we are not off by much at all.)

Solution to Problem A.6

The partial derivatives of F and their values at the point $(x = 2, y = 1, z = 2)$, are

$$\frac{\partial F}{\partial x} = 4x - 2y - 3z, \quad \text{hence} \quad \left.\frac{\partial F}{\partial x}\right|_{(x=2,y=1,z=2)} = 8 - 2 - 6 = 0;$$

$$\frac{\partial F}{\partial y} = -2x + z + 2y, \quad \text{hence} \quad \left.\frac{\partial F}{\partial y}\right|_{(x=2,y=1,z=2)} = -4 + 2 + 2 = 0;$$

and

$$\frac{\partial F}{\partial z} = y - 3x + 6z, \quad \text{hence} \quad \left.\frac{\partial F}{\partial z}\right|_{(x=2,y=1,z=2)} = 1 - 6 + 12 = 7.$$

To be a candidate for a minimum, all three partials must be 0; since they are not, this point cannot be a minimum. In fact, the partials tell us that decreasing z a bit, starting at $(x = 2, y = 1, z = 2)$ while holding x and y at 2 and 1, respectively, causes the function to decrease; more specifically, by moving to (say) $(x = 2, y = 1, z = 1.999)$, the function decreases by approximately $0.001 \times 7 = 0.007$.